Alin Olteanu and Paul Cobley (Eds.)
Semiotics and its Masters

Semiotics, Communication and Cognition

Edited by
Paul Cobley and Kalevi Kull

Volume 36

Semiotics and its Masters

Volume 2

Edited by
Alin Olteanu and Paul Cobley

DE GRUYTER
MOUTON

ISBN 978-3-11-162788-5
e-ISBN (PDF) 978-3-11-085780-1
e-ISBN (EPUB) 978-3-11-090000-2
ISSN 1867-0873

Library of Congress Control Number: 2022949279

Bibliographic information published by the Deutsche Nationalbibliothek
The Deutsche Nationalbibliothek lists this publication in the Deutsche Nationalbibliografie; detailed bibliographic data are available on the internet at http://dnb.dnb.de.

© 2024 Walter de Gruyter GmbH, Berlin/Boston
This volume is text- and page-identical with the hardback published in 2023.
Cover design based on a design by Martin Zech, Bremen
Typesetting: Integra Software Services Pvt. Ltd.

www.degruyter.com

Preface

This second volume of the *Semiotics and its Masters* (sub-)series gathers sixteen papers by leading scholars in semiotics currently. It is based on debates initiated at the 13th World Congress of the International Association for Semiotic Studies (IASS/IAS), which was hosted by the International Semiotics Institute, at Kaunas University of Technology (Lithuania), in June, 2017. It continues the path set by the first volume (Bankov and Cobley 2017), which stemmed from the 12th World Congress of this Association.

As such, this book offers an encompassing picture of state-of-the-art semiotics, both through minute theoretical inquiries and focused analyses. The volume does not target one theme, its rationale being to capture the contemporary trends in, and uses of, semiotics broadly. As the term 'semiotics' always covered a very broad area of scholarship, the papers here form an eclectic collection. They provide diverse but not unrelated insights into the academic salience of contemporary semiotic research. This is reflected, from the start, by the theme of the congress from which they draw inspiration, titled "Cross- Inter- Multi- Trans-" (see Martinelli et al 2018). This enumeration of prefixes that refer to relationality, fluidity, instability and, perhaps more generally, anti-monadism, suggests what is perhaps the most interesting but also problematic feature of semiotics: it evades a strict definition. Semiotics, as evinced here, is one or more of the following and, at times, seemingly none of them:

- the theory of the sign
- the theory of semiosis
- a "sign science" that encompasses all modes of signification
- a concern with codes and decoding
- a branch of, or supplement to, linguistics
- synonymous with "semiology"
- the study of human signification
- the study of comparative *Umwelten*, comprising the signification of all living things (Cobley 2022: x)

The first lesson that the central semiotic concept of *sign* offers, in varied accounts, is not so much that the sign or semiosis are definite entities. It is, rather, that 'stuff' is *about* 'stuff'. The sign, signs and semiosis are not self-enclosed; instead, they are gateways to worlds. Often, those worlds are made up of more semiosis; but they sometimes contain phenomena that are not semiosis – at the very least, they can involve a strong awareness that there is *something* beyond semiosis (Deely 1994).

The effort to focus on the essence of *something* reveals an *aboutness*, referred to in some accounts as *intentionality*, in others as *significance* (see Deely 2001: 404, Short 2006). As we find ourselves in the Anthropocene, a period of uncertainties, semiotics, in its many forms, often lends itself to various other academic disciplines – from philosophy to sociology, communication and media studies and to natural sciences and engineering – as an underpinning framework to reconsider old protocols and destabilize traditional boundaries. The present book unravels such research avenues. It is divided into three sections corresponding to three general ways in which semiotic theories are employed in contributing to the academy. They are respectively titled *Semiotic epistemologies*, *Contemporary schools of theoretical semiotics* and *Applications and practical discussions*.

The first section consists in ample and minute epistemological discussions, the type with which semiotics is often charged. Chapter 1 welcomes the reader to *Semiosistan* through a thought experiment: the creation of a nation entirely composed by semioticians. Massimo Leone reflects on what characteristics the inhabitants of this nation should have. Beyond the formal requirements of a robust engagement with semiotics, the chapter concludes that the most important value in this fictional country would be the commitment to approach the world through language, instead of violence, and to believe in the possibility to cultivate a reasonable community of interpreters. A country for semioticians, therefore, is not needed, since semioticians should, on the contrary, venture into the world and spread their message of trust in the reasonability that underlies the human capacity for language. This announces what the reader is bound to find in a collection of texts by leading semiotics scholars on the state-of-the-art of this subject: challenging but inspiring disagreements.

In Chapter 2, Donald Favareau unfurls the arguments for semiotic realism, as an epistemology that avoids the loopholes left by scholastic nominalism for modern science. He draws on John Deely, who noted that "every substance and every accident is maintained by realities of circumstance and being other than itself" (2001: 228). This implies the view that all things arise and are maintained within a dense web of inextricably interwoven *relationships*. Thus the question for modernist science since at least the time of Ockham becomes whether or not such 'relationships' *per se* can be said to have a genuine, and sometimes end-directed, existence in their own right (the doctrine of *semiotic realism*), or whether they are merely the linguistic and analytical constructions that observers impose upon their acts of apprehending the conjoint activity of particular things (the doctrine of *nominalism*, which today mostly takes the form of *scientific instrumentalism*). Favareau explains that recent advances in both biology and semiotics support the necessity of semiotic realism as an irreducible organizing principle in the living world.

By employing specific semiotic tools, in Chapter 3, Eric Landowski and Jean-Paul Petitimbert observe changes that the idea and method of science have recently undergone, alongside social, technological and environmental changes. Complexity, as a notion stemming from systems theory and of increasing importance for philosophy of science, is discussed in light of regimes of meaning, particularly those of manipulation and adjustment. Incompleteness is considered a key element of scientific inquiry and, arguably, of knowledge in general, underpinning the notions of complexity and emergence which supersede outdated and simplistic pretenses about determinism and indeterminism. The chapter ends by reflecting on the capacity of humans to employ science to survive the sixth mass extinction which we have produced by destabilizing the biosphere into the Anthropocene which we now inhabit.

In Chapter 4, Gary Shank offers a thorough discussion of Peirce's concept of inquiry. He notes that, while Peirce often changed his ideas, he never deviated from the description of postcartesian inquiry introduced in his early work. Shank argues that Peirce considered that the task of inquiry is to pursue a search for meaning, most often in the face of genuine doubt, that would be ultimately validated through the world of experience. Peirce turned from the Cartesian 'cogito' toward a collective model of understanding that leads to truth. Shank builds on these notions to explore just how revolutionary Peirce's turn from Descartes was. In particular, Descartes's project of reducing duality to unity is shifted in the exact opposite direction. Instead of moving from two to one, Peirce showed the way to move from two to three. Shank explains that, by understanding the almost fractal nature of triads in our empirical world, Peirce's ideas can move us from reductionism toward an expansive type of triadic understanding that, by its nature, provides stability.

Basarab Nicolescu explores the possible roles of semiotic approaches in the effort of establishing transdisciplinary science in Chapter 5. Technological singularity is defined as a hypothetical event in which artificial intelligence would be capable of recursive self-improvement or of autonomously building machines smarter and more powerful than itself, up to the point of an *intelligence explosion*, that yields an intelligence surpassing all current human control or understanding. Nicolescu reviews the different opinions expressed around this idea and around the idea of transhumanism. In this endeavour, he ponders on the phenomenon of panterrorism and the theme of the Anthropocene. He posits that the transdisciplinary interaction of philosophy and spirituality with other sciences, exact and human, is the privileged means of resistance to a new barbarism. *Transdisciplinary philosophy*, he argues, must be a philosophy that integrates transdisciplinary methodology.

Section 2 comprises discussions on the actuality of some important semiotic theories from long-enduring traditions, such as the semiotics of A. J. Greimas to new proposals, such as the semiotics of economic transaction, by Kristian Bankov. The first paper in this section, Chapter 6, consists of Andrew Stables' account of the academic trajectory that led to his interest in semiotics and in construing education from a fully semiotic perspective. As such, the chapter offers an insightful account of the semiotic approach to education that, pioneered by Stables, gained much popularity in the past decade. The paper delves into an encompassing discussion of both Western metaphysics in general and, contextually, scholarly trends in British academia, where semiotics is not mainstream, especially given the analytical tradition there. Stables' chapter unfurls the arguments for which semiotics, taking the side of process as opposed to substance metaphysics, can collapse mind/body dualism, in the broader discussion of overcoming the long-standing divide in Western philosophy and science between empiricism and rationalism. The discussion supports a semiotic doctrine of rich empiricism, where the sign is defined as a feature of an event, experience as the subject's implication in events and events as the manifestations of processes. The chapter concludes by pondering on the importance of these considerations for learning and education through the example of educational policy.

In Chapter 7, Kristian Bankov proposes a semiotic theory of economic transaction, as a new approach to the mechanisms of transaction of economic value. Analyzing the nature of the main semiotic device for value transactions – the money sign – Bankov equates the trust in the future of the economic system of exchange and the scarcity of its availability with the condition for its value and meaning. Such characteristics lead to a search for theoretical support in the existential analytics of temporality, as devised by Heidegger, where Bankov finds a homology between economic scarcity and the thesis of the primordial finitude of temporality, namely the scarcity of time. Thus, he distinguishes between two levels of semiotic analysis of transactions: a deep/authentic level of the primordial formation of value and a superficial level of commercial practices of market exchange. From this point of view, the new digital economy seems to bridge the two levels, transforming the availability of time for each person into the major economical resource. The study concludes with some critical remarks, from a semiotic perspective, on neoliberal financial excesses.

Chapter 8 addresses ecosemiotics. Timo Maran argues that addressing ecological problems requires an ontological position that sees environmental processes simultaneously as semiotically mediated and rooted in ecosystems. For example, problems such as the effects of global environmental change, non-human animals coping with urbanized environments and human migration due to environmental degradation, bond sign processes and the flows of matter and energy. According to Maran, ecosemiotics provides a robust conceptual framework for studying these topics. The chapter proposes a toolbox that combines: the ecosemiotic sphere as a general concept for ecosemiotic research; activity centres, which are *loci* in the ecosemiotic sphere with distinct identities and dynamics, bringing along change; relations between activity centres that are the primary object of ecosemiotic study. The proposed framework brings together some specific concepts, such as, among others, affordance, semiotic pollution, ecological code, meaning transfer, semiocide. From this perspective, Maran explains how ecosemiotics holds a good potential for analyzing crucial contemporary environmental problems.

Jacques Fontanille explores, in Chapter 9, the anthropological dimension of Greimas' semiotics, alongside the linguistic and phenomenological dimensions. This inquiry reveals the need to complement this theory with more recent theoretical insights in order to answer more comprehensively to contemporary issues. In this regard, Fontanille draws attention to discussions in media studies on retransmission, remediation and re-enunciation, as well as schemas considered recently in anthropology which can lend themselves to broadening the scope of Greimas' narrative semiotics. While constituting contemporary trends in media studies, the former notions are traceable back to the structuralist semiotic frameworks with which Greimas engaged in debate. As such, they are here discussed in regard to the notion of semiotic regimes. The paper offers an encompassing model for studying human relations by enriching anthropology with narratological concepts as well as *vice versa*.

Eero Tarasti discusses existential semiotics, a semiotic theory that he initiated. Chapter 10 offers an overview of what Tarasti called the Zemic model. As a key concept in existential semiotics, the Zemic model is explained in light of considerations in both semiotics and existential philosophy. By accounting for the transcendence of the human self as a semiotic phenomenon, this notion can be employed in the scrutiny of any human fact. As an important area of application of the Zemic model, the paper concludes with a discussion on forecasting future and emergent reality.

Section 3 of this volume consists in a broad array of practical applications of major semiotic theories to salient contemporary issues. These applications showcase the contemporary epistemological importance of imagery, iconicity, the body and mediality, advocating semiotic rather than analytic approaches to conceptualization and meaning. In Chapter 11, Yunhee Lee offers a semiotic approach to intermedial narratives. She observes that post-classical narratology developed in two directions: contextualism and cognitivism. Contextualist narrative tends to represent the external world by way of cultural and historical parameters, while cognitivist narrative represents the internal world of mental phenomena. Contextualist narratologies harbour a diachronic view, construing narrative as an instrument to contextualize or historicize, whereas cognitivist narratologies regard narrative as embodied in medium specifics. The chapter examines the possible dialogical collaboration of the two directions by looking at the intermediality of narrative between poetry and film. From a Peircean perspective, narrative inquiry has two faces, namely, poetic and rhetoric. The relation between "narrative imagination" in poetry and "imagistic narrative" in film is elaborated, here, from a first-person perspective. Examining their dialogical interaction, the chapter aims to show how narrative form as an impregnator for sense-making is transmitted through medium specifics, entering through poetics and coming out through rhetoric. Lee concludes that intermedial narrative showcases communication media as a condition for identifying selfhood.

Chapter 12 also offers media analyses, but in a different interrogation and with a different scope. By assuming that a city should, first and foremost, be compared with itself, with its own past and with its present ideals and realities, its sources and outcomes, Mariana Neț offers an insightful semiotic outlook on *Belle Epoque* Bucharest. This period of (European) history roughly stretches between 1880 and 1914 and was a turning point in the development of the city of Bucharest. Neț explains how during this time Romania's capital city turned into a modern, Western European type of city in many respects. Histories and monographs account for its rapid progress, its many urban improvements, as several foreign travellers' accounts also do. Neț draws on such texts to testify the plurality of lifestyles and world views in turn-of-the-century Bucharest.

Chapter 13, by Donna West, is a timely study on potential applications of Charles S. Peirce's semiotics in psychology. West explains that Peirce's concept of virtual habit (1909: MS 620) constitutes a scaffold for abductive reasoning. Virtual habits compel the conduct employed to avert anticipated consequences, surfacing as vivid action-images which are so specific that they qualify as determinations, soon to be enacted. The argument is that although they do not rise to the level of habit, in that repetition is not yet materialized, they serve a higher calling, inciting novel hypotheses, particularly in children (habit-change). Vivid, episodic memories emerge at the age of 3;0, when indices differentiate the 'where' of event scenes. These memories are constructed when the index hastens the application of logic to cause-effect scenarios, such that spatial relations suggest a logic for event frames/scenes. Thus, the chapter shows how Peirce's concept of virtual habit (compelling, episodic images) constitutes the most effective preparation for implementing novel inferences.

Juha Ojala tackles the important and complex notion of agency. Chapter 14 provides a naturalist-pragmatist analysis of agency and its development across the continuum of biological and social processes of signification using specific

Peircean tools (phaneroscopic categories, semiotic triangle, the tenfold sign, inquiry, habits, representation and hard and soft facts). Ojala argues that the sensorimotor agent is a simple semiotic system: an organism with "direct coupling" with the environment. The embodied basis of its learning enables the development of agency. Meaning is located in habits of action, as habits allow for the prediction of future. Through hard and soft facts, we negotiate our position in the world. For that, inquiry involves constant evaluation of the relation of the Signs of ourselves and other Objects, including other subjects. Adopting this Peircean perspective, Ojala claims that the communicative revelation empowers the instrumental agent to claim the semiotic space of opportunities to operate with signs for self and for others to interpret, reaching the full extent of semiotic agency.

In Chapter 15, José Enrique Finol showcases how semiotic theory is crucial for understanding the concepts of eroticism and pornography. He proposes a vision of these two concepts, in a semiotic key, in a frame that starts from a phenomenological concept of the body. He correlates these concepts with those of coquetry and flirtation, in a way that reveals a series of cultural ways of looking at the body and of speaking of it. The concepts of body motion and body rest are also employed to frame the senses of eroticism and pornography.

Zdzisław Wąsik takes a historical-evolutionary approach to language as an individual property of speakers and learners, in Chapter 16. The discussion starts against the background of divergent evolutionism and convergent diffusionism, stating that languages have a mixed character. Wąsik claims that the semiotic expressivity of humans manifests in a conflation, or a set of binary relations, formed by multiplicity of interconnected points, or linkage positions, in intentional productions and utilizations of verbal signs, referring to virtual or actual things and states of affairs, which form the signified and communicated reality of everyday life. In this framework, the natural and cultural layers of language are regarded as potential tiers owing to the innate character of the speech faculty as embedded in hereditarily specialized neuronal centers of human brains to communicate by the use of verbal means and through the implementation of certain physiological techniques. Wąsik assumes that these layers might have emerged as a result of evolutionary adaptations of human organisms to their natural and artificial surroundings through the extension of certain communicational abilities.

As with semiotics as a disciplinary field, there is much cross-reference in this volume and the knowledge inhering in it could have been figured in numerous different ways. Yet, like the first *Semiotics and its Masters* volume, the division into *Semiotic epistemologies*, *Contemporary schools of theoretical semiotics* and *Applications and practical discussions* aims to mediate an academic heritage to future generations of semiotics masters, ushering new possibilities for semiotic research and rendering manageable the fecund flux of contemporary semiotic debate without failing to indicate its vibrancy.

Alin Olteanu
Käte Hamburger Kolleg *Cultures of Research*
RWTH Aachen University
Germany
November 2022

Acknowledgement: The Käte Hamburger Kolleg *Cultures of Research*, where Alin Olteanu is based, is funded by the German Ministry for Education and Research (*Bundesministerium für Bildung und Forschung*).

References

Bankov, Kristian & Paul Cobley (eds.). 2017. *Semiotics and its Masters: Volume 1*. Berlin: De Gruyter Mouton.

Cobley, Paul. 2022 (forthcoming). Global semiotics. In Jamin Pelkey (ed.), *The Bloomsbury companion to semiotics* Volume 1, 17–37. London: Bloomsbury.

Deely, John. 1994. *The human use of signs, or Elements of anthroposemiosis*. Lanham, MD.: Rowman and Littlefield.

Deely, John. 2001. *Four ages of understanding: The first postmodern survey of philosophy from ancient times to the turn of the twenty-first century*. Toronto: University of Toronto Press.

Martinelli, Dario, Audronė Daubarienė, Simona Stano & Ulrika Varankaitė (eds.). 2018. *Cross-inter-multi-trans: Proceedings of the 13th World Congress of the International Association for Semiotic Studies (IASS/AIS)*. Kaunas: IASS Publications & International Semiotics Institute.

Short, Thomas L. 2007. *Peirce's theory of signs*. Cambridge: Cambridge University Press.

Peirce, Charles S. 1867–1913. Unpublished manuscripts are dated according to the *Annotated Catalogue of the Papers of Charles S. Peirce*, ed. Richard Robin. 1967. Amherst: University of Massachusetts Press, and confirmed by the Peirce Edition Project. Indianapolis: Indiana University-Purdue University.

Contents

Alin Olteanu
Preface —— V

Section 1: **Semiotic epistemologies**

Massimo Leone
Welcome to Semiosistan! —— 3

Donald Favareau
Beyond teleonomy: Towards a biology of semiotic realism —— 13

Eric Landowski, Jean-Paul Petitimbert
Risky heuristics —— 39

Gary Shank
The semiotic inquirer and the practice of empirical inquiry —— 59

Basarab Nicolescu
Transdisciplinarity as a solution to the challenges of the contemporary world —— 75

Section 2: **Contemporary schools of theoretical semiotics**

Andrew Stables
Notes towards a semiotic theory of learning —— 89

Kristian Bankov
Scarcity and meaning: Towards a semiotics of economic transaction —— 111

Timo Maran
Applied ecosemiotics: Ontological basis and conceptual models —— 129

Jacques Fontanille
The anthropological dimension of Greimas' narrative semiotics. The case of transmission and (re) transmission —— 151

Eero Tarasti
What happens? The Zemic model in existential semiotics —— 169

Section 3: Applications and practical discussions

Yunhee Lee
Intermedial narrative as communication media: Imagination, narrative, and selfhood from Peirce's semiotic perspective —— 207

Mariana Neţ
Icons of modernity in *belle époque* Bucharest. The semiotics of city guides and yearbooks, foreign travellers' *memoirs*, postcards and cinema —— 227

Donna E. West
Glimpses into Peircean event imaging: Episode-simulation as a scaffold for right-guessing —— 249

Juha Ojala
Development of agency as semiotic empowerment: A Peircean analysis —— 273

José Enrique Finol
On the corposphere: Body, eroticism and pornography —— 299

Zdzisław Wąsik
Natural and cultural layers in the discursive becoming of language as a semiotic system —— 311

Index —— 337

Section 1: **Semiotic epistemologies**

Massimo Leone
Welcome to Semiosistan!

Abstract: The article proposes a thought experiment, the creation of a nation entirely composed by semioticians, and wonders what characteristics its inhabitants should have. Beyond the formal requirements of a robust engagement with semiotics, the article concludes that the most important value in this fictional country would be the commitment to approach the world through language, instead of violence, and to believe in the possibility to cultivate a reasonable community of interpreters. A country for semioticians, therefore, is not needed, since they should, on the opposite, venture into the world and spread their message of trust in the reasonability that underlies the human capacity for language.

Keywords: Semiotics, interpretive reasonability, social commitment, violence, unreasonability

> Comment voulez-vous gouverner un pays qui a deux cent quarante-six variétés de fromage ? (Charles de Gaulle)

1 The birth of a nation

Dystopias often tell the story of an invasion. A multitude of strangers swarms into a space, disrupting its values. In countless US early 20th-century novels, Italians, Irish, or Chinese invade America, dispossess the white race, and take control. Toward the end of the century, aliens, monsters, and zombies become the protagonists of catastrophic tales. But in the last week of June 2017, following the decision to organize a world congress of semiotics in a city like Kaunas, a new dystopia arose: the invasion of semioticians. They were everywhere in the centre of the city: jogging along the Neman river at dawn, sipping coffee in bars in the morning, strolling along the elegant boulevards in the afternoon, purchasing vast amounts of amber and linen at dusk. In such week, no place in the centre of Kaunas was immune from this overwhelming presence, except, perhaps, some of the deserted parallel sessions of the congress itself.

Disquieting as this image might seem to the lay locals, however, such occupation turns, to the eyes of semioticians, from dystopia to utopia. What if semioticians

Massimo Leone, University of Turin

https://doi.org/10.1515/9783110857801-001

finally take over? What if they federate so as to establish, in 2017 Kaunas, a new country called "Semiosistan", a country entirely governed by semioticians?

2 Choosing a flag

The geopolitical fiction is not entirely fanciful: flicking through the elegant book of abstracts of the congress, one gathers the impression that semioticians can deal with everything, from climate change to terrorism, from vegan food to porn movies. But a number of intriguing questions would immediately arise in Semiosistan. If one looks up a country in Wikipedia, some constant elements characterize it, usually in the right column of the page. The first of them is a flag. How would the flag of Semiosistan look like? Semioticians would fight over the decision: Greimas' semiotic square on a black background would look a little like the flag of ISIS (International Semiotic Institute State), but also Peirce's triangle on a white background would look overly minimalist; and what about keeping the giant "S" of the IASS, also in order to convey the idea that Semiosistan is a country of super human beings? Choosing the coat of arms, the national hymn, the capital (Paris? Bologna? Tartu? Vilnius?), the official languages, and even the demonym of Semiosistan would entail fierce discussions; yet most of these questions could be settled quite rapidly, during a IASS assembly, for instance.

Two further questions, instead, would stay unsettled, demanding a much longer and deeper reflection on the nature of the new nation. The first question would be: who is a citizen of Semiosistan? In other words, how does one earn the right to name themselves a national of such a utopian country? Would, for instance, marrying a famous semiotician be sufficient to receive a semiotic passport? The second question would be: what are the values of Semiosistan? In other words, what kind of future does Semiosistan depict for itself and strive for?

3 Defining citizenship

As regards the first question, some funny tests virally circulate through the web, with such titles as "What Nationality Are You Subconsciously?" or, more peremptorily, "What Should Your Nationality Be?" We all know these tests and have fallen for them at least once: replying to a series of questions, such as "What's the most important thing in society?" or "How important are tradition and family?", one is progressively oriented toward the conclusion that, despite what one's passport says, one actually is Italian, or French, or German at heart. It is somehow an injustice that such tests never allow one to find out that one is, for instance, Lithuanian at heart. But let's just imagine, for once, that one of these tests also considers small countries or countries overlooked by Eurocentric history, and even includes such a newly established and tiny country as Semiosistan. Answering what questions, and how, would someone be declared a "semiotician" at heart?

Depending on how the test is designed, it could be surprising in both ways: on the one hand, someone who has believed to be a historian, or a sociologist, or a musicologist all her or his life, would be suddenly put in front of the sheer truth: you are a semiotician at heart my friend, please accept it and learn the new hymn (composed by Eero Tarasti of course). On the other hand, however, the test would also reorient toward a new spiritual country those researchers who, despite calling themselves semioticians, teaching semiotics, participating in semiotic congresses, and even wearing semiotic t-shirts, actually are sociologists, or psychologists, or historians at heart, or even belong to the stateless community of cultural studies, or to the displaced community of philosophy. What questions, then, would unmask both the crypto-semiotician and the pseudo-semiotician?

Some of them would detect immediate signs of national belonging, like the one hundred questions that the US Government used to print on the back of yellow pages so as to help prospective applicants for citizenship to become good nationals. As a mild provocation, I shall now dare to formulate some of the hundred questions for obtaining the citizenship of Semiosistan. The first question would read as follows: "Dear participant of the 2017 IASS Congress, please reread the text of your paper; does it explicitly mention the word "semiotics" or its derivatives at least once? If not, then I'm sorry, but you are maybe at the wrong congress. Second: please reread the footnotes and bibliography of your paper; do they contain references to the names of some of the founding fathers of the discipline, for instance Saussure, Greimas, Barthes, Peirce, Eco, Lotman, etc.? If not, then I'm sorry, but you are maybe at the wrong congress again. Third: does your paper substantially mention some specifically semiotic concepts, such as semiosis, signifier, signified, connotation, denotation, semiosphere, semiotic square, interpretant, object etc.? If not, I'm sorry for the third time, but your paper should have been presented at another congress. Fourth: when you come across another congress participant, do you obsessively engage a conversation on the destiny of semiotics? If not, you should leave Semiosistan immediately".

4 The values of a nation

Besides these immediate signs of recognition, however, the citizenship of Semiosistan should depend on something much deeper and difficult to pinpoint: that is, one's adhesion to the values of the nation. Indeed, it would be possible for someone to never mention the word "semiotics", never quote its masters, never fidget with its concepts, and never ponder its fate, and still deserve full citizenship, exactly by virtue of one's adhesion to the central values of the nation. What values, then, earn one honorary citizenship in Semiosistan? What brings us together, fellow semioticians and Semiosistanians, despite our differences of origin, language, semiotic faith, and, increasingly, dietary restrictions (by the way, Dario Martinelli and I are currently writing a book entitled *How to Travel with a Gigantic Piece of Seitan*)?

I shall now conclude the slightly tongue-in-cheek section of this paper by reminding you that, some years ago, at a lengthy symposium, I tried to wake up myself and the audience through proposing a Decalogue on "How to Become a Semiotician"; here it goes, written on digital stones:

1. You shall study semiotics; choosing a good university course with a good teacher; reading books, articles, essays; going back to the classics, avoiding compendiums, readers, and also most online materials: they are not good (for the moment);
2. You shall practice semiotics; initially through purposeless analysis; through interpretation for the sake of interpretation; annoy your friends with semiotics;
3. You shall befriend other semioticians; meeting them regularly not only on the web, but also in congresses, symposia, colloquia; remember to celebrate semio-festivities;
4. You shall not turn semiotics into a rhetoric; semiotics' purpose is to help other people to understand meaning, not to convince them that you understand it better than them;
5. You shall not turn semiotics into magic; semiotics is a discipline, one should be disciplined in learning and in practicing it;
6. You shall not turn semiotics into religion; semiotics is only one out of a multitude of options; respect other disciplines and ask respect from them;
7. You shall not turn semiotics into science; let's face it: semiotics is part of the humanities; thank god meaning will never be ruled by the laws of necessity;
8. You shall not turn semiotics into mystery; if nobody understands you but other semioticians, you are a failure;
9. You shall not turn semiotics into bar conversation; if everybody appreciates you except other semioticians, you are a failure too;

10. You shall not be worried that your mother doesn't understand what you do; most people who do new things have skeptical mothers.

I still believe in this Decalogue, although compendiums of semiotics have considerably improved in the meantime, as well as attempts at making it closer to natural sciences. Articulate as it might read, however, such list of commandments would still not fully grasp the deep values of Semiosistan; the injunctions of the Decalogue, indeed, would probably work for all humanities. What is it, then, in the rarefied sphere of academic values, that sets semiotics apart?

5 Why Greimas matters

At the Semiotics World Congress, in Kaunas 2017, I was invited to participate in a roundtable to commemorate Algirdas J. Greimas and to propose my ideas on the current relation between semiotics and society. I was, I must confess, deeply humbled to enjoy this plenary space, meaning that my audience had no alternative but to listen to me or play with a smartphone. Moreover, I was even more humbled to share this plenary roundtable with such distinguished colleagues as Jacques Fontanille and Eric Landowski. Despite having met them personally a number of times, including at breakfast, these two names still mainly sound not as names of colleagues but as names of central semiotic authors. Fontanille, to me, is not as much a person I come across at breakfast time in my hotel as a recurring item in my bibliographies. Yet, something fundamental set us apart in this task of both commemoration and reflection. Unlike them, I never met Greimas as a person. I met him, instead, as an author, when my mentor Omar Calabrese first suggested to me, then a young student at the University of Siena, to read *Du sens*. Therein I was shocked to discover Greimas' (1970: 7) most famous sentence: "Il est extrêmement difficile de parler du sens et d'en dire quelque chose de sensé" ("it is extremely difficult to talk about meaning and to say something meaningful about it"). The English translation does not fully capture the semantics of the original French, but gives at least an idea of why Greimas is, still nowadays, a fundamental author whom we should all read, and have our students read, independently from our semiotic denomination.

The importance of Greimas, as well as the importance of semiotics, stands out especially if one plays with the most famous sentence of the Lithuanian (or Franco-Lithuanian) scholar in a structural way, for instance, through exploring its antonyms. The main problem of our times, indeed, is not that saying something meaningful about meaning is difficult, but that saying something meaningless about meaning is becoming increasingly easy. In 2015, I had the great honour to bestow an honorary degree on Umberto Eco; it was certainly more an honour for me than for him, for whom it was honorary degree number forty-two. At the end of the ceremony, there was a press conference and, on that occasion, Eco pronounced a sentence that then created turmoil in the media (e.g. Nicoletti 2015) and still remains a sort of a motto of that Turin celebration: "I social media danno diritto di parola a legioni di imbecilli"; "the social media give the right to speak to legions of imbeciles". Many young bloggers attacked Eco as though he were a senile academic at the end of his career, hammering the new media of his time out of nostalgia. The founding father of Italian semiotics, however, was bashing social media not from the point of view of a reactionary intellectual, but from that of a progressive thinker. Eco, it is well known, extolled the value of lowbrow culture during all his life, continuously mixing it with elite and highbrow culture in his works. In bashing the imbeciles of social media, Eco was actually trying to defend the intellectual value of mass culture.

6 On imbecility

Who is, indeed, an imbecile? How do you say imbecile in the languages of the IASS? *Imbécile, imbécil, schwachsinnig, imbecille*: in the traditional etymology of the word, an imbecile is someone who is "*sine baculo*", that is, "without a staff" or "without a stick", i.e. someone who cannot support him- or herself. Social media have extended, to a mass of imbeciles, the possibility to speak publicly because many, if not most, speakers in the social media have no arguments to support what they say but also, more pathetically, because they possess no other weapon than their unfounded imbecilities. As a consequence, today, it is extremely easy to talk about meaning and to say something meaningless. That is so because it is increasingly hard to single out, pinpoint, and debunk meaninglessness. I see it clearly in the domain that I study the most, that of religious fundamentalism and its digital expressions. While I, the semiotician, am painfully striving to demonstrate, for instance, through the application of the Greimassian method, that a radically violent interpretation of a 'sacred' text is unfounded, the fundamentalist imbeciles will have already polluted the web with their unsupported interpretations, often generating millions of copycats: the word "bacillus", too, comes from the Latin "baculus", "stick" or "staff": the stick of imbecility frequently goes viral.

One of the primary values of Semiosistan should therefore be, beyond any difference of semiotic affiliation, that of resisting, exposing, and banning imbeciles. What does that mean, in semiotic terms?

7 The potential of semiotics

Greimas' famous sentence is intrinsically optimistic. It states, as recalled earlier, that it is "extremely difficult to say something meaningful about meaning"; but that implicitly entails that it is, indeed, *possible* to say something meaningful about meaning. It entails, that is, that the field of human experience that we call "meaning", and that seems to represent a large part if not the totality of it, is not subject to chaotic, capricious, and unpredictable forces. On the contrary, it is characterized by patterns endowed with regularity. Observed, described, and analyzed through a specific method, these patterns allow the semiotician to say something meaningful about them. That which matters the most, however, is not the content of what is said. That which matters the most is the possibility of saying it. Throughout the history of semiotics, several methods for grasping and pinpointing signification have been devised. Greimas' generative semiotics is certainly one of the most articulate among them, but it cannot certainly claim with certainty to be neither the best, nor the only one. As a consequence, so as to belong to Semiosistan, one should be required not to swear allegiance to such or such a method, but to the fact itself that a method exists, that is, that human beings are able to develop a meta-discursive framework in which they can reasonably argue about meaning and hopefully reach a peaceful conclusion. In other words, a citizen of Semiosistan must believe that, despite all oddities, idiosyncrasies, and tragedies, the human predicament essentially is language, that is, a domain in which and about which we human beings can emerge from our existential solitude and share a common symbolical ground.

8 Looking for aliens

Worried, like most of my colleagues, about the viability of semiotics, I am always extremely pleased when present-day popular culture hints at this arcane discipline. In a 2016 movie by Denis Villeneuve, *Arrival*, a linguist is contracted by the army for the purpose of deciphering the mysterious language of some monstrous aliens that have just landed on planet Earth. Since the aliens seem to express themselves through secreting a black substance similar to ink into bizarre and irregular circles, the linguist realizes that she has to turn into a semiotician if she wants to interpret the language. The most relevant aspect of this decoding, however, is not the deciphering itself, but the assumption that these black circles can indeed be decoded and associated with meaning through a reasonable procedure of interpretation. Such an assumption is even more relevant when the movie's spectator realizes that the strange aliens and their mysterious language are nothing but a sci-fi metaphor concerning the past, memory, and trauma. There is a way to attach a reasonable meaning to the memory of existential pain, the movie subtly suggests.

When we, the semioticians, commemorate and celebrate the lives and scholarly efforts of deceased colleagues such as Greimas or Eco, we should, therefore, invoke their example as an antidote against those socio-cultural forces that, on the contrary, push human beings to semiotic nihilism. Confronted with the alien, the citizen of Semiosistan seeks to understand it – for it assumes that even the alien, in its need to interact with other aliens and with the environment, exudes meaning. When the imbecile, whose impotent ignorance threatens Semiosistan, is confronted with the alien s/he does not seek to understand. The imbecile shoots. Imbeciles shoot whenever they encounter something that exceeds their meagre capacity for spotting and articulating patterns and regularities in the environment. They shoot and are prey to shooting propaganda – for imbeciles are exactly that: human beings that, for one reason or another, have abdicated the human inclination to exist in language, to reasonably seek a regular correspondence between a sign and its object.

9 Expats forever

After all, it might not be such a good idea to establish the new nation of Semiosistan. I wouldn't like to live in a country where fellow citizens constantly analyze the meaning of my tie. But establishing the new country would not be such a good idea especially because it would represent a slightly cowardly move. Semioticians today do not need to venture into a new world but they need to adventure in the old one. They need to take their sophisticated toolboxes and face the unpleasant feeling of exploring a social reality that increasingly rejects semiotics because it increasingly rejects the idea of a reasonable community of interpreters. We need to face the fundamentalists, the trolls, and the conspiracy theorists of this world. We need to go out there to find our own aliens. It is a risky task, of course. While we strive to interpret the alien, the alien will seek to shoot at us. But if we endure, and above all if we stay united, as in our fantastic congresses, we might one day leave the world with the hope that, like our prestigious predecessors Greimas, Eco, Peirce, etc., we somehow contributed to make it a more intelligible, and therefore a more livable place.

References

Greimas, Algirdas Julien. 1970. *Du sens: essais sémiotiques*, Volume 1. Paris: Éditions du Seuil.

Nicoletti, Gianluca. 2015. Umberto Eco: "Con i social parola a legioni di imbecilli", *La Stampa* 11 June. https://www.lastampa.it/cultura/2015/06/11/news/umberto-eco-con-i-social-parola-a-legioni-di-imbecilli-1.35250428 (accessed 11 January 2022)

Donald Favareau
Beyond teleonomy: Towards a biology of semiotic realism

Abstract: "In actual existence," notes John Deely "every substance and every accident is maintained by realities of circumstance and being other than itself" (2001: 228). Accordingly, all things – including and, perhaps most especially, organisms – arise and are maintained within a dense web of inextricably interwoven *relationships*. Thus the question for modernist science, since at least the time of Ockham, becomes whether or not such 'relationships' *per se* can be said to have a genuine, and sometimes end-directed, existence in their own right (the doctrine of *semiotic realism*), or whether they are merely the linguistic and analytical constructions of we observers, which we impose upon our acts of apprehending the conjoint activity of particular things (the doctrine of *nominalism*, which today mostly takes the form of *scientific instrumentalism*). Recent advances both in biology and in semiotics, it is argued here, support the necessity of semiotic realism as an irreducible organizing principle in the living world.

Keywords: telonomy, finiousity, semiotic realism, teleodyamics, being towards another

1 Introduction: The erasure of semiosis from biology

When the modern discipline of biology was formalized, along with a number of other contemporary scientific disciplines, in the early years of the 19th century, pioneering naturalist Gottfried Reinhold Treviranus (1776–1837) conceived of the project thus:

> The objects of our research will be the different forms and manifestations of life, the conditions and laws under which these phenomena occur, and the causes through which

---

Acknowledgment: Research for this article was funded and conducted under the auspices of National University of Singapore ACRF Research Grant #A-0003116-00-00.

Donald Favareau, University Scholars Programme, National University of Singapore

https://doi.org/10.1515/9783110857801-002

they have been effected. The science that concerns itself with these objects we will indicate by the name Biology [*Biologie*] or the doctrine of life [*Lebenslehre*] (Treviranus 1802: I:4, quoted in Richards 2003: 16).

Yet, despite the broad and holistic purview with which it was thus inaugurated, with the increasing success of material reductionism in Physics and Chemistry at the beginning of the 20th century, the newly-formed discipline of biology slowly began to morph from the search for the *principles* by which living beings act and are organized, to the search for the *mechanisms* by which living beings act and are organized – a subtle but important distinction that was well-documented by Nobel prize winning microbiologist Carl Woese's (1928–2012) observation that:

> The 19th was biology's defining century. There, for the first time, biology's great problems lay scientifically outlined and assembled, with all of them effectively in early stages of development. Nineteenth century biology was a potpourri of problems in that some (like the natures of the gene and of the cell) cried out for dissection, analysis in terms of their parts, whereas others (such as evolution and morphogenesis and the significance of biological form in general) were holistic, metaphysically challenging, and *not* fundamentally understandable as collections of parts. . . . [but] given the temper of the times, the entry of chemistry and physics into biology was inevitable. The technology that these sciences would introduce was not only welcome but very much needed. But *the physics and chemistry that entered biology (especially the former) was a Trojan horse, something that would ultimately conquer biology from within and remake it in its own image*. . . . [for its] fundamentalist reductionism (the reductionism of 19th century classical physics), is in essence metaphysical. It is *ipso facto* a statement about the nature of the world: [i.e., that] living systems (like all else) can be completely understood in terms of the properties of their constituent parts. This is a view that flies in the face of what classically trained biologists tended to take for granted, *the notion of emergent properties* (2004: 184–185; 175, italics mine).

Such a situation led Woese to lament, in an article that he wrote towards the very end of his forty-year career in biology, entitled and calling for *A New Biology for A New Century*, that:

> It is instructive to catalog some of the changes that fundamental reductionism wrought in ourperception and practice of biology. Chief among these is that *the biologist's sense of what is important and what is fundamental was retooled to conform to the classical physicist's perception thereof.* [It is because of this that] biology today is no more *fully* explanatory in principle than physics was a century or so ago. In both cases, the guiding vision had (or has) reached its end, and in both, a new, deeper, more invigorating representation of reality was (or is) called for (2004: 173–175).

While Woese's paradigm-changing rallying cry is relevant to the project of biosemiotics – the notion of "emergent properties" that Woese decries the erasure of, I will argue, is nowhere more critically needed for understanding and explaining life than in the emergent relations of *suprasubjectivity* and *being towards another* that constitute the *ontological grounding* of *sign relations*.

It is important to note that this conceptual erasure has serious consequences not just for practicing biologists, but for all of us, as scientific understandings come to influence cultural understandings and vice-versa. For, indeed, the subsuming of biology, whose purview is the study of the living world, to the methods and analyses proper to the study of the non-living world, has resulted in deleterious changes not only in the biologist's, but also in the average layperson's concept of organism in regards to, as Woese warns,

> his or her view of what constitutes an explanation, in what constitutes a 'comprehensive' understanding of biology, in what biology's relationship to the other sciences is, in what biology can tell us about the nature of reality, in what biology's role in the society is, and in what biology's future course will be (Woese 2004: 174).

This historically contingent supplanting of a holistic approach with a reductionist one in turn produced

> changes in how biological knowledge is organized – the structure of academic curricula, the nature and purview of biological disciplines and text books, the priorities of biological funding agencies – and an overall change in the perception of biology by the society itself. [As a result], all has by now been set in stone. It is impossible to discuss modern biology without the cacophony of materialistic reductionism throughout (ibid).

If this Woese's contention is indeed the case – and the experience and expression of more and more prominent biologists (e.g., Deacon 2011, Hoffmeyer 2008, Kauffman 2016, Noble 2008) increasingly suggest that it is – then a particularly pressing question for science then becomes: how can a biology built on such materialist reductionist foundations ever find a way to deal with something as central to life itself as the immaterial relationality of signs?

For, whether it is the genome, the proteome, or the connectome project, contemporary science can only use the tools that it already possesses to try to understand the dynamics of the living world. Accordingly, the majority of science's explanations remain stuck at the physical and chemical level of analysis and it has neither the vocabulary nor the conceptual tools that would allow it to investigate organisms as other than so-called "soft machines". As a result, and as Frederik Stjernfelt noted at a roundtable on biosemiotics at the IASS Congress in 2007:

> If you take any textbook in contemporary Biology – on any level from Bio-Chemistry and Molecular Biology and all the way up to Ecology and Ethology – and pick some arbitrary page, you'll find semiotic terminology. You'll find biologists talking about *signals* and *codes* and *communication* and *information* – and the strange thing about it is that these

> concepts in ordinary textbooks do not appear as technical concepts. They appear [instead] as straight-off, commonsense concepts. Yet, in many cases, if you go up to the person that wrote that textbook and ask them: "What do you mean by 'stands for' or 'signal' or 'message transfer' and so on?" they will answer, "Well that's just a sort of metaphor; sort of an image. If I tried, I could explain the same phenomenon without using any semiotic terminology." And so the obvious counter-question to that is: "Then why don't you do it?" (Favareau et al. 2008: 7)

Yet so great is the resistance to introducing anything that might be seen as "unscientific" – within a paradigm that has, perhaps mistakenly, defined "scientific" as that which can be explained in exhaustively in terms of matter and energy relations, much in the way that the physics and chemistry of the non-living world can be – that today it is more the norm than the exception for university Life Science majors to be instructed right at the outset of their studies that

> science only studies observable phenomena. It functions in the realm of matter and energy [and therefore] it is a serious mistake to think that the methods of science can be applied in areas of investigation involving other aspects of human experience, e.g., matters of the mind" (Miller and Harley's *Zoology*, 1994: 11).

Similarly, writes Nobel Prize winner Eric Kandel at the conclusion of his authoritative *Principals of Neural Science:* "most neuroscientists and philosophers now take for granted that all biological phenomena, including consciousness, are *properties of matter* . . . and some philosophers and *many neuroscientists* believe that *consciousness is an illusion*" (2000: 1318, italics mine).

Thus, while the sign relation of 'standing for' is ubiquitous in the biological world and most certainly in that subset of the biological world that is the human species, the resistance to studying sign processes in nature *as* genuine *sign* processes – as opposed to just studying the interactions of their material substrates – has a long and principled history in science (a history that I tried to sketch out in its broad strokes in Favareau 2010). Not surprisingly, then, the serious effort to investigate 'subjective experience' *per se* – which is also an undeniably ubiquitous characteristic of all living systems (provided that one does not conflate all kinds of organismic experience with the all but anomalous minority instance of self-conscious, language-employing human subjective experience) has likewise been shunned in natural science as a subject of inquiry in its own right.

2 The inescapable persistence of semiosis in living systems

Throughout the history of modern science, however, there have always been alternative thinkers arguing against the attempt to analytically reduce biological relations to physical and chemical ones. One such thinker was the cybernetician Gregory Bateson (1904–1980) who drew an analytical distinction between the organization and behaviour of what he called, using terminology that he took from Jung, systems of *Pleroma* versus systems of *Creatura*.

For Bateson, Pleroma was the realm of the non-living world wherein causation is unaffected by subjectivity, with all change and being taking place strictly as determined by the mechanistic causality of unthinking material and efficient cause and effect. Creatura, on the other hand, characterizes the mode of causation that is distinctive of the living world – i.e. systems whose organization and action are the result of establishing and detecting system-relevant *differences* and acting volitionally upon such distinctions made from stimuli (Bateson 1972: 462–465; 486–487). Creatura systems are, of course, a special case sub-set of Pleroma systems, in that both are purely physical systems, subject to the same sets of material and energetic physical laws, with the primary distinction being that in inanimate (Pleroma) systems, traditional Newtonian "billiard-ball mechanics" are responsible for all changes of state and position that happen to the system, whereas living (Creatura) systems self-initiate action in response to various stimuli, and have the agency to make (if only in the most primitive sense) decisions in their movements.

Put simply: in the non-living world, inanimate objects are pushed and pulled about by forces and impacts that can be well described and fully explained by the laws of motion, mass and physics. Yet when a living system as simple as a bacterium moves up a sugar gradient, it is not because the sugar molecules are actively pulling it in the way that the gravitational force of the moon pulls the ocean tides; rather, the bacterium is directing a motive power within itself to generate an end-directed movement that has been established not by the physical laws of motion themselves, but by the historical contingency of its lineage's past actions in the world within an evolutionary dynamic.

This is a crucially important ontological distinction that the biosemiotican Jesper Hoffmeyer (1996: 46) captures well when he notes that

> most of what happens between animals themselves or between animals and their environment is triggered by or carried by stimuli which, from a physico-chemical point of view, are negligible when set against the volume of matter and energy thus activated.

The muscle contractions of a 100 pound dog, who takes off running at 15 mph upon the detection of an odorant molecule, are not propelled by the infinitesimal amount of ATP that can be catalyzed from the reception of that molecule (to use Hoffmeyer's example), any more than a classroom of students standing up at their teacher's request are being physically pulled up out of their chairs by the sound waves of the teacher's voice. In both cases, the living Creatura system – unlike a non-living Pleroma one – is using *signs* to guide its actions, and is initiating its own forces according to not just a material-energy dynamic, but according to a *semiotic* dynamic that has emerged as a higher-order organizational and behavioural level for the volitional control of matter-energy expenditure and directedness.

Indeed, as the early 20th century animal physiologist and proto-biosemiotician Jakob von Uexküll (1864–1944) reminds us, in the world of non-living nature we find only *objects* being pushed and pulled by forces; but in the world of living nature we find only *subjects* that are initiating their own actions based on signs. Yet this distinction becomes a problem for the contemporary biologist who, as Woese reminds us, is literally trained in the *erasure* of subjective (and therefore semiotic) experience in his or her explanatory hypothesizing. For this kind of self-initiated, purpose-driven, end-directed action has no comfortable place in the so-called "objective" explanations of science – or at least not in a science that is taking its cues from the Pleroma-examining methods and concepts of contemporary Physics and Chemistry. In Batesonian terms: the biology-ruling paradigm of *materialist physicalism* that Woese decries is the attempt to explain the living world of *Creatura* entirely in terms of the non-living world of *Pleroma*.

Nevertheless, biological (Creatura) systems clearly exhibit not only the specifically end-directed *behaviour* that Uexküll points us to, but specifically end-directed *organization* as well, in the form of functional and purpose-serving proteins, cells, organelles, tissues, organs, and organ systems. "The occurrence of goal-directed processes is perhaps the most characteristic feature of the world of living organisms" wrote the evolutionary biologist Ernst Mayr (1904–2005), whose own work in the establishment of neo-Darwinism, paradoxically, did much to reduce such end-directedness to blind programming, as we shall see. The importance of end-directedness is echoed by his contemporary, the chronobiologist Colin Pittendrigh (1918–1996) who, in a correspondence with Mayr, went so far as to assert that "the objects of biological analysis are *organizations* ([the biologist] calls them *organisms*) and, as such, are end-directed. Organization is more than mere order; order lacks end-directedness; organization *is* end-directed." (Mayr 1974: 98, 115, final italics in the original). The question for science then becomes: who or what is doing the end-directing and how could such end-directedness arise (and continue to take place) in an otherwise utterly non-end-directed universe of Newtonian mechanics?

3 An attempt to square the circle: The non-semiotic concept of teleonomy

Teleological explanation, with its Aristotelian implication that "ends" (*telos*) are operative in the organization and operation of nature, was assumed to have been banished from modern science, first in physics, with the rejection of the authority of the ancient and scholastic thinkers at the outset of the Scientific Revolution, and later in biology, with the rejection of the arguments for end-directed or intelligent design brought about by Darwin's evolutionary theory.

Accordingly, by the middle of the 20th century, the increasing difficulty of maintaining such cognitive dissonance in the life sciences in the face of what clearly seemed to be intelligent and end-directed behaviour evident throughout the animal kingdom, led biologists to explicitly distance themselves from even being mistakenly tagged with the dreaded stigma of "teleology." It was Pittendrigh himself – in response to J.B.S. Haldane's (1892–1964) much-quoted observation that "teleology is like a mistress to a biologist: he cannot live without her, but he's unwilling to be seen with her in public" (quoted in Mayr 1974: 115) – who came up with the more respectable-sounding concept of *teleonomy*. Wrote Pittendrigh (1958: 320):

> Biologists for a while were prepared to say "a turtle came ashore *and* laid its eggs [instead of *to* lay its eggs]." These verbal scruples were intended as a rejection of teleology but were based on the mistaken view that the efficiency of "final causes" is necessarily implied by the simple description of an end-directed *mechanism*. . . . The biologists longstanding confusion would be removed if all end-directed systems were described by some other term, e.g., *teleonomic,* in order to emphasize that recognition and description of end-directedness does not carry a commitment to Aristotelian teleology as an efficient causal principle.

What Pittendrigh, as well as his fellow biologists who adopted the term, such as Ernst Mayr and Jacques Monod (1910–1976) – was attempting to do with this neologism was to preserve what they never fail to qualify as the "apparent" purposiveness of animal behaviour and the "seemingly" intelligently designed organization of organisms within the Neo-Darwinian 'accident and post-hoc genetics' attempt at explaining "evolution without meaning" in the memorable words of biosemiotician Kalevi Kull (*personal communication*). Accordingly, the problems that it was meant to pre-empt, according to philosopher of science Colin Allen (2009), were the charges of:
1. Creationism (of animal organization and behaviour by a supernatural Designer)
2. Vitalism (positing some special ends-seeking "life-force" within living systems)

3. Backwards Causation (invoking future outcomes in explaining present behaviour and the evolution of traits)
4. Incompatibility with Mechanistic Explanation (because of 2 and 3)
5. Mentalism (attributing the action of mind or foresight where there is none)
6. Empirical Untestability (for all the above reasons)

Animal organization and behaviour *do* exhibit "apparent" end-directedness under the teleonomic view of living systems, but the "ends" are not ones that exist as the result of intentional purposes, wants, goals, or future states to be desired, explored or realized. Instead, the teleonomic view proposed that such seemingly "end-directed behavior" are nothing more than the mechanical working out of evolutionary "programming" that itself arose without any purpose, intention or foresight and that has become fixed as a result of the blind, purposeless, post-hoc organizing process of natural selection.

Mayr makes this point about programming explicitly and maintains it as central to his whole understanding when he writes that: "A teleonomic process or behaviour is one which owes its goal-directedness to the operation of a program . . . [and] each particular program is the result of natural selection, constantly adjusted [again, in a completely blind, post-hoc operation] by the selective value of the achieved endpoint" (1974: 99). Such programs, defined as "coded or *prearranged* information that *controls* a process (or behaviour) leading it toward a given end" are, he argues,

> either entirely laid down in the DNA of the genotype ('closed programs') or are constituted in such a way that they can incorporate additional information ('open programs') acquired through learning, conditioning or through other experiences . . . [and] once the open program is filled in, it is equivalent to an originally closed program in its control of teleonomic behaviour" (1974: 103, italics mine).

Thus, by explaining the end-directedness of living systems as an epiphenomenon of evolutionary programming via blind allele removal, neo-Darwinist biologists can then proceed to acknowledge and investigate all the "apparently" end-directed behaviour and organization of organisms with a clear conscience, knowing that they are not going to be charged with any of the six objections that Allen lists above, and that, just as in Stjernfelt's account, all talk about future "ends" directing current behaviour (much less of "codes", "information" and "signals", which Mayr invokes repeatedly throughout his argument, without reflecting upon their semiotic provenance), "is all just a sort of metaphor; sort of an image", which, if they tried, they "could explain without using any semiotic [or teleological] terminology."

Once again, however, the problems caused by such an evasion of the reality of meaning-making by and between living systems go beyond the world of working biologists but proceeds, via the schools and popular media, directly into the (mis)understandings carried and acted upon by the members of the broader culture itself. "The hypothesis that adaptations arise without the existence of a prior purpose, but by chance may change the fitness of the organism" is how the widely-assigned *Oxford Dictionary of Zoology*, for example, defines *teleonomy* for its life science student readers (Allaby 2003:50). Meanwhile Wikipedia, which is one of the main resources through which the average person comes in contact with the 'authority' of science, neglects to even designate the idea as a "hypothesis", presenting it instead as if it were an ontological fact of nature:

> Teleonomy is the quality of only *apparent* purposefulness and of goal-directedness of structures and functions in living organisms that is brought about by natural laws (like natural selection). Teleonomy is sometimes contrasted with teleology, where the latter is understood as a purposeful goal-directedness brought about through *human or divine intention*. Teleonomy is thought to derive from evolutionary history, adaptation for reproductive success, and/or the operation of a program.

What follows logically from the acceptance of such premises is the familiar litany of implications that biosemiotics has long been arguing against:

(1) that the purposiveness and end-directed actions of "living organisms" (which must, of course, include ourselves) is only "apparent" or illusory purposiveness: e.g., the mechanical working out of programs;
(2) that adaptations in the natural world arise by "chance" – the purposive actions of organisms play no role in shaping natural selection (other than in mate selection and geographical distribution, which likewise are reducible to either chance or to the mechanical working out of internal programs);
(3) that for reasons that remain utterly unexplained (and, in fact, directly contradict what is being implicated in point 1), "human" goal-directedness is assumed and unproblematic, while animal goal-directedness is not (this, in an "evolutionary" account of teleology, no less!) and
(4) that the only conceivable alternative to explaining animal purposiveness as being illusory is human anthropomorphizing or an appeal to supernatural forces.

By contrast, the idea that "end-directedness" of all kinds in the living world[1] – functions, goals, purposive action, intentionality (whether explicitly mentalized or otherwise), the active negotiation of multiple possibilities, etc. – is ineluctably bound up with the nature and use of *sign* processes, is widely recognized in the biosemiotics community, where Hoffmeyer (2008), Markoš (2002), Kull (2014), Brier (2008), Barbieri (2003), Bruni (2015) and Stjernfelt (2014) – to name just a few – have contributed important ideas on the as yet under-examined roles of *semiotic scaffolding, biohermeneutics, non-Darwinian evolution, cybersemiotic signification spheres, natural conventions, heterarchical semiosis* and *natural propositions*, respectively, as naturally arising phenomena in the organization and action of living systems. Such ideas may serve as at least preliminary conceptual frameworks to help us better understand the reality of living systems' integral end-directedness, while yet scrupulously avoiding the six "fallacies of teleology" listed by Colin Allen above. For clearly, a purely reductionist approach of the kind used in traditional chemistry and physics is going to be necessary but insufficient in describing and understanding the relationships whereby living systems have learned (whether over evolutionary or ontogenetic time) to turn environmental cues into signs for self-initiated action.

Outside of the biosemiotics community proper, too, interest has been growing in challenging the dominant neo-Darwinist evolutionary paradigm that 'accidents happen and become fixed' largely through the processes of random mutation and mate selection, so as to acknowledge and to better understand the contributing role that an organism's own actions in the world play in shaping the course of evolution, rather than reducing animals and their behaviour to the mere vehicles for gene transfer. Physiologist Denis Noble (2008), microbiologist James Shapiro (2011), and the members of the Third Way of Evolution group (http://www.thethird wayofevolution.com) have been at the forefront of this movement, just as theoretical biologists Terrence Deacon (2011, 2013) and Stuart Kauffman (1996, 2016), each in their own way, have been working to develop models of biological evolution in which "ends" are real products of animal behaviour and organization that can be

---

[1] And here is where the distinction between Pleroma and Creatura becomes particularly salient, for even Mayr acknowledges that there are processes in the inanimate world – such as gravity and the second law of thermodynamics – which lead to "end states", but these states are reached "only in a passive, automatic way, regulated by external forces or conditions" and are not, crucially for him, governed by the active working out of a "program." Mayr christens these processes *teleomatic* ones and acknowledges that the processes found in living nature "are of an entirely different nature than *teleomatic* processes" (1974: 98). Terrence Deacon's current project (2011) is to show how such *teleomatic* processes can, under the right conditions, lead to *teleodynamic*, genuinely end-directed and even semiotic processes – but that discussion would need an entire paper of its own.

accounted for naturalistically, and are not just the working out of "coded and pre-arranged programs" that have been "built in" to organisms as the accidental result of genetic recombination alone, as Mayr would have it.

All of the above researchers have important and innovative ideas to contribute towards developing a more accurate and nuanced understanding of the concept of "teleology", or end-directedness, in nature. Since the current volume is devoted to contemporary semiotics, I would like here to focus instead on one powerful and much-needed argument that comes not from a biologist at all, but from the philosopher and semiotician John Deely (1942–2017). I hope to show how that argument can inform and is congruent with the work of some of today's cutting-edge scientific thinkers in better understanding and explaining the characteristic end-directedness we find in living systems.

4 An alternative approach to understanding end-directedness: Semiotic realism

Deely was trained as a Thomist, and no matter how far his own investigation into the actions of signs took him, his works suggest (at least to me) that throughout his career, he is consistently arguing – albeit in a massively more updated, complex and sophisticated way – for Thomas Aquinas' anachronistically post-modern understanding that: "Sign relations partake of a dual being: one in singular things, another in the soul, and each contribute their respective accidents to it" so as to result in a genuinely distinct ontological state of being-towards-another, or mediative third ([1252]/1965: ¶57, as paraphrased in Favareau 2015a: 240).

Indeed, it is precisely the modernist divide of dichotomized mind-dependent and mind-independent reality that Aquinas radically opposes in what is, ultimately, a biosemiotic perspective. Likewise, it was part of John Deely's career-long mission to combat the erroneous

> common usage of the terms 'object' and 'subject', with their derivatives, [which are] the outcome of three centuries of modern thought wherein philosophy sought to distinguish so-called "epistemology" from "ontology" in order to show that the former alone could establish the foundations for human knowledge from purely within the knowing subject (Deely 2009: 14).

Deely was convinced that ontology itself, and not just epistemology, can and must be implicated in the actualisation of knowledge, if we and all other animals are to have any true knowledge of the world at all (even if just true enough to live in it). With Peirce, Deely consistently argued for a doctrine of *semiotic realism*, wherein sign relations are understood to be, in the first instance, not the mental constructions of human (or even animal) minds, but instead are genuinely existing relations that humans and animals *may come to know as* sign relations, through their own actions in the world of mind-independent reality. The relevance of such a nuanced understanding as Deely offered, for biology (and for science in general, in justifying its claims about the nature of mind-independent reality) cannot be overstated. For it is only by the adoption of such a semiotic realism that one can account for the ability of mind-dependent activity to veridically align with mind-independent reality, while still acknowledging the ineliminable role that our mind-dependent activity plays in shaping our perceptions of mind-independent reality. "If the image that a bird gets of the insects it needs to feed its progeny does not reflect at least some aspects of reality," Nobel prize winning cellular biologist François Jacob (1920–2013) reminds us "there are no more progeny [and] if the representation that a monkey builds of the branch it wants to leap to has nothing to do with reality, then there is no more monkey" (1982: 56). Similarly, the pioneering electro-physicist Heinrich Hertz (1857–1894), in his widely influential *Principles of Mechanics*, expressed the modern scientific doctrine of "experimental interactionalism"[2] this way:

> We form for ourselves images or symbols of external objects; and the form that we give them is such that the *logically necessary consequents* of the images in thought are always the images of the *necessary natural consequents* of the thing pictured. . . . For our purpose, it is not necessary that the images should be in conformity with the things in any other respect whatever. As a matter of fact, we do not know, nor have we any means of knowing, whether our conception of things are in conformity with them in any other than *this one fundamental respect* ([1894]/1899: 1–2, *italics mine*).

Hertz's crucially important caveat in the second half of the quote recalls, of course, Peirce's Pragmatic Maxim that, in our search for clarity regarding the way things really are in the world, that we "consider what effects, that might conceivably have practical bearings, we conceive the object of our conception to have. Then, our conception of these effects is the whole of our conception of the object" (CP 5.402).

What Deely's doctrine of semiotic realism, as developed from the ideas of Peirce and Poinsot, further adds to this common-sense refutation of radical idealism is the even more subtle understanding that neither mentally internal

---

[2] The term is Michael Heidelberger's, which he uses to characterize the post-Kantian approach to scientific veracity advocated by Hertz' mentor, Hermann von Helmholtz (1821–1894) that Hertz developed even further in the direction of what we are referring to here as "semiotic realism" (1998: 13, 23).

"images" nor consciously accessed "representations" (as the term has traditionally come to be defined) are fundamental to the establishment and successful use of sign relations. For both 'images' and 'representations' are inescapably *relational* phenomena that, as such, *inherit* whatever informational potential that they have from the pre-requisite existence of genuinely form-giving relations in the world itself. "In actual existence," notes Deely "every substance and every accident is maintained by realities of circumstance and being other than itself" (2001: 228).

Accordingly, all things – including and, perhaps most especially, organisms – arise and are maintained within a dense web of inextricably interwoven *relationships* – and the question for modernist science, since at least the time of Ockham, notes Deely, becomes whether or not such relationships *per se* can be said to have a causative (and sometimes end-directed) existence in their own right (the doctrine of *scientific realism*), or whether they are merely the analytical (or linguistic) constructions of we observers in our acts of apprehending the conjoint activity of particular things (the doctrine of *nominalism*, which today mostly takes the form of *scientific instrumentalism*).

As the ample evidence earlier in this paper attests, both the concepts of *genuine end-directedness* and of *sign relations* have been consigned to the realm of scientific instrumentalism in contemporary biology. Understanding the scepticism with which such talk about the causal organizing potential of "suprasubjective relationship *per se*" would be met by scientists (as well as non-scientists), Deely made it an integral part of his grand project to attempt to establish the reality of mind-independent sign relations as a unique category of actually existing, causally operative influences in the lives of living beings, without reifying such 'sign action' (as he called it) as if it were some kind of mysterious and independently subsisting causal force.

For "of course", acknowledged Deely, sometimes sign relations.

> may not be in the order of [mind-independent reality] at all. Relations as 'between' subjects may simply result from comparisons made by some mind – our own, say – when two subjects are considered together. This is what the modern philosophers generally would come to think (2009: 23).

Deely, however, like Aristotle, took extraordinary pains to establish that 'relations' *per se* "are not *in* the substances that are related", such as 'in minds' or 'in genes', as most of contemporary science would have it. Rather, stressed Deely

> Relations are over and above [their component relata] *tout court*. Relations, if they are anywhere in *ens reale* [the realm of mind-independent being] are *between* individuals, and 'between' is not a subjective mode of 'in', as *'in se'* and *'in alio'* are subjective modes

of 'in': what is in between two [individuals] is in neither of the [individuals]. It is over and above them, *suprasubjective*, if you like . . . [and thereby constitutes] a distinct *category of ens reale* [mind-independent being] under *to Ên* [the more encompassing category of Being], and not merely a perspective of thought (*ibid*) (2009: 22–23).

Deely's ideas and writing, as can be clearly seen above, are grounded in a deep acquaintance with the full sweep of Western philosophy, and, as such, can make for daunting reading and easily be misunderstood. Invoking a pre-Cartesian tradition in thinking, wherein the terms 'subject' and 'object' had not yet been burdened with the dualistic connotations of "living knowers" and "inanimate things" that arose from Descartes' binary sundering of the world into the mutually exclusive domains of *res cogitans* and *res extensa*, respectively, Deely realizes that the passive acceptance of those terms of the debate *as such* forecloses the possibility of ever resolving the epistemological paradoxes that are engendered by adopting them. Accordingly – and as part of his efforts to research and to convey to us the ways that scholars were thinking *before* modernity made its "wrong turn" into Cartesian dualism, so as to better equip our own efforts to devise a more explanatorily satisfying overarching conceptual framework for the understanding of life and mind – Deely instead uses the term 'subject' throughout his writings to mean individual entities or "substances . . . things separate from one another and [in a qualified and relative sense] existing in themselves" (2014: 593).³

"Intersubjectivity", then, in Deely's terms, denotes merely any action taking place between subjects, while "suprasubjectivity" denotes the relation *qua* relation that is thereby established by that interaction and that is (or at least can be) consequential *per se* in organizing future such interactions. Deely notes that "social norms" have this character of immaterialy existing, but potentially materially

---

3 Indeed, even the more technical modern senses of the word 'subject' "relating to philosophy, logic, and grammar are derived ultimately from Aristotle's use of *to hupokeimenon*, meaning 'material from which things are made' and 'subject of attributes and predicates'" but that which itself cannot be the predicate of another (Oxford Dictionary of English 2010: 1773). Correspondingly, an "object" in the Deelyan terminology always refers to an "object of experience" (again, from the Latin *objectum* or 'thing presented to the mind') and thus, "far from being a mere alternative or synonym for "thing", is simply a disguised way of saying 'something signified', or 'significate'" (2014: 598). As such, "objects" are agent-created sign constructs partaking both of the agent's biology and its world, and joined recursively by the actions of that biology on that world, as vice-versa, in the manner of Uexküll's 'functional circle' (Uexküll 1940). Further discussion in this direction, while germane, will lead us too far astray from the more limited objectives of the present paper, so the reader is encouraged to consult Deely 2009 for his fullest discussion of the relationships between subjects, objects, signs and things.

organizing consequentiality. So, of course, do the "natural conventions" that have evolved to organize animal development and interaction. Let us next consider a relatively simple example from nature to help us to better comprehend what Deely means by this concept of "suprasubjective" relations as immaterial relations that come into being *between* individuals (or entities), but which then can exert a causal or organizing effect on the subsequent material interactions of those entities.

5 Biosemiosis via suprasubjective relationship: The dead horse arum

An elegant example of the kind of suprasubjective sign relationships that are operative in organizing species' behaviour and morphology even in the non-human world is the thermogenic Mediterranean lily *Helicodiceros muscivorus*, known more commonly as the Dead Horse Arum. Found on gull colonies where rotting bird corpses and their attendant carrion-eating blowflies are abundant, these gruesome-smelling plants precisely mimic the sight, odour, texture and even the temperature of the flesh of a rotting gull corpse, releasing a putrid odour that is similar in its chemical composition to that of decaying flesh, which attracts the nearby blowflies deep into its flesh-colored and textured, prison-like chambers – where it traps them, deposits its pollen on them and then finally releases them to carry away its male gametes and, ideally, unknowingly pollinate a receptive conspecific (Kite 2000, Stensmyr et al 2002, Angioy et al 2004).

Examples of such fine-grained mimicry abound in nature; but what is most relevant to our present discussion is the acknowledgement that the brain-free Dead Horse Arum cannot in any psychological or conceptual way "know" what a rotting gull corpse looks like, smells like, feels like, or what a gull's body temperature is upon recent expiration. Indeed, it can have no knowledge 'in' it that there even exist things like gulls, or flies, or even itself or any other Dead Horse Arums. Yet the precise reproduction of all these 'unknown and unrecognized' properties of smell, sight, touch, texture and temperature constitute the critically important *signs* that the arum uses in successfully exploiting the carrion fly.

Clearly, then, this manifestly effective instance of successful "sign use" has come into being not from the plant's 'epistemology' but from its ontology (and so, too, for the blowfly, whose 'epistemology', such as it is, likewise derives from its ontology – which is itself the product of prior semiotic action in the world). For were sign relationships not genuinely grounded as suprasubjective *Thirdness relations*, having "one foot in inside the organism and one foot in the world outside it" – an "outside" which includes, without exception, the organization and action of other animals and the suprasubjective relations that are organizing *them* – then such semiotic engagement with the world could never be successful, as Jacob and Hertz, remind us.[4]

This is the real-world sense of 'being', John Deely argued, in which a sign relation proper exists: i.e., not in either of its termini, but in the suprasubjective relations of Thirdness that genuinely do hold over and between them, whether or not any given individual in the relationship realizes it or not. Such relations in the biosphere are those whose essential characteristic "consists in a reference or *being toward another*, those features of being which one cannot, even by an abstraction, omit reference toward" (2001:228) and which interweave to form the causal texture, the warp and woof, of agents, signs and actions that constitutes the biosphere.

Adopting a Peircean perspective also, yet coming from a rigorously scientific, as opposed to a rigorously philosophical background, theoretical biologist Terrence Deacon's coining of the neologism *ententional* to denote "all phenomena that are intrinsically incomplete in the sense of being in relationship to, constituted by, or organized to achieve something non-intrinsic" (2011:27) shares much in common with Deely's notion of *being towards another* as an organizing principle in living nature. Such phenomena include "functions that have satisfaction conditions, adaptations that have environmental correlates, thoughts that have contents, purposes that have goals, subjective experiences that have a self/other perspective, and values that have a self that is benefited or harmed" (2011:27). What makes entential processes appear so cryptic, notes Deacon, is the fact that "they exhibit properties that appear merely superimposed on materials or physical events, as though they are something *in addition to and separate from* their material-physical embodiment" (2011:57, italics mine).

Deely's discussion of 'relation' as a unique category of ontological being and about 'being *in futuro*' (2015: 344;355) as a viable way of thinking about potential interpretants that have not yet resulted from a situation in which "dyadic interactions bring about existence of a new condition or state which (by definition) does not reduce to dyadic interaction" (2015:356) may seem somewhat mystical or obscurantist upon first acquaintance. Yet, I want to argue, the naturally occurring state of affairs in the real world that these ideas are pointing to is the same naturally occurring state of affairs that Deacon's work on ententionality is pointing to,

---

4 "Thirdness", of course, is Charles Sanders Peirce's term for the phenomenon of "lawfulness" that emerges from repeated or habitual interaction between entities and that then comes to mediate their subsequent interaction.

as well as is the work of his fellow theoretical biologist Stuart Kauffman, with his notion of "the Adjacent Possible" (see Favareau 2015b for a fuller discussion of this latter congruence) and that – most importantly to our present discussion – is exactly the real-world phenomena that mechanistic notions such as *teleonomy* fail to capture (or to actively erase).

In short – and as Deacon's 2011 magnum opus, *Incomplete Nature*, argues in such fine-grained and convincing depth: "The paradoxical intrinsic quality of existing with respect to something missing, separate, and possibly nonexistent is irrelevant when it comes to inanimate things, but it is a defining property of life and mind" (2011: 3). This "quality" is an utterly non-mysterious product of what John Deely has been calling "suprasubjective" relations in nature and that sees its ultimate realization in what Peirce called *finiousity*, or

> that mode of bringing facts about according to which a general description of result is made to come about, quite irrespective of any compulsion for it to come about in this or that particular way; although the means may be adapted to the end. The general result may be brought about at one time in one way, and at another time in another way. Final causation does not determine in what particular way it is to be brought about, but only that the result shall have a certain general character (CP 1.211).

For Deacon, that "general description" consists in the series of physically embodied "constraints" that, taken together, form a kind of negative template of "constitutive absences" biasing and delimiting the degrees of freedom that a given system has regarding what possibilities it may and may not actualize, and how.[5] While for Kauffman (2016), what is most ontologically unique about living systems is the radical "openness of possibility space" that is brought into being with the actualization of any given previously finious "end".[6]

In the next and final section, I want to briefly review Peirce's notion of *finiousity* especially for whatever biologist readers that this article may have and to suggest that its time has come to replace the outdated notion of *teleonomy* as a more fertile scientific concept for the investigation and understanding of living systems.

---

[5] Again, this short paper can in no way to justice to the depth and complexity of Deacon's argument, nor is it its intent to, wishing merely instead to note its congruence with Peirce's and Deely's ideas here. Readers interested obtaining in a fuller understanding of Deacon's argument may want to begin with Sherman's (2017) authorized and relatively more accessible explication, before moving on to the primary materials.

[6] The most simplified account here might, again, be Favareau (2015b), although in this case, even stronger would be the suggestion for the interested reader to go to the original sources, particularly Kauffman (1996) and (2016), after beginning with Kauffman and Gare (2015).

6 Peirce's naturalization of the concept of final causation

In three classic papers on the topic, Hulswit (1996) and Short (1981 and 1983), explicated Peirce's concept of final causation, or what he would later call *finiousity*, for their fellow Peirce scholars, and I want to draw from their work extensively in this section in doing the same for biologists. Short's (1983) thumbnail sketch of the matter, in fact, can hardly be improved for concision and is thus worth quoting here in full: "The classical conception of teleology, found in Plato's dialogues and perhaps earlier still, was most clearly formulated by Aristotle", he writes, and from it we may derive these propositions:

> Teleological explanation is explanation by final causes. Final causes are abstract types that so *influence processes of mechanical causation* that they tend to bring about their own actualization. (It follows that descriptions of final causation as "backwards causation" are mistaken. *A final cause is not a future actuality: it is a present possibility.* That the merely possible should influence the actual is still a paradox, from the mechanistic point of view.) While final causation thus involves mechanical (or efficient) causation, neither is reducible to the other. Final causes are required to explain what mechanical causation by itself cannot explain, namely, *the emergence of order from disorder or of uniformity from variety*. (1983: 311, italics mine).

Now the concepts of the "emergence of order from disorder" and, as Peirce will go so far as to define his concept of finiousity later, of "those non-conservative actions which seem to violate the law of energy" by bringing about relatively negentropic states of "irreversible" order (CP 7.471) are all familiar to us today through the work of Prigogine (1984), Kauffman (1996), Deacon (2011) and others. Yet the reference here to "abstract types" may strike contemporary ears as somewhat mystical, making the whole idea, again, quite suspect and not at all a suitable concept for incorporating into contemporary science.

As is usual with Peirce, however, there is an utterly naturalistic understanding to be had here, once one digs deeply enough into his vast corpus of writings to unearth it. Hulswit's choice of the word 'general' instead of 'abstract' when he writes that "final causes are general types that tend to realize themselves by determining processes of mechanical causation" (1996:188) is much more in keeping with Peirce's own lifelong insistence on the reality of "generals" – or genuinely formative Thirdness relations – in nature. (e.g. CP 5.312, 5.431). Here, again, it is the insistence upon the word *relations* that cannot be under-appreciated. These "generals" or "types" are not self-subsisting Platonic entities – Peirce himself makes this distinction explicit when he disparages such a naïve and reifying view as "nominalistic Platonism" (CP 5.503).

"The realist," Peirce writes, "does not say that any generals *exist* [as self-subsisting entities] . . . what he says is that some generals, such as the law of gravitation, are *real*" (R 290:15–16, 1905, italics in the original).

Here, as has often been remarked, Peirce's use of medieval and ancient terms can be misleading to modern ears: Peirce's reference to "generals", as can be seen from the quote above, derives from medieval scholarship debates about the notion of *universals* – the 'horseness' of a horse, for example, and whether or not we are justified in positing that 'horseness' as something more than our own mental category making. Indeed, notes Peirce, natural "law or regularity"– a set of *relations* that, in interaction with one another, are determinative (such as the laws of gravitation noted here) – "are the kind of universals to which modern science pays the most attention" (CP 4.1, 1898). Understood in this context, we can see that precisely what Peirce is *not* positing with his notion of finiousity is any kind of "essence bestowing" cosmic entity or force. If anything, it has more in common with the modern-day understanding of "emergent order" and "facilitative constraints", as we shall see.

Likewise, and as Hulswit (1996:186) points out, Peirce.

> calls the 'tendency toward an end state' a *cause* because he attaches great value to the original meaning of concepts, [and] according to its original, Aristotelian, meaning, a cause is some kind of *condition* without which a thing would not be what it is. Thus, Peirce's notion of cause is much more general than the modern notion, which restricts the term to the [exclusively] Aristotelian efficient cause.

Too, like Aristotle, notes Short, "Peirce argues that processes of final causation are observable. They exhibit striking empirical patterns which would be too improbably coincidental if there were no final causes that explained them" (1981:370). Importantly, adds Short, "Peirce does not believe, any more than Aristotle did, that final causes can work without the cooperation of efficient causes" (1981:370).[7] Rather, that they are mutually dependent aspects of the same one process. Indeed, in what is again a striking contemporary understanding of the process of *emergence*, Peirce writes that:

> Efficient causation is that kind of causation whereby the parts compose the whole; final causation is that kind of causation whereby the whole calls out its parts. Final causation without efficient causation is helpless; mere calling for parts is what a Hotspur, or any man, may do; but they will not come without efficient causation. Efficient causation

---

7 Short does an excellent job, especially in his 1981 article, explicating the crucial differences between Aristotle's more 'good'-realizing notion of final causation and Peirce's more statistical mechanics-inspired one, but this discussion, too, falls too far afield of our present purposes.

> without final causation, however, is worse than helpless, by far; it is mere chaos; and chaos is not even so much as chaos, without final causation; it is blank nothing (CP 1.220).

Again, the idea of an aspect of a process "calling out its parts" is strikingly prognosticative of Terrence Deacon's (2011) equally non-mystical notions of "constitutive absence" and generative "incompleteness" in nature. There, as here, final causes are not future events or states of being, but instead are a state of "emergent dynamics... organized around and with respect to possibilities" – including, critically, for Deacon, the possibilities that are foreclosed and not realized, so as to issue in a stable, self-reinforcing system state (2011: 16) "The laws according to which objects behave are not accidental features of objects, but *essential* features of objects" is how Peirce scholar Aaron Wilson describes Peirce's rationale for the defense of the reality of generals (2012: 182). Also, "by a tendency to an end," Peirce himself clarifies,

> I mean that a certain result will be brought about, or approached, and in such a way that if, within limits, its being brought about by one line of mechanical causation be prevented, it will be brought about, or approached, by an independent line of mechanical causation (1902 [1976]: 65)

– as is well evidenced throughout the processes of biological development and as Deacon's autogen experiments are meant to model.

Peirce also states that "The relation of a law, as a cause, to the action of force as its effect [i.e., efficient causation] *is* final causation" (CP 1 .212, 1902) and nowhere is this better seen than in the biological realm of Bateson's Creatura systems which are distinct from the mere Pleroma systems from which they arise *precisely* in their ability to develop and propagate form-giving "laws" of their own. *Auto-nomous* is the entirely apt description of entities and systems that are able to, in Hoffmeyer's wording, "impose a new set of boundary conditions or constraints on their individual components... and in so doing establish a set of hitherto nonexistent rules" (2008: 292).

Such *finiousity* is completely un-mysterious, even if the exact details of its abiogenesis and its constituent efficient processes are still being worked out and debated by scientists – not the least of whom is Deacon himself, who, in defining the still under-developed concept of "emergence" as "unprecedented global regularity generated within a composite system by virtue of the higher-order consequences of the interactions of composite parts" notes that, most importantly: "here, it is the *relational properties* of the constituents (as opposed their primary or intrinsic properties) that constitute the higher order" (2006: 122, italics mine). Such emergent regularities (or what Hoffmeyer calls 'rules') "focus energy flow and agency of the system or subsystem upon a *constrained repertoire of possibilities"* in the summary of Claus Emmeche, "thus guiding the system's behaviour to follow a more definite sequence of events" (2015: 275).

It is precisely *the configuration of present possibilities* being realized in a system, and *the generative constraints immanent in that configuration* that bias them more towards one general end-state than another, I would argue. It is these that best define the modern-day equivalent of Peirce's concept of 'final causation' without the positing of some kind of ghostly, time-travelling and "backwardly causal" future actuality. It is precisely here – in the physical "configuration of present possibilities" in any given system that is realized first and foremost by the *relations* between the constituents, more so than by just the intrinsic properties of the constituents themselves, as Deacon points out – that Deely's notion of *relation* as an ontological category of its own gains its scientific imprimatur. In so doing, as Cobley and Stjernfelt point out: "Deely has rescued the ontology of the sign from the grasp of dualism – and even dogmatic triadic thought – through his stress on *relation* over and above the sign's components" (2016: 330).

Similarly, and perhaps most importantly for our project of replacing the mechanism of *teleonomy* with the genuine end-directedness of *finiousity* as a legitimately explanatory scientific concept, both Hulswit and Short also note that in the process of being realized, the final causes themselves may change. "During the realization of a final cause," writes Hulswit, "there is always the confrontation with the material world. This is the ground for the evolution of new final causes. New [ends, as well as means towards ends] do not happen just by chance, but as a response to an actual problem" (1996: 213fn). Accordingly, concludes Short, Peirce's notion of final causation "thus results, not in the dead uniformity of a single plan, but in the unpredictable heterogeneity of enterprises, personalities, and species that fill our world" (1994: 406). Surely such an understanding is a more accurate and fertile way of approaching the reality of animal organization and interaction than is the idea of reducing it to an inbuilt set of control programs.

7 Conclusion: "Calling out its parts"

We began this discussion of the road not (yet) taken from *telonomy* to *finiousity*, and from a metaphysics of only "apparent" purposive action in living systems to one of semiotic realism in biology, with a consideration of Nobel laureate Carl Woese's 2004 call for "a new biology for a new century." It may be germane here to note that 20 years earlier, a group of scholars who would lay the groundwork for the current biosemiotics project issued much the same clarion call, envisioning a transdisciplinary effort to develop an understanding of the role of sign relations in living systems that would

> provide the human sciences with a context for reconceptualizing foundations, and for moving along a path which avoids crashing into the philosophical roadblock thrown up by forced choices between [naïve] *realism* and *idealism*, as though this exclusive dichotomy were also exhaustive of the possibilities for interpreting experience" (Anderson, Deely, et al. 1984: 8).

Today, in 2022, both projects (if, indeed, they do not turn out to be the same project, as I suspect they will) remain far from seeing their own envisioned endstates accomplished.

That said, perhaps they, and we their supporters on the sidelines, may take some small comfort in Thomas Kuhn's (1982:16–17) prediction that, with scientific revolutions

> the central change cannot be experienced piecemeal, one step at a time. Instead, it involves some relatively sudden and unstructured transformation in which some part of the flux of experience sorts itself out differently and displays patterns that were not visible before.

Absential relations, semiotic realism, and the notion of *the adjacent possible* are all fine candidates for just such a paradigm-changing transformation in how biology views animal being. Perhaps the place to begin the conversation with mainstream biologists, so as to allow those concepts their proper hearing is, paradoxically enough, with a more Peircean inspired understanding of the reality of "possibilities" as instantiated biologically in organisms via the evolution and development of suprasubjectively established 'ends' – in other words, of semiotic *finosuity*. Only then, with the unequivocal incorporation of semiotic analysis into biology, can "a new biology for a new century" truly begin.

References

Allaby, Michael. 2003. *Oxford Dictionary of Zoology*. Oxford: Oxford University Press.
Allen, Colin. 2009. Teleological notions in biology. In Edward N. Zalta (ed.), *The Stanford Encyclopedia of Philosophy*. Accessed online February 19, 2017 at: https://plato.stanford.edu/archives/win2009/entries/teleology-biology
Anderson, Myrdene, John Deely, Martin Krampen, Joesph Ransdell, Thomas A. Sebeok, Thomas & Thure von Uexküll. 1984. A semiotic perspective on the sciences: Steps toward a new paradigm. *Semiotica* 52(1/2). 7–47.

Angioy, Anna Maria, Marcus Stensmyr, Isabella Urru, Monica Puliafito, Ignazio Collu & Bill Hansson. 2004. Function of the heater: The dead horse arum revisited. *Proceedings of the Royal Society of London B: Biological Sciences* 271 (Suppl 3). 13–15.

Aquinas, Thomas. [1252] 1965. *Aquinas on being and essence: A translation and interpretation*. Joseph Bobik (trans.), Notre Dame: Notre Dame University Press.

Barbieri, Marcello. 2003. *The organic codes: An introduction to semantic biology*. Cambridge: Cambridge University Press.

Bateson, Gregory. 1972. *Steps to an ecology of mind*. Chicago: University of Chicago Press.

Brier, Søren. 2008. *Cybersemiotics: Why information is not enough*. Toronto: University of Toronto Press.

Bruni, Luis. 2015. Heterarchical semiosis: From signal transduction to narrative intelligibility. In Peter Pericles Trifonas (ed.), *International handbook of semiotics*, 1079–1097. Dordrecht: Springer Science.

Cobley, Paul & Frederik Stjernfelt. 2016. Sign, object, thing: An eternal golden braid. *Chinese Semiotic Studies* 12(3). 329–334.

Deacon, Terrence. 2006. Emergence: The hole at the wheel's hub. In Philip Clayton and Paul Davies (eds), *The re-emergence of emergence*, 111–50. New York: Oxford University Press.

Deacon, Terrence. 2011. *Incomplete nature: How mind emerged from matter*. New York: W.W. Norton.

Deacon, Terrence & Tyrone Cashman. 2013. Teleology versus mechanism in biology: Beyond self-organization. In Brian G. Henning & Adam Scarfe (eds.), *Beyond mechanism: Putting life back into biology*, 287–289. Lanham, MD: Lexington Books.

Deely, John. 2001. *Four ages of understanding: The first postmodern survey of philosophy from ancient times to the turn of the twenty-first century*. Toronto: University of Toronto Press.

Deely, John. 2007. *Intentionality and semiotics: A story of mutual fecundation*. Scranton: University of Scranton Press.

Deely, John. 2009. *Purely objective reality*. Berlin: Mouton de Gruyter.

Deely, John. 2014. Subjectivity, suprasubjectivity and semiosis. *Chinese Semiotic Studies* 10(4). 593–604.

Deely, John. 2015. Building a scaffold: Semiosis in nature and culture. *Biosemiotics* 8(2). 341–360.

Favareau, Donald. 2010. The evolutionary history of biosemiotics. In Donald Favareau (ed.), *Essential readings in biosemiotics: Anthology and commentary*, 1–87. Dordrecht: Springer.

Favareau, Donald. 2015a. Symbols are grounded not in things, but in scaffolded relations and their semiotic constraints. *Biosemiotics* 8(2). 235–255.

Favareau, D. 2015b. Creation of the relevant next: How living systems capture the power of the adjacent possible through sign use. *Journal of Progress in Biophysics and Molecular Biology* 119(3). 588–601.

Favareau, Donald, Claus Emmeche, Jesper Hoffmeyer, Kalevi Kull, Anton Markoš & Frederik Stjernfelt. 2008. The IASS roundtable on biosemiotics: A discussion with some founders of the field. *The American Journal of Semiotics* 24 (1–3): 1–22.

Jacob, François, 1982. *The possible and the actual*. London: Pantheon Books.

Heidelberg, Michael. 1998. From Helmoltz's philosophy of science to Hertz's picture-theory. In Davis Baird, R.I.G. Hughes & Alfred Nordmann (eds.), *Heinrich Hertz: Classical physicist, modern philosopher*, 9–24. Dordrecht: Springer Science.

Hoffmeyer, Jesper. 1996. *Signs of Meaning in the Universe*. Bloomington: Indiana University Press.
Hoffmeyer, Jesper. 2008. *Biosemiotics: An investigation into the signs of life and the life of signs*. Scranton: Scranton University Press.
Hertz, Heinrich. 1894 [1899]. *The principles of mechanics*. D.E. Jones and J.T. Walley (trans.). London: MacMillan and Co.
Hoffmeyer, Jesper. 2014. Semiotic scaffolding: a biosemiotic link between sema and soma. In Kenneth R. Cabell & Jaan Valsiner (eds.), *The catalyzing mind: Beyond models of causality*, 95–110. Dordrecht: Springer.
Hulswit, Menno. 1996. Teleology: A Peircean critique of Ernst Mayr's theory. *Transactions of the Charles S. Peirce Society* 32(2). 182–214.
Gilbert, Scott & David Edel. 2015 [1985]. *Ecological developmental biology: The environmental regulation of development, health, and evolution*, 2nd edn. Oxford: Sinauer Associates.
Kandel, Eric, James Schwartz, & Thomas Jessell. 2002. *Principles of neural science*. New York: McGraw-Hill.
Kauffman, Stuart. 1996. *At home in the universe*. Oxford: Oxford University Press.
Kauffman, Stuart. 2016. *Humanity in a creative universe*. Oxford: Oxford University Press.
Kauffman, Stuart & Arran Gare. 2015. Beyond Descartes and Newton: Recovering life and humanity. *Progress in Biophysics and Molecular Biology* 119(3). 219–244.
Kuhn, Thomas. 1982 [2002]. What are scientific revolutions? In James F. Conant & John Haugeland (eds.), *Thomas Kuhn, the road since structure: Philosophical essays, 1970–1993*, 13–32. Chicago: University of Chicago Press.
Kite, Geoffrey C. 2000. Inflorescence odour of the foul-smelling aroid *Helicodiceros muscivorus*. *Kew Bulletin* 55(1). 237–240.
Kull, Kalevi. 2014. Adaptive evolution without natural selection. *Biological Journal of the Linnean Society* 112(2). 287–294.
Markoš, Anton. 2002. *Readers of the book of life: Contextualizing developmental evolutionary biology*. Oxford: Oxford University Press.
Mayr, Ernst. 1974. Teleological and teleonomic: A new analysis. In Robert S. Cohen & Marx W. Wartofsky (eds), *Methodological and historical essays in the natural and social sciences*. Boston Studies in the Philosophy of Science Volume XIV, 91–117. Dordrecht: D. Reidel.
Miller, Stephen A. & John P. Harley. 1994. *Zoology*. 2nd edn. Dubuque, Iowa: Wm. C. Brown Publishers.
Noble, Denis. 2008. *The music of life: Biology beyond genes*. Oxford: Oxford University Press.
Oxford Dictionary of English, 3rd edn. 2010. Angus Stevenson (ed). Oxford: Oxford University Press.
Peirce, Charles S. 1866–1913 [1931–1935]. *Collected Papers of Charles Sanders Peirce, vol. 1–6*. Harvard University Press, Cambridge, MA.
Peirce, Charles S. 1866–1913 [1958]. *Collected Papers of Charles Sanders Peirce, vol. 7–8*. Harvard University Press, Cambridge, MA.
Peirce, Charles S. 1902 [1976]. *The new elements of mathematics, volume 4: Mathematical philosophy*. Carolyn Eisele (ed.). The Hague: Mouton Publishers.
Pittendrigh, Colin. 1958. Adaptation, natural selection, and behaviour. In Anne Roe & George Gaylord Simpson (eds.) *Behaviour and Evolution*, 390–416. New Haven: Yale University Press.
Prigogine, Ilya, & Stengers, Isabelle. 1984. *Order out of chaos: Man's new dialogue with nature*. Toronto: Bantam Books.

Richards, Robert. 2003. Biology. In David Cahan (ed.), *From natural philosophy to the sciences: Writing the history of nineteenth-century science*, 16–48. Chicago: University of Chicago Press.

Stensmyr, Marcus, Isabella Urru, Ignazio Collu, Malin Celander, Bill Hansson & Anna Marie Angioy, 2002. Rotting smell of dead-horse arum florets. *Nature* 420. 625–626.

Shapiro, James. 2011. *Evolution: A view from the 21st century*. Upper Saddle River, NJ: FT Press.

Sherman, Jeremy. 2017. *Neither ghost nor machine: The emergence and nature of selves*. New York: Columbia University Press.

Short, Thomas Lloyd. 1981. Peirce's concept of final causation. *Transactions of the Charles S. Peirce Society* 17(4). 369–382.

Short, Thomas Lloyd. 1983. Teleology in nature. *American Philosophical Quarterly* 20(4). 311–320.

Short, Thomas Lloyd. 1994. 31. Review of Carl Hausman's Charles S. Peirce's Evolutionary Philosophy. *Transactions of the Charles S. Peirce Society* 30(2). 401–413.

Stjernfelt, Frederik. 2014. *Natural propositions*. Boston: Docent Press.

Treviranus, Gottfried. 1802. *Biologie; oder, Philosophie der lebenden Natur für Naturforscher und Aerzte*. Göttingen: Röwer.

Uexküll, Jakob von, 1934 [1992]. A stroll through the worlds of animals and men: A picture book of invisible worlds. (trans. Claire Schiller). *Semiotica* 89(4). 319–391.

Uexküll, Jakob von, 1940 [1982]. The theory of meaning. *Semiotica* 42 (1), 25–87.

Ulanowicz, Robert. 2009. *A third window: Natural life beyond Newton and Darwin*. West Conshohocken, PA: Templeton Foundation Press.

Wilson, Aaron. 2012. The perception of generals. *Transactions of the Charles S. Peirce Society* 48(2),169–190.

Woese, Carl. 2004. A new biology for a new century. *Microbiology and Molecular Biology Reviews* 68(2). 173–186.

Eric Landowski, Jean-Paul Petitimbert
Risky heuristics

Abstract: This article seeks to determine whether the concept of meaning is relevant in hard sciences and, if so, under which of the four semiotic regimes that are now firmly established in the field of interactional research . The study starts with the one whose main feature is insignificance. Called programming, it best accounts for the scientific epistemology according to which, during ages, scientists refrained from attributing the least signification to the regularities (and corresponding "laws") that sciences were discovering. The opposite stance, focussing on unpredictability, leads to another semiotic vacuum, nonsense. All interpretations of reality as a produce of pure chance fall under this regime of assent to the accidental. After a brief survey of these options, we concentrate on the remarkable illustrations that contemporary sciences, via their most advanced postulates (incompleteness, complexity, emergence), provide in terms of manipulation and adjustment, two regimes which entail positive modes of significance but are much more risky as heuristic devices.

Keywords: complexity, regimes of meaning, philosophy of science, manipulation, adjustment

1 Introduction

In 1977, the Nobel Prize-winning physicist Steven Weinberg (1977: 149) concluded his book *The First Three Minutes* with this statement: "The more the universe seems comprehensible, the more it also seems pointless". Forty years later, the neuroscientist Antonio Damasio (2018, quoted in Georgesco 2017: 3; our translation) wrote in the same vein: "It is true that there was a Big Bang, it is true that there was a beginning of life, but can we make sense of it all?" What both these quotes point at is the double quest that seems to have subtended scientific research for more than two millennia. The object of the first – more overt – programme is, needless to say, explanation. The purpose of science is, first and foremost, to discover what things and beings in the world surrounding us are made of; it is to describe, analyse and understand the processes by which they function and interact, to draw the laws which govern their behaviour and thereby make it

---

Eric Landowski, Centre National de la Recherche Scientifique (CNRS), Paris, France
Jean-Paul Petitimbert, Ecole Supérieure de Commerce de Paris (ESCP), Paris, France

predictable and manageable. But what those statements also reveal is that science seems to be pursuing at the same time another – more covert – object that is no longer the elucidation of phenomena, but rather their signification.

Many will, of course, argue that this second programme is *a priori* excluded from the field of exact sciences insofar as they are not, in principle, supposed to be interested in the meaning of the objects that they study. Many researchers would postulate that their studied objects have no meaning (which reduces Weinberg's quote to a mere statement of the obvious). Although this traditional posture was recently given a facelift under the NOMA acronym (Non Overlapping Magisteria), coined by the paleontologist Stephen Jay-Gould, the fact remains that, even without straying from their "magisteria", both above quoted scientists, along with many others, seem to have been tempted to cross that dividing line and to ask further, more philosophical – nay semiotic – questions as a result of their research. In fact, this has been the case from the very birth of science as we know it today. Alongside the desire to understand and explain the complex pragmatic processes which govern nature, the question of the *meaning* of life and of the existing universe was already what prompted scientific inquiry when it first appeared in Ancient Greece, with the intuitive developments of the atomic theory initiated by Leucippus, Democritus or Epicurus. The central purpose of these early efforts towards rational thinking was to give human's existence and environment another meaning than that forged by naive beliefs in divine interventions. It was to replace a system of beliefs by another, supposedly less irrational. The double effort of elucidating phenomena *and* questioning their significance has always been at the heart of the human search for knowledge.

2 To mean or not to mean?

In this broad context, the scientifically widespread belief in the likelihood for the world to be *devoid* of signification is, just as well as attributing it a meaning, a way (paradoxical as it may be) to solve the problem as to whether meaningfulness should be considered as an effective or an illusory dimension of life. But it is not the sole one since less negative hypotheses are also defended within the scientific community. At that level, scientists do not differ from the rest of the population. When it comes to deciding whether, and on which grounds a signification might, or not, be given to natural phenomena, the variety of positions they adopt does no more than reflect a range of possibilities already identified, in their basic principles, by socio-semiotic modelling (see Fig. 1 below), as applied in other fields (on the French conception of socio-semiotics and its development, see Landowski 2017, 2015). More precisely, the way their positions differ from one another corresponds to the criteria of distinction between four *regimes of meaning* that a deductive procedure allowed defining within the framework of a general model of interaction which interconnects the conceivable manners of addressing the question of significance at large, in whatever domain of knowledge or action (cf. Landowski 2005). Before envisaging the options that hard sciences have taken regarding meaning, and their relationships with its various regimes, it is necessary to present the basic principles of this model which is going to serve hereafter as our conceptual guideline.

The standard scientific option – what we may call the meaninglessness hypothesis – echoes the characteristics of the specific regime which deserves to be introduced first, for the simple reason that in almost all domains it tends to be put at the forefront by our science-impregnated culture (an orientation itself anthropologically explicable in terms of its "naturalistic" epistemological stance – cf. Descola 2013). Under its rule, according to the Hegelian postulate that "the real is rational", things and beings obey necessary and constant laws. And insofar as these laws (be they natural, social, psychological, etc.) are accessible to human understanding, their knowledge makes the behaviour of the agents they regulate predictable and thereby minimises the risks of misunderstandings and failure when interacting with them. Thus, there is a regime of "programming". It is based on the recognition of the regularities which somehow "program" and, up to a certain point, explain the course of things and actions. But recognising the regularity of a given behaviour does not amount to giving it a meaning. On the contrary, as long as under this regime one has to do only with actors – be they human or not, whose behaviour is reduced to the execution of immutable algorithms deriving from their submission to a form of determinism – their lack of a proper will and of a degree of autonomy – in other words their quality of non-subjects – excludes, by definition, on their part, any form of the reflexivity which is presupposed by the very notion of a "meaningful" behaviour. Indeed, the sciences never stop bringing to light new laws, the subtlety of which may amaze even the scientists; but, in accordance with the mainstream epistemology attached to their profession, they scrupulously refrain from attributing them the least signification. To their eyes, the order of the world is meaningless. The regime of programming thus appears at the same time as that of the maximum of *security* in terms of risks and, in terms of meaning, as that of pure *insignificance*.

Paradoxical as it may seem to start the presentation of a theoretical construction about significance with a reference to a regime whose main feature is insignificance, we shall have to pursue for a moment that very line. For logical reasons, the next regime to be introduced at that point is in effect that of *nonsense*, another semiotic vacuum or dead-end point, although no longer produced by strict regularity but by its opposite. Indeed, focusing on *irregularity* and the unpredictability that it entails represents another important option which is at the root of another series of culturally attested manners of answering – although negatively once again – the question of the world's significance and of the meaning of life. In daily affairs, fatalism appears as one of its most common forms: "So it happens, there is no reason for it. Don't ask why, it's just so!" Such an intellectual attitude, which ignores or denies the existence of laws that might make what happens minimally predictable and what exists a little more understandable falls into what we call the regime of assent to the accidental, or simply of *accident*. It encapsulates all kinds of conceptions according to which reality is either the absurd product of pure chance or ruled by factors that escape all power or influence, or actors whose designs lay beyond human cognitive grasp, as alluded to by the phrase "*credo quia absurdum*" (cf. Landowski 2012a). This regime thus implements a complementary form of negativity as regards signification: whereas in programming, insignificance originates from an insufficiency – the lack of a meaning that one would have expected and searched for – under the regime of accident, negativity is due to an excess, that of the frightening, blinding, paralysing presence of nonsense.

These two opposite ways of construing the relationships between guiding principles of interaction and significance, which presuppose each other (as do the contraries in a semiotic square), are sufficient to account for classic scientific viewpoints. We will introduce the other two regimes – manipulation and adjustment which, semiotically speaking, are less paradoxical but much riskier as heuristic devices in the field of hard sciences – when we address advanced contemporary theories.

3 Chance and Necessity

The title of Jacques Monod's famous volume, *Chance and Necessity*, could very well be the catchphrase that sums up the scientific paradigm that prevailed in the western world from the Renaissance until the middle of the 20th century (cf. Monod 1971). Its antithetic terms, abruptly brought together, establish the two pillars upon which science leaned until recently and summarise the classic worldview proposed by scientists. "Necessity" refers to what science is meant to achieve, *i.e.* the discovery of the immutable principles presiding over phenomena and therefore allowing those phenomena to be explained; "chance" is an expedient used to cover whatever scientific procedure finds itself simply incapable of explaining.

The former is a synonym for *determinism*, that is to say, the notion according to which the phenomena studied by science are bound to abide by stable causal laws, be they known and established – therefore allowing for predictability – or still to be discovered. One of the extreme paragons of such a vision is the Marquis de Laplace, a 19th century French astronomer, physicist and mathematician. According to him (2007: 4), the human mind, having

> succeeded in referring to general laws observed phenomena, and in foreseeing those which given circumstances ought to produce, we ought to regard the present state of the universe as the effect of its antecedent state and as the cause of the state that is to follow. An intelligence knowing all the forces acting in nature at a given instant, as well as the momentary positions of all things in the universe, would be able to comprehend in one single formula the motions of the largest bodies as well as the lightest atoms in the world, provided that its intellect were sufficiently powerful to subject all data to analysis; to it nothing would be uncertain, the future as well as the past would be present to its eyes.

The discoveries or hypotheses that fall within this regime are legion in the history of sciences. From Newton's universal gravitation, Marcelin Berthelot's predictive analyses of chemical balance, Hilbert's rightly named "programme" proposed by this German mathematician with a view to demonstrating the completeness of logic, down to Einstein's restrained and general relativity.

In this ocean of determinism, *chance* won its spurs thanks to Charles Darwin who enthroned it in his understanding of nature. His theory of evolution, despite its implacable programmatic law of natural selection, favouring the "most fit" over the "less fit" in the struggle for survival, also turns chance into a major factor in his general equation. It makes it responsible for the great number of inexplicable (and adventitious) variations that appear in the course of the development of species. Indeed, according to Darwin, the causes of these variations remain unknowable, "and the reason for the unknowability of such causes is not lack of human understanding but rather *a lack of a directing rational agency*" (Johnson 2014: xiii; our emphasis). In other words, randomness and happenstance offer an explanation – so to speak – for the sudden first appearance of innovative individual differences that, by chance, will be better adapted to the environment and will therefore be hereditarily transmitted from one generation to the next. From a socio-semiotic standpoint, such a belief in nature viewed as a gigantic gambling table falls into what the interactional model calls the regime of *accident*, or of assent to what luckily (or unluckily) happens. Ultimately, a comprehensive description of Darwinism as a theory results in the acknowledgement that its principles can be reduced to a combination of programmatic necessity, as far as natural selection is concerned, *and* accidental contingency when it comes to accounting for the irruption of evolutionary innovation.

Is the role of chance in Darwinian evolution a hapax in the predominantly determinist paradigm of the history of sciences? This question was certainly answered in the affirmative until the advent of quantum mechanics. Albert Einstein himself, however productive his works had been in the development of this new research area, strongly resisted the elements of randomness that quantum physicists would repeatedly posit when describing the behaviour of the elementary particles of which matter is made at the scale of the infinitesimally small. In one of his letters to Max Born, a leading pioneer of these discoveries, he wrote his now famous – and often ill quoted – statement: "The theory [*quantum mechanics*] says a lot, but does not really bring us any closer to the secret of 'the Old One' ['*des Alten*', i.e. *God*]. I, at any rate, am convinced that *He* does not throw dice." (4th December 1926) (Einstein 1971. The original text reads: "Die Theorie liefert viel, aber dem Geheimnis des Alten bringt sie uns kaum näher. Jedenfalls bin ich überzeugt, daß *der* nicht würfelt").

Yet, despite these resistances, quantum physics kept moving forward and evidenced that the depths of subatomic matter abide by rules that happen to be contrary to the predictive linear determinism that prevails in our macroscopic world. One of the main principles that has been brought to light is that of *discontinuity* (or *rupture*), according to which the quantum world is composed of integers only. There is no such thing as decimals or intermediary steps between two values. Not only are elementary particles indivisible, but they behave and move by jumps, without any gradual transitions. Between two positions of one given particle there is absolutely nothing because its movements are made by discontinuous leaps (hence the expression "quantum leap" that everyday language has adopted). The other main disconcerting feature of the quantum world is the fundamental indeterminism that reigns over particles. This characteristic leads to the impossibility of predicting experimental results, even if the experiments are repeatedly and rigorously conducted in the exact same conditions. The quantum world only allows probabilistic measures: happenstance and discontinuity semiotically doom the researcher to give assent to what randomly happens before their eyes.

From this standpoint, it is undeniable that Jacques Monod's formulation is a lapidary synthesis of the two regimes of interaction and meaning (or lack thereof) that have long supported the modern scientific paradigm: the insignificance of programmatic causal determinism along with the meaninglessness of blind assent to probabilistic randomness. Hence, comes this somewhat despairing conclusion at the end of his essay: "Man knows at last that he is alone in the universe's unfeeling immensity, out of which he emerged only by chance" (Monod 1971: 180), underlining the absurdity of the human condition and the meaninglessness of human existence.

However, at the beginning of the 20th century another two new trends progressively emerged amongst the sciences. Even though it was not their objective, Gödel's theorem, first, and complex systems theories some decades later, completely renewed the scientific landscape. As regards our topic, they had the effect of opening radically new ways of envisaging the relevance of meaning within the scientific sphere. In this context, for instance, the renowned physicist

Bernard d'Espagnat was led to contemplate the possible intervention, behind observable phenomena, of a "veiled reality" whose agency would impart to those phenomena a form of significance (Espagnat 1995). Somehow, meaning might thus be relevant! our world might after all, even scientifically speaking, *have a signification*, life might *make sense* . . . In comparison with all previous scientific doctrines, such hypotheses are testament to an authentic epistemological revolution.

4 Coincidences vs. interaction

This radical reorientation may be paralleled with the qualitative changes which, in semiotic terms, accompany the passage from the above-mentioned regimes of programming and accident to the two complementary ones, namely "manipulation" and "adjustment". These latter should now be considered in order to account for the mode of approach to meaning in today's most advanced scientific theories.

According to the former two regimes, the universe is populated only with agents which blindly implement what would be called, in Greimassian narrative semiotics, their "thematic roles" (cf. Greimas and Courtés 1983). Whatever their nature – social actors behaving in accordance with their status or physical elements composed of matter and energy – they all unconditionally comply with the functions and follow the trajectories assigned to them by society or nature. Strictly speaking, one should in fact say that rather than actually "inter-acting", agents merely endure the effects of *"co-incidences"* between their own predefined routes and the equally fixed and necessary trajectories of the neighbouring agents. When a tile falls on a passer-by's head, such a collision is viewed as a random coincidence of trajectories and is called an *accident* (an accident that, incidentally, disturbs not only the passer-by but also the tile, since it spoils the aesthetic perfection of its normal curving path through space). However, if it were possible to demonstrate that the mishap endured by the passer-by had been arranged by some mischievous third agent informed of both the poor condition of the roof and the customary routes of the passer-by, then everything changes. The passer-by would no longer have been merely the victim of bad luck. He would have fallen in a sort of ambush or trap deliberately devised by an anti-subject. Instead of looking purely accidental, the coincidence would then appear to have been *programmed*. It would be programmed, moreover, on the basis of the bad intentions of some malevolent agency. In other words, we would thus pass from the logic of coincidences (either predictable because conditioned by already recognised regularities, or unpredictable because apparently due to pure chance) to a veritable syntax of *inter-action*. (On these two facets of the notion of *coincidence* and their philosophical interpretation, see Jullien 2017: especially 25–36). In the strict socio-semiotic use of the term, "interaction" involves "subjects" – that is to say no longer the kind of figures that conform to predefined roles and routes but syntactic actants whose agentivity admits some degree of autonomy, however minimal. Such an autonomy may take an infinite variety of forms but, in all cases, it will mobilise either one or the other (or, in certain cicumstances, both) of the two distinct principles on which may be grounded a subject's propensity and capability (or in one sole word, semio-narratively speaking, "competence") to interact with other subjects and more generally with the environment: intentionality and sensitivity.

Intentionality, a mix of volition and cognition (although not necessarily implying clear "conscience"), is the basic principle of interaction and meaning that founds the regime of "manipulation". A "manipulator" is someone who aims at making other persons accept to do things that they would not do unless feeling impelled or tempted to do them by the former's manoeuvres (such as threats or promises, provocations or flatteries). Far from following a predefined algorithm, *doing* consists, in the first place, in *deciding* to do. This entails that intersubjective relationships will essentially take the shape of a syntax of reciprocal persuasion among willing subjects-of-reason. In turn, this supposes that although each agent pursues his/her own aims and objectives, all of them ought to share to some extent a common set of values permitting them to negotiate in order to achieve their respective goals by means of agreements with possibly cooperative partners. Such a logic of interaction begs the question of the origin of the subjects' intentions or "will" which appear as necessarily subtending their moves under this regime. Although individual or collective self-determination is not excluded (at least at the most superficial level of observation), the key element that guarantees the efficacy of that regime consists in the recognition by those whose interactions it regulates, of some transcendent agency – what narrative semiotics calls the "sender" – be it named and revered as "God", "Providence", "Reason", the "Party", the "master" or the "father" (among other culturally widespread figures liable to feature this meta-actant). It is ultimately that hierarchically superior agency that defines, for the sake of the community, good and evil, right and wrong, thereby providing its members with a common system of reference and evaluation, and founding the common sentiment of a meaningfulness of the whole construction.

One of the main defining features of the regime of "adjustment" is, by contrast, the absence of any such transcendent level of reference. In its context, what might rule the interaction and ensure its meaningfulness stems from the interactive process itself. The principle which founds this possibility consists in a mutual *sensitivity* which enables the interactants to feel one another's feelings, combined with a disposition to welcome opportunities that the context unexpectedly may offer rather than pursuing previously settled plans – an innate *availability* in the face of propitious circumstances (the *"kairos"*). Laurence Sterne's Yorick, in *A Sentimental Journey*, perfectly incarnates this posture. In such conditions, interaction being neither ruled by inescapable regularities nor submitted to the "decrees" of chance, and not dependent either on some transcendent figure whose volition would overrule that of the subjects, interaction may ideally take the form of a kind of dance. In such a dance the moves of each acting subject are inspired by the others' moves, in such a way that through mutual coordination the very process of interaction continuously invents and transforms its own functioning conditions and recreates its immanent meaning. In order to consolidate and illustrate the semiotic principles of such an interactional syntax and, in particular, the idea of an immanent productivity of meaning and value attached to the intrinsic dynamics of interaction, anthropology provides an extremely rich and diversified material with especially the works of Marcel Detienne and Jean-Pierre Vernant or François Jullien in France, as well as those of Victor Turner, Tim Ingold or James Clifford (cf. Detienne and Vernant 1974; Jullien 2000; Ingold 2000; Turner 1986; Clifford 2013).

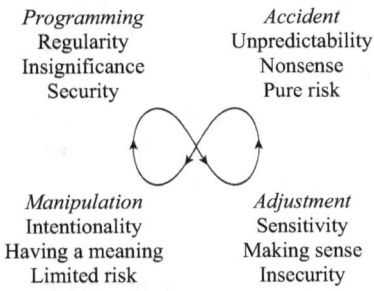

Programming
Regularity
Insignificance
Security

Accident
Unpredictability
Nonsense
Pure risk

Manipulation
Intentionality
Having a meaning
Limited risk

Adjustment
Sensitivity
Making sense
Insecurity

Fig. 1: The socio-semiotic interactional model: four regimes of interaction, meaning and risk. The relationships symbolised by the orientated ellipse that joins the four positions of the diagram are those defined by (Greimas and Courtés 1983: 359–361).

In spite of all their differences, manipulation and adjustment share important characteristics which sharply separate them from the two former regimes. In particular, as opposed to sheer irregularity and unpredictability, which doomed the regime of accident to nonsense, the basic principle of manipulation – intentionality – with its cognitive dimension shared by interactants, ensures that their respective purposes *have a meaning* (and a value, positive or negative). Interactants can recognize this meaning. Likewise, as opposed to strict regularity which led programming to insignificance, under the regime of adjustment, sensitivity ensures that the subjects' moves *make sense* for each other, although no longer as the result of a cognitive "reading" but through a sensitive "grasping". These differences of actantial status and modal competence separate the type of blind agents that are involved in programming and accident from the intentional and/or sensitive subjects interacting in manipulation and adjustment. Until recently, they marked the threshold between the realms of natural and human sciences. Of course, a major part of cultural production, from myths and folktales to literature at large, ignores this borderline and anthropomorphises all kinds of natural elements or artefacts. On another level, in philosophical appendices seeking to "give a meaning" to their scientific discoveries, it has also been possible to witness that important scientists apparently transgress the same borderline by metaphysically attributing some kind of design to nature. Currently, being faced with speculative discourses in which "humans and non-humans" are granted the same interacting competences within a sort of vast post-modern melting pot is a commonplace à la Latour, as we might say by allusion to the sociologist of that name (cf. Sokal 1997; Sokal and Bricmont 1998: Chapter 5).

While such forms of anthropomorphisation have little or nothing to do with scientific conceptualisation, it is with great surprise that, on attempting to semiotically analyse how natural processes are described – and given a meaning – in the most advanced sciences, we discovered a striking *formal homology* between the principles of interaction construed as governing natural processes and the interactional syntaxes that characterise each of the two semiotic regimes we just introduced. The most rigorous forms of scientific modelling, devised in order to account for natural phenomena, thus seem to rejoin the grammar of the most ordinary cultural forms of making sense of life and the world, based on intentionality and sensitivity. Insofar as such a formal homology might be confirmed, it would mean that a common grammar of meaningful interactions equally pervades these two areas of knowledge, whose objects have been considered, for centuries, as ontologically distinct by nature.[1]

---

[1] A different yet comparable approach to this question which amounts no less than to seeking to unify sciences is to be found in Jean Petitot's works on the homomorphisms that allow the principles of René Thom's mathematical theory of catastrophes with the elementary structures of meaning as explored by structuralist linguistics and semiotics from Saussure and Jakobson, Hjelmslev and Brøndal to Lévi-Strauss and Greimas, to be connected – cf. Petitot 2003, 2002.

5 Incompleteness and teleology: The regime of manipulation

As we said, the first trend which originated this revolution and retrospectively makes it understandable stems from Gödel's theorem and its application beyond the sole field of mathematics. In a broad-brush way, this theorem posits that any coherent axiomatic system contains at least one proposition that is contradictory and undecidable. In other words, the consistency of a system necessarily entails its *incompleteness*. As the physicist Thierry Magnin explained: "Classic science, with its dream of perfect predictability, claimed to construct an exhaustive system of representation. Gödel's works have brought this ambition to a close. Quantum physics is the field par excellence where incompleteness, this 'something that escapes us', is most highlighted" (Magnin 2010: 173; our translation). This theory leads to the conclusion that it is illusory to believe that everything can be fully demonstrated, which incidentally renders "Hilbert's programme" entirely vain. Therefore, science today knows perfectly well why it shall never know certain things: not only why it is impossible to produce any system that is both consistent *and* complete, but also why the simultaneous position *and* momentum of a given particle cannot be exactly determined and measured together (according to Heisenberg's uncertainty principle), etc.

At the same time, it also knows that at quantum scale Aristotle's logic is seriously jeopardised, as evidenced by the wave-corpuscle duality. This strange and mind-boggling property of the elementary components of matter shows that, although behaving like a wave or behaving like a corpuscle are two mutually exclusive modes of being, any given particle is both a wave *and* a corpuscle. Along the same line, one could also evoke the quantum superposition of states, popularised by the famous thought experiment known as Schrödinger's cat.

Science is now also aware that the interactions between elementary particles transcend the limits of time and space. In 1982, Alain Aspect experimentally proved that if a pair of initially correlated particles (*e.g.* two photons emitted from the same atom) are separated from one another by a distance that can go so far as several light years, they will continue to interact as though they had never been separated. Repeated measurements across other similar experiments made by other researchers have constantly shown that what happens to one particle impacts the other instantaneously, *i.e.* faster than the speed of light, thus violating the limit imposed by Einstein's general relativity. Based on this mind-bending paradoxical phenomenon, known as *entanglement* or *nonseparability*, another physicist, Olivier Costa de Beauregard hypothesised what he called *backward causality* or *retrocausation* whereby an effect can occur before its cause, or in other words whereby the future can affect the present, and the present can affect the past. He went so far as to write: "The past, present and future of the universe exist simultaneously, not now of course, which would be contradictory" (Beauregard 1995: 58; our translation). Albeit somewhat controversial, this theory is nonetheless of current concern (cf. AAVV 2011).

Faced with so many counterintuitive properties, contravening the classical laws of physics and logic, but also faced with this incompleteness – that is to say, with the irreducible incapacity of sciences to come up with a comprehensive explanation of the world – a number of researchers have started to infer the hypothetical existence of a level of ("veiled") reality that *transcends* those that our senses, apparatuses and calculators can apprehend. That is, for instance, the case with the anthropic principle developed in astrophysics. According to this theory, if the fine-tuning of the fundamental constants of the universe is so minutely precise, it is *in order to* create the conditions needed to generate and accommodate life and consciousness. Recently, computer technology was used to generate virtual models of universe, as it now allows the modelling and simulation of the possible developments of the universe by varying its fundamental constants (gravitation, density, speed of light, speed of expansion, etc.). It turns out that none of these alternative scenarios would allow for any form of life to hatch: they would all be infertile.

What can be deduced from these experiments? The conclusions go in two directions. One possibility is that there exists an infinity of parallel universes (a *multiverse*) and by chance we happen to be in the only one that is viable. The alternative is that, according to the principle of Ockham's razor, it can be postulated that there is only one universe. In this latter option, the probability for such a minute fine-tuning to be a mere coincidence is close to zero (approximately $1/10^{60}$). The astrophysicist Trinh Xuan Thuan compares this probability to the odds for an archer to shoot an arrow and hit the bull's eye of a $1cm^2$ target placed at a distance of 15 billion light years (Xuan Thuan 1991: 302). It then becomes possible to infer a primary cause, to hypothesise some *intentionality* upstream of such an accurate natural process and to adopt a teleological point of view by ascribing a *purpose* to it: the advent of a conscious observer. As the physicist Freeman Dyson puts it: "I do not feel like an alien in this universe. The more I examine and study the details of its architecture, the more evidence I discover that it is likely to have been awaiting our arrival" (Dyson 1986: 293; our translation).

Moreover, the fact that all the current physical theories collapse from the moment that they try to describe the universe beyond what is known as the 'Planck wall' (*i.e.* 10^{-43} seconds after the beginning of the supposed Big Bang), when 'something' emerged in the absence of any other thing – that is to say from nothing – leaves the door open to all kinds of speculations, the most extreme of which, that must be discarded as pseudo-science, are supported by the neo-creationist proponents of the theory of the so called *intelligent design*.

This re-evaluation of the omnipotence of chance, inherited from Darwin, has permeated even disciplines formerly of strong Darwinian tradition. A number of researchers in these areas, *e.g.* the biochemist Michael Denton or the paleontologist Simon Conway-Morris among others, are now reducing the role of chance in favour of the concept of *convergence*, that would prevail over the former (Denton 1998). Their research findings point at the existence, across evolution, of *types* or *archetypes*, "analogous to attractors", that, they purport, have channeled the evolutionary trajectories and the development of species by pulling or guiding biological systems forward, despite the vagaries of history. According to Conway-Morris, "the evolutionary routes are many, but the destinations are limited" or, in other words, all roads lead to Rome (Conway-Morris 2003: 145). He goes even as far as to argue that the functional forms (*e.g.* the structure of the eye) have been preset from the beginning of the universe : "It is my suspicion that (. . .) the nodes of occupation [*i.e.* where the functional forms can exist] are effectively predetermined from the Big Bang" (Conway-Morris 2003: 30).

By downsizing the realm of possibilities and by confining contingency mostly to minor details, this theory also allows the sensing and positing of some form of upstream *intentionality*. Those types, or attractors, would be the marks that it has left in the history of evolution, thus relegating chance to a secondary auxiliary position. Extending Einstein's metaphor of the dice, the Nobel Prize winning physiologist Christian de Duve is said to have quipped: "God plays dice with the universe because He is sure to win" (quoted in Kostro 2013: 486). The "evolution dice" would therefore be loaded and rigged. More seriously, he wrote: "Conscious thought belongs to the cosmological picture, not as a random epiphenomenon that would be peculiar to our biosphere, but as a fundamental manifestation of matter". He adds: "I opted in favour of a universe *with a meaning* and not devoid of sense. Not because I want it to be so, but because that is how I interpret the scientific data at our disposal" (Duve 1996: 493–494 ; our translation; emphasis added).

Semiotically speaking, this recent teleological trend – although far from being shared by all researchers despite its being born from the general acknowledgement of the inaccessibility of certain levels of reality and the subsequent notion of incompleteness – can be reduced to two main components: the dismissal of pure randomness as the sole primary factor of change in the cosmos and the hypothesis of the possible existence of some transcendent intentionality. The regime of interaction that these characteristics fall into is that of manipulation.

6 Complexity and emergence: The regime of adjustment

As we already mentioned, not all scientists follow that teleological line of thought and a number of them have chosen the path of discoveries made in many disciplines (mathematics, chemistry, neurosciences, ecology, economy) from the analyses of complex systems. Contrary to the linear reasoning of the Laplacian causal determinism that claims to be totally predictive, the analysis of complex systems, particularly those known as complex adaptive systems (CAS) or nonlinear dynamical systems (NLDS), reveals that they are characterised by a "non-predictive determinism" whose most famous example is the metaphor of the butterfly effect. It illustrates the idea that a complex phenomenon will remain unpredictable even if all its initial variables are known. Systems theory argues that any system, even if reduced to a few simple constituents, may evolve over time in an unforeseeable way, either towards stability or towards instability.

Determinism relies on the "reassuring" idea of the regularity of phenomena and the equilibrium of the world resulting from it. Conversely, complexity takes an interest in the disequilibrium of the systems that it analyses and, by taking into account the instability of such objects, it recognises the insecurity and risks inherent in them.[2] They are conceived as unstable autonomous organisations whose development depends on their initial conditions and on the interactions between their own components as well as with their environment. According to such a conception, the more variables interact in a system, the more it becomes unpredictable and chaotic (which does not necessarily mean disorganised). The principles of complexity are therefore the complete antithesis of those of pure determinism and, among them, of reductionism in particular for which, according to Descartes, the whole is mechanically nothing but the sum of its parts. This reductionism having shown its limits in a great number of areas, the theory of complexity comes to mitigate the failure of the classical, analytical and logical scientific thought. A perfect understanding of the parts composing a system does not entail a perfect understanding of how the whole system will behave or develop.

Indeed, most of the properties of complex systems fly in the face of reason and defy common sense. As complexity often counters standard logic, it sometimes

---

[2] This dimension is no less fundamental for the socio-semiotic approach of interactions since the four regimes of meaning and interaction which compose the model are interdefined at the same time as tantamount "regimes of risk". Cf. above, Fig. 1, and Landowski (2005: 54–57, 72, 91).

becomes necessary to call upon nonlinear mathematical models and use computer methods to which certain disciplines, such as biology, are not accustomed. In the same vein, because complexity places more emphasis on interactions than on objects, its methods have become transdisciplinary, which is not without causing some difficulty: cooperation between disciplines, redivision of research fields, cultural antagonisms between traditions, and even overt polemic as soon as it comes to transposing concepts from exact sciences to human and social sciences. It is then justified to claim that the understanding of the laws of complexity is still in its infancy. Nevertheless, despite these difficulties, it is receiving sustained attention in many areas. Among the most famous researchers and thinkers who made complexity their battleground, we can mention the Nobel Prize winning chemist Ilya Prigogine, the biologist Henri Atlan, or the philosophers of science Edgar Morin and Philip Clayton.

The key concepts that complexity brought to light are those of *self-organisation* and *emergence*. The self-organisation of complex systems is a process of coordination within the elementary components of a given system which, by adjusting to one another, reduce the system's entropy, that is, the tendency to disorganisation and disorder. In astrophysics, for example, the opponents of the anthropic principle consider the present state of the universe as the result of such a complex process of disentropy (or negative entropy).

The other striking property of complex self-organised systems is their capability to adequately respond to situations for which *they have not been programmed*. They can develop surprising innovative features that science calls emergences: "A property or a process is said to be emergent at a given level of organization if, although it is in principle reducible to the properties of its lower level constituents, its occurrence seems impossible to predict *a priori* on the basis of what is known about these initial properties" (Mayet 2005; our translation). In other words, an emergent feature is a new global quality or property, created by a given complex system, that has the characteristic of being unknown to the local parts which compose it and have produced it through their stochastic (nonlinear) interactions. The most mundane and simplistic example is water. Water has a wide range of remarkable distinctive characteristics but these are totally impossible to predict in the sole light of those of its two elementary components. Yet their adjustment to each other gives rise to something that is both absolutely unprecedented and totally unpredictable. Emergence therefore counters reductionism insofar as the whole (global level) is no more equal to the sum of its parts (local level). It also objects to determinism insofar as it generates stability out of instability, so to speak.

For example, among the proponents of complexity, the mathematician and biologist Stuart Kauffman (1995: vii–viii) strongly argues that:

> Another source – self-organisation – is the root source of order. The order of the biological world, I have come to believe, is not merely tinkered, but arises naturally and spontaneously because of these principles of self-organisation – laws of complexity that we are just beginning to uncover and understand. (. . .) The complex whole, in a completely nonmystical sense, can often exhibit collective properties, emergent features that are lawful in their own right.

In another area, the paleoanthropologist Ian Tattersall considers that the appearance of language among *Homo sapiens* is a typical phenomenon of emergence and not the result of a gradual process operating over a long period of time in accordance with the programmatic principles of Darwinian selection. For his part, the paleontologist Stephen Jay Gould argues that such emergent properties, that cannot be reduced to the organisms that constitute a species, may account for the sudden evolutionary leaps, separated by long stages of equilibrium, that punctuate evolution.

However, emergence is also somewhat of a paradoxical phenomenon. It generates order and stability in a given system, but the interactional process by which it achieves it is chaotic. Halfway between order and disorder, this generative property of complexity called emergence takes place at the "edge of chaos", *i.e.* "in the boundary between rigidity and randomness" (Pascale 1999: 91). And, indeed, the study of complexity also highlights the existence of critical tolerance thresholds of disorder which, once crossed, turn the temporary stability of a system into a highly unstable state. In this case, local disorder also generates global disorder. This is particularly evident in ecosystems. The *anthropocene,* which is on its way to being officially recognised by the scientific community as an epoch of planetary history, is the living proof of that flip side of complexity (cf. Petitimbert 2017). In the Earth system, the nature of the interactions that so far ensured its equilibrium have changed and a number of thresholds have been crossed. At the scale of the entire planet, a point of no return has been reached: scientists now know that some of the brutal and sudden changes we are witnessing are irreversible. From the point of view of complexity, before reaching a more or less stable state, the timeline of which is unpredictable, planet Earth has now entered an uncontrolled chaotic phase. The anthropocene, the cause of which is, as the Greek etymology of the word indicates, humankind itself, threatens therefore the survival of the entire human species. The complexity of this highly serious critical situation requires the invention of similarly complex solutions; but this is another debate.

Coming back to our main topic, the general principles that subtend this last contemporary scientific trend seem to converge towards the actantial syntax of *adjustment*. The first principle of complexity that we retain is its non-predictive character, which places this theory in a position contradictory to the programmatic Laplacian conception of science as based on the principles of continuity and regularity. Knowing that the very definition of the semiotic syntax of adjustment, as we defined it in previous works, makes it a mode of interaction of which neither the form nor the outcome are entirely knowable in advance, because under this regime it is the sole dynamic of the interaction itself that delineates the modalities and the finalities of its own development (cf. Landowski 2012b), one can see that this regime could very well be part of the conceptual arsenal of complexity.

Moreover, since the regime of adjustment excludes any instrumental aim among actants and is devoid of any transcendent sender to set the meaning and value of the transformations, self-organisation, as a *sui generis* process, echoes the peculiarity of this regime, and places complexity in the opposite position with respect to the previous teleological tendency.

Thirdly, the anti-reductionist concept of emergence appears to reflect this singular property that adjustment has, allowing for a real *creation* of meaning and value in the form of an *unprecedented* dynamic unfolding among actants – each being considered as a reserve of potentialities – which, as it develops, *invents* its own form and establishes its own order of meaning and value (Landowski 2012b).

Finally, because complexity analyses the imbalances that unfold against a backdrop of instability and insecurity, it considers that the relationships between the dynamic objects that it studies are situated, as in the logic of adjustment, at the edge of chaos, on the threshold of accident (Landowski 2007). That this accident, the risk of which nothing allows to avoid, may unfortunately eventuate, is currently evidenced in full sight by the anthropocenic changes that jeopardise human existence on planet Earth.

The above elements of correspondence between the scientific notion of complexity and the semiotic definition of adjustment may appear a trifle broad-brush and certainly need a more rigorous and in-depth exploration. Even so, why not acknowledge that we feel comforted by the result of this first confrontation between our model and these varied scientific proceedings which result in the elucidation of meaningful dynamic patterns immanent to natural processes? The series of convergences we observed show that the heuristic approach that we adopted almost two decades ago when we embarked on constructing deductively our model starting from Greimas's standard narrative grammar (at that time still restricted to a syntax of manipulation) was not completely vain, risky as it may have been. It seems, on the contrary, to be somehow validated by the formal homologies, even incomplete and still too superficial for the present incursion in scientific theorising to bring to light. The next step should be to learn the lesson that we must consolidate the model, refine and revise it where necessary, according to what this exploration has taught us. No doubt "hard" scientists have extremely little to expect from social "sciences". We, on the contrary, know that we have everything to gain by learning from the extraordinary intellectual audacity and creativity of today's scientific theoretical imagination.

7 Conclusion

In this early third millennium, it seems that a mutation of the world of the sciences is taking place. Despite the resistance exercised by those who, whatever their motives, have chosen to stick to the established principles dating back from Laplace or Darwin – and according to our interpretation, to the corresponding regimes of programming and assent to the accidental – more and more scientists tend to concur in delineating a new paradigm. This new paradigm encompasses hypotheses corresponding to the other two socio-semiotic regimes of interaction and meaning: that of manipulation (by a transcendant level of reality posited from the irreducible incompleteness of models) and that of adjustment (evidenced by the emergent phenomena taking place in self organised complex systems).

Only a few years after the publication of Jacques Monod's book and in response to it, Ilya Prigogine and the philosopher of science Isabelle Stengers wrote: "The opposition between determinism and randomness is being undermined. (. . .) From now on, our descriptions of the world will be organised through the notions of stability and instability, and not through the opposition between chance and necessity."[3] From the perspective of incompleteness, albeit being an ardent defender and torchbearer of the theory of complexity, Edgar Morin does not hesitate to state in one of his latest books, *Connaissance, Ignorance, Mystère* that: "The mystery [incompleteness] does not devalue the knowledge that has driven to it. It makes us aware of the occult powers that command us, which are not primarily determinisms, but which are like *Daimon*, interior and exterior to us, *who possess us and lead us to folly, exhilaration or raptures*".[4]

It may well be that the notions of incompleteness and complexity will cohabit in the future in very much the same way as chance and necessity did in the past. After all, it may also simply be that the sciences will now have to harness the four regimes altogether in order to eventually be able to give meaning to or to discover what makes sense in those findings that would otherwise only seem to be either insignificant or meaningless. Only the future will tell us if, by

---

[3] Prigogine, Stengers (1978: 13–14) (our translation).
[4] Morin (2017: 174) (our translation and our stress).

means of some adjustments with nature, our species succeeds in surviving the sixth mass extinction that is programmatically announced to take place sometime in the course of the anthropocene.

References

Aavv. 2011. *Quantum retrocausation: Theory and Experiment, American Institute of Physics Conference Proceedings 1408*. New York: Melville.
Clayton, Philip. 2004. *Mind and Emergence: From Quantum to Consciousness*. Oxford: Oxford University Press.
Clifford, James. 2013. *Returns: Becoming Indigenous in the Twenty First Century*. Cambridge MA: Harvard University Press.
Conway-Morris, Simon. 2003. *Life's solution: Inevitable humans in a lonely universe*. Cambridge: Cambridge University Press.
Costa de Beauregard, Olivier. 1995. *Le corps subtil du réel éclaté*. Saint-Barthélemy-Lestra: Aubin.
Damasio, Antonio. 2018. *The Strange Order of Things. Life, Feelings and the Making of Cultures*. New York: Pantheon.
Denton, Michael. 1998. *Nature's destiny: How the laws of biology reveal purpose in the universe*. New York: Free Press.
Descola, Philippe. 2013 [2005]. *Beyond Nature and Culture* [Par-delá nature et culture]. Chicago: University of Chicago Press.
Detienne, Marcel & Jean-Pierre Vernant. 1991 [1974]. *Cunning Intelligence in Greek Culture and Society*. [*Les ruses de l'intelligence. La metis des grecs*]. Chicago: University of Chicago Press.
Duve, Christian de. 1996. *Poussière de Vie*. Paris: Fayard.
Dyson, Freeman. 1986. *Les dérangeurs de l'Univers*. Paris: Payot.
Einstein, Albert, *The Born-Einstein letters*. 1971. Translated by Irene Born. New York: Walker and Company.
Espagnat, Bernard d'. 1995. *Veiled reality: An analysis of present-day quantum mechanical concepts*. New York: Basic Books.
Georgesco, Florent. 2017. Antonio Damasio dans l'inconnu de la vie. *Le Monde*. supplement "Le Monde des livres", 1st Dec. 2017.
Greimas, Algirdas J. & Joseph Courtés (eds.). 1983 [1979]. *Semiotics and Language: An Analytical Dictionary* [Sémiotique: Dictionnaire raisonné de la théorie du language]. Bloomington, Indiana University Press.
Ingold, Tim. 2000. *The Perception of the Environment. Essays on Livelihood, Dwelling and Skill*. London: Routledge.
Johnson, Curtis. 2014. *Darwin's dice: The idea of chance in the thought of Charles Darwin*. New York: Oxford University Press.
Jullien, François. 2000. *Detour and Access: Strategies of Meaning in China and Greece*. Translated by Sophie Hawkes. New York: Zone Books.
Jullien, François. *Dé-coïncidence*. 2017. Paris: Grasset.

Kauffman, Stuart. 1995. *At home in the Universe: The search for the laws of self organization and complexity*. New York: Oxford University Press.
Kostro, Ludwig. 2013. Are life, consciousness and intelligence cosmic phenomena? In Richard L. Amoroso, Louis H. Kauffman & Peter Rowlands (eds.), *The physics of reality: space, time, matter, cosmos. Proceedings of the 8th symposium honoring mathematical physicist Jean-Pierre Vigier*. Singapore: World Scientific Publishing.
Landowski, Eric. 2005. *Les interactions risquées*. Limoges: Pulim.
Landowski, Eric. 2007. Ajustements stratégiques. *Actes Sémiotiques*, 110 (http://epublications.unilim.fr/revues/as/66).
Landowski, Eric. 2012a. *Shikata ga nai* ou Encore un pas pour devenir sémioticien. *Lexia*, 11–12, Culto, pp. 63–88.
Landowski, Eric. 2012b. Jacques-le-juste. *Actes Sémiotiques*, 115 (http://epublications.unilim.fr/revues/as/2722).
Landowski, Eric. 2015. The Greimassian Semiotic Circle. In M. Grishakova (ed.), *Theoretical Schools and Circles in the Twentieth Century Humanities*. London: Routledge, pp. 84–98.
Landowski, Eric. 2017. Interactions (socio) sémiotiques. *Actes Sémiotiques*, 120 (http://epublications.unilim.fr/revues/as/5894).
Laplace, Pierre-Simon de. 2007. *A philosophical essay on probabilities*. Translated by F.W. Truscott & F.L. Emory. New York: Cosimo.
Magnin, Thierry. 2010. La contradiction en physique quantique et en théologie, in Bernard Guy (ed.) *Ateliers Sur la Contradiction*, proceedings of the March 2009 symposium held in the *École Nationale Supérieure des Mines de Saint Étienne*, Paris, Presses des Mines.
Mayet, Laurent. 2005. L'émergence d'une nouvelle science ?, in L'énigme de l'émergence, Sciences & Avenir, special-issue 143, p. 5.
Monod, Jacques. 1971. *Chance and necessity: an essay on the natural philosophy of modern biology* [Le hasard et la nécessité: essai sur la philosophie naturelle de la biologie moderne]. New York: Alfred A. Knopf.
Morin, Edgar. 2017. *Connaissance, ignorance, mystère*. Paris: Fayard.
Pascale, Richard T. 1999. Surfing the edge of chaos. *MIT Sloan Management Review*, 40(3). 83–94.
Petitimbert, Jean-Paul. 2017. Anthropocenic Park: 'humans' and 'non-humans' in socio-semiotic interaction. *Actes Sémiotiques*, 120. 1–12. (http://epublications.unilim.fr/revues/as/5816).
Petitot, Jean. 2002. Mathematical Physics and Formalized Epistemology. In M. Mügur-Schächter and A. van der Merwe (eds), Quantum Mechanics, Mathematics, Cognition and Action. Kluwer: Dordrecht.
Petitot, Jean. 2003 [1985]. *Morphogenesis of Meaning* [Morphogenèse du sens]. Bern: Peter Lang.
Prigogine, Ilya & Isabelle Stengers. 1978. *La nouvelle alliance*. Paris: Gallimard.
Sokal, Alan. 1997. Professor Latour's Philosophical Mystifications. http://www.physics.nyu.edu/sokal/le_monde_english.html.
Sokal, Alan & Jean Bricmont. 1998. *Intellectual Impostures*. London: Profile Books.
Sterne, Laurence. 1938 [1768]. *A Sentimental Journey through France and Italy*. Harmondsworth: Penguin Books.
Turner, Victor W. 1986. *The Anthropology of Performance*. New York: PAJ Publications.
Weinberg, Steven. 1977. *The first three minutes: A modern view of the origin of the universe*. New York: Basic Books.
Xuan Thuan, Trinh. 1991. *La mélodie secrète: Et l'homme créa l'univers*. Paris: Gallimard.

Gary Shank
The semiotic inquirer and the practice of empirical inquiry

Abstract: Peirce often changed his ideas but he never deviated from his description of post-Cartesian inquiry introduced in his early work. He saw the task of inquiry was to pursue a search for meaning, most often in the face of genuine doubt, that would be ultimately validated through the world of experience. He turned from the Cartesian 'cogito' toward a collective model of understanding that leads to truth. I hope to build on these notions of semiotic inquiry to explore just how revolutionary Peirce's turn from Descartes was. In particular, Descartes's project of reducing duality to unity is shifted in the exact opposite direction. Instead of moving from two to one, Peirce showed the way to move from two to three. By understanding the almost fractal nature of triads in our empirical world, Peirce's ideas move us from reductionism toward an expansive type of triadic understanding that, by its nature, provides stability.

Keywords: Peirce, inquiry, semiotics, Postcartesian models

1 Introduction

Charles S. Peirce is well known for changing his ideas: his models, his terms, and his architectonic, among others. However, he never deviated from the model of the post-Cartesian empirical inquirer that he introduced in his early work. He saw that the task of the empirical researcher was to pursue a search for meaning, most often in the face of genuine doubt, that would be ultimately validated through its application within the world of experience. Unlike Descartes, he turned away from the individual 'cogito' toward a collective model of understanding that leads to truth. This paper will build upon these well-known aspects of semiotic inquiry to explore just how revolutionary Peirce's turn from Descartes can be. In particular, Descartes's project of reducing duality to unity is shifted in the exact opposite direction. Instead of moving from two to one, Peirce showed the way to move from two to three. By understanding the almost fractal nature of triads in our empirical world (a world, by the way, of length and breadth and height), Peirce's ideas move us away from reductionism toward an expansive

---

Gary Shank, Center for Qualitative and Semiotic Inquiry, USA

https://doi.org/10.1515/9783110857801-004

type of triadic understanding that, by its nature, provides stability. This can be pulled together with a thought experiment. Descartes, whether he meant it or not, redefined the domain of 'objectivity' as materialist in nature. This has been an ongoing disaster for the natural and human sciences. By moving away from this dead end, it is possible to re-conceptualize the empirical inquirer as a semiotic being, and not, by taking Descartes to his logical end, an inquiry 'machine.'

2 Peirce and the nature of human cognition

Anyone who has conducted even a cursory look at the body of Peirce's work can see that his thinking, his terminology, his philosophical and theoretical orientations, among other things, were constantly shifting and morphing and evolving throughout his long career (Brent, 1998).

But there is one set of ideas that never changed, and it took on its full form in some of his earliest work (Peirce, 1868a/1992; Peirce 1868b/1869/1992). In these early articles, Peirce lays out his case both for the four "incapacities" which, he claimed, inescapably shape us as inquirers, as well as laying out a refutation of the Cartesian model of the inquirer.

Below are the four incapacities briefly stated in contemporary paraphrase, as I understand them:
1) When we appear to be looking inward as an act of introspection, we are actually reasoning hypothetically based on our knowledge of external facts;
2) Every cognition we have is determined logically from our previous cognitions;
3) There is no thinking without signs; and
4) We cannot use our cognitive powers to grasp anything that cannot yield to cognitive understanding.

3 The problem with Descartes

Peirce's departure from Descartes occurred very early in his work, and persisted throughout the rest of his life. As a young man, he reported being captivated by Kant, to the point of probably memorizing Kant's *Critique of Pure Reason* (Brent, 1998). But as his formidable mind continued to grow and develop, Peirce saw that the gap between the noumenal and the phenomenal was an unresolvable barrier for grounding a complete and thorough worldview with empirical inquiry playing its own part (Kant, 1781/1998). Rather than blaming Kant directly, he searched for the origins of the ideas that grounded Kant's work. The very things that made Kant's work untenable in Peirce's eyes were first found in Descartes. In particular, Descartes used his Method of Doubt as a starting point for grounding what will come to be known as Modern Philosophy in general, and modern metaphysics in particular.

Toulmin (1990) points out that Descartes's project did not occur in a vacuum, but instead was a representation of the change in Western thought from the 15th and 16th centuries into the emerging 17th century. Briefly, that era started with the European discovery of America and ended with the Thirty Years War of the early 17th century. It was a period of great material abundance. Such abundance tends to generate free play, exploration and tolerance in both thought and actions. Here is where we find the work of Shakespeare, Michelangelo, and Montaigne, just to name a tiny few. But as the wealth from America started drying up, and the newly established Protestant movement contributed to creating new and fierce wars of intolerance, the basic tenor of European thought changed as well. There was a strong need to re-establish convergent thought and a strong sense of certainty, and it was in that milieu that Descartes created his Method of Doubt. It is important to look at the issues above in order to see both the goals of Descartes's project as well as the intensity of the need for such a project in the first place.

In Descartes's method, doubt is extended until it leads him to the famous *Cogito ergo sum*. At this point, Descartes's doubt ends and he has his firm and certain foundation for what will come to be known as Modern thought. This foundation did not come without its costs, however. By grounding certainty in a mental act, Descartes first changed the fundamental form of inquiry from the search for reality to the search for knowledge. (Incidentally, this is the reason that, in most works of philosophy and foundations of the social sciences today, "epistemological this" and "epistemological that" recurs: these inquirers can see no other conscious frame for reality, and this in turn leads to major consequences in inquiry). Most importantly, by relying on the mental act of knowing as his starting place, Descartes created a problem in trying to deal with the physical world as well. That is, unless Descartes accepted that all reality is a mental construction, an option he seems to assiduously avoid, he had to acknowledge that the physical and the mental, the objective and the subjective (as he eventually defined these terms in variance with their original understandings [cf. Deely, 2001]), have been split asunder to create an apparent duality of reality.

From this vantage, the noumenal and phenomenal of Kant's model are a direct and obvious extension. Furthermore, the project of trying to reduce Cartesian duality back into some form of unity has dominated Western philosophy ever since.

When Peirce tackled this Cartesian problem, he did so in a totally unique way. The problem with Descartes's method of doubt, he argues, is that it was only pretend doubt. That is, Descartes never really doubted the things he claimed to doubt, and he did not set aside his use of this method until he restored all the things he had claimed to doubt (Peirce, 1868a/1992; Peirce, 1877/1992).

Thus, according to Peirce, Cartesian doubt is not a proper place to begin inquiry. It is both artificial and self-contained. A much better approach is to look at the nature of human beings in general, and discover how this general nature is translated into the conduct of inquiry in particular. The application of both his ideas about incapacities and his rejection of the Cartesian method combine to form his understanding of how we use logic and inquiry as human beings, while being cognizant of human skills and weaknesses.

Peirce then tackles the question of how human beings reason in the real world. He looks at how human beings seek to build their knowledge and understanding of the world while still acknowledging their incapacities and characteristics as human beings (Peirce, 1877/1992; Peirce, 1878/1992). Rather than starting with the Cartesian absolute of the knower as the center of the pursuit of truth, Peirce instead grounds human inquiry squarely in the notion of doubt as a real problem in the world. This is not pretend Cartesian play doubt. Instead, he calls it Genuine Doubt and rightly states the fact that Genuine Doubt is disorienting. That is, we seek to get out of Genuine Doubt and back into the overall state of belief that allows us to function in the world at so many levels. Here, I shall not concentrate on his four methods of fixing beliefs, but instead acknowledge his claim that the highest form of action to lead us from doubt to belief is to ground our actions in our beliefs while being nevertheless ready to change those beliefs when and if consequences warrant us to do so. In order to make this process universal, Peirce goes on to say that meaning, which is both the foundation and target of beliefs, is found not in words but in actions and practices. We do not state our beliefs but put them into action. This greatly expands the domain of beliefs. As one example, when we walk across the floor and pay no attention to where we place our feet, we are doing so because we believe the floor is solid. That is, this act of walking is itself a belief statement.

This notion of human beings starting in the world as believing creatures who modify their beliefs (as primarily manifested in their actions and practices in the world) is our starting point for the eventual formation of a Peircean model of what itself will ultimately become a semiotic model of the empirical inquirer.

4 Peirce's model of the inquirer

Descartes and Peirce diverge in their views relating to both the nature of the inquirer and the goals and tasks of inquiry. Descartes was concerned with the acquisition of facts and knowledge to create a firm and certain starting place for our actions. Once we have that firm foundation, then inquiry is of two parts. The first part is to gather true facts from the world. The second part is to put those true conclusions together to form more and more comprehensive statements of knowledge about the world. Meaning is then considered to be an emergent property of these knowledge statements.

It is easy to see how the processes above could be developed in both algorithmic and mechanical forms. In principle, this most certainly could lead to the creation of an Inquiry Machine. De la Mettrie (1748/1912) brought this approach home very early on in his book *Man A Machine*. To take this notion to its logical extreme, if we create sufficiently accurate and well-programmed data-collecting devices, and program them with algorithms to organize these data into knowledge bases, then we can actually replace the human inquirer with what I call the Inquiry Machine. At this point, we remove the last traces and vestiges of human imperfection in our quest for knowledge, and the human inquirer is rendered fundamentally obsolete.

On the other hand, Peirce assumed the search for meaning to be fundamental. From his point of view, empirical inquiry is inescapably human and builds upon collective understandings of meaning. There is no Inquiry Machine, but human beings doing inquiry for human beings and addressing genuine human doubts.

5 From duality to triadicity

How is the Peircean approach to inquiry fundamentally different from Cartesian inquiry? To get ahead of ourselves, we need to replace duality with triadicity. We can start by making the case that Cartesian duality is woefully inadequate as a comprehensive approach. Before we do this, we need to acknowledge where duality seems to work. Cartesian inquiry is most effective when dealing with unmediated circumstances. For instance, the time that a ball takes to fall from the top of a building to the ground is determined only by the height of the building and the gravitational constant. Everything else can be ignored. Granting that this unmediated process can work quite well in these types of situations, it however becomes less and less useful as things grow more complex, especially when looking at living things in general and humans in particular.

The followers of the Cartesian view explicitly acknowledge that duality is not something they seek to preserve, but something they seek to reduce to some form of convergent unity. This problem was known to Descartes at the outset. His project was to replace duality models with unity models. Such actions seem to require convergence toward a final established and certain point. This is a task worthy of an Inquiry Machine. The essence of the Cartesian orientation is that dualities need to be replaced with unity. Is there an alternative?

Let us consider the basic experience of being a human being in the world. What is the one orientation that all human cultures and societies share? As has been mentioned, all humans live in a world of three stable dimensions; length, width and height. The key concept here is "stable". If humans live in a stable world, then the likelihood of Genuine Doubt being present is greatly diminished. Yet it is not eliminated; hence the necessity of inquiry. The Cartesian basis for stability is the pursuit of underlying unity; but does this truly promise stability? Instead, it seems to be a fixed and static point that may be stable indeed, but only because it is unchanging.

6 Human incapacities and empirical inquiry

At this point, I return to Peirce's list of the four incapacities of human cognition (Peirce 1868a/1992; Peirce, 1868b/1992). This is important because human cognition is the species' primary tool for inquiry. In general, these incapacities point out that, as inquirers in a world of experience, we have no ability to apprehend directly the nature of anything. Furthermore, we can only move into the unknown from the known. Therefore, the fruits of inquiry are gained only by our ability to reason from what we have based our experiences on and our current understanding of what those experiences mean. So, rather than looking at meaning as an emergent property, Peirce put it front and center (1877/1992). Our inquiry is not just for ourselves or for some ideal, but it is a way for us collectively to understand and deal with both current and future practices.

Human inquiry, it would seem, is oriented toward using reasoning as a guide toward a meaningful and stable picture of the world. This is clearly a more contingent goal than Cartesian inquiry but, then again, human experiences are contingent. If human work continues to be collective and ongoing and if it diligently practices self-correction, then there is no reason to assume that humans will not end up in a world of experience that is both meaningful and stable and most likely true.

7 Human inquiry and the sign

Perhaps the most explicit and clear incapacity that Peirce cited is the notion that there is no thought without signs. The essence of triadicity in inquiry is the sign. Also, according to Peirce, signs are everywhere. Furthermore, when humans inquire, they are not only perceiving signs but also creating signs. That is, any stable and meaningful understanding humans produce will be some collection of human thoughts, and there are no thoughts without signs (Peirce, 1868a/1992; Peirce, 1868b/1992).

When does it make sense to use triadic methods in conducting empirical inquiry, then? To begin with, the same consideration must be addressed regarding dyadic or Cartesian, models of empirical inquiry: where does it make sense to use them? In fact, when dealing with unmediated statics and dynamics all that is needed is a dyadic model. For instance, in order to perform the famous high school physics experiment where a steel ball is released and rolls down a ramp, very little data is needed in order to predict how far will it roll, when it will come off the ramp and when it will move along the smooth black marble top of the lab table. In fact, all that needs to be known is the mass of the steel ball, the gravity constant and the angle of the ramp. Of course, there are any number of observable or measurable phenomena that could be tracked. What about, say, the color of the steel ball? The answer to this question must be: it is totally irrelevant. The barometric pressure in the room? Well, this is an intervening variable, sure, but so miniscule as to be negligible. The coefficient of friction can be kept low by using smooth marble, but there will be inevitably some tiny such effect. Since the measuring tools are not sensitive enough to pick up such tiny effects, they can easily be ignored. Just to be on the safe side, the ball should be rolled a number of times and the average distance reported.

If this logic is carried over into work with living creatures, right away there will be problems in any attempt to treat the ensuing phenomena as unmediated processes. The sign becomes the lynchpin of empirical inquiry that deals with living creatures, at least, because all actions of living creatures are mediated and therefore triadic.

In summary, the sign is a versatile tool because it can be dialed back to work with unmediated phenomena, but can readily and naturally be extended to its full potential to deal with mediated phenomena. So one can safely bid adieu to unmediated phenomena at this point and move forward to look at signs in their full triadicity.

8 Implementing triadic methods in empirical inquiry

What does a sign look like as an empirical tool, then? To answer the question, consider Peirce's ten classes of signs. They create a limited but powerful set of inquiry tools, particularly for inquiry into living creatures.

At first blush, Peirce's ten classes of signs look like an odd sort of categorization (Shank, 2003; Shank, 2006). After all, what use is there in labelling, say, a weathercock, as a Dicent Indexical Legisign (Peirce, 1903/1955, p.119)? Yet, drawing back from these apparently tortuous details, the ten classes manifestly limit both the types and natures of signs. This is an extremely useful and practical finding, since the scope and spread of signs appear to be vast. By working out these classes, Peirce did a further service for empirical inquirers. The classes allow empirical inquirers, among others, to create direct links between the various ways humans reason about the world and the sorts of things they can say about the various things in the world (Peirce, 1897/1955).

There is mathematical precision in Peirce's ten classes of signs. They are a consequence of three different systems that are always present in a sign. The first system deals with the way in which the sign is grounded in the world. This grounding aspect identifies a sign as either being a qualisign, sinsign or legisign. The second system deals with how the sign represents its object. This representational aspect identifies a sign as either an icon, an index or a symbol. The final system deals with how the sign operates as a sign. This manifesting aspect identifies a sign as either a rheme, a dicent or an argument. The three trichotomies give rise to combinations of signs; however, certain combinations are not allowable, because as signs get more abstract they get more limited in their scope. Using a monotonic reduction system, Peirce (1897/1955) created the following list of classes of signs that are allowable:
1) Rhemic Iconic Qualisign
2) Rhemic Indexical Sinsign
3) Rhemic Symbolic Legisign
4) Rhemic Indexical Sinsign
5) Rhemic Symbolic Legisign
6) Rhemic Iconic Qualisign
7) Dicent Indexical Sinsign

8) Dicent Indexical Legisign
9) Dicent Symbolic Legisign
10) Argument Symbolic Legisign

It is hard to blame anyone in the least for taking a look at this list, shrugging their shoulders, and walking away. It is a classic case of how Peirce's neologistic terminology sacrifices familiar, but potentially misleading expressions, for precision.

Nevertheless, for the sake of using these classes in the conduct of empirical inquiry *only*, I suggest a more clear terminology consisting in specialized uses of the classes, as opposed to generalized ones. It would be inappropriate to generalize them to all situations of use.

Starting with the ground of a sign, we can ask whether that grounding is possible, singular, or general. Because the first type of grounding is not specific but only possible, I refer to it as Open. Because the second type of grounding is specific but only in the case at hand, I refer to it as Single. Finally, because the third type of grounding is based on rule or convention and not any given sign *per se*, I refer to it as General.

Moving on to the representational nature of a sign, the next question to ask is whether that representation is iconic, indexical, or symbolic. These terms are quite familiar in everyday speech in English. Because the first type of representation is based on a possible representation or mimesis, Peirce refers to it as an Icon. Because the second type of representation is based on the fact that it points to its object in some perceivable or specific way, he refers to it as an Index. Finally, because the third type of representation is based on rule or convention and not any given sign per se, Peirce refers to it as a Symbol.

Finally, looking at the manifestations of a sign, the question arises whether that manifestation is possible, singular or general. Because the first type of manifestation is not direct but only possible, Peirce refers to it as a Tone. Because the second type of manifestation is specific but only in the case at hand, Peirce names it a Token. Finally, because the third type of manifestation is based on rule or convention and not any given sign *per se*, he refers to it as a Type.

Now, consider the classes as formulated for use by empirical inquirers:
1) Open Iconic Tone
2) Open Iconic Token
3) Open Iconic Type
4) Open Indexical Token
5) Open Indexical Type
6) Open Symbolic Type

7) Single Indexical Token
8) Single Indexical Type
9) Single Symbolic Type
10) General Symbolic Type

Rather than fleshing out the nature and uses of these empirically oriented classes of signs, it is useful to take a cursory look at two of the most important processes that might be used by empirical inquirers.

The first process deals with the orientation of researchers and how that orientation impacts the process of empirical inquiry in general. The second process involves the specific modes of reasoning used to operationalize the first process.

I will start with the Tenth and final class of signs that that might be encountered or used by empirical inquirers. A General Symbolic Type is actually a Law. The main dynamic of a Law is that it is certain. Empirical inquirers would like to think that they are in pursuit of Laws but have not yet found one. The closest the inquirer comes to Laws is when s/he creates mathematical theorems. Mathematics is true by fiat, meaning that this form of inquiry allows inquirers to deduce further understandings from the accumulated body of theorems and conjectures. This is the only example I can think of that resembles a Law and it is the only place where pure deduction can be used. That is, when an inquiry dealing with General signs is conducted, Deductive reasoning is used, or Reasoning to the Law.

Classes Seven, Eight, and Nine are the Single classes. As such, they start with actual specific items in the world of experience and then build from there. The main dynamic of Single signs is that of Probability. As more and more similar items are gathered, the probability that the inquirer is pursuing something systematic in the world of experience increases. Inquiry dealing with Single signs employs the process of Inductive reasoning. But each is inductive in a different way.

Single Indexical Tokens are best thought of as Facts. Facts are regularities in the empirical world that are probably consistent. However, each fact stands on its own platform, so to speak. The form of inductive reasoning used when the targets of inquiry are facts is such that the inquiry concerns the probability that what has been found is not a coincident but has some real link to the inquiry. It is the case, say, that gun is found at a murder scene. Whether or not this gun was the murder weapon is a fact that needs verification in some way before the investigation can move on. This form of empirically-based Induction is Reasoning to the Fact.

Single Indexical Types are best thought of as Hypotheses. Once a certain amount of facts is gathered, the inquirer can start to make probable guesses about whether or not those facts are related. When enough facts are gathered and the inquirer can surmise that they are related, then the inquirer is in a position to hypothesize connections. Again, the empirical truth of these hypotheses is probable, since they are inductively generated. Is there a pattern here in this specific case, or are all these things coincidentally present? This form of empirically-based Induction is Reasoning to the Hypothesis.

Single Symbolic Types are best thought of as Theories. A theory is inductively generated, as are judgments about probable facts and hypotheses. Theories, though, can be made to travel beyond the specific data to look at potentially cohesive bigger pictures. The most tested theories can be treated as quasi-laws, although they are in principle only one conflicting observation away from being found to be false. When theories are treated as quasi-laws, then the process that modern science calls the hypothetico-deductive process can come into use. The Theory of Evolution and the Theory of Relativity are examples of theories that are well grounded in ongoing inductive evidence. This form of empirically-based Induction is Reasoning to the Theory.

Before leaving this topic, it should be noted that there is not just one form of induction that is often contrasted with deduction, but three specific sub-classes of Induction. Each sub-class deals with different starting points and reaches different probable conclusions.

This finally leads to the Open classes of signs. Semiotic theory asserts that the guiding mode of reasoning in this form of empirical inquiry is Abduction (Peirce, 1903/1998; Shank, 1998; Shank, 2001). Because abduction deals with possibilities and not probabilities *per se*, it has much more variability and, as such, it accommodates the actual majority of sign classes. That is, while there is only one empirical approach based on deduction, and three approaches based on induction, there are actually six approaches based on abduction, thus completely explicating the approaches grounded on the ten classes of signs (cf. Shank, 2003 for a more extensive explication of this point). The six "tools" will be considered in turn.

The first sign class in this area is the Open Iconic Tone. Its open character means it is strictly in the realm of possibility and the fact that it is a tone means that it has no specific manifestation in the world of experience. For all intents and purposes, an Open Iconic Tone is the possibility of a possible possibility. The only thing that keeps this class of signs as worthy of consideration is the fact that, ultimately, not all things are possible. So it does make a divide, in a way, within the world of experience.

Open Iconic Tones are best thought of as Hunches. This is an important finding, since it brings the hunch squarely into the realm of reasoning in empirical inquiry. Hunches are iconic because they are triggered by something that the sign user will see or hear or smell or touch or taste that stirs a loosely formed possibility that there just might be something that demands attention. For instance, an archeologist may be walking along a creek in an area where Native Americans were thought to live and hunt. She would like to start a dig, but she has to decide where. Finally, she sees a low and level place along the bank which might have been the sort of place where they might have made camp. This is not so much a guess as it is a legitimate logical inference performed in very open conditions and leading to very open possibilities. This empirically grounded type of abduction is Reasoning to the Hunch.

Open Iconic Tokens are best thought of as Omens. An omen is more than a hunch because it is grounded in something that is actually manifested in the world of experience. It encourages looking at something as a harbinger of something else, but only as a possible indicator. Again, it is iconic because it is based in either resemblance or mimesis. Consider, now, two different examples of omens. In the first cases, a farmer is out plowing her fields with her new and expensive and delicate tractor. She is in a part of the field that is furthest from the barn, which serves as the shelter for her beloved tractor. All of a sudden, a bank of dark and ominous clouds roll in and the wind picks up. Because she wants to protect our new tractor, she reasons that these clouds might be an indicator of a coming rainstorm, so she heads back to the barn as fast as she can. Is it actually going to rain? At this point, it is difficult to say. Like most omens, the rain cloud points to a possible future event. That does not mean that it is certain that it is going to rain. It is still just a possibility.

Not all omens are grounded as clearly as the example above. Tarot cards and other fortune-telling procedures foster the idea that there will be future outcomes. These are omens as well. There is no guarantee that an omen is sound and useful and valuable. This empirically-grounded type of abduction is Reasoning to the Omen.

Open Iconic Types are best thought of as Metaphors. Metaphors are the most abstract and theoretical products of abductive reasoning. Lakoff and Johnson (1980) have called metaphors the basis of cognition. Metaphors allow juxtaposition of seemingly disparate things and allow the discerning of connections that are often surprising. Metaphors also facilitate the creation of possible models of intelligibility that can be used in attempts to incorporate new and often difficult information. This empirically-grounded type of abduction is Reasoning via the use of Metaphors.

Open Indexical Tokens are best thought of as Clues. Clues often resemble facts and sometimes grow up to be facts. Considered in and of themselves, they are markers that are possibly meaningful in the search for information and understanding in any empirical inquiry. It is impossible to overestimate the value of clues in empirical inquiry, so it is important to understand what they really are and how they really operate. This empirically grounded type of abduction is Reasoning to the Clue.

Open Indexical Types are best thought of as Patterns. Pattern formation seems to be wired into the human nervous system. Cognitive science in particular shows that there is a strong psychological compulsion to form and find patterns. Yet patterns, like all other forms of abductive reasoning, have their properties and values as forms of possibilities. When there is an array of clues and which may be taken to be related to each other, the best test of this idea is to see if the clues do, indeed, form a pattern. This empirically-grounded type of abduction is Reasoning to the Pattern.

Open Symbolic Types are best thought of as Explanations. For the sake of simplicity, an explanation can be considered as a conjecture. It holds together well enough to bring together a lot of information; but it is not sufficient to support a lot of predictions. This empirically-grounded type of abduction is Reasoning to the Explanation.

To conclude this section on Abduction, it should be emphasized that when these various modes of reasoning in approaching empirical work are employed, it is possible to greatly expand awareness and subsequent use of all these modes of reasoning when and where they are called for. Equally important is the fact that this indicates that there are a finite number of reasoning tools that can be used. This insight is useful therefore in a different way, marking the parameters of reasoning and inquiry. Finally, there is any number of insightful and practical connections among these modes of reasoning that cannot be explored in depth here for reasons of space. Nevertheless, the connections still exist.

9 Beyond the inquiry machine

To conclude, I will return to Toulmin's (1990) rather unflattering picture of the beginnings of Modernism and the so-called Enlightenment. While the Enlightenment was the birthplace of contemporary technology, it has been a dead end in the search for a means of understanding the natures and worlds of living creatures, humans included. The era that Modernism replaced was an era of abundance, in terms of exploration, curiosity and tolerance. Modernism replaced all of this with its fear-driven search for absolutes and certainty. Abundant and tolerant patterns of thought and practices were replaced by a mindset of scarcity where the only guarantee for survival was making sure everything that was said or done was unassailable.

Contrast the pessimism of Modernism and its Cartesian roots with the promise of semiotic inquiry in search of meaning that can be put to any variety of uses. When the concept of the sign is allowed into methodology, with its forms of clues, omens, metaphors, patterns, fables, riddles, and the like, the resultant vision allows the crafting of a divergent but increasingly meaningful and stable look at the world. Furthermore, by including new tools that allow inquirers to confront the types of signs above and more, humans' reach is likewise expanded as well. So it remains necessary to preserve the limited tools of Modernism which allow humans to tackle unmediated issues, but also to move forward into these vast and rich new lands. Semiotic inquiry acknowledges that the world of experience is not a place of scarcity but a place of abundance, particularly when the search for meaning is involved. As a result, the semiotic inquirer revels in the joy of working with meaning and belief in the world.

My last example comes from personal experience. When I lived in northern Illinois, I was working with people who ran the educational outreach of Fermilab. Fermilab, before it was replaced by CERN, was the largest and most powerful cyclotron (particle accelerator) in the world. Its ring was buried underground, forming an earthen ridge whose radius was five miles long. At any given time, there were flags of over fifty nations on display, signifying the nationalities of the researchers who were currently on site. Their electric bill was over a million dollars a week. This was a big league place.

Yet, the director, Leon Lederman, was concerned with more than chasing subatomic particles. He had created a place that celebrated the life of the mind. Each elevator had a blackboard, and they were constantly in use. Every office looked out into the open inner space of the 14-story building, where a Foucault pendulum ceaselessly traced its path. Every table in the cafeteria had pads and paper. Every middle school kid who came on tour got to ask any questions they wanted to actual physicists who volunteered eagerly to respond.

I remember standing with Dr. Lederman, a winner of the Nobel Prize in Physics for his research characterizing the nature of neutrinos and quarks, on the 14th floor, looking out over the ring and the restored prairie that housed it. A herd of buffalo wandered about. Lederman was taking in the whole scene with a rapt expression.

"How would you describe this place to someone who has never been here," I asked.

He grinned. "I would tell them that this is the world's biggest and coolest sandbox. And we get to bring our pails and shovels and play here every day."

Within the dour confines of Modernism, he had found abundance. How much farther is it possible to go, when methods and perspectives that bring abundance to the forefront, are put into place?

References

Brent, Joseph. 1998. *Charles Sanders Peirce: A life*. Bloomington, IN: Indiana University Press.
Deely, John. 2001. *Four ages of understanding*. Toronto: University of Toronto Press.
de la Mettrie, Julien Offray. 1942 [1748]. *Man a machine*. La Salle, IL: Open Court.
Descartes, René. 2003 1637. *Discourse on method and meditations*. NY: Dover.
Kant, Immanuel. 1781 [1998]. *Critique of pure reason*. Cambridge: Cambridge University Press.
Lakoff, George & Mark Johnson. 1980. *Metaphors we live by*. Chicago: University of Chicago Press.
Peirce, Charles S. 1992 [1868a]. Questions concerning certain faculties claimed for man. In Nathan Houser & Christian J. W. Kloesel (eds.), 11–27. *The Essential Peirce: Volume I*, Bloomington, IN: Indiana University Press.
Peirce, Charles S. 1992 [1868b]. Some consequences of four incapacities. In Nathan Houser & Christian J. W. Kloesel (eds.), *The Essential Peirce: Volume I*, 56–83. Bloomington, IN: Indiana University Press.
Peirce, Charles S. 1992 [1869]. Grounds of validity of the laws of logic. In Nathan Houser & Christian J. W. Kloesel (eds.), *The Essential Peirce: Volume I*, 109–123. Bloomington, IN: Indiana University Press.
Peirce, Charles S. 1992 [1877]. The fixation of belief. In Nathan Houser & Christian J. W. Kloesel (eds.), *The Essential Peirce: Volume I*, 124–141. Bloomington, IN: Indiana University Press.
Peirce, Charles S. 1992 [1878]. How to make our ideas clear. In Nathan Houser & Christian J. W. Kloesel (eds.), *The Essential Peirce: Volume I*, Bloomington, IN: Indiana University Press.
Peirce, Charles S. 1998 [1903]. Pragmatism as the logic of abduction. In Peirce Edition Project (eds.) *The Essential Peirce: Volume II*, 226–241. Bloomington, IN: Indiana University Press.
Peirce, Charles S. 1955 [1897]. Logic as semiotic: The theory of signs. In Justus Buchler, (ed.), *Philosophical Writings of Peirce*, 98–119. NY: Dover.
Shank, Gary. 1998. The extraordinary ordinary powers of abductive reasoning. *Theory and Psychology*, 8, 841–860.
Shank, Gary. 2001. It's logic in practice, my dear Watson: An imaginary memoir from beyond the grave. *Forum for Qualitative Studies*, 2 (1). Online at: http://qualitative-research.net/fqs/fqs-eng.htm

Shank, Gary. 2003. Peirce's ten classes of signs and the empirical researcher. Paper presented at the Annual Meeting of the Semiotic Society of America, Ottawa, Ontario, Canada, October 2003.

Shank, Gary. 2006. Praxical reasoning and the logic of field research. In Dick Hobbs & Richard Wright (eds.), *Handbook of Fieldwork*, 23–36. London: Sage.

Toulmin, Stephen Edelston. 1990. *Cosmopolis*. Chicago: University of Chicago Press.

Basarab Nicolescu
Transdisciplinarity as a solution to the challenges of the contemporary world

Abstract: Technological singularity is defined as a hypothetical event in which *artificial intelligence* would be capable of recursive self-improvement or of autonomously building machines smarter and more powerful than itself, up to the point of an *intelligence explosion*, that yields an intelligence surpassing all current human control or understanding. In this paper, I review the different opinions expressed around this idea and around the idea of transhumanism. I also analyze the phenomenon of panterrorism and the theme of the anthropocene. I formulate the hypothesis that the transdisciplinary interaction of philosophy and spirituality with other sciences, exact and human, is the privileged means of resistance to the new barbarism. I call *transdisciplinary philosophy* the philosophy which integrates transdisciplinary methodology.

Keywords: singularity, transdisciplinarity, artificial intelligence, panterrorism, Anthropocene

1 Introduction

I would like to start with a simple question: can we really dialogue?

The word "dialogue" emerged at the foundation of modernity, but it initially referred only to nature (Galilei 1962).

Now, each person has his/her prejudices, his/her convictions, and his/her subconscious representations. When two people try to communicate there is inevitably a confrontation: representation against representation, subconscious against subconscious. As this confrontation is subconscious, it often degenerates into conflict rather than dialogue.

Language is the vehicle of these subconscious representations. Interlocutors might use the same words, but they might mean radically different things.

Acknowledgement: I would like to thank Professors Paul Cobley and Dario Martinelli for their kind invitation to give a keynote at the very important and stimulating 13th World Congress of Semiotics.

Basarab Nicolescu, International Centre for Transdisciplinary Research (CIRET), Paris, France

https://doi.org/10.1515/9783110857801-005

Arguably, we are manipulated by our own representations. Dialogue is strictly impossible in the absence of a *methodology* of dialogue. We can only monologue. It is impossible to be in the other's place.

The same considerations apply in the case of nations, cultures, religions and spiritualities: interest against interest, representation against representation, dogma against dogma, hidden spiritual assumptions against hidden spiritual assumptions. This situation is aggravated by the large number of languages (more than 6000), which each display their own system of representations and values. A completely accurate translation from one language to another is impossible.

The situation is also aggravated by the immense contemporary means of destruction and the continuing destruction of the environment. A new model of civilization is necessary, where the keystone is dialogue between human beings, nations, cultures and spiritualities for the survival of humanity.

We have therefore to face a number of important questions:
- What is the methodology of dialogue?
- Is a suspension of our prejudices necessary to arrive at a "fusion of horizons" (Gadamer 1960)?
- Is the abandonment of the binary logic and the adoption of non-classical logic necessary?
- Can we dialogue without first identifying the levels of Reality involved in the dialogue?
- How can we take complexity into account?
- Are the transcultural and the trans-spiritual crucially important for a methodology of dialogue of cultures and of spiritualities?
- Is dialogue between cultures a social or a political gamble?
- Is the danger of the dissolution of cultures in the context of globalization real?
- Are there big cultures, small cultures and falling cultures?
- Are peoples of the world prepared for a real dialogue of cultures?
- What is the role of the spiritual dimension in this dialogue?

This paper argues that we can begin to address all these questions by adopting the methodology of transdisciplinarity.

2 The new barbarism

From my point of view, we live in a time of a new barbarism which might be characterized by three words: Panterrorism, the Anthropocene and Transhumanism.

I introduce the neologism *Panterrorism* to describe a new form of terrorism, without any connection to any religion. Its aim is to kill the other in order to impose its own power. On 13 November 2015, Paris was hit by blind force of hate. It was a massacre of innocents. What was intended was to kill a certain way of life, the symbol of which is Paris. In this new form of terrorism, the battle does not consist in soldiers confronting other soldiers. There are only killers who blindly exterminate what is, to them, an anonymous mass. Panterrorism is more and more common on our planet. By killing the other, the desire of omnipotence reaches an unpredicted climax. The French philosopher Marcel Gauchet (2016) noted in a recent conference that jihadism is, not just for the obvious reasons, a disconcerting phenomenon in the West. Jihadism is, after the fall of the Nazi and Communist totalitarianism, a new form of totalitarianism that uses religion as a political project. This new form of totalitarianism will inevitably use the new technologies – including 3D printing in order to produce arms and bombs, the Internet of Things (IoT) in order to commit mass crimes, electronic chips implanted in the human body in order to dispose of a fabulous quantity of information, etc.

The second word, the *Anthropocene* is a neologism designating a new geological era, characterized by the fact that the actions of the human species have become the dominant geophysical force on our planet as compared with natural geological forces. There is a danger today, for the first time in history, concerning the extinction of the entire human species (see, for example, Latour 2014: 27–54). The survival of the human species is, for a good number of scientists and philosophers, the most important issue of our time.

As the well-known Australian climatologist Clive Hamilton writes in his book *Requiem for a Species* (2010a), it is difficult to accept the idea that human beings can change the composition of the Earth's atmosphere at a point of destroying their own civilization and also the human species. One can predict sea level rise of several meters during this century due to the dissolution of Arctic sea ice in one or two decades. One can even predict that the ice on the entire planet will disappear in several centuries, leading to rising sea levels by about 70 meters. Unexpected phenomena will occur: domestic animals will turn into wild animals and grown plants will disappear (Hamilton 2010a: 44). The consequences for the security of nations will be huge: waves of refugees from climate-disadvantaged countries will immigrate to climate-favored countries, which will cause unprecedented conflicts. International organizations are not prepared to face such a situation: they are not really concerned with the security of the planet, but with the security of regions of the planet.

One thing is certain: *in the Anthropocene, the old and persistent radical distinction between nature and culture is no longer valid.* Culture changes nature. Desecration of nature thus reaches its peak.

How can this terrible catastrophe be avoided? In the US, many politicians are convinced that it can be avoided by technological solutions and there have been formed several committees of specialists to find such solutions. A new discipline was born which is very prosperous today: geo-engineering, whose object is manipulating the environment to counter-balance the climate change caused by the human species. The goal is to transform the chemical composition of the atmosphere so that one can adjust at will the temperature of our planet.

Paul Crutzen, the Dutch winner of the Nobel Prize for Chemistry, proposed in 2006 to introduce aerosols into the atmosphere to reflect sunlight (Crutzen 2006). This suggestion has spawned a research trajectory, supported by prestigious institutions such as the US National Academy of Sciences and the Royal Society (Hamilton 2010a: 202). The idea is to inject sulphur dioxide into the stratosphere, in gaseous form, at an altitude of 10–50 km, thus forming sulphate aerosol particles that can reflect sunlight (Hamilton 2010a: 198). Crutzen remarks in passing that the diurnal sky will become permanently white, a grim perspective in aesthetic terms. It is impressive that scientists of the stature of Edward Teller (co-founder and director of Lawrence Livermore National Laboratory in San Francisco) and Lowell Wood (researcher at the same laboratory and influential scholar at Pentagon) are among the staunch followers of this technological solution. Wood even remarked that "We've engineered every other environment we live in – why not the planet?" (quoted in Hamilton 2010b). Yet, as Hamilton, argues, it is not technology that will save our species, but a radical change of our vision of Reality.

Based upon the transdisciplinary approach, I shall present some brief considerations about Transhumanism and its connection with what is called "technological singularity". *Technological singularity* is defined as a hypothetical event in which artificial intelligence would be capable of recursive self-improvement or of autonomously building smarter and more powerful machines than itself, up to the point of an *intelligence explosion,* that yields an intelligence surpassing all current human control or understanding. Because the capabilities of such superintelligence may be impossible for humans to comprehend, a technological singularity is the point beyond which events may become unpredictable. What is being defined here is an *essential singularity in the history of the human race beyond which human affairs, as we know them, could not continue* (More and Vita-More 201).

The term 'technological singularity' was coined by the mathematician, computer scientist and science fiction author Vernor Vinge (1993), who argues that artificial intelligence, human biological enhancement, or brain–computer interfaces could be possible causes of the singularity. Futurist Ray Kurzweil (2005) predicts that singularity will occur around 2045, whereas Vinge predicts it sometime around 2030.

The basic idea is that although technological progress has been accelerating, it has been limited by the basic intelligence of the human brain, which has not changed significantly for millennia. Many writers tie singularity to observations of exponential growth in various technologies, using such observations as a basis for predicting that singularity is likely to happen sometime within our century.

Kurzweil reserves the term "singularity" for a rapid increase in intelligence (as opposed to other technologies), writing for example that "The Singularity will allow us to transcend these limitations of our biological bodies and brains [. . .] There will be no post-Singularity distinction, between human and machine" (2005: 9). The suggestion seems to be that while the human brain is far from simple, massive redundancy in the brain makes it much simpler than might be expected. He defines his predicted date of the singularity in terms of when he expects computer-based intelligences to significantly exceed the total sum of human brainpower. Kurzweil's analysis of history concludes that technological progress follows a pattern of exponential growth, following what he calls the "Law of Accelerating Returns". Whenever technology approaches a barrier, Kurzweil writes, new technologies will surmount it.

The huge literature around the concept of the technological singularity puts the accent on the bright, attractive and utopian side of technology. Here, I choose to discuss its dark side.

From the numerous books, articles and internet documents, I conclude that all this discussion of "the technological singularity" is not rigorous. Science-fiction is not science and wishful thinking is not a serious thinking. In fact, the technological singularity is not a singularity in the mathematical meaning of this word. Exponential behavior does not mean singularity. All these arguments, in my view, appear to constitute an excuse to dissimulate the basic ideology behind all the discussion: the advent of *transhumans*. "Singularity" is used as a metaphor to suggest the jump from humans to transhumans. In other words, the technological singularity is the basic ground of what is called *Transhumanism*.

If the transhumanist project will be achieved, human beings will become increasingly more machine and the machine will become increasingly more human. The international cultural and intellectual movement of transhumanism advocates the use of biotechnology to improve the physical and mental characteristics of human beings. Ageing and death, in this configuration, are considered undesirable and should not be inevitable. Likewise, natural selection is considered obsolte and to be replaced by technological selection. The major project is to remove any transcendent force and replace it with the human-machine of superhuman intelligence, master of his/her/its life. Transhumans, "improved humans" or "ameliorated humans", will constitute a new, bio-technological species. Future society will be divided between "transhumans" and "old humans". The old humans will inevitably be servants of the transhumans.

It is evident that to meet the triple threat – Panterrorism, the Anthropocene, and Transhumanism, humanistic claims alone are totally inefficient. My hypothesis is that the transdisciplinary interaction of philosophy and spirituality with other sciences, hard and humanistic, and with literature and art, is the privileged means of resistance to the new barbarism. I call *transdisciplinary philosophy* the philosophy which integrates the transdisciplinary methodology.

There spiritual poverty currently on our Earth. It is manifested in fear, violence, hate and dogmatism. In a world with more than 8000 academic disciplines, more than 10000 religions and religious movements and more than 6000 tongues, it is difficult to dream about mutual understanding and peace. There is a need for a new spirituality, conciliating self-serving technoscience and altruistic wisdom.

The first motivation for a new spirituality is technoscience, associated with fabulous economic power, which is simply incompatible with present spiritualities. It drives a hugely irrational force of efficiency for efficiency's sake: everything which can be done will be done, for the worst or the best. The second motivation for a new spirituality is the difficulty of the dialogue between different spiritualities, which often appear as antagonistic.

Simply put, we need to find *a spiritual dimension of democracy*. Social and political life goes well beyond academic disciplines, but they are based upon the knowledge generated by them. The only way to avoid the dead end of the new barbarism is to adopt *transdisciplinary hermeneutics*. Transdisciplinary hermeneutics is a natural outcome of transdisciplinary methodology.

3 Transdisciplinary methodology

The methodology of transdisciplinarity (Nicolescu 2002) is founded on three postulates which are concerned with Reality. The definition of Reality will be offered shortly, but the postulates concerned with it are as follows:
1. The ontological postulate: *There are, in Nature and in our knowledge of Nature, different levels of Reality of the Object and different levels of Reality of the Subject.*

2. The logical postulate: *The passage from one level of Reality to another is insured by the logic of the included middle.*
3. The epistemological postulate: *The structure of the totality of levels of Reality is a complex structure: every level is what it is because all the levels exist at the same time.*

The first two postulates received, in the 20th century, experimental evidence from quantum physics, while the last one has its source not only in quantum physics but also in a variety of other exact and human sciences.

The key concept of transdisciplinarity is the concept of *levels of Reality*.

"Reality", first of all, designates that which *resists* our experiences, representations, descriptions, images, or even mathematical formulations.

Insofar as reality participates in the being of the world, an ontological dimension should be assigned to this concept. Reality is not merely a social construction, the consensus of a collectivity, or some inter-subjective agreement. It also has a trans-subjective dimension: for example, experimental data can ruin the most beautiful scientific theory.

The meaning we give to the word "Reality" is therefore pragmatic and ontological at the same time.

We have to distinguish, in order to avoid further ambiguities, the words "Real" and "Reality". *Real* designates that which *is*, while *Reality* is connected to resistance in our human experience. The "Real" is, by definition, veiled for ever (it does not tolerate any further qualifications) while "Reality" is accessible to our knowledge. Real involves non-resistance while Reality involves resistance.

By "levels of Reality", I mean a set of systems which are invariant under certain general laws (in the case of natural systems) or general rules and norms (in the case of social systems): for example, quantum entities are subordinate to quantum laws, which depart radically from the laws of the macrophysical world. That is to say that two levels of Reality are different if, while passing from one to the other, there is a break in the applicable laws and a break in fundamental concepts (like, for example, causality). Therefore there is a *discontinuity* in the structure of levels of Reality.

Every level is characterized by its *incompleteness*: the laws governing this level are just a part of the totality of laws governing all levels. And even the totality of laws does not exhaust the entirety of Reality: we should also consider the Subject and its interaction with the Object. *Knowledge is forever open.*

The zone between two different levels and beyond all levels is a zone of *non-resistance* to our experiences, representations, descriptions, images, and mathematical formulations. Quite simply, the transparency of this zone is due to the limitations of our bodies, of our sense organs and of our brain, limitations which apply regardless of what measuring tools are used to extend these sense organs. We therefore have to conclude that the topological distance between levels is finite. However, this finite distance does not mean a finite knowledge. Take, as an image, a segment of a straight line – it contains an infinite number of points. In a similar manner, a finite topological distance could contain an infinite number of levels of Reality.

The unity of levels of Reality of the Object and its complementary zone of non-resistance constitutes what I call *the transdisciplinary Object*.

The different levels of Reality of the Object are accessible to our knowledge thanks to the different levels of perception which are potentially present in our being. These levels of perception permit an increasingly general, unifying, encompassing vision of Reality, without ever entirely exhausting it. In a rigorous way, these levels of perception are, in fact, *levels of Reality of the Subject*.

As in the case of levels of Reality of the Object, the coherence of levels of Reality of the Subject presupposes a zone of non-resistance to perception.

The unity of levels of Reality of the Subject and its complementary zone of non-resistance constitutes what I call the *transdisciplinary Subject*.

The two zones of non-resistance of transdisciplinarity, Object and Subject, must be identical for the transdisciplinary Subject to communicate with the transdisciplinary Object.

Knowledge is neither exterior nor interior: it is simultaneously exterior *and* interior. The study of the universe and of the human being sustain one another.

The zone of non-resistance plays the role of a *third* between the Subject and the Object, an Interaction term which allows the unification of the transdisciplinary Subject and the transdisciplinary Object while preserving their difference. I call this Interaction term the *Hidden Third*.

The transdisciplinary Object and its levels, the transdisciplinary Subject and its levels and the Hidden Third define the transdisciplinary Reality. It is important to note that the Hidden Third restores the continuity of Reality.

The incompleteness of the general laws governing a given level of Reality signifies that, at a given moment of time, one necessarily discovers contradictions in the theory describing the respective level: one has to assert A and non-A at the same time.

It is the included middle logic (Lupasco 1951) which allows us to jump from one level of Reality to another level of Reality.

Our understanding of the axiom of the included middle – there exists a third term T which is at the same time A and non-A – is clarified by the notion of "levels of Reality".

Representing the three terms of the new logic – A, non-A, and T – and the dynamics associated with them by a triangle results in a clearer image of the included middle. In this triangle, one of the vertices is situated at one level of Reality and the two other vertices at another level of Reality. The included middle is in fact an *included third*. If one remains at a single level of Reality, all manifestation appears as a struggle between two contradictory elements. The third dynamic, that of the T-state, is exercised at another level of Reality, where that which appears to be disunited is in fact united, and that which appears contradictory is perceived as non-contradictory. In other words, the action of the logic of the included middle on the different levels of Reality is able to explore the open structure of the unity of levels of Reality.

All levels of Reality are complexly interconnected. From a transdisciplinary point of view, complexity is a modern form of the very ancient principle of universal interdependence. The principle of universal interdependence entails the maximum possible simplicity that the human mind could imagine, the simplicity of the interaction of all levels of Reality. This simplicity cannot be captured by mathematical language. It can only be captured in non-mathematical symbolic language.

The human person appears as an interface between the Hidden Third and the world. The erasing of the Hidden Third in knowledge signifies a one-dimensional human being, reduced to its cells, neurons, quarks, elementary particles and electronic chips.

The Hidden Third between Subject and Object is rational but it denies any rationalization. The Hidden Third is not the opposite of reason: to the extent that it ensures the harmony between Subject and Object, the Hidden Third is part of the new, complex transdisciplinary rationality.

4 Conclusions

A new spirituality, free of dogmas, is already potentially present on our planet. There are exemplary signs and arguments for its birth, from quantum physics to theatre, literature and art (Nicolescu 2014). We are at the threshold of a New Renaissance, which asks for a new, 'cosmodern' consciousness comprising scientific knowledge and spirituality (Nicolescu 1994). Paradoxically, though, the new Renaissance is potentiality overshadowed by the violence of the new barbarism.

Etymologically, the word "barbarian" means one who is a stranger, an alien, who belongs to an uncivilized world. In this context, the new barbarism introduces a radical newness, for it means that *the alien is not outside us but within us*. We are our own barbarians.

There is an *ontological barbarism* consisting in the desire to reduce everything to a single level of Reality, a *logical barbarism* consisting in the refusal of any other logic than that of the excluded third, and an *epistemological barbarism* consisting in the refusal of complexity, of the interconnection between different levels of Reality.

The three tentacles of the new barbarism – transhumanism, panterrorism, and anthropocene – is a result of this triple barbarism – ontological, logical and epistemological. They have in common the fact that they are based on an updated model of Reality, reducing all levels of Reality to one.

Transdisciplinary hermeneutics will lead to the *fusion of horizons* that, with reference to Gadamer, was mentioned at the outset: a fusion not only of science and spirituality but also of all the other fields of knowledge, like arts, poetry, economics, social life and politics. Transdisciplinary hermeneutics can avoid the trap of trying to formulate super-science or super-spirituality. Unity of knowledge can only be an open, complex and plural unity.

This transdisciplinary methodology is the foundation of a new era – the cosmodern era. *Cosmodernity* (Nicolescu 2014) means essentially that each entity in the universe is defined by its relation to the other entities. *The idea of cosmos is therefore re-emphasized.* This is the reason why I introduced the word "cosmodernity" in 1994, in a book of aphorisms called *Théorèmes poétiques* (translated recently in English under the title *The Hidden Third* [2016]; see also Moraru 2011).

The cosmodern mind is a "vehicle for a new togetherness for solidarity across political, ethnic, racial, religious, and other boundaries". A "new geometry of 'we'" and a powerful *with-ness* distinguish cosmodernity from modernity or postmodernity. All cultures are inter-related. Cosmodernity is, by its very nature, transcultural, trans-spiritual and transreligious. Modern rationality is metamorphosed in relationality. Moraru coins the very evocative word "poethics" and he stresses that " . . . cosmodernism is best understood as an ethical rather than "technical" project. This project has considerable bearings on how we think not just about the subject but also about discourse, history, culture, community, patrimony, and tradition." The ethical imperative of cosmodernity is that of togetherness. The entire world, our world, is a "web of ideas and images", of people, cultures, religions, and spiritualities (Moraru 2011: 5, 23, 57, 55, 316, 304, 312).

Transdisciplinary philosophy is the privileged means of resistance to the new barbarism and it could educate the young generations in the spirit of this resistance. Its main outcome is the vital necessity of dialogue. Of course, we cannot dialogue with murderers but we can dialogue with potential killers, these young people living in our own countries, who, by taking their particular view of the world as an absolute view, become fanatics of panterrorism. We can dialogue with young and old people and try to give a meaning to the dangers of Anthropocene and Transhumanism. Only through transdisciplinary dialogue can we face the challenges of the contemporary world.

References

Crutzen, Paul. 2006. Albedo Enhacement by Stratosferic Sulphur Injections: A Contribution to Resolve a Policy Dilemma, *Climatic Change* 77(3–4): 211–220.
Gadamer, Hans-Georg. 1960. *Gesammelte Werke, Hermeneutik I. Wahreit und Methode*. Tübingen: J. C. B. Mohr.
Galilei, Galileo. 1962. *Dialogue Concerning the Two Chief World Systems, Ptolemaic and Copernican*. Berkeley: University of California Press. Translation by Stillman Drake. Foreword by Albert Einstein. The first edition appeared in 1632, year which could be considered as the birth date of modernity.
Gauchet, Marcel. 2016. L'attraction fondamentaliste. Paper presented at the workshop *La psychanalyse et le fait religieux*, Campus des Cordeliers, Paris. https://www.youtube.com/watch?v=T00PrHsmoL8&feature=youtu.be (accessed 3 July 2019).
Hamilton, Clive. 2010a. *Requiem for a Species – Why We Resist the Truth about Climate Change*. London: Earthscan.
Hamilton, Clive. 2010b. The powerful coalition that wants to engineer the world's climate. *The Guardian*. 13 September, https://www.theguardian.com/environment/2010/sep/13/geoengineering-coalition-world-climate. (accessed 1 July 2019)
Kurzweil, Ray. 2005. *The Singularity is Near: When Humans Transcend Biology*. New York: Penguin.
Latour, Bruno. 2014. L'Anthropocène et la destruction de l'image du Globe. In Émilie Hache (ed.), De l'univers clos au monde infini, 29–56, Paris: Éditions Dehors.
Lupasco, Stéphane. 1951. *Le principe d'antagonisme et la logique de l'énergie – Prolégomènes à une science de la contradiction*. Paris: Hermann & Cie.
Moraru, Christian. 2011. *Cosmodernism – American Narrative, Late Globalization and the New Cultural Imagination*. Ann Arbor: The University of Michigan Press.
More, Max and VITA-MORE, Natacha (ed.). 2013. *The Transhumanist Reader – Classical and Contemporary Essays on the Science, Technology, and Philosophy of the Human Future*. West Sussex: Wiley-Blackwell, John Wiley & Sons.
Nicolescu, Basarab. 1994. *Théorèmes Poétiques*. Monaco: Rocher.
Nicolescu, Basarab. 2002. *Manifesto of Transdisciplinarity*. New York: State University of New York Press. Translation from the French by Karen-Claire Voss.
Nicolescu, Basarab. 2014. *From Modernity to Cosmodernity – Science, Culture, and Spirituality*. New York: State University of New York Press.
Nicolescu, Basarab. 2016. *The Hidden Third [Le Tiers* Caché: Dans les Différents Domaine de la Connaissance]. Translation by William Garvin. New York: Quantum Prose.
Vinge, Vernor. 1993. The Coming Technological Singularity: How to Survive in the Post-Human Era. In Landis, G. A. (ed.) *Vision-21: Interdisciplinary Science and Engineering in the Era of Cyberspace*, pp. 11–22, NASA Publication CP-10129.

Section 2: Contemporary schools of theoretical semiotics

Andrew Stables
Notes towards a semiotic theory of learning

Abstract: This article explains the academic trajectory that led to his interest in semiotics and construing education from a fully semiotic perspective. This involves an encompassing discussion of both Western metaphysics in general and, contextually, scholarly trends in British academia, where semiotics is not mainstream, especially given the analytical tradition here. The article unfurls the arguments for which semiotics, taking the side of process as opposed to substance metaphysics, can collapse mind/body dualism, in the broader discussion of overcoming the longstanding divide in Western philosophy and science between empiricism and rationalism. The discussion supports a semiotic doctrine of rich empiricism, where the sign is defined as a feature of an event, experience as the subject's implication in events and events as the manifestations of processes. The paper concludes by pondering the importance of these considerations for learning and education through an example of educational policy.

Keywords: education, learning, thick empiricism, process metaphysics, dualism

1 Introduction: Personal history

As semiotics is not established as a self-standing discipline in British higher education, my route into semiotics was not a formal one. It is a field that British scholars most likely encounter in their work in literary, film or media studies, or in advertising or marketing. Some may come across semiotics through studies in pragmatist philosophy; others through interests in structuralism across a wide range of areas in the performing arts, humanities and social sciences; a very few through related interests in psychology (such as ecology of mind), engineering (cybernetics), biology (animal communication) or theoretical physics (the idea of observer dependence). The semioticians and semiotic conceptions encountered through these various routes may sometimes seem a fragmentary and random collection to those with a formal training in the field. On the other hand, entering the field with a set of perspectives drawn

---

Andrew Stables, Roehampton University

from other disciplines can provide insights that challenge conventional assumptions. Indeed, all encounters with semiotics offer the promise of theoretical frameworks that can cross more established disciplinary boundaries: at the very least, to make sense of verbal and non-verbal signs within different textual practices; perhaps even to offer some kind of unifying perspective that can cross the notorious divide between the humanities and the physical sciences.

Bridging the arts-science divide has always been of personal interest, informing my work on the relationship of culture and environment from the 1990s (e.g. Stables, 2003a, 2006). My own interests have always been eclectic. My first degree was in English literature (with a little philosophy); my graduate studies introduced me to social science research; I have taught English and drama at high school level, and philosophy, research methods and educational discourse at university level. My most enduring interests have been in the history of ideas and in music. Much of my life has been spent trying to make sense of the apparently conflicting experiences of, for example, listening to music, walking in the countryside, and thinking in words. Earlier in my academic career, I played with the boundaries of textuality, writing *inter alia* about forms of environmental literacy (Stables, 1998; Stables and Bishop, 2001), and about schools as discursive communities (Stables, 2003b/2009). It was only in about 2004 that I began to pursue these interests fully as an adventure in semiotics.

Since 2005, I have been working on a claim I made in my first explicitly semiotic publication, the book *Living and Learning as Semiotic Engagement*. The claim was in two parts: first, that all living (whatever exactly that means) is semiotic engagement, and second, that this proposition ('all living is semiotic engagement') has the potential to become 'a foundational statement for a postfoundational age' (Stables, 2005:11). The case for semiotics as the only feasible interdisciplinary discipline is not, of course, original: it is at least implicit in the work of Peirce, Sebeok and Deely, to name but three. Any claim to originality in my own work comes partly by default, as most of my engagement with these seminal figures has been in more recent years (though semiosis is always an act of forgetting as well as remembering, and of excluding as well as including: in biological terms, who we are is not determined solely by our genes but also by the epigenetic processes that enable certain genes to be activated at the expense of others). My motivation also comes from a longstanding desire to find a framework that eschews Cartesian mind-body dualism in as thoroughgoing a manner as possible, and a feeling that Peirce, Deely and Sebeok did not go as far as is feasible in this respect. By assuming a distinction between semiotic and pre-semiotic activity, and in failing to question certain aspects of the uniqueness of the human condition, it seemed to me that Peirce's followers were not escaping this dualism quite as radically as they claimed.

The exploration of a 'fully semiotic' position within my work since 2005 arises from a desire to test the feasibility of an account in which the universe may be actually constituted by rather than merely 'perfused' with signs (Peirce, 1906: 394), on the grounds that there is no sound basis on which to separate semiotic from non-semiotic, or pre-semiotic activity. I have explored the implications of this in relation to childhood (Stables, 2011, 2013), the state of being, or becoming, human (2012) and, most recently, theories of learning (Stables, Nöth, Olteanu, Pesce and Pikkarainen 2018). In the present paper, I will attempt to justify the foundations of this position before realising its implications for semiotics and, finally, educational theory. The argument develops the one presented in my 2016 paper in the *Semiotica* special edition on edusemiotics.

2 Semiosis as rich empiricism

Theoretical semiotics, on this account, is a form of philosophy grounded in a rich conception of experience, as opposed to the view of experience in the classical empiricism of Locke as the direct apprehension of the inherent qualities of external entities. Philosophy tends to appeal to abstract truths, and to networks of conceptions. Semiotics appeals to what happens: to significance and experience.

A fully semiotic position does not reject mind-matter dualism by merely privileging one side over the other: it is neither a mind-in-charge (idealist) nor a matter-in-charge ([thin] empiricist) position. Rather, it construes 'mind' and 'matter' as contingent explanations, to enable us to differentiate between a thought and a punch, for example, or between a dreamt and a waking encounter. The process of nature is simultaneously both mind and matter and neither mind nor matter: it is semiosis. Our experience is our implication in that process (so it is 'real'). Furthermore, a view of natural process as semiosis has implications for all the divisions of classical philosophy: metaphysics, ontology, epistemology, ethics and aesthetics.

In general, the modern philosophical tradition, characterised by its bifurcation into idealism and classical (or thin) empiricism, is widely recognised as 'a series of footnotes to Plato' (Whitehead, 1978: Pt. 2, S.1, Ch. 1). That is, it responds to the debates in Plato's Socratic dialogues around the true nature of fundamental concepts such as beauty and justice. While Plato favoured dialectical approaches to these challenges, his pupil Aristotle stressed the importance of the empirical. This account gives Plato the seminal role in idealist philosophy and his pupil, Aristotle, similar status with respect to empiricism.

A fully semiotic position, however, must surely start with a recognition of the given not as some ideal form, nor as the inherent qualities of external entities, but rather as that which is unquestionably given: for example, the word (in a specific language) 'beauty' or 'justice'. In experience, a sign is first and foremost a sign, not that which it denotes or connotes. Indeed, denotations are often disputed and various; connotations always are. If we want to know how best to educate our children, for example (surely a valid, indeed inevitable, aspiration), the starting point has to be what we already mean by 'education' – how the sign 'education' operates in real experience – rather than what we should mean, as though the sign merely represented some indisputable conceptual or material entity. *Contra* Plato, there can be no feasible faith that the result of this journey will be some kind of understanding of a 'real, best education', even though the aim may be to produce 'the best possible education for us' (in the near future). Whatever next steps are taken, they will be contextually grounded and contingent. What passes as a good education in one context may be quite different in another. Of course, we will bring many resources to bear on the question of how we should best educate our children, but one we cannot rely on is the assumption that there is a perfect form of education 'out there', the meaning of which we can grasp either by rigorous quantitative study or by trained philosophical means of concept clarification.

A concept can only be made clearer for us, here-and-now, to use in relation to our own goals. The clarification of concepts is, then, an empirical matter, but in a rich sense, not in the tradition of empiricist philosophy. We bring our experience as a whole, including our desires, injuries, thoughts and dreams, to the quest for clarification. Furthermore, the quest for clarification does not, perhaps counterintuitively, always result in greater clarity. Sometimes the outcome is an appreciation of vagueness. The more we look into a political rallying cry such as 'equality of opportunity', for example, the more we realise that its force comes from what Norman Fairclough has called its 'ambivalence potential' (Fairclough, 1995: 113): its capacity to 'mean all things to all men' (see also Stables, 1996). In clarifying concepts, then, we are really seeking to determine appropriate levels of clarity and vagueness or openness, for concepts, like everything else on a fully semiotic account, are open systems, for signs are not anchored in a world of discrete entities, conceptual or material, that is pre-semiotic.

A fully semiotic approach is therefore anti-Platonic, insofar as it traces mind-body dualist thinking back to Plato. Such an approach also needs to avoid two other forms of absolute dualism that lack warrant: those of substance and process, and of space and time.

The metaphysical debate between substance and process metaphysics may seem of little direct relevance to semiotics. However, I argue that it serves to muddy the water. The view of the universe as comprising substances that move and interact is grounded in Aristotle. Aristotle's account runs up against the problem of the prime or unmoved mover, which (or who, in some religious accounts) causes movement in other substances but cannot be moved by any prior substance. A process metaphysical account removes this problem by construing substances as temporary manifestations of energy flows and the forces that arise from them. This account also removes the problem of deciding the point at which something gains substance, for substances vary greatly in terms of both robustness and duration: consider water as ice, liquid and gas, for example. Ironically, while modern physicists may be quite comfortable with this account, the language they employ, even at the sub-atomic level – the language of 'particles', and even 'strings' – is strongly grounded in the language of substance metaphysics. This may be the cause of certain problems in quantum mechanics that it is not pertinent to explore here.

Another potential weakness of substance metaphysics is its assumption of quantity. When Kant wrote of the world beyond our senses, he employed the plural term *noumena*, implying not only that there is a world beyond experience, but that this world comprises discrete entities (Kant, 1998). A fully semiotic position is not anti-realist; it does not deny a noumenal world as the flow of energy and the interaction of forces. However, any assumption that Kant has about discrete entities in that world are unwarranted, and do not hold up on a process account. We have no way of ascertaining whether the items we perceive exist independently of us or whether they are rather manifestations of our own modelling of the effects of physical forces. Certainly, from the human perspective, natural forces cohere into entities of different types and durations, as perceived and experienced, but all these are constantly in flux. Even if we grant that, say, solidity will be experienced as much by an elephant as by a human, it cannot be validly inferred from this that the elephant models the world as the human does.

This has implications for a worldview that sees mathematics as fundamental (as did Plato's). It raises the danger of mathematisation: that is, of the inappropriate or excessive use of mathematics. An example of this will be given at the end of this paper with respect to educational policy. The contents of the universe cannot simply be counted, even though the interactions of forces might be understandable in terms of mathematically expressed relationships. As with 'mind' and 'body', we use arithmetic terms for pragmatic uses (and not always consistently, as in one pair of trousers, or claiming that 2+2=5 for higher values of 2). Arithmetic is a tool; we have no evidence that the universe is fundamentally arithmetical or even mathematical in a broader sense. If semiotics is fundamental then mathematics cannot be: it must rather be a sign system among other sign systems.

In semiotics, a view of the sign as substance is also common and can, perhaps, be equally as misleading. The fully semiotic account proposed here has signs (including sign-as-particle and sign-as-string) as features of events. Events are the experienced manifestations of processes. Processes (for example, ageing) are manifested in events (for example, birthday parties). Our experience, on this anti-dualist account, is our implication in events, not our human gloss on events. As modern physics has suggested (Rickles 2018), events are observer-dependent, though we do not only 'observe', for we are not merely observers so much as participants. Events and experience are determined by the encounters of prior events and experiences with new contexts. They are not merely the products of 'mind' or 'matter' on the dualist account.

Events, and therefore experiences, are also simultaneously and always here-and-now. Another unwarranted assumption underpinning modern philosophy (though not modern natural philosophy, in the form of theoretical physics, since Einstein) is that space and time are entirely separate schemas, as Newton supposed and Kant argued. It is now accepted that space cannot move without time and *vice-versa* (Taylor and Wheeler 1992). Time, in the form of clock time (the Greek *chronos*, as opposed to *kairos*: the time of significance) can certainly be a useful form of measurement but processes do not happen merely in time but in space-time. We find the legacy of the Greek dual conception of time in the contrast of, for example, 'It is three o'clock' and 'It is time I went'. 'Time I went' is not determined by the mere 'now' of clock time alone but by the progress of events in the here-and-now.

The here-and-now both enables and constrains our experience. Space-time frames significance, hence the paradox of the present, which can never be pinned down, although we always live in it; we are in it, yet its meaning is always and already deferred. This acknowledgement may have been little explored in theoretical semiotics to date; yet it has significant philosophical implications, not least in placing a higher value on the collectivity of subjective experience than on the objective truths derived from telescope, microscope or statistical calculation.

3 Modifying conceptions of the sign and semiosis

3.1 Limits of existing models

Given the above, it is not surprising that I find neither Peircean nor Saussurean formulations of the sign and semiosis entirely satisfactory. Indeed, it would be counter to any conception of semiosis that any previous explanation could ever be entirely convincing, because the context of reception has changed.

Saussurean semiology gives us a view of the sign as 'signifier' and 'signified' (according to the 1959 translation into English of Saussure's *Cours*). This division is empirically verifiable insofar as I can be aware directly of both a dog and what the term 'dog', whether read or heard, makes me imagine. However, the arbitrary relations of signifier to signified and of both to external referent render this view one in which human culture apparently floats free from any biophysical reality beyond itself. (Poststructuralists would ditch the dyadism and think in terms of the Derridean free play of signifiers). On my proposed fully semiotic account, the world of natural forces results in likely similarities or overlaps between aspects of modelling both within and between species (for example); for instance, an asteroid impact on the Earth is likely to impact not only on humans; plus, other entities will recognise that something is going on irrespective of whether they account for it as asteroid impact. Structuralism cannot easily embrace such apparently pre-semiotic phenomena, even though they clearly contribute to more conscious behaviour. The relationships of the signifier 'asteroid impact' the signified and the external referent are not arbitrary even though we cannot assume them to be either fixed or given prior to experience.

Peirce gives us a triadic formulation that connects human culture to everything else but only through the assumptions of Firstness and Secondness that are not empirically verifiable, as everything is known at the level of Thirdness. As Colin Koopman has argued, Firstness implies philosophical givenness just as much as naïve empiricism (Koopman, 2009). Saussure explains our conscious experience, but not how it must relate to that which is other; Peirce explains everything but only formulaically through a model that defies empirical testing in a rich as well as a thin sense.

3.2 Alternative account

As response, I suggest that
1. We take a process metaphysical view: we prioritise Process over Substance;
2. We regard significance (meaning) as meaning-in-use, not as imperfect understanding of some ideal form;
3. We make no assumption of individual entities at noumenal level, and we do not regard experience as dependent on the inherent qualities of entities; and
4. We reject entirely mind-body substance dualism

Taken together, these moves imply that there are no grounds for separating semiotic from pre-semiotic or human meaning making (and language) from natural processes.

On this basis, I offer an alternative conception of the sign as a feature of an event. The steps of this argument are as follows:
- Universe is process
- Process comprises processes
- Processes comprise events
- Signs are features of events (prompts, but not substitutions; signs do not require objects; and a sign can be seen as both confluence, drawing from previous signs, or 'traces', and influence)
- The sign is not ultimately quantifiable; we need not conceive of it as consistently either monadic, dyadic or triadic (so we can avoid mathematisation; Peirce was a mathematician and generated a mathematically regular semiotics; however, if semiosis is fundamental, then mathematics is a sign system among others, not the foundation of sign systems, and semiotics does not need mathematical regularity).

Let us just consider for a moment how different the above formulation is from Peirce's:

> I define a sign as anything which is so determined by something else, called its Object, and so determines an effect upon a person, which effect I call its interpretant, that the latter is thereby mediately determined by the former.' (Peirce 1908: 478)

Note the traps from which Peirce cannot escape: the singularity of the Object, and the implied humanism of 'upon a person' (though he himself was unhappy with this, as he wrote to Lady Welby).

3.3 Language and humanism

One of the potential obstacles to developing a version of semiosis that does away entirely with mind-body dualisms is the issue of language. Is not language something that only human beings possess and thus is not full semiosis only possible for humans? (Of course, if we allow this, we have to face some pretty intractable questions about the point at which this specifically human, linguistic consciousness arose.)

One way out of this is simply to see the basic structure of language as analogous to the basic structure of all processes: that is, to acknowledge that everything that happens is the result of expectation, or repetition, or habit, encountering the unexpected, the different and the challenging: of Subject (the recognised) operating in a new context (the Predicate). At the most basic level, we do not live in a frictionless universe, and friction means that what happened last time will not be possible in exactly the same way next time. No pendulum will swing evenly forever, for example. Without friction, without the unexpected, there would be no change, no evolution, and no us. Our moods are lifted or dampened, our expectations are modified, and the rock is gradually eroded by wind, sun and microbes. Everywhere conditioned response is challenged by new circumstances, in the face of which identifiable entities either adapt or perish. Whether or not entities are conscious of that (whatever consciousness is) is not the issue of primary importance. This model certainly applies to more than human response, though it does explain that. In the animal world, for example, the cat sees the familiar mouse (Subject) running apparently towards that bush over there (Predicate) so decides to pounce.

On this account, without the basic mechanism that underpins grammar at the deepest level, nothing is. Semiotic processes have the structure of propositions. Wittgenstein's claim at the beginning of the *Tractatus* that 'The world is all that is the case' (Wittgenstein, 1974: 5) has strong resonances with what is being argued here, except perhaps that Wittgenstein was arguably considering things in relation to facts rather than propositions. (Wittgenstein's work remains open to a variety of interpretations.) On this account, the sign says something to something (or someone) about something known (S) doing something unknown (P). This position is analogous to that of Stjernfelt (2011).

Although the main focus of this paper is the implications of this view for theories of learning, it should be noted at this point that to claim that the S-P structure is inherent in all processes is effectively to remove one of the major arguments for humanism: that what separates humans from other animals is not utterance, communication, nor even modelling, but grammar and syntax. On this account, specific forms of grammar and syntax, such as ordering of subject and predicate or noun and verb, may be particular to human language (though there is variation between languages), but at the level of deep structure there is no need to account for anything 'deep-wired' into the human brain. This gives credence to claims such as that of Lyn Miles that great apes, such as Chantek the orangutan, have language (Miles, 2014). Indeed, the argument could be extended to the claim that the 'personhood' Miles argues should be attributed to Chantek is an empty one as 'personhood' is an expression of discredited humanism. In effect, Miles undermines her own claim in any case by arguing that parrots can understand as well as mimic, but not claiming personhood for these. If the S-P structures we recognise are simply elaborations of all semiosic activity, then we are not justified in even starting our arguments about the status of animals by considering whether they reach some kind of threshold in terms of language use in the most general sense, for there is nothing qualitatively distinct about human language. (Of course, gorillas are less good at English than readers of this paper.)

While the remainder of this paper focuses on the implications of a fully semiotic view of learning for relations in the human world, therefore, it should be borne in mind that there is no assumption that the model is only applicable to the human.

4 Semiosis/change/learning

We shall now begin to apply this model and move towards a fully semiotic theory of learning.

At the most basic level, Outcome (O) is the result of Habit, or Conditioning (Cd) encountering new context (Cn), such that O = (Cd + Cn).

However, as signs do not come singly, we can understand Progress (P) or Change (C) in an individual or society as the result of semiotic responses continually modified by signs appearing in new combinations, such that $P/C = (Cd + Cn)^n$.

Let us add a level of specificity to this, as we need to consider the conditions under which habitual responses are altered.

First we can claim that Outcome is the result of habit encountering new context, where Outcome relies on the sum of, or a selection from, previous evocations (Cd) in terms of what works in the present context, such that O = (Cd [selection] + Cn).

But how do we make that selection? Recognition/ familiarity must play a role here, so we can say that Outcome is the result of habit encountering new context where Outcome relies on the strongest resonance of the new item to known items

(Cd) and then selection or modification of one or more of those resonances to make possible best sense of new context (Cn), such that O = (Cd[analog] + Cn).

While not really a Peircean model, this account follows Peircean scholars who have recently taken a strong iconic turn (Stjernfelt, 2007; Olteanu, 2014) insofar as we select from our repertoire of habituated responses those that most resonate with the demands of the new context. We are guided by similarities. Note that (on Peirce's account), a symbol (perhaps, a flag) or an indexical sign could fulfil this 'iconic' role. For example, if one had previously been unpleasantly treated by Right Wing nationalists, one might seek to avoid a nearby street demonstration at which a lot of national flags were being carried. The (symbolic) flag here would not have a vastly different effect from the placing of a purely physical barrier between oneself and the demonstrators: evocations cannot be so easily separated into sign types.

Let us illustrate the above with the simple example of encountering a dog one has not met before. It seems self-evident that our initial response to a new canine acquaintance (O) will depend on our prior experience of dogs (Cd) and the aspects of that prior experience that most seem to be reflected in the new doggy companion. Thus if all our experiences with dogs have been safe and friendly, we may be inclined to pat the new animal; if all our experiences have been fearful, we will be fearful again; yet if we have had experiences of both joy and being bitten, we will scan the new dog for the features or 'traces' (to use Derrida's term) that indicate friendliness or aggression.

Moving onto an explicit concern with learning, therefore, we can speculate on the kinds of encounters that will modify habit.

A particular habit is therefore reinforced (+) or problematised (?) with each new encounter, such that outcome (O) is the result of the reinforcement or readjustment of a habitual response (HR+/HR?). A positive encounter (cn+), largely predictable even if not necessarily desirable, strengthens habitual response (HR+) while a problematic (though not necessarily negative) encounter (cn?) diminishes it (HR-). Thus (N.B. iff = 'if and only if')

$$O = (HR+) \text{ iff } (cd + [cn+])$$

while

$$O = (HR?) \text{ iff } (cd + [cn?])$$

This raises a challenge for educators. While psychological research shows that motivation is produced by success, change arises only from challenge. On this model, teaching is more or less controlled identity disruption rather than identity reinforcement. Students will not necessarily learn more because they feel happy and confident in what they are doing. (Note that from a Buddhist perspective, learning might be understood as a form of disillusionment: realising that what was taken as concrete is in fact ephemeral.) However, balance is crucial here. Organisms either adapt to new contexts or die. Students either respond positively to new challenges or, if too strongly challenged, retreat from them. Certainly, if teaching is too predictable, the danger is that an illusion of success is maintained that cannot be transferred from the classroom or school context or, indeed, adapted to any new situations. On the other hand, students must feel that challenges are within their potential grasp, or they will become alienated and disheartened. Teachers, of course, are not 100% in control of the student's context of reception, but they – like parents and any other authority figures – exert considerable responsibility over the situations their charges find themselves in. Teachers do not determine students' prior habits but they have great power over the contexts in which they must work.

An important feature of this model is that it does not differentiate between kinds of change, or between change in the human or non-human realm, or even between change in living and non-living entities. Indeed, if adopted, it effectively problematises these distinctions.

For many semioticians, change is a necessary but not sufficient condition of learning or indeed semiosis. From these perspectives, the 'fully semiotic' approach developed here may not be acceptable as 'semiotic' at all. Nevertheless, it seems inescapable that there is no space in this model for a discretely identifiable process of learning. This does not mean that 'learning' is meaningless, but it is meaningless to say, as the school inspector might, 'there is good learning going on in this classroom'. What is going on is semiosis and change, and just as there is no good reason to understand semiosis in terms of Firstness, Secondness and Thirdness, so there is no good reason to make an absolute qualitative distinction between semiosis and change. This is not to dispute that human beings are extremely complex and are dealing with large numbers of sign reactions more or less simultaneously, whereas certain natural responses are much simpler, but it would not be a valid inference from this model that more complex patterns of recognition and response equate to specifically human attributes such as mind, consciousness or reason.

In effect, change might or might not be construed as learning, which seems to be a judgment we make about certain kinds of change. 'I learnt something today', I might say, just as I might say, 'I have made up my mind'. Like decisions, learning is a retrospective gloss on an outcome. What teachers do with students is to engage in practices. They cannot predict exactly what students will learn from that engagement. We speak of learning from events of social or personal significance: 'I learnt Maths at school', but also 'I learnt a lot from that failed relationship' – but we do not speak of all change as learning, for 'learning' is a social judgment we apply to certain kinds of change.

In short:
- All living is semiosic
- All living produces change
- so there is no conceptual space for 'learning' as a form of life
- Rather – learning is retrospective judgment on significant events.

5 Education

5.1 Implications for teaching and learning

'Education' is, like 'learning' or 'semiosis', a contested term. However, in general use the term is often used to refer to the institutions and practices associated with the development of skills and understanding, often but not exclusively of the young, and generally outside the narrowly domestic sphere where childrearing is also, in part, concerned with the growth of these attributes. A very thin conception of learning in the abstract has been developed, but in educational contexts the teacher-learner relationship offers an alternative perspective. Even if students do not actually learn as a practice, or activity, all educational actors are judged with reference to what students are deemed to have learnt (as retrospective judgment). Thus, how learning is construed in educational theory is of importance even where 'learning' is an empty category when viewed as a form of practice.

My argument is that the philosophical choices we make about the sign and semiosis are highly significant to our understanding of the teaching-learning dynamic and the practical effects of that understanding, including the training of teachers.

For example, a substance metaphysical account will tend to a view of teacher, student and subject matter as essentially closed systems that interact. These systems are subject to change through relation on this substance account, rather than being temporary states in the context of change and relation on the process account. On the substance account, the sign relates to either a material entity, a conceptual entity, or a conceptual entity implying certain material entities; it has reality in and of itself, even though it may depend on other entities, and it can therefore be understood or misunderstood. Meanwhile the subject matter (that-which-is-to-be-learnt) has considerable stability and enduring value, and can be learnt and taught about more or less in isolation, while student and teacher are substantive entities who can be understood primarily as persons in their own right, and who can both be understood or misunderstood, and can understand or misunderstand that-which-is-to-be-learnt.

The above account tends to a view of the learning process as strongly bifurcated: the student either understands or does not understand. We can contrast this with a view grounded in the process account I have proposed, according to which all systems are open. On this account, the sign only makes sense in relation to its spatiotemporal context, has no firm reality in itself other than as experienced, and can therefore never be either fully understood or fully misunderstood. That-which-is-to-be-learnt now gains salience from its context, is always open to interpretation, and can never be taught or learnt in isolation. Finally, both teacher and student are regarded as in transition, themselves relational, and each incapable of ever having either a complete understanding or no understanding at all of that-which-is-to-be-learnt.

Under both idealism and classical empiricism, a unit of knowledge is a discrete entity, either conceptual or material. Similarly, the learner is a person at a particular stage of their development who is therefore 'ready' or not to take on board a particular concept. Furthermore, because knowledge is fairly fixed, it is possible to 'atomise' and 'step' the curriculum: that is, split the content into small elements that can be introduced along a continuum from simplicity to complexity. In some ways, this makes teaching a relatively straightforward process, while teacher training can concentrate largely on two areas of understanding: the construction of the subject matter, and the readiness of the student to receive it, grounded in theories from developmental psychology (often Piaget). In short, on the substance metaphysical view, that-which-is-to-be-learnt can be regarded as a discrete entity, the nature of which can be imparted by the teacher, who understands this entity, to the student, who does not yet understand it and will end up either understanding or misunderstanding it; there is no middle way.

On the second, process account that has teacher, student and that-which-is-to-be-learnt as shifting sets of relations, the teacher, who usually has more experience related to the topic, guides the student, who is usually less experienced, to explore that-which-is-to-be-learnt, thus increasing understanding, and, in a very small way, modifying that-which-is-to-be-learnt.

This process account does away with two assumptions that bedevil education, alienating students: the assumptions that there is a complete understanding of anything (and conversely that anyone can have no understanding whatsoever, for that also is impossible), and the assumption that one's response can be entirely meaningless or wrong. These can be summarised as the Complete and Correct Understanding Fallacy (or CCUF) and the Meaningless Sign Fallacy MSF). The child who claims that water is white, for example (Olteanu, Kambouri and

Stables), is making a logical inference from previous experience. The teacher should regard this as a starting point for further exploration rather than merely dismissing it as 'wrong'.

5.2 The aims of education

As this model has developed over the past few years, several colleagues have expressed their fear that it does not offer a sufficiently normative context for teaching.

It is indeed the case that the model I propose undermines any conviction that teachers, or policy makers, can determine exactly what students will learn, any more than parents can determine how their children will turn out. Thus the 'learning outcomes' model of curriculum planning is invalid, a symptom of the narrow performativity that Lyotard (1986) warned would become the standard approach of the postmodern institution in a world in which discussion of higher aims or purposes has become impossible. It follows, also, that however much policy makers try to prescribe the curriculum, what actually happens in the interactions between students and teachers cannot be so clearly determined. There is an inevitable unpredictability about the process that might be seen as a valuing of professional judgment rather than anarchy.

On the other hand, no teaching-and-learning encounter happens in a vacuum, either synchronically (that is, irrespective of environment) nor diachronically (that is, irrespective of tradition). The choices that policy makers, teachers and students make are all guided by often implicit beliefs about what constitutes human progress. When we, as teachers, engage with practices with our students, we are always doing so with some end in sight, some conception of what progress means for us.

In broad terms, it might be argued that history offers us the following models of human progress:
- material and bodily development, measured by progress in life expectancy, physical health and material possessions, and developed through practices including sport, medicine, and various forms of lifestyle enhancement through acquisition;
- rational and logical development, measured in terms of progress in science, and applied as technology (often in the service of 1. above);
- moral and ethical development, understood in terms of growth in human virtues and social justice, and applied in personal choice and social action;
- aesthetic development, understood in terms of the depth and breadth of human response, sensitivity and engagement, and practised through

involvement with the arts and with other creative enterprises that allow for self-expression; and
- ecological development, understood in terms of human custody of the Earth and its resources – and arguably, in future, of resources beyond Earth – and practised through human engagement with the natural world and through lifestyle choices with respect to pollution, energy use and biodiversity.

It is possible to regard the account of learning I have offered as closer to behavioural and (thin) empirical accounts than to those that are psychologically cognitivist and philosophically idealist, as everything hinges on human experience. However, I am arguing for rich empiricism. On this account, experience is construed in the broadest possible manner: it includes and does not exclude thought, empathy or evaluation. For example, when we are habitually guiding our students in a certain direction through the activities we are engaging in with them, we are also habitually balancing certain longer-term objectives and ingrained assumptions. Our experience, in the broadest sense, is not free of our deepest wrestlings with meaning and conscience but incorporates them. The resources at our disposal include the deepest questions we can formulate about where we are trying to go and how we want the world to change. We are all trying to adapt, survive and flourish and are constantly addressing the question of how. Our teaching, therefore, is guided by strong normative assumptions that are deeply culturally ingrained irrespective of how prescriptive the curriculum is at a detailed level.

Are we exercising free will in doing this? Well, if a God's-eye view were possible, this account tells us we are not: we are habituated and responsive in relation to that habituation. However, we feel free, and we cannot ever have this view from nowhere. We are certainly responsible. It seems to me, therefore, that to enact social policy on any other basis than this feeling of freedom and responsibility would be quite wrong. The irony is that this arguably fatalistic account is greatly more empowering than models of semiosis and learning which are trapped within essentialist assumptions.

5.3 Recommendations for educators

The final section addresses, in broad terms, the practical implications of the position developed here for those with educational responsibilities.

The model posits teaching-and-learning as joint exploration rather than the delivery of pre-set truths. This may seem easier said than done, as the dynamics of the school classroom or university lecture hall often do not allow for much free-ranging discussion or active learning. There is no proposal here to rid the world of formal lectures or teacher explanation, however. These activities are part of the great 'conversation of mankind', to use Oakeshott's term (Bakhurst and Fairfield 2016). However formal the setting, though, it should be borne in mind that this is ultimately a communicative process, and that it is interpretive all the way down. That is, the teacher's interpretation of the subject matter will be interpreted by the student. In the context of primary and secondary schooling, it is the teacher's responsibility to acknowledge the interpretations of the students and to guide them to challenge those interpretations in the light of received wisdom (as interpreted by the teacher). In the more formal aspects of higher education, lecturers may not feel that they have direct responsibility for students' interpretations, but the dynamics are the same nonetheless, and the wise teacher will present the material in such a way as to make the most of her students' worldviews. Thus, in both contexts, teachers should be as learner-aware as possible, but not in the rather abstruse sense of regarding the student as a learner at a given developmental stage, as in Piagetian or other psychological stage models.

It is also important to remember that all teaching, whether it appears directly informative or not, is concerned with the development of practices. The formal history lecture is part of the process of developing students as historians. Teachers of all sorts can work with an awareness of this, and use student activities (whether formal essays, presentations or other sorts of project) to gauge how their input is being interpreted by students as they engage in the practice in question on their own terms. This element of 'publication' (Harré, 1983; Stables, Jones and Morgan, 1999) is a very important aspect of the process of appropriating the subject matter, through testing one's appropriations against some form of peer or external judgment. Thus, feedback on students' interpretations, from informal conversation to formal essays, is very important in negotiating and developing practice.

As far as possible, students' opportunities here should not place them in the situation of feeling crushed or rejected. Of course, one is always free to criticise a student for perceived laziness or failure to engage with the material, but to dismiss a conscientious student's interpretations as merely incorrect can prove very inhibiting. Rather, the good teacher will try to see 'where the student is coming from' and use that as a prompt to further guidance. This is difficult for many teachers; it requires thought and sensitivity beyond the baseline requirements in many higher education contexts, if not in schools.

In relation to this, note that certain activities are more amenable than others in terms of the possibility of valuing student interpretation. The mathematics teacher who focuses on merely getting the right answer will struggle to understand the student who does not arrive there, but the teacher who focuses on students explaining their reasoning will be able much better to appreciate the student's approach and will therefore be much better fitted to helping them. Where feasible, teachers can consider activities that allow maximum scope for student interpretation with little attendant danger that the student will be inhibited by the fear of 'getting it wrong': activities such as role plays, historical re-enactment, and simulations, for example. Such activities offer extensive opportunities for teacher support and information, while ensuring quite complex forms of student engagement.

5.4 Educational policy implications

If semiotics is foundational, no other discipline is. I alluded briefly earlier to the dangers of mathematisation: the misguided assumption that the qualitative can be understood quantitatively. Mathematisation, thus styled, is a near relative, or version, of scientisation. Teachers, and particularly teachers of the humanities, are often aware that both their masters and their students expect both that educational progress can be validly quantified and that all curriculum subjects can follow 'scientific' rules on this naïve understanding. So, for example, when we introduce Shakespeare, or poetry in general, to students in our high schools, they are overly concerned with what each line 'means' and assume that there is always one, incontrovertible, meaning to be understood. Teachers may sometimes fall into the trap of acceding to this wish, thus giving the impression of Shakespeare as a one-dimensional, perhaps deliberately difficult author.

Of course, teachers are very aware that what makes Shakespeare a great writer is the range of responses some of his lines can evoke. For example, when Falstaff, in Act 5, Scene 3 of *Henry IV Part 1*, declares that 'the better part of valour is discretion' (often cited as 'discretion is the better part of valour'), we are aware that there are at least three voices here: that of Falstaff, that of Shakespeare (in whose authorial voice lurk those of his other characters, including Prince Hal), and that of the reader. Furthermore, the character of Falstaff is ambivalent insofar as he is both a coward and, to some extent, an astute and sympathetic observer of human affairs, some of whose remarks (such as against the quest for 'honour' and the 'bubble reputation') resonate strongly with Millennial sentiments. Thus, it is a denigration of Shakespeare's work to argue that this line 'means' one thing: it means both that Falstaff is a coward and that Falstaff may be wise; it is both ironic and literal (as Falstaff is effectively running away); it arouses both sympathy and disgust in the reader – and perhaps more.

In short, scientisation bedevils education, and sometimes it takes a specifically mathematical form, as in the construction of league tables of various sorts. This is not to argue that there is no value in comparing quantitative outcomes: the problem arises when it is assumed that such outcomes are also valid qualitative judgments.

A specific example of mathematisation in educational policy arises from the way foreign interventions are assumed to be of value in local contexts. Say, for example, that School A (in its own distinct context) adopts a new teaching method X. There is a measurable improvement from state A to state AX. School B (in its own distinct context) is assumed to be underperforming, so it is recommended that it adopt intervention X. The naivety here is in assuming that the improvement from B to BX will mirror that of A to AX. However, as contexts A and B remain different, in effect this is unlikely to happen:

$$A \rightarrow AX \neq B \rightarrow BX$$

It is, of course, awkward for policy makers, and even teachers, to take this realisation on board in the current performative policy context. However, a more qualitative, semiotically sensitive approach need not be at odds with the desire to show value for money in public services. Instead of beginning with the assumption that the qualitative can be quantified, it would be possible to reverse the polarity, for instance by asking social actors how well spent they feel a certain amount of public money in a certain area has been. The assumption here is not that people are predictable machines, but that they are necessarily varied semiotic engagers in a much broader sense.

References

Bakhurst, David & Paul Fairfield (eds.). 2016. *Education and Conversation: Exploring Oakeshott's Legacy*. London: Bloomsbury.
Fairclough, Norman. 1995. *Critical Discourse Analysis*. London: Longman.
Harré, Ron. 1983. *Personal Being: a theory for individual psychology*. Oxford: Blackwell.
Kant, Immanuel. 1998. (ed. Guyer, P. and A. Wood) *Critique of Pure Reason*. Cambridge: Cambridge University Press.
Koopman,Coopman. 2009. *Pragmatism as Transition: historicity and hope in James, Dewey and Rorty*. New York: Columbia University Press.
Lyotard, Jean-François. 1986. *The Postmodern Condition: a report on knowledge*. Manchester: Manchester University Press.
Miles, Lyn. (2014) *Chantek: the first orangutan person*. TEDx talk, Retrieved from https://www.youtube.com/watch?v=q2pisrdO2TQ 20 August, 2017.

Olteanu, Alin. 2014. The Semiosic Evolution of Education. *Journal of Philosophy of Education* 48/3, 457–473.
Olteanu, Alin, Maria Kambouri & Andrew Stables. 2016. Predicating from an early age: Edusemiotics and the potential of children's preconceptions. *Studies in Philosophy and Education* 35, 621–640.
Peirce, C. S. (1908). Letter to Lady Welby (23 December 1908). Reprinted, 1998. In Charles S. Peirce, *The Essential Peirce* (Volume 2), 478–481. Bloomington IN: Indiana University Press.
Peirce, Charles S. 1906. The Basis of Pragmaticism in the Normative Sciences. Reprinted, 1998. In C. S. Peirce, *The Essential Peirce* (Volume 2), 371–397. Bloomington IN: Indiana University Press.
Rickles Dean. 2018. World Without World: Observer-Dependent Physics. In Anthony Aguirre, Brendan Foster & Zeeya Merali (eds.) *Wandering Towards a Goal. The Frontiers Collection*, 101–108. Dordrecht: Springer.
Stables, Andrew, Winfried Nöth, Alin Olteanu, Sébastien Pesce & Eetu Pikkarainen. 2018. *Semiotic Learning Theory: new perspectives in philosophy of education*. London: Routledge.
Stables, Andrew. 1996. Paradox in Educational Policy Slogans: evaluating equal opportunities in subject choice, *British Journal of Educational Studies* 44/2, 159–167.
Stables, Andrew. 1998. Environmental Literacy: functional, cultural, critical. The case of the SCAA guidelines, *Environmental Education Research* 4/2, 155–164.
Stables, Andrew. 2003a. Environmental Education and the Arts-Science Divide: the case for a disciplined environmental literacy. In Adrian Winnett, A. & Alyson Warhurst (eds.), *Towards an Environmental Research Agenda: a second selection of papers*, 49–59. Basingstoke/New York: Palgrave.
Stables, Andrew. 2003b. School as Imagined Community in Discursive Space: a perspective on the school effectiveness debate, *British Educational Research Journal* 29/6, 895–902.
Stables, Andrew. 2005. *Living and Learning as Semiotic Engagement: A New Theory of Education*. Lewiston, NY/ Lampeter: Mellen Press.
Stables, Andrew. 2006. On Teaching and Learning the Book of the World. In Sylvia Mayer & Graham Wilson (eds.), *Ecodidactic Perspectives in English Language, Literatures and Cultures*, 145–162. Trier: WVT.
Stables, Andrew. 2009 (first published 2003). School as Imagined Community in Discursive Space: a perspective on the school effectiveness debate, reprinted in Harry Daniels, Hugh Lauder & Jill Porter (eds.), *Knowledge, Values and Educational Policy: a critical perspective*, 253–261. London: Routledge.
Stables, Andrew. 2011. *Childhood and the Philosophy of Education: an anti-Aristotelian perspective*. London: Continuum.
Stables, Andrew. 2012. *Be(com)ing Human: Semiosis and the Myth of Reason*. Rotterdam: Sense.
Stables, Andrew. 2013. Conceptions of Childhood and the Educational Rights of the Child. *Philosophy Study* 3(9): 857–866.
Stables, Andrew. 2016. Education as Process Semiotics: towards a new model of semiosis for teaching and learning. *Semiotica* 212, 45–58.
Stables, Andrew & Keith Bishop. 2001. Weak and Strong Conceptions of Environmental Literacy: implications for environmental education, *Environmental Education Research* 7(1),89–97.

Stables, A., Sonia Jones & Carol Morgan. 1999. Educating for Significant Events: the application of Harré's social reality matrix across the lower secondary school curriculum, *Journal of Curriculum Studies* 31/4, 449–461.
Stjernfelt, Frederik. 2011. Signs Conveying Information. On the Range of Peirce's Notion of Propositions: Dicisigns, *International Journal of Signs and Semiotic Systems*, 1(2): 40–52.
Stjernfelt, Frederik. 2007. *Diagrammatology: An Investigation on the Borderlines of Phenomenology, Ontology and Semiotics*. Dordrecht: Springer.
Taylor, Edwin & John Archibald Wheeler. 1992. *Spacetime Physics: Introduction to Special Relativity*. New York: W H Freeman.
Whitehead, Alfred North. 1978. *Process and Reality*. New York: Free Press.
Wittgenstein, Ludwig. 1974 [1922]. *Tractatus Logico-Philosophicus*. Trans. D.F. Pears & B.F. McGuinness. London: Routledge.

Kristian Bankov
Scarcity and meaning: Towards a semiotics of economic transaction

Abstract: The semiotics of economic transaction is here presented as a new approach to the mechanisms of the transaction of economic value. After analyzing the nature of the main semiotic device for value transactions – the money sign – we identify, at its core, the trust in the future of the economic system of exchange and the scarcity of its availability as a condition for its value and meaning. Such characteristics lead us to search for theoretical support in the existential analytics of temporality devised by Heidegger, where we find a homology between economic scarcity and the thesis of the primordial finitude of temporality, which is a scarcity of time. Thus, we distinguish between two levels of semiotic analysis of transactions: a deep/authentic level of the primordial formation of value and a superficial level of commercial practices of market exchange. From this point of view, the new digital economy seems to bring closer the two levels, transforming the availability of time for each person into the major economical resource. The study ends with some critical remarks from a semiotic perspective on neoliberal financial excesses.

Keywords: economic value, time, temporality, experience economy, money

1 Introduction

There is an apocryphal saying which goes like this:

> If you have an apple and I have an apple and we exchange these apples then you and I will still each have one apple. But if you have an idea and I have an idea and we exchange these ideas, then each of us will have two ideas.

Most of the existing semiotic paradigms fit well with this aphorism. They fit in the sense that most of them examine the production of meaning, the processes of understanding, the exchange of messages, the forms of expression of ideas, etc. No semiotician would consider the apple part of the aphorism as related to semiotic theory (if not considered as a gift exchange) and that would be quite correct. The semiotic approach which considers something different from exchange

---

Kristian Bankov, New Bulgarian University

https://doi.org/10.1515/9783110857801-007

of (meaningful) ideas is pragmatics. In pragmatics, words are not used to exchange ideas, but to do things. If two lovers exchange the idea "I love you", "I love you, too", that will not be a waste of time as it would partake of the logic of the aphorism. They are exchanging the same idea, but actually the thing that matters is the establishment (or reconfirmation) of the reciprocity of their relation. The transaction semiotics that I would like to outline here is different from pragmatics, although the premises are similar. If "How to do things with words" is the slogan of pragmatics, "How to get things with signs" should be the slogan of transaction semiotics.

But why should getting things with signs be an important issue? Apparently, buying something from the shop with money is not a major semiotic challenge. But here I claim that the challenge for semiotics comes from the fact that *in the last two decades we have become immersed in an economic reality where buying material products with material money signs becomes less and less frequent.* One smaller semiotic challenge is to try to model the new forms of electronic money and their relation to economic value – the entity they stand for in some respect within the transactions. A bigger challenge is to understand, semiotically, the so-called "dematerialization of the economy". Under that label there is a great deal of semiotic scholarship focusing on the symbolic value of consumption which determines market and social relations beyond the utilitarian logic of economic models. Here is situated the gift economy as well, which, as we shall see, is the twin-antipode of our proposal. But transaction semiotics necessarily probes deeper into the new economy. Rather than goods in the new economy, people are buying access to services and experiences. Much commerce is taking place because of the internet and the role of wired and wireless communicative interaction is fundamental. The existence of this economic reality is supported by a new type of value transaction, which challenges not only the logic of the old style monetary transactions but also the notion of reception and consumption of economic value itself. The rise of the shared economy, for instance, is reducing the dependence of business on the centralized banking system and state control; but the price to pay is a much bigger communicative involvement of the participants. The overall benefit is that the existing material infrastructure is used much more efficiently. Also, how might it be possible to account for the amazing services that we have for free, such as social media platforms and search engines? They seem to be free but actually "search results are becoming increasingly personalized and so-called 'free' services are being paid for with information on our browsing behavior" (Olsthoorn 2011: on the cover). Companies in the new digital economic environment are "extracting" value from our online activities (data mining) as the oil companies are extracting oil from the earth. "Data is the new oil", according to one of the maxims of the new economy and in the same way as once there were petrol derivatives in every single production industry, today practically there is no business without internet value transactions involved.

The ambition of this paper is to uncover the semiotic mechanisms behind the transaction of economic value – an aspect of our social life which has not been investigated deeply in the age of conventional "property exchange" economy, but which is far more semiotically challenging today in the age of the internet and the access economy. The purpose is not so much to discover the hidden principles of the new economy, unknown to business professionals and consultants, *but to open a semiotic perspective on an interesting and important social reality from within our discipline and encourage semiotic and semiotically oriented interdisciplinary research about economic value*. That is why the conceptual apparatus of my proposal comes from semiotics, in particular the way in which Umberto Eco synthesized structuralism with pragmatism, but also from ideas of the structural hermeneutics of Ricoeur and from Derrida and Heidegger, as well as from some classical socio-economic insights to be found in the work of Mauss and Rifkin. As a method, transaction semiotics draws objectivity from a different source, compared to cognitive (phenomenological) semiotics which is obsessed with perception and generative semiotics, obsessed with the deep structures of language. Transaction semiotics may rely on the socially-constituted objectivity of the market, where needs, desires, products, services, dreams and experiences meet in the unified system of the economic transaction. It draws objectivity, as well, from the formal characteristics of the money sign, which is in continuous evolution and reflects the characteristics of the entirety of socio-economic reality.

2 Economic value, money and temporality

An inspiring study of the monetary history of the major regions of the world shows that money and finance are crucial for "the ability of humans to imagine and calculate the future" (Goetzmann 2016: 2). Such a statement announces an important bridge between philosophy and economics, encouraging the semiotically-minded reader to explore the consequences from the side of semiotics that are left unexplored by the Goetzmann. Another statement in the same book is even more suggestive, although it refers to something already well accepted: that financial arrangements are the basis of one of the most remarkable of humanity's inventions, namely writing (21–22). Semiotics of transaction makes a particular contribution to literary studies, where this historical fact is insufficiently acknowledged.

With writing and temporality viewed in such a way, the proposed theory appears to entirely belong to Western metaphysics; but this is not bad news as far as our purpose is to set up a research field, particularly given the overwhelming insistence on criticism as a play of deconstruction in the last decades.

So, how exactly does this interweaving of economic value, temporality and writing work? The first recorded forms of economic exchange, dating from prehistory – barter and gift exchange – represent a special semiotic relevance. While gift exchange practices are a fascinating topic, they have overshadowed the far less exciting course of development of the economic means of exchange. Mauss was criticized from various perspectives, but his core assumption opened a powerful research direction (Graeber 2001: 171ff). The "total social prestation", which overwhelms the utilitarian value of gift exchange, includes temporal, existential and economic implications; but these are difficult to separate and formalize. This is why our semiotic approach to transactions finds far more useful the line of development from barter exchange to the present-day monetary forms of market exchange.

The barter principle consists of a rudimentary semiotic function of *renvoi*, but without a foundation in inscription. The bartering subject acts economically with regard to a short-term project where his/her present resources (tradeable goods) and future needs are planned with the intermediation of an expected exchange. Economists explain the advent of money signs as a natural optimization of barter exchange (Jevons 1875, Menger 1892). The increased exchange of certain goods makes those goods more desirable than others, often resulting from a combination of their utility and durability. Such is the case with grain, cattle and salt, goods which offer the certainty to their owners that they will always be in demand. This scenario allowed the economic exchange system to further detach itself from the immediacy of needs and consumption. So-called "commodity money" was possessed by participants to trade even without the need to consume the respective money. Various metals, ornaments and shells were among the most evolved forms of commodity money and they gradually changed the logic of the money sign. The utility function was substituted by the scarcity principle. Later in this paper I will show that this principle is very important for the present considerations.

While commodity money was evolving, trading practices developed other, semiotically more advanced means for the transfer of economic value, namely receipts. These were part of the Sumerian clay tables, but also took the form of ox-hide shaped ingots of copper and other materials on which it was possible to write symbols or imprint seals. In many developed regions in the ancient world, writing started in this way, both for characters and numbers (Goetzmann 2016: 27ff). The semiotic advantages of commodity money and receipts gave rise to what was destined to become the major form of economic exchange for the next two millennia, namely *the coin*. Coinage started in the 7th century BC in Lydia. It was "the invention of the print" in the economic field, having an impact comparable to that of the Gutenberg's machine. Iconic and graphic symbols were printed on a standardized piece of very durable metal whose availability was scarce. Compared to the previous forms of money, coins were countable and not to be measured with reference to quality and quantity. As a formal principle, coins introduced *fungibility*, which changed the way economic value was conceived. The fungibility of coins introduced a new level of rationality and calculability in the administration of society. This is, probably, what made the adoption of the coin a global phenomenon. The coin changed the meaning of wealth as well, optimizing the efficacy of war campaigns. We may generalize that the introduction of the coin extended the temporal span of the politico-economical projects of societies.

The pursuit of the *langue* of money signs, in Saussure's (1986 [2016]) terms, a system underlying particular instances of use, continues with paper money. As a semiotic form, paper money also synthesizes the advancement of many financial notation practices parallel to coins, emerging with the advent of the first banks in Renaissance Italy. Paper money was first adopted in China around the 11th century AD, but the origin of contemporary paper money is to be found in 17th century Sweden. Paper money represents a further semiotic advancement of the money sign towards the properties of the linguistic sign – its sign vehicle is much more arbitrary than the sign vehicle of coins. At its first appearance, paper money was representative money: standardized anonymous receipts for deposits of precious metals. If we apply Eco's definition of semiotics as the study of "everything which can be used in order to lie" (Eco 1976: 7), then paper money is more adequate for semiotic study than the previous financial notation systems. Paper money prevented the inconvenience of the transfer of big quantities of metal coins in commerce; it improved the means for communicating economic value, especially amidst large urban areas emerging in the industrial revolution. But the control of economic value behind money signs became a central issue of governance. In these circumstances, national central banks were born. Paper was not itself a scarce material; it was a representation of a scarce material in the safety vault of the banks. The authenticity of banknotes – the sign vehicle of economic value – was at stake.

The rest of the financial history is a process of liberation of the money sign from the representative function. The process is complex and varies from country to country, but the fall of the Gold Standard in 1971 in the USA stands out as a landmark. Such money, the value of which depends entirely on a government decree, is called "fiat money" and "a legal tender". This step introduces further flexibility in financial arrangements from the top governmental level to everyday payments. Although credit cards and electronic transfers started during the first years after the Second World War, "intangible" electronic payments became a global phenomenon in the mid-1980s, as a direct consequence of this new financial paradigm. This paradigm heralded the age of the internet in finance, the place where our considerations commence.

3 Trust and scarcity

The passage from commodity money to intangible electronic payments took more than ten thousand years. During this time, economic activities profoundly changed, as well as trading practices and money forms. Changes took place in the human understanding of what economic value is and, most of all, where the value of money *comes from*. The intangible flat money in global electronic circulation today crystallized what, I would argue, is the essential, as well as the semiotic definition, of money: namely "trust inscribed" (see Ferguson 2008: 30 ff.).

Why, then, does "trust inscribed" capture the essence of money? It means that the value of money is not, for example, an intrinsic property of the money sign as mercantilists and many others had thought about gold. Nor is the value of money to be identified in incorporated labour, as Marx proposed. The value of money comes, instead, from *the trust we have in the future of the whole economic system*. The value is a common bet among the interested economic actors that trade with available goods, services and any other product of our work that will meet our future needs and desires. Money – and, more generally, finances – is the regulative principle of the bet, the means that makes it possible. The entity of the wealth of nations (or better – of corporations) depends on the temporal range of economic predictability. In premodern societies, the majority of people lived on an annual period of planning which multiplied with the number of inhabitants forming the economic exchange. In modern society, both parameters have grown exponentially, hundreds of times. It is precisely the objectified and abstract trust in the future, inscribed in money, that makes possible present-day investments concerning the needs and desires of future generations of people. With the gift economy, the trust inscribed in the offer was personalized and concrete; the "return of the investment" was conditional and uncertain.

Herein lies the basic question of the value of money. Long term economic predictability, which is the origin of global wealth, depends on the stability of the value of money. This stability is not given for granted. Actually, there are many institutions like the World Bank and central national banks that are responsible for keeping the value of money stable. Although the issue is much more complex, maintaining the value of money stable effectively means preventing governments from being tempted to emit more money than the real state of the economy presupposes and preventing banks giving credit to large numbers of unreliable debtors. *In contrast to the linguistic sign, the money sign cannot be reproduced in arbitrary quantity.* The money sign is a carrier of value which is always scarce in respect of the needs and desires of people. As Sexton (2008: Ch. 3) explains, scarcity is the fundamental economic problem of having seemingly unlimited human wants in a world of limited resources. Money, to keep its value, must be scarce and must correspond to the objective scarcity of production. Hence, a crucial part of our trust in the economic system, even when we are not aware of it, is concerned with the scarcity of money in circulation. When the amount of money in circulation increases considerably, people assume a higher propensity to have property and provisions rather than money, and prices increase. When this happens, our trust in money declines, it loses value and meaning together with our trust.

I illustrate these dependencies with the case of Bitcoin. Bitcoin is a decentralized digital currency that appeared in 2009, soon after the world financial crisis started. There was no valuable asset, gold or other, to provide Bitcoin with its value. Bitcoin was independent from the centralized banking system and probably this was an auspicious moment for it to start. The value of Bitcoin started to rise by being adopted by people, initially programmers from the circles of the mysterious inventor of the currency, known as Nakamoto, and then other experienced programmers and users. A few years after the first introduction of the currency, some large companies adopted it as a way of payment and commercial exchange with bitcoins reached hundreds of millions of dollars. Again, behind this real commercial value of hundreds of millions of dollars there was nothing tangible. As Bitcoin.org explains, "all that is required for a form of money to hold value is trust and adoption" (https://bitcoin.org/en/faq#why-do-bitcoins-have-value). *It was the algorithmic solution of the problem of the scarcity of bitcoins, combined with peer-to-peer economic transactions and independence from banks that generated the value of this currency* and made it preferable to other forms of money. The scarcity of bitcoins is guaranteed by its basic algorithm, which allows a small number of bitcoins to be generated on a regular basis. This process is programmed to end in 2025 when the number of bitcoins in circulation will reach 21 million. But this does not mean that the growth of the value of bitcoins and the commercial range will come to a halt. On the contrary, the programmed scarcity of bitcoins is far more reliable as a deposit of value than state money.

During the world financial crisis of 2007–2008, for example, many governments behaved quite irresponsibly in regard of the scarcity of their currencies (see section 6 below). If the trust and adoption of bitcoins grows after the halt of its emission, its price will grow. Hypothetically, one bitcoin may reach the value of 1.000.000 dollars and thus a value in circulation of twenty-one trillion dollars and an unlimited range of commercial exchange according to how often people use it. This is not a pure fiction. Consider the example of one of the early adopters of bitcoin, a Norwegian student writing a thesis on encryption who, in 2009, bought 5 bitcoins at the price of about 5 dollars each and forgot about them until 2015, realizing then that he was a wealthy man with a fortune of $886,000 (https://www.theguardian.com/technology/2015/dec/09/bitcoin-forgotten-currency-norway-oslo-home).

4 Scarcity and finitude

The case of Bitcoin illustrates well the most semiotic of the definitions of money – *trust inscribed*. Returning to the notion of semiotics of transactions we may try now to go one level further in the analysis of what exactly is transferred with the transactions of economic value. But, before that, some conceptual support from the side of semiotics and philosophy will be necessary in order to construct a theoretical bridge equally grounded in economics and humanities.

Most semiotic approaches to economic value evince a Marxist and generally critical orientation and/or a more technical comparison between the communicative function of the general signs and financial ones (Bankov 2017). Among the non-critical contributions (but still influenced by Marx) one is particularly appropriate for the purposes of this paper. The title is "Making Semiotic Sense of Money as a Medium of Exchange" (Dyer 1989). The aim of Dyer's paper is to reveal the deepest levels to which the meaning of money is rooted in the mind of those who live in a pecuniary culture. In the same way in which philosophers before the linguistic turn considered language as a neutral means of expression of thought, today money is considered as a neutral means of economic exchange. Dyer (1989: 505) proposes something similar to the linguistic turn in the analysis of money in modern life: "By re-presenting objects and experiences as comparable containers of exchange value, money symbolically transforms life and, thus, mediates our understanding of it." The statement is quite strong insofar as it presupposes that there are important realities in our social experience that are beyond the grasp of language, of a different nature, but still articulated in a socially shaped formal system and that only money can be their symbolizing system. He even claims that money is "a primary vehicle through which meaning is constructed in a pecuniary culture" (ibid). As theoretical support, Dyer uses the notion of "symbolization" from the American thinker, Walker Percy, who sees the notion as a universal cultural phenomenon and the only way to "make the world accessible to human purposes" (Percy 1975 quoted in Dyer 1989: 505).

Dyer's short article opens this important perspective, but leaves it unexplored. In particular, it leaves the temporal dimension untouched. Money signs are constitutive for the worldview in the pecuniary culture, they are a mediator for our shared understanding of reality; but there are no hints at the transaction of value and the imagination and calculation of future.

Derrida offers some important insights on the transaction of economic value in a temporal perspective in one of his least famous books. In *Given Time: 1. Counterfeit Money* (Derrida 1992) the overall intention of the French philosopher (if we can speak at all about intentions in Derrida) is to deconstruct "econologocentrism" – i.e. of *Homo economicus* as self-present, rational agent of contractual exchange in liberal capitalist society (Holland 1994: 559). The twisted play of deconstruction starts with one important axis of confrontation – that of gift exchange versus monetary exchange.

Derrida begins with long reflections on one sentence, taken from a letter of the historical figure Madame de Maintenon. She writes: "The King takes all my time; I give the rest to Saint-Cyr, to whom I would like to give all" (Derrida 1992: 1). The deep insight, which made me pay much attention to that text is that *behind each transaction of value there is a transaction of time, or rather an economically assessed time*. Derrida's deconstructive play goes in the opposite direction, though, and he entertains his reader by explicating all possible metaphysical implications of the idea that time can be given as a gift (for a superior exploration of the same ideas, but without theoretical implications, see Avni 1985). Fuel for that play is the double meaning of the word "present" – a gift and the temporal dimension of now. For Derrida, following his master, Heidegger, at the core of of Western metaphysics is the failure to understand authentic temporality.

The central object of the book concerns another of the leading topics in our inquiry – counterfeit money. The term comes from Baudelaire's prose-poem with the same name, written in and about an interesting *époque*: a time when money was becoming increasingly powerful in French society but also increasingly unstable, with the founding of new institutions of credit and new practices of speculation. A small accident with counterfeit money takes place around a tobacco shop in the poem and, as Derrida argues (107–116), tobacco symbolized (for Baudelaire as well as his era) an excessive, gratuitous commodity that defies the norms of utility, just as counterfeit money defies the norms of signification and propriety. The key episode occurs as one of the main characters gives a counterfeit coin to a beggar they encounter outside the tobacco shop "getting for free the title of a charitable man" (Holland 1994: 558–559). Then, during long deconstructive speculations, Derrida involves the semiotic transaction of value with the confrontation of symbolic gift-exchange and rational-economic exchange. His purpose is to defeat common sense and to explicate the inconsistencies of the presupposed meanings which brought him to claim that the gift is not only impossible, but it is The Impossible (Derrida 1992: 5), as well as to englobe the whole endeavour as "the madness of economic reason" (34 ff). This leads to the most important part of my observation: in order to develop the deconstructive play in this book, Derrida uses the figure of the circle, which is discovered every time an exchange takes place, but is also seen as the essence of economy. This figure comes from the ordinary metaphysical concept of time (Derrida 1992: 7), inherited from Heidegger, to oppose time to the authentic temporality of *Dasein*. *But why not take the concept of the authentic temporality of Heidegger to develop the philosophical grounds of the constitution of economic value?*

At the core of the authentic concept of time in *Sein und Zeit* lies "the thesis of the primordial finitude of temporality" (Heidegger 1996 [1927]: 330). "Primordial" would mean that the comprehension of the problem of time is not a question of knowledge, but a mode of being and such a mode is inescapably being-towards-end with predilection of the future in respect of the present and past. According to Heidegger, such conditions of finite time for our existence – the finitude of temporality – allow all other everyday or scientific temporalizations of time, which are inauthentic (as the circular one). It precedes them, it is their condition of possibility (1996 [1927]: 250–252, 331).

Finitude, in this sense, is something quite close to the notion of scarcity. This finitude is the scarcity of time which every human being has to face, the unavoidable end of our life which eventually comes. If we follow Heidegger's analysis of primordial finite temporality, such a condition determines the meaning of all things that fill everyone's existential project. Even if we imagine an infinite time and aspire to an eternal life, the meaning of such fantasy comes from the primordial finitude of our temporality.

Now, economic discourse seems to be a completely different universe; but if we look at the definition of scarcity, actually some homology starts to appear: scarcity is the fundamental economic problem of having seemingly unlimited human wants in a world of limited resources. (Sexton 2008: Ch. 3) *My proposal is that at the core of economic value is the condition of perpetual struggle with scarcity/finitude in which our being is primordially situated.* On the surface of the problem this homology is expressed with the cliché "time is money", but such simplification does not account for the nature of value and the deep meaning of transaction. Oscar Wilde puts this distinction quite well: "Nowadays people know the price of everything and the value of nothing" (Wilde 2006: 42). Trivial economic thought, observing the exteriority of market activities, considers time, money, goods and services as objects among other objects, objectified by the price and rational calculus. Semiotics of transaction combines this with the deep levels of value exchange, the meaning of our needs as resulting from the struggle with scarcity, expressed on the surface of the market through our wants and desires.

5 Time and economy

This inquiry started with Goetzmann's argument that money and finance are at the core of the ability of humans to imagine and calculate the future (Goetzmann 2016: 2 ff). If language is the house of being, as Heidegger (1998) considered, writing should be the house of our economic being. This does not apply to writing in general, but to the origins of writing and the evolution of the money sign, which is an evolution of the writing system of money and finances. In the predilection for the future in both authentic human temporality and the essence of money (as trust inscribed) we have a fertile horizon for analysis, which we can only outline here. In his fundamental work *Time and Narrative*, Paul Ricoeur provides a notion of *emplotment*, which brings together the temporal perspective of the hermeneutic phenomenology of Heidegger and the theory of narrative (Ricoeur 1984). Emplotment "configures events, agents and objects and renders those individual elements meaningful as part of a larger whole in which each takes a place in the network that constitutes the narrative's response to why, how, who, where, when, etc." (Atkins 2005). Emplotment is a matter of how the human's ongoing experience with reality assumes narrative form thanks to its temporal constitution. The content may vary from culture to culture, from epoch to epoch, from individual to individual, but narrative emplotment is what makes the world accessible to human purposes. With the exception of Derrida, economic discourse has never been interesting to the hermeneutic phenomenologists; but I think we have enough evidence that it deserves the same type of attention as the philosophic, literary or artistic discourses. The specificity of economic value as emplotted in the meaningful whole of our grasp of reality represents its own deep semio-narrative structures and superficial discursive levels. As Ricoeur says "the authentic is what is most concealed" (Ricoeur 1988: 64). The authentic in the transaction of economic value is what concerns the temporalization of economic time. Then this temporalization appears on the surface level as a socioculturally determined form of commerce and market exchange.

Now let us return to where we started. Our initial observations were about how, in the age of the internet, the market changes, access substitutes the deal with ownership change, commodities and products are substituted by services and experiences. The temporal aspect of economic value starts to dominate the observable level of the market. The digital age, in a way, brought the deep and the superficial levels closer and made this phenomenon more transparent for semiotic analysis. For instance, the ideologists of the so called "Experience economy" define the evolution of business in this way:

> If you charge for stuff, then you are in the commodity business.
> If you charge for tangible things, then you are in the goods business.
> If you charge for the activities you execute, then you are in the service business.
> *If you charge for the time* customers spend with you, then you are in the experience business.
>
> (Pine and Gilmore 1999: 194, emphasis mine)

Considering time as the core of economic value is not a discovery of the digital age. Already in the early 1960s, economists observed the changing proportion between work and leisure time and realized that the latter was becoming more important for the economy than the former (Mincer 1963; Becker 1965). With such an approach, the source of the household's welfare was seen rather in its activities than in the goods and commodities themselves. Activities mean *combination of goods and time*. Hence, the utility of a good was seen as a complex combination of time-saving performance and the income of the household which was rating the price of the time saved.

Thus, the further course of development of the economy in advanced consumer societies optimized the time-saving performance of goods and the concomitant rise in the value of leisure time. Initially, this led to the development of the service sector – a time-saving substitute for goods – which came to cover 75% of the GDP of these economies. Afterwards, the experience economy developed, where time became the central issue of profit and economic value.

Today, the most precious economic resource is the time of the customer. Many businesses provide, for free, devices which were hitherto expensive, such as smartphones, printers, home theatres, etc., just to assure a long term contract for the service that is sold through them.

The "lords" of the Time economy, however, are *Google* and *Facebook*. They conquer our time by providing previously unthinkable services for free, selling afterwards the collected data of our time spent on these services to other companies, who become in their turn more competitive in anticipating our desires and availability.

Such approximation of the deep level of economic temporality and the surface commercial practices is not without ethical consequences. Jeremy Rifkin sees this process as the absorption of the cultural sphere into the commercial sphere (Rifkin 2000: 11). When the economy was less developed, the non-commercialized time people were spending was the source of their cultural diversity which he claims is the lifeblood of civilization (12). Today, with the internet and the new communication technologies, paid-for services and experiences penetrate all of our available time, even the most intimate moments. Thus the new economy "threatens to destroy the very social foundations that give rise to commercial relations" (ibid). The extreme consequences of this process are well illustrated in a dystopic sci-fi movie from 2011 called *In Time* where, in an awful future society, time itself is adopted as currency – the time each character still has to live. The movie presents time as transferable from person to person and from the state to people and, thus, earned through work, spent for consumption and used as a gift among people.

6 The critical perspective

The main purpose of this paper is to open a new theoretic approach towards economic exchange. The text, however, would be incomplete without a few considerations on how semiotics could enrich the critical awareness of what happened in the financial world during the financial crises since 2008. The way many governments behaved and, especially, the anti-crisis measures of the Federal Reserve, revealed unprecedented financial flexibility and emission of huge amounts of money, unthinkable for the times of the Gold Standard and the standard notion of scarcity. There is no unanimous judgement whether this was the best possible way to overcome the crisis or just a placebo, postponing even worse crises. For many, it was a striking injustice to see how banks and their managers, led by lust for profit, made gross errors of judgment yet, instead of bankruptcy, they received support from governmental funds, i.e. the money of those who were the victims of the errors, and who effectively lost their houses, jobs and savings. While generally truthful to the facts, such a perspective opens room for many further explanations and analysis.

Two very insightful articles which use an explicitly semiotic interpretation offer profound explanations of the vicious mechanisms that caused the crisis. In his "Rethinking money and the state: a semiotic turn" (2013), David Gleicher examines a split in the meaning of economic value, which the financial means represent. During the years of the New Deal and the postwar economic boom in the United States, economic growth was supported by a harmonious growth of financial means. "In semiotic terms, the money, endogenously created, communicated both commodity credit and debt ownership" (Gleicher 2013: 348). After the growth of the real economy reduced its pace and the Gold Standard was suspended, financial speculations started to develop their own logic, independent of the productive economy, or as the author calls it – "commodity credit". The economic value, generated by the latter was measurable in wages, prices of goods and services, production costs, etc. This is comparable with each individual's experience with the market system, the commonly accepted "grammar of money" (353), which has been explicated in the previous sections, above. But the economic value of the pure money capital, subject of the stock markets and the financial speculations at large, emerged as a completely different system, a different language, according to Gleicher, and the big troubles started because of the interference of this latter logic into the former one:

> The oligopoly now creates massive amounts of money by purchasing derivatives, including hedges (themselves backed by derivatives or simply naked), and also by financing corporate (more generally, institutional) mergers and acquisitions. These purchases inject new deposits into the oligopoly as a whole. The bulk of the new money is pumped into the issuers of the debt, for the most part corporate investment banks (kissing cousins of the oligopoly), hedge funds, and equity firms all of whom leverage the money they borrow (Gleicher 2013: 353).

Similar to a Ponzi scheme (known also as a Financial Pyramid), this system injects a "cancer-like growth of financial capital" (347) into the overall economy, with a perpetual result of domino-like crises. Contrary to the financial language of our everyday market experience and our respective ability to plan our future "the pure money capital is a language whose words have no meanings" (351).

With similar premises, the research on "Immaterial value and scarcity in digital capitalism" by Michael Betancourt (2010) begins. Here, again, a semiotic interpretation of finances is used to reveal the mechanisms of the present day capitalist system which are hidden from the public as well as some of that system's controllers. Two main contributions of Betancourt to the present research are worth noting: 1) his notion of "futurity" as a new form of economic value; 2) his analysis of the way the digital economy changes the principles of the financial system.

As with Gleicher and many other analysts, Betancourt opposes the phase of the productive economy to that of financial dominance. His explanation of the cancer-like growth of financial capital relies on the nature of the value, as measured by money. During the Golden Age of industrial capitalism, the logic of economic exchanges was based on material assets, accumulation of past labour, present needs and foreseeable future demand. The financial speculations of the last decades moved the barycenter of the system towards an *unforeseeable future*. Betancourt calls this process "semiotic manipulation", "semiotic transactions" and "financialization". As argued above, it is common to sell and invest on the basis of future production; but in this case the selling and reselling enters an infinite spiral of unpredictability. The value of such transactions presupposes future production, but their entity overwhelms by many times the capacity of the productive economy even in the best of possible worlds. What remains at the core of these financial operations is a *pure futurity*, uncontrollable by the scarcity of productive capital. In the case of the 2008 crisis, the expectation of the regular payment of mortgages was sold and resold with so many financial derivatives that the damage, after people stopped paying the rates, was incomparably greater than the assets which provoked it, resulting in a crisis for the whole world.

The second important point in Betancourt's paper regards the role of digital production for reaching the spiral of the futurity market. The advent of digital business and especially the internet created overoptimistic expectations for financial speculators. According to the American theorist "the digital appears as a naturalization of the concentration of capital, since the digital itself poses as a magical resource that can be used without consumption or diminishment, leading to a belief in accumulation without production" (Betancourt 2010) i.e. once the digital product (software, online platform, mobile service, etc.) is created it is infinitely reproducible without further investment and it can reach users without limits. Such a view is quite distorted, but it has unleashed the appetites of the financial operators and made them bolder in reselling the futurities. This vision failed to acknowledge the scarcity of time on disposition of all users, preventing all of them from taking advantage of the benefits of the infinitely available digital products.

7 Conclusions

The dot-com bubble and the financial crisis of 2008 exhibit some extreme consequences of the framework opened in this paper. There are also other non-critical trends that make more transparent the temporal dimension of each transaction of economic value. We trade in a variety of economically temporalized time, both as work/production and consumption/leisure. There are many and growing industries dedicated directly to the extension of human life, long life expectancy being one of the glories of Western consumer societies; but there are also industries dedicated to the distortion of our time perception, for instance extending the present moment, such as alcohol and drugs. There are the "chronotope industries" where fiction transfers us to a distant time and place, and those dedicated to provide the user with sensory experience of parallel possible words, or to augment artificially the experience of the present. Then there are the conventional time-saving industries of utilities, goods and services which have led to the advent of the mass consumer society, which is today entering into a new generation market, known as the Internet of Things – an entire electronic intelligent ecosystem dedicated to integration of all levels of our everyday life, saving time from daily routines much more efficiently than the previous system. There are as well the "Dorian Gray" industries, dedicated to making people look and feel younger – a fake acquisition of temporality at the level of appearance and self-esteem. I also mention the "religious industries", concerned with selling to believers the temporality of the existence after death. The whole phenomenology of commercialized temporality will be a subject of further research.

References

Atkins, Kim. 2005. "Paul Ricoeur (1913–2005)". *The Internet Encyclopedia of Philosophy*. http://www.iep.utm.edu/ricoeur/ (Accessed 27/3/2017).

Avni, Ora. 1985. The Semiotics of Transactions: Mauss, Lacan and the three Musketeers. *Modern Language Notes*, Vol. 100, No. 4, The Johns Hopkins University Press. French Issue (Sep., 1985), pp. 728–757.

Bankov, Kristian. 2017. Approaches to the semiotics of money and economic value. *Signs & Media*. 15: 178–192.

Becker, G. S. 1965. A theory of the allocation of time. *Economic Journal* 75: 493–517.

Betancourt, M. 2010. Immaterial value and scarcity in digital capitalism. www.ctheory.net/articles.aspx?id=652 (Accessed 20 August 2017).

Derrida, Jacques. 1992 [1991]. *Given Time: 1. Counterfeit Money*. Trans. Peggy Kamuf. Chicago and London: The University of Chicago Press.

Dyer, Alan W. 1989. Making semiotic sense of money as a medium of exchange. *Journal of Economic Issues*, 23(2): 503–510.

Eco, Umberto. 1976. *A Theory of Semiotics*. Bloomington: Indiana University Press.

Ferguson, Niall. 2008. *The ascent of money: A financial history of the world*. New York: Penguin.

Gleicher, David. 2013. Rethinking money and the state: a semiotic turn. *Journal of Sustainable Finance & Investment*. 3(4): 344–359.

Goetzmann, William N. 2016. *Money changes everything: how finance made civilization possible*. Princeton, NJ, and Woodstock: Princeton University Press.

Graeber, David. 2001. *Toward an Anthropological Theory of Value. The False Coin of Our Own Dreams*. New York: Palgrave.

Gibbs, Samuel. 2015. Man buys $27 of bitcoin, forgets about them, finds they're now worth $886k. https://www.theguardian.com/technology/2015/dec/09/bitcoin-forgotten-currency-norway-oslo-home. (Accessed 27/3/2017)

Heidegger, Martin. 1996 [1927]. *Being and Time*. Translation by Joan Stambaugh. Albany: State University of New York Press. (page numbers from the original German edition from 1927)

Heidegger, Martin. 1998. Letter on 'Humanism. In William McNeill (ed.), *Pathmarks*. Cambridge: Cambridge University Press, 239–276.

Holland, Eugene W. 1994. Review of Given Time: 1. Counterfeit Money by Jacques Derrida; Peggy Kamuf. *Nineteenth-Century French Studies* 22(3/4): 557–559.

Jevons, W. S. 1875. *Money and the Mechanism of Exchange*. New York: D. Appleton and Company.

Menger, Carl. 1892. On the origins of money. *Economic journal* 2: 239–255.

Mincer, J. 1963. Market prices, opportunity costs, and income effects. In Carl F. Christ, Milton Friedman, Leo A. Goodman, Zvi Griliches, Arnold C. Harberger, Nissan Liviatan, Jacob Mincer, Yair Mundlak, Marc Nerlove, Don Patinkin, Lester G. Telser & Henri Theil (eds.) *Measurement in Economics: Studies in Mathematical Economics and Econometrics in Memory of Yehuda Grunfeld*. Stanford: Stanford University Press, 67–82.

Olsthoorn, Peter. 2011. *The Price We Pay for Google*. Eburon Elements.

Percy, Walker. 1975. The Message in the Bottle. New York: Farrar, Straus and Giroux.

Pine, B. Joseph & James H. Gilmore. 1999. *The Experience Economy: Work is Theatre and Every Business a Stage*. Boston MA: Harvard Business School Press.

Ricoeur, Paul. 1984. *Time and Narrative*, Vol. 1. Translation by Kathleen McLaughlin & David Pellauer. Chicago: The University of Chicago Press.

Ricoeur, Paul. 1988. *Time and Narrative Volume III*. Translation by Kathleen Blarney & David Pellauer. Chicago: University of Chicago Press.

Rifkin, Jeremy. 2000. *The Age of Access: The New Culture of Hypercapitalism, Where all of Life is a Paid-For Experience*. New York: Penguin/Putnam.

Saussure, Ferdinand de. 1986. *Cours de Linguistique Générale*. Edition critique établie, introduite et commentée par Tullio de Mauro. Payot: Paris.

Sexton, Robert L. 2008. *Exploring Economics*. Mason, OH: Thomson South-Western.

Wilde, Oscar. 2006. *The Picture of Dorian Gray*. Oxford and New York: Oxford University Press.

Timo Maran
Applied ecosemiotics: Ontological basis and conceptual models

Abstract: Addressing ecological problems requires an ontological position that sees environmental processes simultaneously as semiotically mediated and rooted in ecosystems. For example, problems such as the effects of global environmental change, animals that are coping with urbanized environments and human migration due to environmental degradation bond sign processes and the flows of matter and energy. Ecosemiotics provides a robust conceptual framework for studying these topics. The toolbox proposed in this paper combines the ecosemiotic sphere as a general concept for ecosemiotic research; activity centers, which are *loci* in the ecosemiotic sphere with distinct identities and dynamics, bringing along change; relations between activity centers that are the primary object of ecosemiotic study. The proposed framework gathers some specific concepts, such as, among others, affordance, semiotic pollution, ecological code, meaning transfer, semiocide. I will argue that ecosemiotics holds a good potential for analyzing crucial contemporary environmental problems.

Keywords: ecosemiotics, ontology, semiotic modelling, ecosemiosphere, environmental problems

1 Introduction

To thrive as a discipline in the 21st century, it is essential for semiotics to address problems that contemporary society and culture(s) are facing. This includes both developing theoretical models as well as applying these in analyses of critical topics. A set of issues that has raised a lot of concern in recent decades is the degradation of the natural environment, human-induced climate change, global biodiversity loss, spread of invasive species, accumulation of waste and the connected effects and outcomes. Addressing this set of environmental problems may be challenging for semiotics, since the environment as an object differs from traditional objects of semiotic studies and because environmental degradation appears to be connected with the modernist episteme that has also partly nourished

Timo Maran, University of Tartu

https://doi.org/10.1515/9783110857801-008

20th century semiotics. Such a challenge may, however, also be the catalyst for semiotics to generate new perspectives.

A number of studies and reports from environmental sciences highlight the severe consequences of human impact on the natural environment. To give a few quantitative measurements, the UN Food and Agriculture Organisation reveals in its report "State of the World's Forests 2016" that agricultural land globally covers more than one-third (37.7 %) of all available land and that the number is steadily growing at the expense of forests and other natural landscapes (for instance, in the period from 1990–2015 the global forest area fell by 129 million hectares [FAO 2016: x]). An essential metric of the impact of human industry on the global climate is high concentration of CO_2 in the atmosphere. In April 2016, the Mauna Loa Observatory recorded in the high atmosphere a CO_2 concentration of 410,28 ppm (parts per million), which is the largest concentration of CO_2 in Earth's atmosphere that the human species has ever witnessed (Kahn 2017). Also, the global species extinction rate has accelerated significantly during the industrial era, the process that has been often referred to as the "sixth extinction". It has been estimated, for instance, that "vertebrate species loss over the last century is up to 100 times higher than the [natural] background rate" of extinctions (Ceballos et al. 2015: 1).

These few measurements mark the interconnected set of problems that human civilisation is facing. In 2005, an environmental historian, Jared Diamond, listed 12 challenges that humanity needs to solve for avoiding global environmental crises: destruction of natural habitats, degradation of soil quality, shortage of fresh water, overfishing and overhunting, effects of introduced and domesticated species on native species, human population growth and increased medial impact of people to the environment, global warming, chemical pollution, depletion of fossil fuels, human land use and its effect for Earth's photosynthetic capacity. Acknowledging such challenges also led research communities to issue a number of warnings and pleas for actions (e.g. Ripple et al. 2017).

In recent decades, the awareness of environmental issues has risen in the human sciences under the caption of environmental humanities. Paradigms of environmental history, ecocriticism, human-animal studies, environmental psychology, more-than-human geography and others have been engaged in dialogue to study relations between the human and the non-human world. This development has brought along substantial shifts in underlying scientific presumptions and ontologies for addressing animal or even material subjects. For instance, there has been a considerable interest towards material processes and their possible representations in human discourses. In the 1990's, Actor-Network Theory, led by French sociologist and philosopher Bruno Latour (1993, 1997), aimed towards a "flat ontology" that could incorporate social, material and semiotic processes. Some authors like John Law (2008) called this movement "material semiotics", referring to its origins in Greimasian actant analysis that was later applied to the processes of the material world. Further, material ecocriticism (Iovino and Oppermann 2014) is an approach in literary criticism that has made an attempt to study material entanglements, the agency of things, and the making of meaning out of matter and things. The objects of study could be, for instance, the effects of non-living protagonists (volcanos, climate) on human lives and narratives, or the life-cycles of plastics, radioactive waste and other human-created substances.

In the light of environmental humanities, it becomes legitimate to ask, how could semiotics help in addressing the ongoing environmental change? Apparently environmental degradation has its roots and causes in the semiotic dynamics of culture – what models do humans use to make sense of the environment, what is the position of scientific knowledge in human worldviews, how well do people know their surrounding environment and how do they attribute or transpose meanings to the environmental structures? From the broader biosemiotic perspective, it is also crucial to consider that environmental degradation is in numerous ways related with the activities of other species, e.g. farming and cattle contributing substantially to CO_2 and methane emissions, climate change altering ecological relations and food chains between wild species in countless ways. My belief is that by analysing sign processes, semiotics has a very special contribution to offer to other environmental humanities in the task of understanding the roots of human induced environmental change. In this paper, I make an attempt to delineate some ecosemiotic principles as well as to gather and elaborate conceptual tools that could be used in such a research.

2 The ontological basis of ecosemiotics

From an ecological perspective, life is interactional and bound to material processes on the most basic level as ecological food chains are a part of more overwhelming cycles of the matter and energy of the Earth. In a similar vein, there are interactions between semiotic processes and ecological processes. By the simpler iconic (resemblance-based) and indexical (association-based) sign relations, semiotic processes are connected to the world's structures and patterns (Maran and Kull 2014; Maran 2017b; Kull 2009). This does not entail advocating Newtonian determinism but rather pointing out that semiotic processes are semi-autonomous in regard to the underlying cycles of matter and energy. Semiosis brings a certain flux to the natural world and gives to ecosystems a degree of freedom necessary for balancing external forces and changing conditions.

From this standpoint, ecosemiotics could enquire to what extent human semiotic processes or sign systems are in correspondence and support ecological processes – or to what extent they disrupt and counteract these. Ecosemiotics has a reason to be suspicious of the highly abstract and purely symbolic semiotic structures (e.g. artificial languages and codes) of human culture and to question their ability to sustain living processes. This observation is valid for both the object-level and the meta-level. On the meta-level, ecosemiotics' attention to connections between culture and the environment clearly differs from critical discourses of cultural studies that build their identity on abstracted categories and their ideological oppositions. From an ecosemiotic viewpoint, these are rather ideologies themselves that are highly abstract sign systems expressing human social dynamics. Life, on the other hand, is complex, creates strange configurations and searches, by behavioural and evolutionary means, for ways to overcome strict limitations. Also the recent attempts to connect biosemiotics and the humanities (Cobley 2016; Wheeler 2016) have expressed their worries towards critical discourses and emphasised the role of material and biological processes as a ground in which human culture is rooted.

In its attention to environmental problems, ecosemiotics can rely on a number of thinkers from semiotics and beyond. There has been a tradition of thought in the second half of the 20th century that under different disciplinary labels has addressed relations between semiotic processes (both in organisms and in culture) and their environment. In the 1950–60s, Michael Polanyi (1958, 1966) wrote extensively about the rootedness of individual knowledge in the environment and sketched an entirely new sign type – the *tacit sign* – that connects human cognised experience with precognitive perceptual and biosemiotic processes. A decade later, anthropologist, cybernetic and polymath Gregory Bateson (1980, 2000) studied, among other things, relations between a semiotic entity (a culture or an individual) and its surrounding context in terms of redundancy and complementary relationship and worked out the layered understanding of learning and communication that included their effects on semiotic systems. In the 1980s, perceptual psychologist James J. Gibson (1986) described a keen balance between the agency of environmental structures and the activity of a living organism under the concept of "perceptual affordances". In his view (Gibson 1986: 127), the environment has a strong ontology and indeed affords action and meaning:

> The composition and layout of surfaces *constitute* what they afford . . . . [T]o perceive them is to perceive what they afford. This is a radical hypothesis, for it implies that the

'values' and 'meanings' of things in the environment can be directly perceived. Moreover, it would explain the sense in which values and meanings are external to the perceiver.

Gibson's account is critically important for ecosemiotics, as it facilitates addressing the significance and value of ecosystems separately from human semiosis.

These are a few examples from many authors belonging to or influenced by pragmatics, cybernetics, complexity studies or ecology that can be used as a source of inspiration for ecosemiotics. In wider terms, this intellectual movement can be denoted as "Ecological Postmodernity" after Charlene Spretnak (1997: 73), who characterises this by the following criteria: ecological postmodernity perceives the world as a "community of subjects", considers the primary truth condition to be "the particular-in-context", understands "selves" to be processual, highlights the interchange between body and culture, sees reality as fragmented and therefore drives towards complexity-based scientific description. Indeed, the intellectual approach that stems from these ideas can be considered to be a novel episteme of thinking apart from modernist and postmodernist views.

The intellectual developments of the 20th century have prepared the ground for the ecosemiotic paradigm that formed a subfield of semiotics in the 1990s. The term Ökosemiotik was apparently first used and defined by Winfried Nöth (1996) in a paper published in *Zeitschrift für Semiotik*. A few years earlier, Alfred Lang (1993) used the term "semiotic ecology" and proposed a corresponding research programme rooted in Peircean semiotics, while Swedish anthropologist Alf Hornborg (1996) published a paper on "ecology as semiotics". It was, however, in 1998 when the journal *Sign Systems Studies* (vol. 26) published in English two papers on the topic, one by Nöth (1998), another by Kull (1998) that proposed explicit definitions and delineations of ecosemiotics. This was three years later followed by a special issue of the same journal (Nöth and Kull 2001) that, in its turn, gave rise to a series of conferences and the commencement of university courses on ecosemiotics (for a more detailed overview of the history of ecosemiotics, see Maran and Kull 2014). Ecosemiotics has been thereafter defined, for instance, as "the study of sign processes which relate organisms to their natural environment" as interpreted by Winfried Nöth (2001: 71) or as the semiotic discipline investigating "human relationships to nature which have a semiosic (sign-mediated) basis" (Kull 1998). More recently, we have specified ecosemiotics as "a branch of semiotics that studies sign processes as responsible for ecological phenomena" (Maran and Kull 2014: 41). It may also be said that ecosemiotics is concerned with the semiotic processes that relate to or address the broader context of living biological processes (Maran 2017a: 5).

Based on the earlier studies, we can sketch four basic properties to characterise the ecosemiotic understanding of its research domain: dynamicity; historicity; multilayeredness; and contextualisation.

1) Dynamicity means here that the ecosemiotic sphere is not static but changing and that this change arises from the inner dynamics of the objects. In other words, the ecosemiotic sphere brings along its own character to the research situation. This dynamicity arises from the interplay between multiple actors: forces of material nature, agencies of different biological species and human groups and cultural texts.

2) This dynamics of the ecosemiotic sphere is not, however, occasional or incidental but derives from the earlier stages of the system. In biosemiotics a similar idea was described by Jesper Hoffmeyer (2014) as "semiotic scaffolding", where the semiotic development of an organism prepares the ground and makes possible the future developmental directions of the same organism. The ecosemiotic sphere has *historicity* or descendance, whereas its past is not external but rather forms a memory, being a source of interpretation, autocommunication and recoding.

3) The ecosemiotic sphere has layers with different semiotic complexities and levels of abstractness that are simultaneously present and partly interwoven. The ecosemiotic sphere contains the semiotic potentiality of the physical environment, the communicational activities of humans and other species as well as symbolic representations of the environment in human sign systems. There are different types of connections and relations between these layers.

4) The ecosemiotic sphere is contextualised. This means that the ecosemiotic sphere as the object of study is situated in the broader environmental context. The boundaries of the ecosemiotic sphere are not strict but rather semi-surpassable and allow it to obtain identity within a broader semiotic environment through the flows of information and matter (here we might take inspiration from Lotman's [2005] semiosphere concept). Such partial closure is characteristic of ecological systems – water, flocks of birds and plant seeds are able to enter into and exit an ecological system – and the same principle should characterise the object of ecosemiotic studies.

These four properties give to the ecosemiotic approach a distinct identity. Ecosemiotics, as I perceive it, affirms the existence of objects with hard ontology but at the same time considers these as semiotically active, dynamically changing and having fluid connections with surrounding environments. We can think of the ecosemiotic sphere as described here in terms of ecosemiosphere – the concept that was proposed by the American medievalist and ecosemiotician

Alfred K. Siewers. According to Siewers, "an ecosemiosphere literally means an ecological bubble of meaning (borrowing the term 'semiosphere' from semiotics). It involves not a 're-enchantment' of nature, but recognition of nature as a meld of physical and cultural communication, which can be considered spiritual as well as material" (Siewers 2014: 4), and the term also "extends earlier definitions of specific symbolic cultures as semiospheres, or meaningful environments, into physical environments. It also extends onto a regional level the description in ecosemiotics of 'nature-texts' integrally related to physical environment" (Siewers 2011: 41). Siewer's ecosemiosphere is characterised by spatial organisation and localisation, which could help to delineate the otherwise amorphous object of study.

3 Conceptual toolbox for ecosemiotics

Ecosemiotic studies would benefit from an open epistemological stance since the environment and other objects of ecosemiotics tend to be more complex than our descriptions of these. Therefore we should not postulate strict typological distinctions but rather rely on *ad-hoc* approaches where conceptual tools and methods will be constructed in the course of the case study in solving particular problems. Conceptual tools and typologies themselves are modelling devices of the human species, encumbered with particular cultural, ideological and historical backgrounds, and should therefore be used carefully. Objects of ecosemiotics are, however, "strange" in the sense that they have their own structure, memory and often their own Umwelt or Umwelten. The autonomous nature of the research object means that relations between the object and the researcher need to be reciprocal and dialogical and hence the open epistemological approach is suitable. Open epistemology, however, does not mean relying on incidental or ambivalent metalanguage. There is still the possibility to develop a concrete conceptual framework. What is specific for this approach is treating concepts and methods like tools in the toolbox that are used, combined and modified according to the requirements of the specific research task at hand.

In the following, I will arrange a set of concepts and models for practical ecosemiotic analyses. In doing so, I will review existing research literature in ecosemiotics and beyond and also draw examples from my earlier studies on nature writing (analysis of the works of an Estonian author, Fred Jüssi, and nature representations of the Eastern Estonian region Alutaguse, [Maran 2014; Maran and Tüür 2017]) and human-animal relations (cultural reactions to the emergence of the golden jackal in Estonia, changing relations to jackdaws in

Tartu, [Maran 2015; Maran 2016]). The approach that I use here combines three types of entities: the *ecosemiotic sphere*, which is considered to be a general concept for the ecosemiotic research domain; *activity centres*, which are the loci in the ecosemiotic sphere that have distinct identity and that bring along dynamics and change; *relations* between activity centres that are the primary object of the ecosemiotic study. I do not make a clear-cut division between the object-level and meta-level as the proposed research models and concepts themselves are the derivatives of the underlying cultural and academic tradition (thus having connection to the object level).

There seems to be three types of activity centres in the ecosemiotic sphere: 1. Semiotic potentiality of the material environment; 2. Communicative relations between individuals and groups belonging to different biological species (including humans); 3. Human cultural texts with their structure and memory. The extent and reach of effects of these types of activity centres differ: the semiotic potential of the material environment is local and spatially limited, whereas textual structures are able to bridge different cultures and cross large spatial and temporal distances. The three types of activity centres combine into two contact zones: 1. The material environment as a vehicle of mediated communication; 2. Cultural representations of the environment as a means for social communication. These contact zones need special attention as the processes in these thresholds are major sources of dynamics and change in the ecosemiotic sphere (see Fig. 1.).

2.1. Semiotic potentiality of the environment	2.2. Environment as a vehicle of mediated communication	2.3. Direct communicative relations among humans and animals	2.4. Environmental representations as means for social communication	2.5. Human cultural texts in their relations with environment
Perceptual affordances	Environmental mediation	Biotranslation	Semiotic modelling	Replacement of 0-nature
Resource criterion	Semiotic pollution	Umwelt transition	Transposition of meaning	Nature-text
Ecofields	Semiocide	Ecological codes	Dissent	Representational / Mimetic / Complementary / Motivational relations
Environmental signs	Semiotic allowance			Forest model

Fig. 1: Types of ecosemiotic activity centres, their contact zones and the placement of conceptual tools.

The focus of ecosemiotics is intrinsically dynamic and aimed at interactions, influences and hybridisations between different activity centres in the ecosemiotic sphere. In a particular research situation, the entering point, from which the ecosemiotic sphere is approached, may be different (as mapping a spatial region, focusing on the particular cultural text, or describing a case of human-animal communication). From this starting point, however, the scope of analysis should be broadened to cover all other activity centres and their possible relations.

3.1 Semiotic affordance of the material environment

Describing the material environment, its structures, patterns, and potential to induce semiotic relations is an essential part of ecosemiotic study. Patterns and structures of the material environment endow *perceptual affordances* (*sensu* Gibson 1986) to humans and animals, as well as related sign processes. For analysing affordances of the environment, it is not enough to describe environmental structures, yet these need to be juxtaposed with animal physiologies, behaviours and ecologies, following Jakob von Uexküll's (1982) Umwelt analysis. Incorporating animal Umwelten allows the bringing forth of detailed correspondences of meaning between animal and environment. Describing relevant resources for an animal in the given environment can be done systematically by the concept of *resource criterion* (Farina 2012), which describes an environment by locating different resources – either material, biological or cultural – that its inhabitants need and for which they seek. Farina's view is a semiotic one, as resources are not considered as immediately available for species but mediated through the interfaces or *ecofields*, as Farina has named these. Adopting Uexküll's view, Farina describes eco-fields as "space configuration meaning carriers" (Farina 2006: 32). Eco-fields depend on both the physical shapes and structures of the landscape as well as on the perception and life functions of the given species. An important issue becomes, therefore, how well species recognise ecofields, what could be their obstacles in recognising relevant ecofields (e.g. human induced noise and other disturbances). Such a resource-centred view can also be used for pinpointing areas in which different species meet and indicating the grounds for conflicting relations between species.

For more detailed analysis of ecofields, we may benefit from typological analysis of the environmental sign, deriving from indexicality in Peircean terms. Many semiotic authors have elaborated on specific sign types suitable for analysing environmental semiosis. Charles Peirce's classification of indexical signs distinguishes between designators and reagents (CP 8.368 fn23): designators point to something in the environment, whereas reagents are based on true causal connection. Thomas A. Sebeok (2001: 93) lists "symptom, cue, clue, track, trail" as types of index in the environment. A possibility for describing different *environmental signs* would be focusing on the relationship between the object and the representamen, whether it is easily accessible or not, whether it is particular or abstract/manifold (cf. Maran 2017b). For instance, animal tracks and seasonal change are both indexical signs in the environment, but they have very different dynamics. Animal tracks are specific patterns that have a strict causal connection with the animal that has left them and have therefore also a particular and well-limited sign relation to the object. Seasonal change, on the other hand, is a process manifested in many perceivable changes in the environment and its object is an ambiguous, more compound object than a singular entity. It should be noted that there is indeed a broad variety of semiosic processes in the environment that may require a more detailed description.

3.2 Material environment as a vehicle of mediated communication

Another semiotic process in relation to the material environment that ecosemiotics should address is *environmental mediation,* as the question of how animals and humans mark their presence, express their identity and communicate though changing material environments. There are many possible examples of such processes from territory markings of carnivores to fences and gardens built by humans. In environment-mediated communication, the altered semiotic structures as messages become semi-independent. The semiotically altered environment has semiotic potentiality and an effect outside of the temporal frame of communication, and their effects may also be different from what the communicator has intended. This brings us to the question of *semiotic pollution,* where the activities of one species in the environment changes its qualities to the extent that it starts to disturb the semiotic processes of other species. Semiotic pollution was a concept proposed by eminent German semiotician Ronald Posner (2000) to describe the breakdown of sign systems and sign mediation due to internal or external disturbance. Examples of semiotic pollution are the effect of noise on the semiotic processes and overregulated communication codes that obstruct the normal sign processes. We may see, for instance, the effects of noise in the environmental realm in a situation where artificial light sources disturb newly hatched turtles on beaches (Kamrowski et al. 2012). Sea turtles have an inborn urge to move towards the brightest light source that in the natural conditions would help them to orient into open ocean. But the same instinct leads them in human-altered environments to asphalt roads, where they get killed by vehicles.

A type of the semiotic pollution is *semiocide* where, through environmental change, the impact of one participant upon another is intentional and detrimental and where a semiotic subject is actively aggressive towards the other semiotic subject. According to the author of the concept, Ivar Puura (2013: 152), semiocide is "a situation in which signs and stories that are significant for someone are destroyed because of someone else's malevolence or carelessness, thereby stealing a part of the former's identity". The concept of semiocide would provide ecosemiotics with a good tool for analysing conflictual relations between different species and human groups that are mediated by the environment. For instance, closing openings of the ventilation shafts in flat-houses to expel nesting swifts, jackdaws and other birds can be considered semiocidal activity.

To sum up, the role of environmental structures in semiotic processes is manifold. Environmental structures have the potentiality to trigger different types of sign relations in accordance with the specific animal Umwelten. On the other hand, animals are able to change the environment for communicative means and, through this influence, the capacities of other animals to engage with the environment. The outcome of these processes is often detrimental as notions of semiotic pollution and semiocide demonstrate; but, in principle, it could also be beneficial to other participants. Through the mild human influence on the natural environment, it is possible to create novel ecofields that other species can recognize and use. The corresponding semiotic process could perhaps be named *semiotic allowance* and it requires analyzing and modelling both the Umwelten of the involved species as well as the properties of the material environment. Finding and using such new potentials to mitigate environmental conflicts could be one aim of ecosemiotic study.

3.3 Direct communicative relations in the environment

Analysing animal communication is a relevant part of ecosemiotic study as communication always happens in a particular environment and is related with this in various ways. If different species and human groups inhabit the shared environment, then their communicative interactions may also influence their being in the environment. In animals, these dynamics can be described by way of the concept of *biotranslation* which was originally understood as the transfer of a message from the Umwelt of one species to another (Kull and Torop 2000). For biotranslation to become possible, there needs to be some connection or overlap between different Umwelten, and therefore biotranslation mostly takes place between species that are ecologically, behaviourally or physiologically close to one another (Kull and Torop used species of tits and their interpretation of a common predator as an example). For analysing the temporal dimension of change in animal Umwelten, the concept of *Umwelt transition* proposed by Morten Tønnessen (2011, 2014) can be used. Umwelt transition describes the difference between two stages of the same Umwelt before and after some decisive event. For the aims of ecosemiotic analysis, we could narrow our attention down and describe the difference between the aspect of animal Umwelt related to environment (which is one of four basic types of Umwelt relations according to Uexküll) before and after biotranslation or some other ecosemiotically relevant event (semiocide, semiotic pollution, etc.). As a communicative event, biotranslation can create connections between different Umwelten and lead to a greater similarity between them in relation to the environmental structures.

Interactions between communication and environment are indeed manifold. There is a rich body of evidence on how the properties of the communication channel influence the properties of the signals conveyed (Bradbury, Vehrencamp 2011). It is also known that species can change their communication modalities depending on how the communication channel is used by other animal species (e.g. Kight et al. 2011). If we further pay attention to ecological communities, we may notice the entanglement between properties of the material environment and messages sent and received by animals in this environment. Thus, there is reason to describe *ecological codes* as communicative regularities specific to the given ecological community. The ecological code can be "defined as the sets of (sign) relations (regular irreducible correspondences) characteristic to an entire ecosystem, including the interspecific relations in particular" (Kull 2010: 354). In my understanding, there are three basic properties of the ecological codes (Maran 2012): 1. Ecological codes are distributed, open and involve different species. As species have different perceptual organs, Umwelten and relation to the environment, no single individual or species has full perception of an ecological code. Instead, every single species and organism involved in an ecological code has a partial variation of the convention. 2. An ecological code is built upon and incorporates the consistencies, constraints and habits existing in a particular ecological community. An ecological code rests on indexical relations, as it is in these that representamen–object relationships surpass and remain independent of any specific interpreter. 3. An ecological code uses different memory types (following Jablonka and Lamb 2005) having both cognitive and non-cognitive (or conscious and unconscious) aspects. A regulation can be fixed in different memory types simultaneously: for instance, it can be fixed partially in the physical regularity, partially in the genetic memory of a species and partially in the cultural memory of another species. The concept of ecological code may help us to describe the communicational integrity of ecosystems and to understand the involvement of human cultural semiosis in these (which may be more or less corresponding).

3.4 Cultural representations of environment as means for communication

As ecosemiotic study embraces both non-human animal and human communication, we also need to address human communicational activities in regard to environmental processes. A lot of research about the spread of knowledge and attitudes on environmental issues among humans has been carried out within the paradigm of Environmental Communication Studies (e.g. Hansen and Cox 2015). The use of language, including specific vocabularies and connotations of environmental concepts, is also studied by Ecolinguistics (e.g. Stibbe 2012, 2015). Here I will shortly discuss some aspects of how human communication interacts through semiotic means with environmental signs and animal communication.

In perceiving, interpreting and representing environmental objects or animals, humans combine the semiotic potential (appearance, biocommunication) of the object with their own cultural presumptions and models. Cultural models provide here a ground of reference for comparisons and generalisations that are often used to give a higher status to the entity under consideration. As a simple example, endurance, long lifespan and crown spread of the oak tree in combination with the underlying cultural model of "stability/timelessness" has given the oak tree the status of a national symbol in several countries. This, in its own turn, has enhanced the protection and cultivation of oaks in urban greenery in comparison with many other tree species.

In animals, the ground of *semiotic modelling* is often anthropomorphism as similarity to humans with attention to special morphological features of large eyes, upright position, digits on first limbs, etc. It can be considered that such animal symbolization in cultural-mythological consciousness forms a part of "the much more general semiotic landscape that influences interpretations of each and every animal species" (Mäekivi, Maran 2016: 214). In addition to anthropomorphism, Czech philosopher of science Stanislav Komárek (2009: 108–116) has described other bases on which animals can be modelled by biomorphism, technomorphism, psychomorphism or sociomorphism. Such modelling appears to have a double effect – on the one hand it accentuates the given species or environmental object in human discourse, but on the other hand it conceals and covers many properties that the animal or environmental object has in its original ecological context.

A notion that can be used for analysing such processes is *transposition of meaning* where cultural meanings that have some social or cultural causes are attributed to the environmental object or animal species. In classical ethology, a phenomenon of the displacement behaviour is known where an animal in conflict or stress reacts towards an object that seems to be irrelevant to the current situation. For instance, a blackbird in a territorial conflict may start lifting leaves up from the ground or start cleaning its feathers, thereby freezing the uncomfortable situation. It seems that there exists a similar conflictual dynamic in human societies. Conflicts between social groups, which might have roots in deep social or historical contentions, are projected onto animal species or environmental objects that do not have any direct relation with the conflict. Morten Tønnessen (2011) described such dynamics with the example of Norwegian wolves, where tensions between local farmers and industrial agriculture have been projected onto the image of the wolf, which stands as a symbol of forests and forestation. In the Estonian context, there is a similar example of the flying squirrel (*Pteromys volans*) and forest management, where the flying squirrel has become a symbol of old forests and afterwards also a symbol of contention between the forest industry and environmental originations. The transposition of meaning may have real-life consequences to the species involved – for instance, through the implementation of species management strategies.

The semiotic activity of the environmental phenomena or animal species and its interpretation by humans may combine differently. In some cases, the environmental object may also demonstrate *dissent* or non-concordance with human interpretation. The concept of dissent was proposed in this context by Australian semiotician David Low (2008) who emphasised the necessity of including the environment as a semiotic subject into the study of environmental communication. He departed from Peircean semiotics and highlighted a split between an environmental process itself and the human interpretation of this as an important characteristic of environmental conflicts. According to his view, environmental processes enter into environmental communication as dynamical objects of the sign *sensu* Charles Peirce. For example, the pollutants in water act as dynamical objects, whereas their perceived characteristics and effects act as immediate objects of the sign. In such situations, people search for the correspondence between dynamical and immediate objects – that is, they adjust and adapt their sign-mediated knowledge towards the environmental processes themselves. The tension between semiotic activities of the environment and human cultural interpretations may unfold differently in different cases. Also, the animal participant may obtain the position of dissent in regard to the environmental discourse. This was the case, for instance, in the emergence of the Golden Jackal (*Canis aureus*) in Estonia (Maran 2014, 2016) with ensuing interplay between the jackal's own communicative and behavioural activities and human interpretation and modelling (relying on the opposition of their own and alien and other models) of the new and strange species. For ecosemiotics, such a frame of analysis would mean working simultaneously on different hierarchical levels and analysing transferences and attributions of meanings across scales.

3.5 Dynamics between cultural texts and environment

Another locus of ecosemiotic analysis is texts and textual representations, covering a number of cultural artefacts from nature essays and field guides up to journal articles and visual media content. What makes textual representations specific as a research object is their distinct structure. Representations usually have structural, compositional and narrative consistency deriving from the codes and languages used for creating them, which also gives texts a certain relative autonomy and independence. Nature representations may easily outlast the environments they are representing. This endurance of texts is similar to the understanding of symbols as being 'alive', that is, symbolic signs having something approaching their own subjectivity and agency that may alter the surrounding culture (Nöth 2014). Texts with their own agency can influence the human understanding of nature and, through human action, change the material environment by replacing this with human altered environments. This dynamic has been described in detail by Kalevi Kull (1998: 366) as *replacement of 0-nature* (nature as it is) by 2-nature (nature remodelled by humans).

However, we may also see that relations between environmental semiosis and cultural semiosis are often not so straightforward. The relationship between texts that represents nature and its object(s) of representation is not always univocal, but cultural texts attach themselves to various semiotic anchoring points in the environment. To explicate and explain these interconnections between nature writing and the environment, I have proposed the model of *nature-text* (Maran 2007). According to this model, ecosemiotic research is considered to have at least a double object: "in addition to the written text that speaks about nature and points to nature, it should also include the depicted part of the natural environment itself, which must be, for the relation to be functional, to at least some extent textual or at least textualizable" (Maran and Tüür 2017: 289). The formal characteristics of nature representations – the literary and narrative strategies employed in the text – are often organised and shaped according to the particular environmental relationship it represents. Thus, the nature-text model asks what kind of literary devices convey what kind of human-environment relation (message) in the context of what kind of environment (see Maran and Tüür 2017 for discussion and examples).

From a semiotic perspective, the written text and the environment are tied together in multiple ways: by *representational*, *mimetic*, *complementary* and *motivational* relations (Maran and Tüür 2017). On the most basic level, the nature representation – such as, for instance, a nature essay – *represents* the environment in a certain culture-specific way and through the interpretation of a particular author. Nature writing can be *mimetic* in the sense that the structure or the narrative of the text can repeat certain environmental or physical sequences. For instance, in an animal story the sequence of the events can be determined by the actual biological life cycle or the daily activities of the animal. At the same time, the text and the environment can be in a *complementary* relationship so that the reader's experience of the text and of the environment become actualised simultaneously in the reading process, and mutually support each other. In such a case, not all the meaning relations potentially present in the environment need to be represented in the text, yet the author presumes that his/her readers are familiar with the common characteristics and properties of the environment. In the case of a complementarity relation, interpretative loops emerge between the text and the environment; the text is interpreted with reference to the environmental experience, and the environment is interpreted on the basis of textual knowledge. The environment may also inspire an author to create a specific nature representation, in which case we may talk about the *motivational relationship*; that connects back to the topic of perceptual affordances and environmental signs discussed earlier. Different meaning relations can be active at the same time; they can combine in complex ways and interact with one another – which all create a diverse and multidirectional fabric of meaning between text and environment.

Depending on the type of material we are analysing, there may not be a symmetrical relationship between the text and the environment and the inclusion of other types of theoretical models may become necessary. Especially in regard to a local and place-specific literary tradition, we might benefit from the models that defy the clear structure and limits of the text. With this aim in mind, I have recently proposed to take the metaphor of the forest as a basis of semiotic modelling (Maran 2018). In an ecological sense, the forest is characterized by the extensive presence of decomposers, detritus food changes and organic matter in different stages of decay. As a semiotic system, the forest is unlimited, decentralized, regenerative, and self-organizing. In the *forest model*, we may highlight the following characteristics of the literary object: meanings and codes as shared partially in variations; being in the forest is equal to tolerating meanings and becoming an object of meaning attribution; the basic unit of analysis in the forest is a focal point where semiotic activities and local conditions meet; in forest characters, meanings and qualities have strong ontology and history; and there is a surplus of semiotic material beyond the semiotic processes currently active. As a model, the forest is considered to be locally shaped and regulated, accidental and overwhelming, but at the same time well integrated. This type of modelling has turned out to be beneficial: for instance, in describing a place-specific nature writing of essayists Juhan Lepasaar and Edgar Kask from the Alutaguse region in Eastern Estonia whose work has a heterogeneous structure and reaches beyond the formal dichotomies of author/text, culture/nature, content/form, etc. (Maran and Tüür 2017). To sum up, there appear to be different types of text-environment relations: in some cases, distinctions and oppositions are easy to draw, whereas in other cases, text and environments are more intimately integrated. Studying the dynamics and environmental effects of these different types of texts could be one aim of an ecosemiotic framework.

4 Conclusions: Has the age of ecosemiotics come into being?

Environmental humanities and ecosemiotics have for a long time understood the necessity to overcome the cleavage between culture and nature, between cultural analysis and environmental research. Up to the present, this recognition has led to few practical outcomes, mostly because of the lack of suitable research methods and conceptual tools: hence the call to develop applied ecosemiotics with practically-oriented and robust research methods. In these pages, I have brought together and systematised a number of semiotic concepts that can be used as tools in ecosemiotic research. On a general level, we can bring forth concepts that stress the entanglements between different activity centres (ecological codes, nature-text) and those that retain and strengthen the identities of the semiotic subjects (semiocide, dissent). It is also possible to distinguish between processes that transpose meanings from one activity centre to another (biotranslation, meaning transfer), and those where one activity centre disturbs or challenges the semiotic processes in the other (dissent, replacement of 0-nature). As a combination of these different processes and concepts, the ecosemiotic research area is apparently dynamic. A task of ecosemiotics could be mapping semiotic relations in any given research object, analysing causes of instability in the system and bringing forth possibilities to overcome these.

There are apparently a number of environmental problems that would deserve semiotic attention and where semiotics could provide a new understanding in respect of the underlying causes. The present paper proposed a conceptual toolbox that can be the subject of further elaboration and testing in practical analyses. With the aid of suitable conceptual tools, we could consider developing applied ecosemiotics as a critical discipline of studying human-environment relations. Such an approach might also be able to renew the theory of general semiotics by bringing it closer to the ground, giving it more of a real-life relevance and practical applicability.

References

Bateson, Gregory. 1980 [1979]. *Mind and nature. A necessary unity*. Toronto, New York: Bantam Books.
Bateson, Gregory. 2000 [1972]. *Steps to an ecology of mind*. Chicago, London: The University of Chicago Press.
Bradbury, Jack W. & Sandra L. Vehrencamp. 2011. *Principles of animal communication*. 2nd ed. Sunderland, MA: Sinauer Associates.
Ceballos, Gerardo, Paul R. Ehrlich, Anthony D. Barnosky, Andrés García, Robert M. Pringle & Todd M. Palmer. 2015. Accelerated modern human–induced species losses: Entering the sixth mass extinction. *Science Advances* 19. Jun 2015: e1400253. DOI: 10.1126/sciadv.1400253. (accessed 15. 01.2018)
Cobley, Paul. 2016. *Cultural implications of biosemiotics*. Dordrecht: Springer.
CP = Peirce, Charles S. 1931–1958. *Collected papers of Charles Sanders Peirce, 8. Vol*, vols. 1–6, eds. Charles Hartshorne & Paul Weiss, vols. 7–8, ed. Arthur W. Burks. Cambridge, MA: Harvard University Press. [referred to as CP, followed by reference to the volume and page or pages].
Diamond, Jared. 2005. *Collapse: how societies choose to fail or survive*. New York: Viking Press.
FAO. 2016. *State of the world's forests 2016*. Forests and agriculture: land-use challenges and opportunities. Rome: FAO.
Farina, Almo. 2006. *Principles and methods in landscape ecology: towards a science of the landscape*. Dordrecht: Springer.
Farina, Almo. 2012. A biosemiotic perspective of the resource criterion: Toward a general theory of resources. *Biosemiotics* 5(1): 17–32.
Gibson, James J. 1986. *The ecological approach to visual perception*. Hillsdale: Lawrence Erlbaum.
Hansen, Anders & Robert Cox. 2015. *The Routledge handbook of environment and communication*. Abingdon: Routledge.
Hoffmeyer, Jesper. 2014. Semiotic scaffolding: A biosemiotic link between sema and soma. In Kenneth R. Cabell & Jaan Valsiner (eds.), *The catalyzing mind: Beyond models of causality*, 95–110. Dordrecht: Springer.
Hornborg, Alf. 1996. Ecology as semiotics: outlines of a contextualist paradigm for human ecology. In Philippe Descola & Gísli Pálsson (eds), *Nature and society: anthropological perspectives*. Routledge, London, pp. 45–62.

Iovino, Serenella & Serpil Oppermann. 2014. *Material ecocriticism*. Bloomington and Indianapolis: Indiana University Press.
Jablonka, Eva & Marion J. Lamb. 2005. *Evolution in four dimensions: genetic, epigenetic, behavioral, and symbolic variation in the history of life*. Cambridge, MA: A Bradford Book, The MIT Press.
Kahn, Brian. 2017. We just breached the 410 parts per million threshold. *Climate Central*. 20th April, 2017. http://www.climatecentral.org/news/we-just-breached-the-410-parts-per-million-threshold-21372 (Accessed 08. 02.2018).
Kamrowski, R.L., C. Limpus, J. Moloney & M. Hamann. 2012 Coastal light pollution and marine turtles: assessing the magnitude of the problem. *Endangered Species Research* 19: 85–98.
Kight, C. R., J. M. McNamara, D. W. Stephens & S. R. X. Dall. 2011. Communication as information use: Insights from statistical decision theory. In Ulrich E. Stegmann (ed.), *Animal communication theory: Information and influence*, 89–112. Cambridge: Cambridge University Press.
Komárek, Stanislav. 2009. *Nature and culture. The world of phenomena and the world of interpretation*. München: Lincom Europa.
Kull, Kalevi; Torop, Peeter 2000. Biotranslation: Translation between umwelten. In: Petrilli, Susan (ed.), *Tra Segni*. (= Athanor: Semiotica, Filosofia, Arte, Letteratura. Anno XI, nuova serie 3). Roma: Meltemi editore, 33–43.
Kull, Kalevi & Peeter Torop. 2003. Biotranslation: Translation between Umwelten. In Susan Petrilli (ed.), *Translation Translation*, 313–328. Amsterdam: Rodopi.
Kull, Kalevi. 1998. Semiotic ecology: different natures in the semiosphere. *Sign Systems Studies* 26. 344–371.
Kull, Kalevi. 2009. Vegetative, animal, and cultural semiosis: The semiotic threshold zones. *Cognitive Semiotics* 4. 8–27.
Kull, Kalevi. 2010. Ecosystems are made of semiosic bonds: Consortia, Umwelten, biophony and ecological codes. *Biosemiotics* 3(3). 347–357.
Lang, Alfred. 1993. Non-Cartesian artefacts in dwelling activities: steps towards a semiotic ecology. *Schweizerische Zeitschrift für Psychologie* 52(2). 138–147.
Latour, Bruno. 1993. *We have never been modern*. Cambridge, MA: Harvard University Press.
Latour, Bruno. 1997. On actor-network-theory: A few clarifications plus more than a few complications. *Soziale Welt* 47(4). 1–14.
Law, John. 2008. Actor-network theory and material semiotics. In Bryan S. Turner (ed.), *The new Blackwell companion to social theory*, 3rd ed. 141–158. Oxford: Blackwell.
Lotman, Juri. 2005. On the semiosphere. *Sign Systems Studies* 33(1). 215–239.
Low, David. 2008. Dissent and environmental communication: A semiotic approach. *Semiotica* 172. 47–64.
Mäekivi, Nelly & Timo Maran 2016. Semiotic dimensions of human attitudes towards other animals: A case of zoological gardens. *Sign Systems Studies*, 44 (1/2). 209–230.
Maran, Timo & Kadri Tüür. 2017. From birds and trees to texts: An ecosemiotic look at Estonian nature writing. In John Parham, Louise Westling (ed.), *A global history of literature and the environment*, 286–300. Cambridge: Cambridge University Press.
Maran, Timo & Kalevi Kull. 2014. Ecosemiotics: main principles and current developments. *Geografiska Annaler: Series B, Human Geography* 96(1). 41–50.
Maran, Timo 2017a. *Mimicry and meaning: Structure and semiotics of biological mimicry*. (Biosemiotics 16). Cham: Springer.

Maran, Timo. 2007. Towards an integrated methodology of ecosemiotics: The concept of nature-text. *Sign Systems Studies* 35(1/2). 269–294.
Maran, Timo. 2012. Are ecological codes archetypal structures? In Timo Maran, Kati Lindström, Riin Magnus & Morten Toennessen (eds.), *Semiotics in the wild. essays in honour of Kalevi Kull on the occasion of his 60th birthday*, 147–156. Tartu: Tartu University Press.
Maran, Timo. 2014. Biosemiotic criticism: modelling the environment in literature. *Green Letters: Studies in Ecocriticism* 18(3). 297–311.
Maran, Timo. 2015. Emergence of the "howling foxes": A semiotic analysis of initial interpretations of the golden jackal (Canis aureus) in Estonia. *Biosemiotics* 8(3). 463–482.
Maran, Timo. 2016. Semiotics and the species management discourse: the temporal dynamics of the emergence of new species. In Timo Maran, Morten Tønnessen & Silver Rattasepp (ed.). *Animal Umwelten in a Changing* World. *Zoosemiotic Perspectives* (Tartu Semiotics Library 18), 137–149. Tartu: University of Tartu Press.
Maran, Timo. 2017b. On the diversity of environmental signs: A typological approach. *Biosemiotics* 10(3). 355–368.
Maran, Timo. 2018/2019. Deep ecosemiotics: Forest as a semiotic model. *Recherches sémiotiques / Semiotic Inquiry (RS/SI)* 38/39 (1/2): 287–303.
Nöth Winfried. 2014. The life of symbols and other legisigns: More than a mere metaphor? In: Romanini Vinicius and Eliseo Fernández (eds.), *Peirce and Biosemiotics*, 171–181. Dordrecht: Springer.
Nöth, Winfried & Kalevi Kull. 2001. Introduction: Special issue on semiotics of nature. *Sign Systems Studies* 29(1): 9–11.
Nöth, Winfried. 1996. Ökosemiotik. *Zeitschrift für Semiotik* 18(1). 7–18.
Nöth, Winfried. 1998. Ecosemiotics. *Sign Systems Studies* 26. 332–343.
Nöth, Winfried. 2001. Ecosemiotics and the semiotics of nature. *Sign Systems Studies* 29(1). 71–81.
Polanyi, Michael. 1958. *Personal knowledge: towards a post-critical philosophy*. Chicago: The University of Chicago Press.
Polanyi, Michael. 1966. *The tacit dimension*. Chicago: The University of Chicago Press.
Posner, Roland. 2000. Semiotic pollution: Deliberations towards on ecology of signs. *Sign System Studies* 28: 290–308.
Puura, Ivar. 2013. Nature in our memory. *Sign Systems Studies* 41(1): 150–153.
Ripple, William J. et al. 2017. World scientists' warning to humanity: A second notice. *BioScience* 67(12): 1026–1028.
Sebeok, Thomas A. 2001. *Signs: an introduction to semiotics*. Toronto: University of Toronto Press.
Serenella, Iovino & Serpil Oppermann (eds.). 2014. *Material ecocriticism*. Bloomington: Indiana University Press.
Siewers, Alfred. 2011. Pre-modern ecosemiotics: The green world as literary ecology. In Tiina Peil (ed.), *The space of culture – the place of nature in Estonia and beyond*, 39–68. Tartu: University of Tartu Press.
Siewers, Alfred. 2014. Introduction: song, tree, and spring: environmental meaning and environmental humanities. In Alfred Siewers (ed.), *Re-imagining nature: environmental humanities and ecosemiotics*, 1–41. Bucknell: Bucknell University Press.
Spertnak, Charlene. 1997. *The resurgence of the real: Body, nature, and place in a hypermodern world*. Reading, MA: Addison-Wesley.

Stibbe, Arran. 2012. *Animals erased: Discourse, ecology, and reconnection with the natural world*. Middletown, CT: Wesleyan University Press.
Stibbe, Arran. 2015. *Ecolinguistics: language, ecology and the stories we live by*. London: Routledge.
Tønnessen, Morten. 2011. *Umwelt transition and Uexküllian phenomenology. An ecosemiotic analysis of Norwegian wolf management* (Dissertationes semioticae Universitatis Tartuensis 16). Tartu: University of Tartu Press.
Tønnessen, Morten. 2014. Umwelt trajectories. *Semiotica* 198: 159–180.
Uexküll, Jakob v. 1982. Theory of meaning. *Semiotica* 42(1): 25–82.
Wheeler, Wendy. 2006. *The whole creature. Complexity, biosemiotics and the evolution of culture*. London: Lawrence & Wishart.
Wheeler, Wendy 2016. Expecting the Earth. Life, culture, biosemiotics. London: Lawrence & Wishart.

Jacques Fontanille
The anthropological dimension of Greimas' narrative semiotics
The case of transmission and (re) transmission

Abstract: This paper explores the anthropological dimension of Greimas' semiotics, alongside the linguistic and phenomenological dimensions. This inquiry reveals the need to complement this theory with more recent theoretical insights, so to answer more comprehensively to contemporary issues. Particularly, discussions in media studies on retransmission, remediation and re-enunciation and schemas considered in recent anthropology can lend themselves to broadening the scope of Greimas' narrative semiotics. While currently trends in media studies, the former notions are traceable back to the structuralist semiotic frameworks that Greimas was also involved with. As such, here they are discussed in regard to the notion of semiotic regimes. The paper offers an encompassing model for studying human relations by enriching anthropology with narratological concepts as well as vice versa.

Keywords: Greimas, narrative, retransmission, semiotic regime, schema

1 Introduction

Greimas' semiotics was built on three main pillars: structural linguistics, phenomenology and anthropology. The actualization of the theory and semiotic method requires, thus, half a century later, an update of its relations with these three disciplines, beginning with anthropology, as it presents itself to us today. Narrative semiotics was conceived in a period (that of Lévi-Strauss structural anthropology) in which only the schema of exchange seemed to be able, on the one hand, to support social relations and to support and found collective actants, and, on the other, to explain narrative dynamics. Today, anthropology offers a greater diversity of practical schemas, and especially shows that each of them may configure a specific social bond, characteristic of a type of anthropological collective.

Jacques Fontanille, University of Limoges

https://doi.org/10.1515/9783110857801-009

Rather than drawing a general panorama of the place of anthropology in Greimas' work, I choose to devote my purpose to a particular practical scheme (one of the six schemes of relationship inventoried and systematized by contemporary anthropology), namely that of *transmission*. Particularly, in light of narrative semiotics and structural anthropology, by examining one of its fashionable forms, "**re**transmission", and more generally the "**re**mediations" and "**re**-enunciations", of which today's media specialists are fond.

Is it necessary to point out that these themes are only fashionable insofar as too often we hasten to forget the previous works about them. The topic of "remediation", for example, appears new only if one focuses on the shift from one medium to another, forgetting, for example, the founding works of Kristeva ([1969] 1980), supported by those of Bakhtin (1986), about intertextuality: no text, no semiotic-object can claim *not* to have any relation with other texts, with other semiotic-objects. Of course, something is added when one takes into account the media support of the text, since the presence of other texts in each text implies, then, more or less legible traces of the presence of other supports or a part of their properties in the current text support.

The same situation applies to the "enunciative praxis", which implies that no enunciation can claim to be the irreducible origin of an enunciate, and that any particular enunciation must be situated in a chain of enunciations referring to one another. Regardless of how the problem is approached, the same troublesome question is always raised: if there is no text without mention, quotation, reference or reference to other texts, no mediation without at least potential convocation of other prior or possible mediations, if there is no enunciation without a complex enunciative chain, then, what does the "RE" before "**re**-mediation", "**re**-enunciation" or "**re**-transmission" mean? Or, in other words, on what specific properties should the relevance of the "RE" in "**re**transmission" be founded?

One can begin by examining the most common uses of this term. It is immediately apparent that "transmitting" and "retransmitting" rarely commute, and are not at all in a succession relationship, which would allow the "RE" to be assigned a simple aspectual value of repetition. The broadcasting of a football match on television is referred to as "retransmission" (and never "transmission"), including when it is the first live broadcast, broadcasted at the same time as the match is played, on the stadium. In fact, the "re" of "**re**transmission" expresses here the fact that the match as a show refers to two types of semiotic-objects, for two types of spectators: (i) the live show for the spectators who are present in the stadium, and (ii) the video show for those who are in front of their television. In a completely different context, if I make a report, I have to "transmit it" to my supervisor. Whereas, I may "retransmit" it to another service, to other persons who were not necessarily intended as the receivers of the report.

Thus, we here arrive at the apparent paradox that what would be relevant in the "RE" of **re**transmission would not be the repetition, but the transformation, the reconfiguration, the change of media, format, receiver, point of view, mode of expression, etc. We must therefore suppose that any retransmission presupposes a semiotic mode of existence (anterior or concomitant) which must be different from that which it produces. Since the difference between *transmission* and *retransmission* is due to certain alterations and transformations, we may even imagine that retransmission implies at the limit that in certain cases what is transmitted has to be unrecognizable.

It will therefore be my working hypothesis, that it is possible to have a more anthropological than media-based examination of the question of retransmission, starting with the analysis of a small tale narrated by Lessing.

2 Transmission and inheritance of the past, retransmission and co-construction of the future

In *Nathan the Wise*, Lessing (2007 [1779]) makes Nathan tell a tale in front of his sultan, a tale entitled *The Three Rings*. A father has a ring with a power, which he transmits to one of his sons, and who will do the same in turn. It is therefore the transmission of a power associated with a ring. The central object has a semiotic constitution: an expression (the ring) and a content (a power). This transmission is submitted to a selective rule: each father must choose one of his sons. This rule is perturbed because one of the fathers, of a later generation, refuses to choose between his three sons. Instead, he makes two other rings, and transmits not one but three rings, one for each son. The problem is therefore not that of transmission, but that of its extension, which is compromised by a modification of the rule originally laid down.

The narrative of the three rings is often considered as the paragon of advocacy for tolerance because the three rings and the power transmitted are the analogues of the three monotheistic religions (Judaism, Christianity and Islam).

> A man makes a ring that arouses the love of others for the wearer. He bequeaths it to his favorite son by putting as a condition that he will have to do the same for his own favorite son. The ring is thus transmitted from father to son until the day it falls to a father who has three sons, and who is also attached to the three. He therefore makes two new rings to be made by a goldsmith, and gives one of the three rings to each of his sons, making sure that

> none of them knows who is in possession of the first one. The father dies, the three sons dispute the inheritance, each claiming to hold the original ring and its power.
>
> The situation being insoluble, the brothers ask for the arbitration of a judge. As the ring has the reputation of arousing the love of God and humans in the course of life, the judge recommends waiting to see which of the three rings will be the most effective, and thus incites the three brothers to act so that their own sons and generations to come should be as virtuous as possible, as kind as possible, in order to demonstrate that they are in possession of the true first ring. (My translation).

We can reconstruct the analogy: God loves in the same way the believers of the three monotheistic religions. While they argue and claim to hold the original truth, instead of responding to God's love for them, the fable proposes that they act as worthy beneficiaries of this love, and to become all kind and happy, generation after generation. In addition, metaphor contamination makes it possible to think of the three religions from the Middle East as "sisters", belonging to the same blood family, and called, due to the historical impasse they face, to build a new common future, regardless of their origins and filiation. In the 21st century, the problem is still not solved!

But the narrative must also present and resolve, narratively and figuratively, a deeper conflict of values. As Lessing himself explains in another book, the fable allows us to reconcile what seems irreconcilable within the limits of abstract reasoning: thus the tale facilitates the reconciliation between *reason* and *revelation*; and it allows us to think figuratively the compatibility of faith with the spirit of the "Age des Lumières". Nevertheless, these two dimensions and system of values involve very different temporal regimes: *revelation* refers to a point of origin situated in the past and legitimates a belief in the present, while *reason* contributes to the arrangement of the present with a view to an improvement in the future.

In order to do this, the narrative itself becomes the theater of an axiological transformation based on a reversal of the temporal perspective: the three sons claim an inheritance, and the judge, thanks to an astute argument, proposes them to conceive and build a new future. This reversal is precisely the one that ensures a sustainable, living and adaptive transmission, in which a possible figure of **re**transmission could be recognized: the transmission based on the claim of an inheritance was based on both the past blood links, in an exclusive filiation, and a principle of aboriginal right; the **re**transmission will be based on an emulation open to the totality of each generation, and both individual and collective fulfillment will be based on future social links and on a principle of co-construction of this future.

In other words, simple transmission is first conceived on the same principle as inheritance, from a perspective that derives its legitimacy from a direct retrospective historical filiation, from continuity between fathers and fathers of fathers, and from a never broken relationship with an origin which is buried in the past (this is what distinguishes the first ring from the other ones). When confronted with the two other rings, and faced with the impossibility of proving this relationship at the origin, the tale proposes to reverse the perspective: the proof is to be sought in the future, in what will become of the sons and of the sons of the sons. In the future it will no longer be the origin that will hold the key to the value (of love and happiness), but the merit as manifested in action and behavior. We are dealing here with *retransmission*.

In the fable, the three rings refer to the three monotheistic religions (Judaism, Christianity and Islam): the three great monotheisms would also be historically determined by the links of historical depth, with the ultimate reference to a buried and not directly verifiable origin (the true revelation). This type of transmission, on the same principle as the inheritance and the links of blood, chooses an inaccessible "key", insensitive to reason, definitely closed and intangible. It is the source of intolerance. But religious allegiances can also adopt the other perspective, that of the open future of what is properly called "retransmission".

This short apologue, even beyond the question of tolerance, involves the temporal regime and the mode of existence under which transmission operates:
- relation to an origin VS social link in perspective;
- fragile retrospective continuity VS robust prospective continuity;
- ancestralization VS co-determination;
- linear and transitive succession VS multidirectional reciprocity.

From an anthropological point of view, we can also contrast two collective "ethe" by identifying the secondary practical scheme associated with the main pattern of transmission: the first ethos is that in which transmission is based on the schema of *gift*, and the second one is based on a schema of *production* and *innovation*.

3 Transmission and narrative schemas in Greimas

This last remark calls for another: in the conversion of "transmission" into "retransmission", a transformation takes place, which was not originally foreseen and which, in particular, presupposes a substitution between practical schemas. We can examine this substitution more precisely in the very terms of Greimas's narrative syntax.

In any transmission, especially between generations, some of the actors (the "precedents") are in a position of *renunciation*, and they carry out an *attribution* for the "followers". But all the socio-anthropological studies show that, from the point of view of the followers who are the beneficiaries, transmission only works if they appropriate what is transmitted. In other words, without this *appropriation*, we are dealing only with the transmission of an inheritance, whereas with *appropriation*, it is indeed a (re) transmission. In short, there is on one side a *renunciation* and on the other side an *appropriation*. The association between these two narrative schemas was excluded by Greimas (1983: 188, 229), as not being canonical. For this reason, the link between the *schema of gift* (with *renunciation*) and that of *test* (with *appropriation*) implies a delay and an interval, a negotiation period about values, that is to say a *conversion interval* between the two types of narrative schemas.

In the case of a genuine (re) transmission, we associate two paths which are nevertheless considered as incompatible in the Greimassian deduction: a *renunciation-attribution path* and an *appropriation-dispossession path* separated by a conversion interval in which a ritual, legal or juridico-economic interaction may take place. Following Greimas, this conversion affects actantial syncretisms and narrative points of view: on the one hand, the operator is identified with the disjoint subject, while on the other hand it is identified with the conjoined subject. The shift of narrative points of view takes place precisely during the interval period of conversion or negotiation.

If we now examine the *relationship schemas* such as contemporary anthropology describes them (Descola 2005), *transmission* is treated separately from *gift* or *exchange*. Relationship schemas give form and content to the practical connection between at least two beings (me and some other) or between groups (us and them). The inventory is currently limited to six types: exchange, predation, gift, production, protection, transmission.

The typology established by Descola (2005: 456) is as follows:

Similarity relationship between equivalent terms		Connectivity relationship between non-equivalent terms	
Symmetry	*Exchange*	*Production*	Genetic connexity
Negative asymmetry	*Predation*	*Protection*	Spatial connectivity
Positive asymmetry	*Gift*	*Transmission*	Temporal connexity

The relations of the second group, to which the transmission belongs, are always unilateral and are deployed between non-equivalent actants. The transmission is above all, from an anthropological point of view, what allows the dead to take over the living: the dead are converted into ancestors who are worshipped, a way of uniting in a chain of dependence all the living devoted to ancestralization and the dead who are metaphorically alive, whose power and will are felt in all circumstances. Transmission in the anthropological meaning is therefore a very "retransmission", including a conversion-transformation interval.

A tensive structure is then possible (Fig.1). The two gradients involved are the *similarity of the ontological status* and that of the *reversibility of the narrative roles* in the relation: the first gradient goes from similarity (-) to hierarchy (+), and the second gradient goes from the simple relation of connexity (-) to reciprocal relation (+).

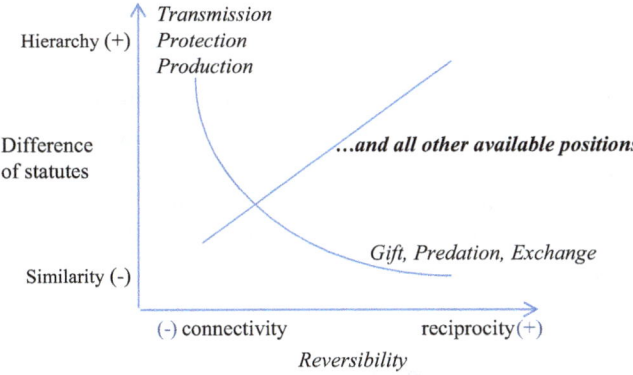

Fig. 1: Semiotic tensive structure of relationship schemas.

The tensive presentation of the typology makes it clear how we may pass, in Greimassian terms, from the *schema of gift* to the *schema of transmission*: (i) by a stronger distinction between the status of partners (on the hierarchical side) and (ii) by a decrease in the reversibility of roles (on the side of simple connexity).

Relationship schemas combine with each other, and each collective privileges one type of relationship rather than another, which gives it an identity, in the meaning of the ethos. But none of the schemas of practice governs on its own the ethos of a collective. In their combinations, each collective chooses a dominant type of relationship, which characterizes a style of manners.

The ethe of transmission are therefore diversified according to the following dominants:
a. Transmission> protection (the transmission protects)
b. Transmission> production (transmission produces specific objects)

c. Transmission> predation (transmission is an appropriation without compensation)
d. Transmission> gift (transmission is a transfer without compensation)
e. Transmission> exchange (transmission is a transfer with compensation).

So, there are instances of "inheritance" (d and e), and of (re)transmission by transformation and conversion (a, b and c).

4 Transmission between the living is a condition for the (re) transmission between the dead and the living

The review of the process should allow us to characterize the conversion or transformation that found genuine (re)transmission. What is transmitted must already be constituted between the living as transmissible; so the question is: how does living prepare them to participate in the specific mode of existence of transmission, through the manipulation of semiotic forms intended to be transmitted, and constituted for transmission?

4.1 The case of the "transmission of cultural practices" between generations

The determinants of the transmission of "taste" for cultural practices are constantly changing: changes in educational methods and processes, technological changes, changes in dominant tastes not only for each generation but for each "age of life" of each generation. In order to recognize how and to what extent a cultural taste has been transmitted, it is therefore necessary to be able to carry out all the transpositions induced by these changes in the transmission process, which also determine the referential of the observer himself.

If we take the example of taste for music, we must therefore distinguish:
- Transmission of the envy for music (appetite)
- Transmission of the hierarchy between types of music: for example, the parents taste for jazz and rock may be equated in the next generation with the taste for hard rock and electronic music.
- Transmission of practices: for example, the conversion of instrumental practice into a music programming practice with a computer.

We understand that the transformations that allow (re)transmission (instead of cultural heritage) are such that content and practices become unrecognizable. It is necessary to accomplish the effort of transformation which makes it possible to pass into the other mode of existence, that of the (re)transmission, in order to recognize that transmission has been effectively carried out. Outside that special mode of existence of transmission, it is impossible to identify the link between the anterior cultural choices and practices and the posterior ones.

4.2 An interactional and transactional conception of transmission

The traditional conception of transmission is generally based on a postulate and condition of homogeneity of norms, values and cultural referents, but it presupposes also their persistence, and so that condition is illusory: in any collective, the confrontation between several cultural systems, several systems of norms and values, and several sets of forms of living, is the general rule. (Re)transmission may only be a transaction between them.

For example, if virginity before marriage is always a principle to be respected for young girls from Maghreb, all surveys show that the meaning of virginity changes from one generation to the next:

> *Preservation of the honor of the family > respect for the moral requirements associated with faith > love relationships under the gaze of God > preservation of oneself for a future love > optimum conditions for establishing a lasting romantic relationship . . . .etc.*

In this chain of reconfigurations, the plane of expression (the observable behavior) is stable, and the plane of the content (notably the axiology) is transformed, with changing isotopies. In other words, the meaning of virginity is renegotiated in a range of transactions that allows for unbroken retransmission. During these transactions, the patterns of relationship change: one passes thus from *protection* (against *predation*) to *gift*, or even to love *exchange*. But the diffusion-conversion phase is an indispensable phase of mediation. It is now possible to propose as hypothesis the following syntagmatic sequence:

CONFIGURATION-PRODUCTION/DIFFUSION-CONVERSION/RECONFIGURATION-TRANSMISSION
/=MEDIATION/

The transactional space is that of the phase of mediation which establishes the special mode of existence where transmission is possible.

4.3 The case of cultural transmission among animals

For several decades, ethologists accumulated evidence that animal behavior is not entirely determined by their genes but also depends on their environment, including social one. Non-human animals use information by observing the behavior of others ("public information", and thus "semiotic" manifestations) in many typical situations, ranging from supply to predator avoidance to the choice of a reproduction place or partner.

For example, when choosing a sexual partner, in many species, females prefer to pair with the more colourful males. However, in experiments in which females are first shown an isolated male with all these attractive characteristics, and a duller male successfully courting a female, the other females then choose the dull male, which they have seen attracting another female. The imitation mechanism explains nothing in this case, since it is necessary to choose between several possible imitation targets. Rather, we should speak of the power of "influence" of a situation, which is based on the "public" and semiotically manifested character of behaviors, and which implies an alteration and a new mode of existence (we are no longer in the genetically programmed behavior, but in the mode of existence of the *influence*).

"Public information", manifested semioses, influences transmission then induces behaviors that differ between populations of the same species and the same field of genetic propagation. We can therefore speak of a social and cultural evolution resulting from a selection exercised on social and cultural variability. This evolution can, if it persists, influence even genetic inheritance. In this case, practical schemes are stable (survival and reproduction behaviors of the species), but their expressions change: hence the need for the mediation phase where the figures of the expression of transmission are negotiated and spread by altering within the collective.

By extrapolating to human collectives, we find the same process, a diffusion-alteration that gives rise to an *influence*, which in turn alters the generational transmission: what is "diffused" within the collective is constituted and validated, because of its persistence, as transmissible between generations; the mode of existence of the transmission is then established. The definition and limits of the collective of diffusion are therefore essential: it is shown, for example, that a given bird species, which hears the song of other species in its environment, produces a song which is inflected by the other songs heard. It has also been shown that elephants can modulate their trumpeting in an environment of tractors and farm machinery. The "collective" in question is therefore far from being limited to congeners, and concerns all beings, even technological ones!

This mediation space is properly semiotic, it is populated by semiosis, influences between semiosis, and alterations of semiosis. This amounts to distinguishing two phases in the great chain of transmission, connected by a mediation:

CONFIGURATION-PRODUCTION /DISSEMINATION/RECONFIGURATION
Mediation: Influence and alterations

To avoid the risky connotations and specificities of the notions of "souls", "spirits" and "ghosts", we could decide to call *"mode of existence of influence"* this mode of existence in which transmission operates between alive and dead, between near or far living beings, between congeners or between heterogeneous beings.

Influence is not manipulation. To use distinctions employed in the work of Landowski, the second occurs under the regime of the junction-programming, while the first occurs under the regime of interaction-adjustment. Influence is an existential alteration, which changes the mode of existence of semiosis and makes semioses fit for transmission.

5 Semiosis of transmission and their alterations

In examining the narrative junction paths proposed by Greimas, we have already identified a particular property of transmission, which consists of a change in narrative regime, operated at a delay of time when ritual, juridical, or socio-economic conversion switches the actantial syncretisms, the viewpoints and the narrative schemas:

RENUNCIATION-DISPOSSESSION {*CONVERSION INTERVAL*} APPROPRIATION-DISPOSSESSION

But this syntagmatic presentation does not account for the semiotic-objects that are involved in the transmission process, and the modes of existence of each.

5.1 Transmission and its semiosis

Transmission is initially a semiotic phenomenon because it operates on semiotic-objects, because it produces the complex semioses that are necessary for it to operate. Transmission requires mediating semiotic-objects.

In social time, this mediation proceeds by "encapsulation": enclosing (or "carring") semiotic-objects provide the conditions for efficiency for the transmission of included (or "carried") semiotic-objects: for example, the *work* can encapsulate the *text*, the *monument* can encapsulate symbols, practices and / or events, the *institution* can encapsulate works, values, forms of living, and / or a story, etc. The carring semiosis (for example: the work, the monument, the institution) are specific to the retransmission process, whereas encapsulated semiotic-objects could be transmitted only as a cultural heritage.

The syntagmatic scheme common to all (re)transmission cases would be, in the terms of the conditions of existence and transmission of semiotic-objects, a hypothetical scheme of persistence which would encounter a hiatus (eg. between generations, between beings, etc.), and which should manage or cancel this hiatus:

> *Replicate (reproduce, alter and innovate), continue (persevere & adjust)*

Most of the sequences proposed or invoked in relation to transmission in the philosophical and socio-anthropological tradition are variants of this elementary schema. Here are some of the most representative models in this literature.

5.2 The syntagmatic variants of the transmission

5.2.1 Transmission by "mass execution" from Saussure (1986) to Sperber (1996)

Following Saussure, the time of the "speaking mass" and of language evolution is unformed and massive, and the principle of the process is the *mass execution of the signs*. The condition of efficiency is the arbitrary and subconscious character of this process (the arbitrariness of the production of the sign, and the massive and unconscious character of social enunciation). This type of process and this condition of success are peculiar to both "sign" (as a type of semiosis) and linguistic value.

But it can also be considered that the "epidemiological" syntagmatic model, inspired by methodological individualism, is a naturalistic variant of the process of transmission by "mass execution". Dan Sperber proposes the following conditions:
– In order to enter the process of epidemiological transmission, the representations must become "public" and "communicated" (in Saussure's term: 'executed'), and consequently they must associate expressions with contents: they are minimal semiosis (signs, objects or practices) that are transmitted.
– After a certain time (which is a function of the number of successive generations), a certain number of replicated and transformed representations can

be concentrated around "poles of attraction". Insofar as representations are transformed to each transmission, these transformations are influenced by the attraction towards these poles.
– Transmission is ultimately explained by transformation, oriented by the relevance of what is transmitted: during replications, there are transformations, and transformations make the areas of greater relevance emerge by concentrating, the "poles of attraction", which are what persists and which enters the chain of transmission.

In the end, the transmission conceived in the perspective of an epidemic of representations takes the following form:

replication and dissemination / transformations and innovations / attraction and concentration

In this process, two points draw attention:
1) Replication induces both transformation and aggregation, the two being indissociable.
2) The process involves thus an adjustment phase, which leads to agglomeration, into wider, encompassing and coherent "signifying sets". Theses agglomerations ensure the "power to exist" of what is transmitted.

It is therefore a process that would favor the gradual integration of lower-ranked semiotic-objects (encapsulated, let us say) within the higher-order semiotic-objects: in particular, integration into forms of living.

5.2.2 The syntagmatic model of tradition (Ricoeur 1991)

According to Ricoeur, tradition can only persist in the present (1) because it selects and reactivates something of the past, and (2) because, in order to reactivate it, it alters and adapts it by re-enunciating it in the present. The central condition of tradition is therefore the periodicity of re-enunciations which guarantees the "power to exist" of contents, for the very value of tradition rests on the possibility of reconstituting a continuity and a saturation of the intermediate enunciative relays. Again, an "enclosing semiotic" ensures the "power of existence" of the included semiotic, and it is for Ricoeur inseparable from our experience of time. The syntagmatic form called *tradition* would consist of the following operations:

(1) sedimentation [(1a) replication & (1b) schematization] and (2) innovation-rewriting.

5.2.3 The syntagmatic model of gift and debt (socio-anthropology of practices)

The process of transmission can also be described as a socio-economy of gift and debt. In Mauss's conception (1923), the sequence of gift, debt and counter-gift invents and articulates social time in general: equivalence (the measure of value) between gift, debt and counter-gift is strictly a function of the time required for each stage of the sequence, and these delays of time depend both on the rules of the social group or on the whole community, on the nature of the gift, on the relations and conventions existing between the partners.

What is transmitted, in particular in the light of everyday practices and, for example, in the case of the transmission of an economic entity or a professional practice, are in particular places, roles and social statuses, places and roles to take or to keep, and in which knowledge and values circulate in time. Each of these, occupying in their turn the place and the role which have been given to them, contracts a debt which leads them to prepare in turn places and roles for the following generations.

In this type of (re)transmission, the transfer of values and roles goes through a phase of uncertainty and intermediate negotiations, on which depend both the acceptance of the gift and the debt, and the return of the counter-gift. The delay of the counter-gift is therefore also that of negotiation (acceptance and assumption of value). Negotiations necessarily relate to the value of the value (its *valency*), to the axiological conditions which frame the transmission. These conditions imply another: the semiotic relation between gift and counter-gift must itself be integrated into a more general semiosis: that of *forms of living*. In short, what is discussed during the period of the return of the counter-gift is also a transition between forms of living.

The syntagmatic form of the transmission is then:

1) gift, 2) latency and axiological negotiation, 3) counter-gift, 4) form of living transition

The latency period is, as in tradition, the critical semiotic moment of the whole process. This is particularly the time of negotiation, or even the choice of the receiver, acceptance or refusal. From the point of view of narrative regimes, this critical moment corresponds precisely to the interval of conversion between the two narrative schemas, which permits the non-canonical chaining of a renunciation into an appropriation (see above).

Finally, we propose a synthesis of transmission types (Fig. 2), which have the form of a tensive structure, one of whose gradients is the intensity of the potential semiosis of manifestation, and the other gradient is the extension of the transmission process, which can be appreciated both in time and space, and in the number of replications, transformations and re-enunciations.

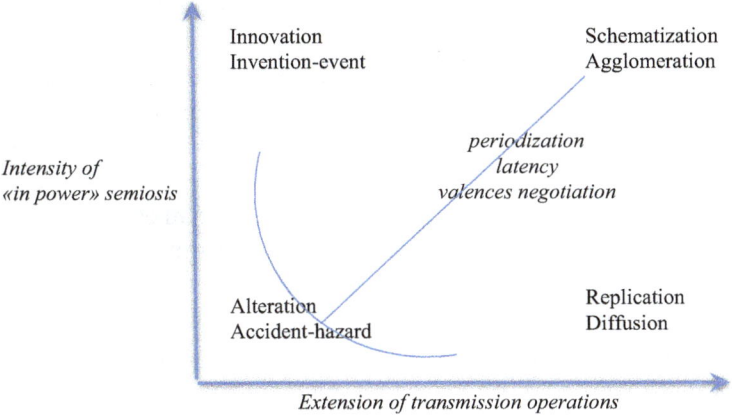

Fig. 2: Semiotic tensive structure of transmission.

6 Conclusion: The efficiency of (re)transmission

The first result of this study is of a syntagmatic and temporal nature: it is neither possible nor relevant to conceive transmission as starting from a point of origin and aiming at a final point of arrival. Transmission is not goal-oriented (it has no "purpose" or "project"). It is always carried, upstream and downstream, in a chain of transmissions. We must therefore conceive transmission on the same principle as enunciative praxis: no origin, no end, no first operation, no closing one. We always transmit *in medias res*. That is why, by principle and by definition, *every transmission is a retransmission*.

The second result concerns the specific semiotic regime of transmission. Retransmission is subject to at least one condition: the encapsulation of semiotic forms within appropriately carrying semiosis: *works* for texts and artistic productions, *institutions* for practices and rituals, *memory* for events and traumas, *narrative dramaturgy* for disasters, etc.

Works, institutions, media, dynamic objects, heritage, memory are all these specific semiosis that integrate and carry other semioses (texts, signs, objects, practices, etc.) to make them transmissible. These encapsulations provide integrated semiosis with additional robustness over time, and resistance to axiological fluctuations related to duration and long-term temporal regimes. Carrying semioses keep the carried semiotics "in power", that is to say, able of being redeployed in a new enunciation. The carrying semiosis has also the role of allowing, without loss of value and continuity, all the transformations and conversions required by (re)transmission.

Indeed, the "power" of these transmitted semiotics is directly determined by the transformative capacity of the carrying semiosis (conversion of narrative points of view, alteration of enunciative positions, modifications of supports, receivers, etc.). In short, not an ability to preserve identically (as in transmission by inheritance), but a capacity for conversion and co-construction of the future.

Finally, the question of (re)transmission extends to all conceivable stages of the semiosis, and adapts itself to all scales of analysis, from the elementary cell and living units, to individuals and generations, and to entire societies. At all scales, transmission involves two fundamental properties, *inheritance* and *variability*. At the cell level, and from a genetic point of view, *inheritance* takes the form of a material (embodied) memory, and *variability* adopts that of a replication code and possibilities of mutation. At an individual level, *inheritance* involves both cumulative learnings and genetic inscriptions, and *variability* allows testing and validation of what will remain for future generations. On the human scale, other dimensions appear, but they concern mainly the lesser or greater sophistication of syntagmatic solutions (see above) that support the process of transmission.

It is particularly noteworthy in this respect that if the encapsulation operation of a semiosis in another semiosis is relatively generalizable, even beyond the anthropomorphic sphere, the syntagmatic schemas of transmission are very specific to the latter. An examination of the different types of syntagmatic schemes shows that even the naturalistic epidemiological one proposed by Dan Sperber, whose operations of expressive publication and agglomeration of attractors might be suitable for all scales of analysis, imposes a criterion of "relevance", that is to say of *meaning*, and not just expression and signal. A fortiori, for the culturalist and / or societal transmission schemes. Whether it is called "relevance," "assumption," "assent," or "construction or reinforcement of value", this criterion of *signification*, particularly *axiological*, implies both a form of reflexivity, and a relation of exchange and/or gift/counter-gift between the poles of the transmission, a fiduciary dimension and modalizations of these two poles: in this case, transmission operates between real anthropomorphic actants.

In any dynamic and evolving collective, balances are established between the anthropological schemes of practice that are stabilized, even frozen, and at least under control, on the one hand, and, on the other hand, those that offer large latitudes of variation and innovation. In short, the distinction is between pregnant and invariant (in the background) practical schemes, actualized by default, and salient and variable (in the foreground), that may be updated at the initiative of actors and networks of actors, and can therefore be carriers of innovations. In a society like that of the first half of the previous century, where transmission processes seemed standardized, intangible and under collective control, the salient and innovative schemes of practice were those of exchange and communication. In contemporary societies, the relation has been reversed: the schemes of exchange and communication are pregnant and frozen by default in a widely shared doxa. It is the schemes of transmission that are subject to variation, which are destabilized and which give way to initiatives and innovation: local institutions such as family and school see their transmission role weakened or disrupted, while other types of institutions, more extensive and more distant, especially social networks, take over.

This study, because it focuses on the anthropological schema of human transmission practices, must therefore be understood in relation to two dimensions in which it derives most of its value: first, the one of differences in analysis scales, where human transmission must be confronted with biological transmission and animal transmission and, secondly, the one of different types of anthropological schemes of practice, where transmission must be thought through its relations, its associations and its balances with generalized exchange, gift-renunciation, predation-appropriation, production or protection.

References

Bakhtin, Mikhail Mikhailovich. 1986. *Speech Genres and Other Late Essays*. Translated by Vern W. McGee. University of Texas Press: Austin.
Descola, Philippe. 2005. *Par-delà nature et culture*. Gallimard: Paris.
Greimas, Algirdas Julien. 1983. *Du sens II, Essais sémiotiques*. Seuil: Paris.
Kristeva, Julia. 1980 [1969]. *Desire in Language: A Semiotic Approach to Literature and Art*, Blackwell: Oxford.
Lessing, Gotthold Ephraim. [1779] 2007. *Nathan Le Sage*. Flammarion: Paris.
Mauss, Marcel. 1923–1924. Essai sur le don. Forme et raison de l'échange dans les sociétés primitives. *L'Année Sociologique*, seconde série.
Ricœur, Paul. 1991. *Temps et récit*. (Temps et récit 1) *L'intrigue et le récit historique*. Points Seuils Essais, Seuil: Paris.
Saussure, Ferdinand (de). 1986. *Cours de Linguistique Générale*. Edition critique établie, introduite et commentée par Tullio de Mauro. Payot: Paris.
Saussure, Ferdinand (de). 2002. *Ecrits de linguistique générale*. Gallimard: Paris.
Sperber, Dan. 1996. *La contagion des idées. Théorie naturaliste de la culture*. Odile Jacob: Paris.

Eero Tarasti
What happens? The Zemic model in existential semiotics

Abstract: This paper offers an overview of what is called the Zemic model. As a key concept in existential semiotics, the Zemic model is explained in light of considerations in both semiotics and existential philosophy. By accounting for the transcendence of the human self as a semiotic phenomenon, this notion can be employed in the scrutiny of any human fact. As an important area of application of the Zemic model, the paper concludes with a discussion on forecasting future and emergent reality.

Keywords: Zemic model, existential semiotics, transcendence, history, future theory

1 What is the 'zemic'?

The zemic is an ontological model which portrays our being. There is no human fact that cannot be scrutinized by it. For instance, every musical utterance is a battlefield of zemic modes, where the weights and markedness values of modes alternate and oscillate, where they struggle against each other to occupy the foreground of the musical message (see Fig. 1).

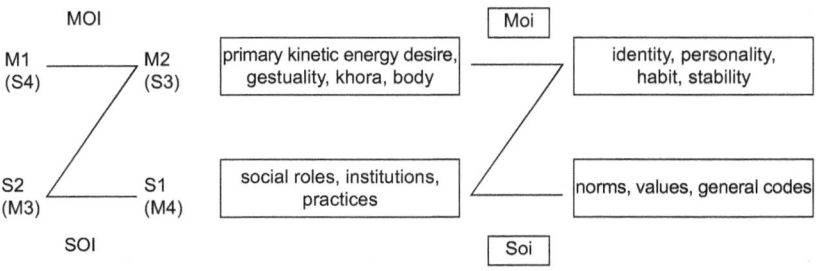

Fig. 1: The zemic model.

Eero Tarasti, University of Helsinki

https://doi.org/10.1515/9783110857801-010

Transcendence, here, concerns the fact that a considerable amount of our existence is in fact absent, should not be left out. We are ready to deny or affirm moments of our being and so to shift to a higher 'suprazemic' level, which I have also called the existential level or existential transcendence, from which the avenue is open towards the highest, radical transcendence (which I plan however to abandon in order to avoid erroneous connotations and by calling that field rather as trans-something, or trans-zemic). Yet, the essential is that the reflective level of the suprazemic is not confused with the abstract conceptual level inside the zemic, *Soi1* where values and ideas appear inside the zemic to the subject. Accordingly, the suprazemic is not any conceptualization of the zemic world, but one that contains that existential moment which is difficult to determine.

I made a list of what the existentially loaded concepts of the suprazemic could be and fell into my own trap. These concepts are: 1) Angst, Kierkegaard's *Begrebet ångest*, a central notion in existential philosophy which does not only have a psychological content as an inner quality of the zemic, for instance, as the accidental of its inner conflictual situation; 2) the theological notion of grace, which appears at this level and is also experienced psychologically in the zemic; 3) belief, about which Gabriel Marcel wrote, *as a broader principle than the Greimassian modality of croire*, which he presumed to be even more fundamental than knowing (*savoir*): "Knowledges are islands in the sea of belief". In fact the modern criticism of positivism also arrived at this concept, namely that knowledge is the same as grounded beliefs, as Karl Popper explained. The fourth concept is 4) **narration**: whether narrative phenomena are suprazemic is a difficult problem due to the category of time. When we move towards transcendence, the role of temporality diminishes: *"L'éternel est tout ce que le temps ne mord pas pas!"* claimed Marcel (Eternal is that which time does not bite). Therefore, I raise the question, how do time, place and actor change in the vertical movement towards transcendence? My answer encompasses: a) in the zemic, each put modes in their positions, places, situations, and to mind, when they adopt existence, from which they are disengaged into metazemic; b) then in the suprazemic, either time destroys or the Proustian theme appears and as in its representation in *Vanitas* paintings, for example, a place is left: *bienvenue/adieux*; c) trans-zemic: these categories do not exist any longer – except in representations like Dante or Michelangelo's resurrection frescos; 5) **organicity** – as a particular aesthetic principle since romanticism, but also in a contemporary admiration of organic life; 6) **identity,** as discussed in Hegel and Later Lévi-Strauss and Kristeva (it is: to belong to some community), 7) **hope:** Ernst Bloch wrote a series of treatises about the topics of the Principle of Hope – how this idea could now be formulated? The principle of hope means perhaps that we believe that the definite affirmation is possible in the zemic world of an experience. This idea is illustrated by, for instance, Dewey's *Art as Experience*, Eino Krohn's 'aesthetic experience' and the 'aesthetic contemporaneity' of Carl Dahlhaus; or experience in Majid Behboudi's *Experience design* project or even in products of consumption. We can experience existential fulfillment, plenitude as early as here and now, *Verweile doch du bist so schön*. Yet, at the same time, we know that this moment can be illusory, vanishing like all in the zemic, or what is present there is *meditatio mortis*, albeit death with the zemic object of our passion, art or subject is the sweet Wagnerian *sinken* . . . *schlafen*, sinking down to something more delicate, in which our zemic entity blends together with transcendence and the 'world soul' (Emerson), that is its final purpose; after such an experience, death is no longer so anguishing, frightening or bitter . . . and not even 'probable' as Marcel Proust said; or to recall what Greimas uttered in his last days: *La mort est effrayante mais mourir est délicieux* (the death is terrifying, but dying is sweet). So I think I may have solved the problem of Ernst Bloch's work which perplexed me for a long time; 8) *memory*, namely the so-called *mémoire involuntaire*, for which memory was completely existential, selecting ability, property of Bergson's *moi profond*; as early as Plato knowing was only *anamnesis* i.e. reminiscent of the world of the ideas; 9) **Sorge**, the Heideggerian principle, and, together with it, the difficult *Befindichkeit*, the general atmosphere or feeling of life, *le presque rien*, which Jankélévitch analyzed with his notion of charm; 10) **cultivation** or *Bildung* or the Greek *Paideia*, just as an internalized erudition and humanity; for instance, Stefan Zweig's *Sternstunden der Menschheit* are just existential moments on the suprazemic level which justifies their choice.

If, therefore, on the zemic level we speak about culture, the Russian theoreticians have the notion of *kulturnost* or culturality, which in Lotman means the essence of a culture, or if we have theatre, we have theatricality, if we have literature we have *literaturnost*, literariness. Yet, with *kulturnost* we have to notice that the anthropological definition of culture as whatever behaviour is not yet a notion of the suprazemic. Only culture defined as an ideal, for which we are striving, as in the Greek *Paideia* or German *Bildung*, or as in the arts education theories of John Ruskin, Konrad Lange or J. Langbehn or the J.A. Hollo i.e. when the culture is experienced as something personal, only then is it also existential and has entrance to our garden of supra-zemic entities.

However, by which method of reasoning have we found those abovementiond concepts, which I thus suggest to be examples and contents of the suprazemic? Again we have to resort to Hegelian logics. It is clear that those concepts listed above stem from the world of being i.e. modes of our zemic (M1, M2, S2, S1). But now they have been picked up from there to the higher level of essence and crystallized into concepts – whether one of those numerous modes of being is elected to represent the whole phenomenal field; or so that they are condensed or focused into one new emergent concept.

Concept is the third entity in the side of being and essence (Hegel 1969: 577). The essence is created when something is either denied or affirmed in the level of immediate being. So emerges the ground: Ground is the unity of negation and affirmation (Hegel/Snellman p. 91), Ground is a reflection which has been expressed, realized; it is reflection as an act. Essence as the ground is the affirmation of vanishing and phenomenal determinant (here: modes of being M1, M2 . . .). Ground is not outside the denied determinant, but the determinant itself is, as denied and abolished, an essence, identical with itself . . . . it is being (existence), which has become reflected in itself. The ground of the existence of some entity is the unity and mixture of all those cognitions, circumstances and states of affairs, which subordinate the existence (Snellman p. 91) – or in this case the unity and synthesis of all zemic profiles as it was stated. Therefore, the alternative of our list above no. 2, *Angst*, has its origins in the numerous situations of zemic worlds in which the *Angst* phenomenon appears by different names or instances as the boredom of an aesthetician. From them, that philosophical umbrella concept is abstracted, like Kierkegaard's *Begrebet ångest*, as the essence of all *Angst* phenomena. History as experienced: the different forms of temporality in the direct world of being, all changes, the time destroys at the end the whole zemic. This process is experienced as history by its essence, like the movement, communication in the work *The leading ideas of mankind's history* by the Finnish classic in history writing, Yrjö-Sakari Yrjö-Koskinen. Or the grace: something inexplicably positive happens in the zemic world. It is received as an act of some 'actor'. This deed objected to a man is felt as grace on the suprazemic level, but its agent disappears in the speechlessness and incomprehensibility of the trans-zemic level. It can be experienced momentarily as an announcement, epiphany.

Nevertheless, now the essential theoretical problem is: how does the movement inside the zemic happen, from one zemic to another, and particularly out of the zemic to the suprazemic? We have to return to many, quite fundamental philosophical problems.

2 Similarity and difference (likeness/unlikeness)

The zemic model is a globe in shape. This leads our thoughts to Plato's dialogue *Timaios* in which the creation of the world is described as follows:

> Now the creation took up the whole of each of the four elements; for the Creator compounded the world out of all the fire and all the water and all the air and all the earth, leaving no part of any of them nor any power of them outside. . . . And he gave the world the figure which was suitable and also natural. . . wherefore he made the world in the

> form of a globe, round as from a lathe, having its extremes in every direction equidistant from the centre, the most perfect and the most like itself of all figures, for he considered that the like is infinitely faire than the unlike (Plato 1953:719).

(Note: what if we would think that our existential primal 'globe' were just body, person praxis and value instead of water, fire etc; moreover, likeness/unlikeness = here also named as similarity/difference?). The globe was completely self-sufficient:

> it had no need of eyes when there was nothing remaining outside him to be seen; nor of ears when there was nothing to be heard; . . . nor would there be any organs by the help of which he might receive his food. . .Creator conveived that as being which was self-sufficient would be far more excellent than one which lacked anything. . ..and in the centre he put the soul, which he diffused throughout the body, making it also to be the exterior environment of it; and he made the universe a circle moving in a circle, one and solitary. Yet by reason of its excellence able to converse with itself, and needing no other friendship or acquaintance. Having these purposes in view he created the world a blessed god (Plato op. cit p. 720).

In this fragment we have already in a nutshell many questions which we now link to our zemic world. First, Plato launches categories, later crucial in Aristotle, of like/unlike, or similar/different. The globe is initially self-sufficient and it enjoys its likeness, similarity. However, then it decides to extend its similarity outside of itsel: "He set up to build the universe similar as far as it was in his power" (ibid.). According to Plato the soul consisted of three parts: same, different and being:

> the soul when touching anything which has being whether dispersed in parts or undivided is stirred through all her powers, to declare the sameness or difference of that thing and some other. . .and as this was an eternal living being, he sought to make the universe eternal, so far as might be. Now the nature of the ideal being was everlasting but to bestow this attribute in its fullness upon a creature was impossible (Plato op cit 723).

Likewise, also the time came to existence:

> He constructed then all arts of time, and the past and future created species of time; which we unconsciously but wrongly transfer to eternal being; for we say that it 'was' or 'is' or 'will be', but the truth is that 'is' alone is properly attributed to it, and that 'was' and 'will be' are only to be spoken of becoming in time, for they are motions, but that which is immovably the same for ever cannot become older or younger by time (Plato op cit 723).

In other words the old saying "All exists always" holds true.

In fact, we have already defined here the relation of zemic to its suprazemic world. What is involved is either the relation of likeness or similarity, when the zemic corresponds to the transcendental suprazemic idea of it, or then difference, unlikeness when zemic tries to adapt to the situation and change itself according to the idea of suprazemic. The bi-levelled nature of Platonian thought is revealed here as Holger Thesleff has shown – as also in our zemic model.

Yet if the zemic world is in fact complete and moves only by rolling around itself, why it starts to move towards another zemic? If we think of world creation myths of many cultures like Kalevala, we meet the story of the maiden of the air who is hovering over water but feels her life to be strange i.e. starts to miss something else. Then we come metaphorically to the basic question, *what is the origin of communication*? This can be explained by the categories of similarity and difference. The opposition seems to be that basic contrast of the universe s1 vs s2 which was later formulated in structuralism. In the dialogue *Parmenides*, Plato deals with the problem again. Socrates says there:

> Things which participate in likeness become in that degree and manner like: and so as they participate in uniqueness become in their degree unlike or again are both like and unlike in the degree into which they participate in both?. . . If a person were to show that all is one partaking of unity, and at the same time many by partaking of plurality, would that be very astonishing, when he wanted to show that I was many he would say that I have a right and a left side, and a front and a back, and an upper and a lower half, for I cannot deny that I partake of multitude (Plato *Parmenides* 1953 vol II, p. 672).

But then Parmenides asks of Socrates: "Tell me now was this your own distinction between ideas in themselves and the things which partake of them? Do you think that there is an ideal likeness apart from the likeness which we possess and of the one and many and of the other things which Zeno mentioned?" (Plato op cit 673). Yes, answered Socrates. Then Parmenides asks: " . . . and would you also make absolute ideas of the just and the beautiful and the good, and of all that class?" Socrates: yes. Parmenides: would you make an idea of man apart from us and from all other human creatures . . . " (p. 673) and later Socrates states: "Ideas are, as it were, patterns fixed in nature and other things are like them and resemblances of them". Then Parmenides questions: Is it possible that idea should not be like the copy, in so far as this has been fashioned in resemblance of the idea? That which is like, cannot be conceived of as other than the like of like." The reasoning continues and at the end Socrates remarks: "But the ideas themselves as you admit do not belong to our world and cannot belong to it." From this they infer the thought that each world stands apart. If God has the most precise knowledge his knowing does not extend to us, and nor is our knowledge any knowing of the divine. Finally, they admit that only a man provided with high gifts by nature can realize that every creature has its species and independent essence. Even more admirable is the one who can teach other to analyze them correctly. This dialogue Hegel considered the ideal example of a philosophical debate.

In fact, what is involved here is the relationship between zemic and suprazemic which has already been discussed. If the ideas of the suprazemic level are 'essences' of the zemic, they represent the unity, oneness, whereas the phenomena of zemic convey multiplicity. The content of the *Soi* of the zemic can be righteousness, whereas the corresponding notion on suprazemic level would be noble-mindedness or generosity. If the notion of zemic is beauty, it becomes on suprazemic level aesthetic experience; for instance, if S1 is the tragic, the equivalent suprazemic quality is catharsis, compassion, purification by the horrible.

Nevertheless, the question remains: why does the suprazemic serve as the model of the zemic world, its principle of similarity to which the zemic has to adjust itself? Did we not already postulate that the zemic itself is a complete globe? Is it like Juri Lotman said in his speech about cultural explosion, that two married people, who have been married all their lives, are like two balls, quite similar, and they do not have anything to say to each other any longer? The plurality, the multiplicity, originates therefore from the fact that the forces of the zemic or different subjects can be and are different. But is it so that we can basically understand only what is like or similar? Which force drives us then towards difference? Which power leads one zemic towards another zemic? Is it desire, *désir*, love, *Trieb*, but also *Sorge*, *Wille* etc.?

When a zemic wants to communicate with another zemic, how does it manage it? It first decides what is common, or like between the two, and then what is unlike. Accordingly it looks after a contact with another (on this subject the Stefanis have published a book *Il contatto*, 2005). It can happen in practice between whatsoever modes: for instance in *Moi1* as corporeal: a therapist touches the patient, a music teacher the pupil; it can occur as 'sympathy of the souls' on the level of *Moi2*, or the character: in colloquial speech one talks about personal chemistry. It can take place at the level of profession, for instance a doctor in an operation, the executor of a police event in the field, in the army; it can happen on the level of values: the participants in a convention of sectarians or a political party session where people find each other and blend into one collectivity. Some zemic inclines to have as its fellow a zemic similar to itself i.e. what is involved is the affirmation of the similarity; some want to have just a difference, a contrast, and so the zemic negates itself at the level of *Moi1*: old is searching for young, (although Hafiz said: "The youth looked at itself in the mirror and did not recognize itself. Only the second youth is a right one"); *Moi2*: the experienced looks after the inexperienced (in order to be brilliant in his eyes, to become its idol); *S2*: the unskilled to the skilful in order to learn a certain practice: master/student, pupil/mentor; and *S1*: a dissident is searching for an opponent, muslims the hindus, shias the sunnis etc. Here the idea of Lotman on culture is valid, i.e. culture which needs a non-culture in order to be built: the Greek the barbarians etc. But are there zemics who are afraid of difference? The autists? The internet addicted?

What are finally those modes contained in the zemic? In addition to the fact they stem from Hegel – which many consider doubtful – can they be approached empirically? For the first, it is clear that they have not constituted themselves by themselves inside the zemic, although according to Plato it had to be most perfect by itself in the world (see Fig. 2). They have rather merged when one zemic encounters another one or when they get in contact or communication with each other. Consequently, they are categories which by dialogue have penetrated into the zemic – or rather, in its touch with the exosemiotic world, the endosemiotic world has taken its shape. It is therefore not the case that the zemic would have grown in isolation from other zemics like *l'enfant sauvage* of Truffaut's movie, emerging as a competent cultural creature. Or like in the opera, the *Legend of Czar Saltan* by Rimsky-Korsakov: the prince is closed after his birth in a barrel with his mother and put to float in the ocean – in the hope the barrel would sink – but instead it arrives at a shore of a miraculous island and from the barrel hatches a handsome prince to perform heroic deeds. No, it is the dialogical principle portrayed by Bakhtin and its all-encompassing power which has effectuated the

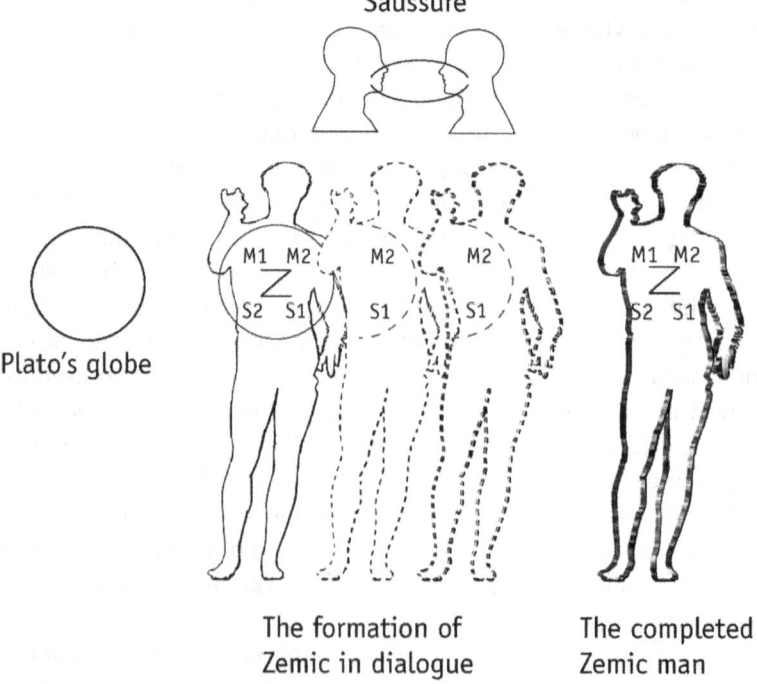

Fig. 2: The development of the zemic via three phases.

action regarding the zemic. One's own speech has adopted elements from an alien speech. The Saussurean model of a dialogue between Mr A and Mr B in *Cours de linguistique générale* is one variant of this idea. Hubert Herman's school of the dialogical self is a contemporary extension.

Also the modes are in a dialogue among themselves, accordingly; for instance, the body with a person or autocommunication among four modes. There exists, perhaps, a model of zemic thinking or reasoning. If *M1* announces that 'p', it has to be taken into account on the level of *M2*, for instance if p = hunger. Then *M2* stops all other activity, and *S2* stops his role, for instance, working, the pauses, and the values of *S1* are pushed to the background. Is the zemic reasoning or its own logics such as Peirce's abduction, deduction, induction – or exduction to use the term by a Turkish philosopher Capuano with his principle of *l'attente de l'avenir*. How far can the modes develop in their individuality and stand conflicts i.e. what is the inner tolerance of the zemic model? If the borderline is transgressed, what happens? If, for instance, *M2* is in conflict with *M1*, *S2* and *S1*, does it give up its demand to be heard and get subordinated under the power of other modes, for instance, without abandoning itself in favour of the dominant *S1*? *Vissi d'arte* principle (*Tosca*) i.e. someone lived only for his/her art or career, abandoning his private happiness: or the body is superior (passion makes one forget even the person). Is there a hierarchy of zemic modes? Is the mind of an individual or culture characterized by a certain preference, for instance is there a culture in which *M1* = 1, *S2* = 2 *S1* = 3 and *M2* = 4, in the ranking order?

How like a glimpse one zemic mode is revealed under another one. In Plutarch's biographies of illustrous men, in the chapter *Antonius* the titular subject's behaviour in a sea battle is portrayed: " . . . Antonius has take to a ship, but Cleopatra he was not allowed to meet and she could neither come to see him. When he had moved to the front Antonius remained there his head upon both hands sitting silent and alone . . . " (p. 67). Antonius is presented mostly as a chief of war, or in his role of *S2*, although he has also been described as the lover of Cleopatra as M2. But, suddenly, when he is sitting in a boat and leaning on his hands in despair, he is again *M1*. In turn, Cicero – the splendid *S2* – is described as possessed by an excessive egoism regarding *M2*, and his egocentrism spoils everything. Alcibiades is an intriguer as *S2* but as *M1* (body) and *M2* (person) he is enchanting i.e. the modes focus in them (also in the dialogues of Plato). The character of Alexander the Great as *M2* is dominated by ambition, but there is also friendship or *vouloir-conjonction*, and cruelty or *vouloir non-S2* (will to negate another). Thus we get several logical cases for how *M1*, *M2*, *S2* and *S1* behave in relations to each other:

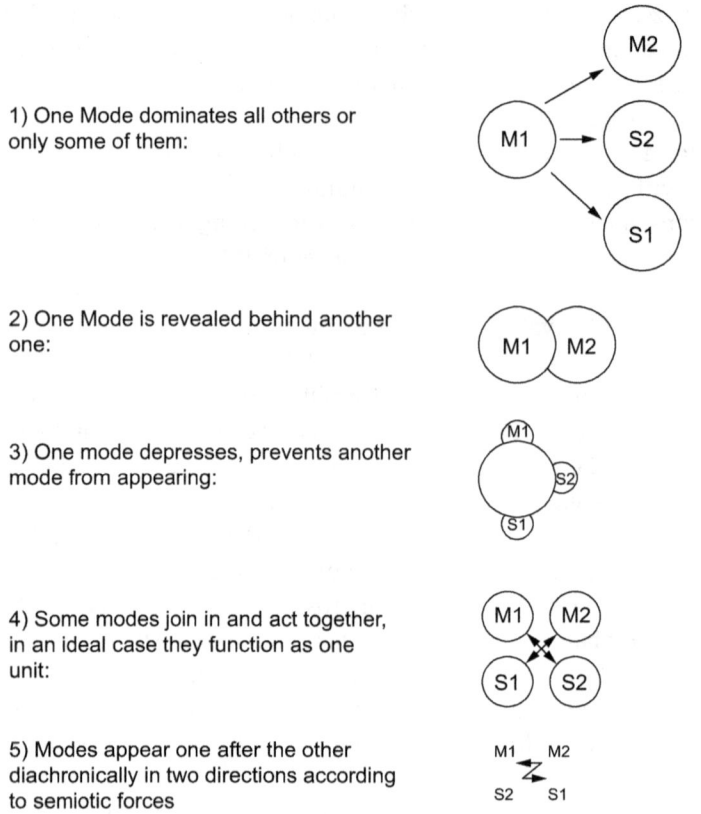

Fig. 3: Five cases of the interaction within the zemic.

Yet, what are basically those modes: body, person, praxis and values? Are they, in spite of their mobility perhaps mental dimensions of the factor analysis which is studied by Guilford in his famous work *The Nature of Human Intelligence* (I am grateful to my student Markku Sormunen for this reference)? Factor analysis has become a well-known and much used test method of psychology. Could the content of our zemic be pursued in a similar manner to such experiments? Piaget is naturally a great authority, here, to be remembered in the history of semiotics as the founder of genetic structuralism. Concerning intelligence, he distinguished three aspects: content, which means observable behaviour; function, which means vast principle of intellectual activity, which is valid for all (zemic modes?); and structure, which varies with tage and action. Yet for why would we need those factors? To explain the difference and unequalness of behaviour in a human population. Guilford mentions the idiot learning cases: one 11-years old passed some tests but failed some others. He was quite musical and recalled words and particularly numbers well. But he was lacking social consciousness and the IQ of his verbal tests was 50. One brilliant pianist mastered and remembered well huge quantities of music, his visual memory was weak and while his verbal IQ was 92, otherwise he got from his IQ domain assignments 52 (Wechsler scale).

The whole method is thus based on tests of type: which letter combination does not belong to other combinations:

PXNQ VRIM AGES GUVC

The right answer is 3 because it has two vowels whereas the others have only one. Another example: what is common to these numbers: 15,110, 85? (answer: they can all be divided by five). Furthermore. which pair of numbers does not belong to the series: a) 2–6, b) 3–9 c) 4–12 d) 6–15? (where the answer is d, because in all other pairs the second number is three times the first). Guilford thus presents the model of his SI theory (where SI means: Structure of Intelligence):

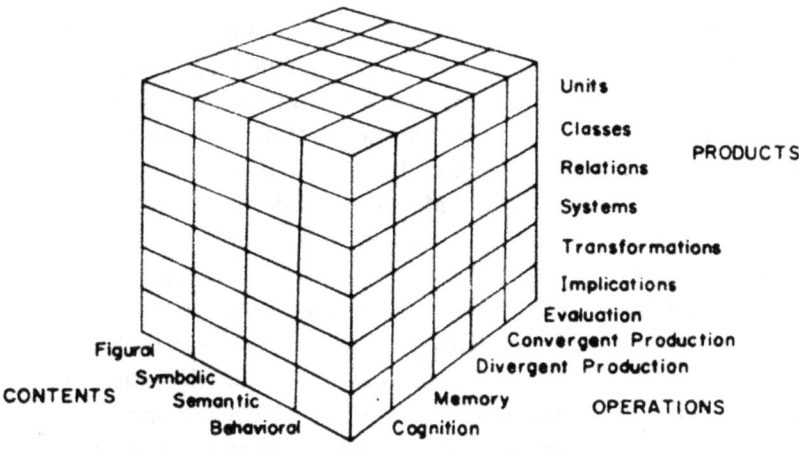

Fig. 4: Structure of human intelligence according to Guilford.

In the model, 120 cubes represents human intelligence and its various factors. Guilford admits that there can be even more abilities and, on the other hand, that some are overlapping. His three main categories portray the groups of various factors or abilities as follows. Operation represents intellectual activities or processes i.e. matters that an organism makes in order to process the information. The contents again manifest vast and substantial basic fields of information. The products constitute forms of information whereby an organism elaborates them. Markku Sormunen proposed to relate the Guilford model to the zemic model; one might ask if they have some connecting point. The epistemic start point of the Guilford model is the dissolution of human intelligence into numerous sub-capacities: there seem to be as many as the tests and one may ponder, at the end, whether factors are found by the tests or whether tests are made according to factors? The view of the human mind is really like the pile of buckshot mentioned by Bertrand Russell, i.e. a conglomeration of detached properties to which we can reduce the functions of the mind. Guilford admits to certain dangers in this method immediately when we go beyond the ordinary statistic observation. There are theoretical difficulties, he states (p. 34). Factors are individual functional structures which are in the background of certain behaviours, he presumes. Yet, it is interesting to juxtapose so different a theory of the human mind with the zemic, in order to clarify in which kind of theoretico-scientific environment this theory could be developed.

3 What Aristotle said

The metaphysics of Aristotle is the canon of Western philosophy, gaining impact via the Persian philosopher Avicenna who learned it by heart. When it is now juxtaposed with our zemic theory, one notices that it can be completely interpreted in the light of it. Yet, the central ideas of the work emerge little by little, fragment. The anthology edited by Umberto Eco and Riccardo Fedrigas *Storia della Filosofia dall'antichità al Medioevo* (Editor Laterza 2004) is here helpful. One of the central notions is Aristotle's concept of substance. How is it related to the zemic and suprazemic? In the text written by Enrico Bert about the main ideas one may find a chapter *Sostanze e accidenti*. In Aristotle's treatise, *Categories*, he distinguishes beings (*enti*) which exist as such, like a man, from beings which exist in others, for instance the colour white, and he calls the first mentioned 'substances' and the second 'accidents'. Among substances which exist in themselves, Aristotle distinguishes principles and substances, with single individuals – for instance, a certain man, like Socrates or Kallias; secondary substances are the universal predicates of a single individual, like 'man', or species which are evoked by them, like the species 'animal'. Primary substances are the precondition of the existence of all others, both secondary substances and accidentals. They do not have any contrary opposition, nor number, but they can gather around them contrary predicates (op it 137–138).

On the side of the notion of substance, Aristotle has the notion of category, which appears in accidents and in their nine species, which are quantity, quality, relation, must, whenness, maintenance, possessing, acting and suffering or being an object of action (*agire/patire*). In my own theory, the zemic world is, of course, a primary substance and its reflection in existential transcendence is suprazemic or the same as Aristotle's secondary substance. Or, in fact. even that is not enough. If Socrates is an accident or concrete primary substance or zemic, then Socrates the man is a reference to his secondary substance or suprazemic. Yet, ultimately, we had reserved our suprazemic level not so much to represent whatsever conceptual naturesthat we find in zemic in the box *Soil!*, but the concept in its existential standpoint in motion towards transcendence or from transcendence towards the zemic world. Such a third degree or ternary substance would then be, for instance, entities containing humanity, certain values, emotions, experiences. In turn, to the Aristotelian categories or principles correspond the following categories of our own zemic mode. Each category is provided with its own formal symbol in order to facilitate their use in analytic Figures and illustrations:

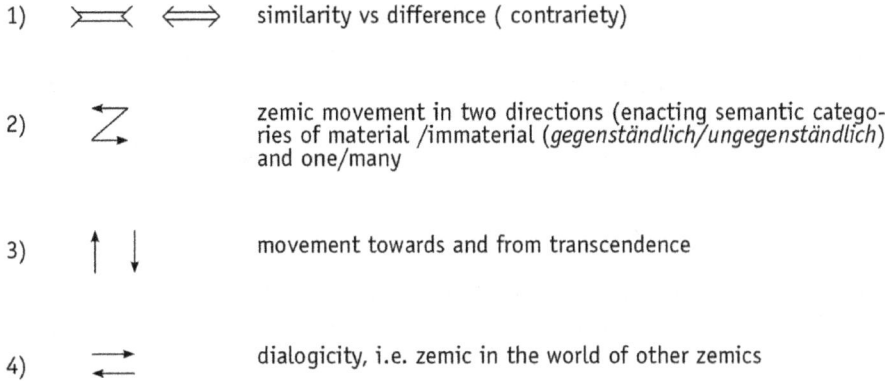

1)   similarity vs difference (contrariety)

2)   zemic movement in two directions (enacting semantic categories of material /immaterial (*gegenständlich/ungegenständlich*) and one/many

3)   movement towards and from transcendence

4)   dialogicity, i.e. zemic in the world of other zemics

Fig. 5: Inner, existential categories of the zemic model.

Furthermore, elements of which Aristotle speaks, also, are content or $M1$ = body, $M2$ = person, and $S2$ = praxis and $S1$ = values. An essential issue in his metaphysics is whether its point of departure is one or two. Aristotle adheres to the second one or the idea that reality consists of oppositions. The structuralist tradition of semiotics owes much to Aristotle for this idea, as do the bits 0/1 of the computer. He presents in his first book ten principles in a list of pairs: limit – limitless, pair- pairless, one – many, right – left, masculine –feminine, resting – moving, right – curved, light – darkness, good – bad, square-rectangular. He argues that those who presume that universe is one and that it has by its nature always one thing as its matter commit a mistake in several respects. Aristotle criticizes many theories of his time from Empedocles to the Pythagoreans who consider their principle the right one but do not explain how there can be movement if limit, limitless, paired and unpaired are the only grounds. Aristotle speaks about birth and disappearance. It is clear that the zemic world is vanishing, and so the distinction between disappearing and eternal things holds true here i.e. zemic = disappears, suprazemic = eternal. If something partakes of this double distinction it is also partaking of the eternal, but only accidentally (Aristotle, p. 27). For instance, some in their zemic reach the level of the suprazemic and at the same time are present in both levels when they reflects their being. Ideas influence the observable things, either eternal – i.e. emerging or disappearing – yet they are not the causes of their movement. In other words, the diverse movements of the zemic world are stem not from the ideas of the suprazemic, but are something else. However, on Plato's *Phaedon* Aristotle remarks: ideas exist as causes of both emergence and being. When substances are reduced to their principles we get the line and level (how close this is to the later Kandinsky's theory of point, line and level). If there are elements, only substance can have them and they appear only in substances. For Empedocles, number is the essence and substance of a thing. Here, the later important notion of essence already emerges (cf. Hegel): Hegel said in his *Logics* that the truth of Being is essence.

Moreover, Aristotle ponders the inner movement of the zemic, from our point of view (p. 33). One emerges from another: the boy becomes after his development a man; what is involved is becoming of something into something, something becoming and something becoming complete. A student is becoming erudite. In other words, a boy (*M1*) becomes a man (*M2*) and *M2*, man becomes an erudite. Yet, Aristotle understands the adherents of likedness and unlikedness, since " . . . we want to hear such things to which we are acquainted and what is different, is felt unlike, incompetent and strange due to our unfamiliarity. Therefore it is easier to understand what we have become accustomed" (p. 35). The same was later stated by Mikhail Bakhtin with his distinction of alien and native speech.

In the third book, Aristotle presents the basis of the whole of semiotics when he ponders what science has to investigate: ". . . likeness, unlikeness, similarity, difference, contrariety, primary and secondary." Does everyone have one contrary opposition? (How close this is to the semiotic square of Greimas): Are the principles of the vanishing and un-vanishing same or not? Are also the principles of the vanishing vanishing? Are principles universdl or individual things, are they actual or potential, are they this or that in other ways than regarding the movement? (p. 37). When Aristotle here speaks about potential and accidental, it can be illustrated by our model in the following:

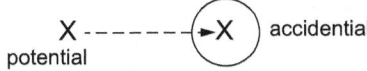

Fig. 6: Potential and accidental according to Aristotle.

Or do the vanishing laws of zemic hold also in the suprazemic?

The principle of the movement includes in our own model several movements – like Z motion; shifts to transcendence and from transcendence; the dialogical movement among different zemics. Are they all ultimately reduced to the same category of movement, one might now ask? Essence cannot be proved (op. cit. p. 40); this is a good observation: distinction is conceptual and happens in our discourse or in language. According to Aristotle, nothing is so strange than to argue that in the visible universe there were still other universes and that they were same as conceivable creatures, except that the latter were eternal, but the first mentioned vanishing. What exist are the man himself, the horse itself and health itself. Such hypotheses are eternal beings. We could interpret this so that we absolutize the properties of our zemic or accidental and call them suddenly universals. How could we then believe in that thesis? Which science could study it? Would there, for instance, be some 'mediate medicine' in addition to the one we know? In addition to the observed healthy and the healthy itself there would be still some other healthy. The solution would be that there are things between ideas and conceivable things, but not as separate from the observable things, but included in them. In other words, in our own discourse we are all altogether citizens of zemic, but on the same suprazemic level, which illuminates our whole being,

Why are some of the beings consisting of the same elements vanishing while some are eternal? Empedocles supposes that the cause of vanishing is a quarrel i.e. unlikeness and difference elevated to the level of action (p. 46. and 47). One may say that zemic is, as a particular being, vanishing (Socrates) but that its categories – S1 vs S2, Z movement, up and down, dialogicity – are not. Many think that being and substance consist of contrasts. All can be reduced to being and not-being or to one and many, for instance, the rest to one and movement to many. There are limitlessly accidental properties, so we cannot list them all. This criticism holds true directly for a science which only gathers and accumulates quantitative data, for instance, for factor analysis, called nowadays 'dataism'. The adherents of such a science reject the idea that there is something like an essential man. Aristotle also reflects upon negation and affirmation (p. 62). Reason can either deny or affirm all what is thinkable and comprehensible (p. 71).

We have to study whether the essence and everyone with such one, be same or different things. Actuality is better and more valuable than good potentiality –

that is clear to Aristotle (p. 165). "Life is the best time of man", said the world ski jump champion, Matti Nykänen (among his immortal aphorisms). All who have an ability for something also have an ability for something opposed. For instance, we can both be ill and healthy, but only actuality or health is good, not a potentiality. What is the nature of wisdom as a science dealing with principles? Is wisdom a science which deals with all substances or not? Does wisdom only deal with substance or also predicates? At least it does not deal with substance conceivable by senses, since they are susceptible of vanishing. (Eino Kaila, a Finnish philosopher, would have said: they are not invariants). One might also ask (p. 186–187) whether the science we are looking after has to deal with principles, which some call elements, since all believe they are included and active in their combinations. However, in the zemic theory, elements are contents: $M1$, $M2$ etc principles are in the structure of the zemic model as categories. Aristotle aspires in his treatise towards a solution to the problem that there is a particular substance between conceivable and concrete substances. We seem to look after some other substance; we have to note, whether there is something which can be separated in itself and not belonging to anything conceivable by sense. Aristotle confirms this. How can there be an order unless there is something eternal and keeping it separate? The problem lies in the fact (p. 189) that knowledge is knowing about universals, but substance does not belong to universals – rather it is some 'this' and exists independently. From here he can argue the principle 'thisness', *hicceitas* and *Quiddité*.

Every contrast can be reduced to primary difference, which are many, and unity or similarity and different or some other difference. In our zemic model, therefore, the contrast is individual = one and a collectivity = plurality, and, on the other hand, materiality = vanishing and immateriality = eternal. Aristotle climaxes the discussion of substance in his XII book to the consideration of conditions: if the universe is some whole and substance is its first part (zemic), and if it is unified on the basis of its consecutive order. Substances are perceivable or zemics and vanishing, but the other species is un- vanishing, or at the level of the suprazemic. The perceivable substance is changeable: body transforms into person etc. There are four kinds of changes: the ones of essence, quality, quantity and place, the change regarding 'this' is birth or disappearance (therefore in relation to potential suprazemic), change in quantity is growth or diminishing i.e. + or -. The change of quality is that a property becomes something other and, regarding the place, the movement. Yet, all changes are changes into contrary oppositions – a semiotician might judge with relief.

4 The concepts of the zemic

Now it is proper to analyze conceptually what happens in the reality around the zemic, namely on the level of suprazemic and in relation to their representations of the zemic. Thus we encounter three different zemic worlds. If we observe merely the role of concepts in them or the mode of *S1* we notice the following: in the zemic world *S1* represents primary notions like worry, beauty, goodness, justice. When the zemic is represented in a discourse, in a text, *S1* appears also as a concrete object or text although it represents something abstract: for instance social care, *schöne Seele* (Goethe), mountain sermon and a law book. But then there is the level of our zemic reflection which represents existentiality; it is the essence or Hegel's *Wesen*, it represents concepts as experienced entities *als Erfahrung* and *Ich-bezogen*, in relation to the I. Yet this *Ich-Bezogenheit* is also negation of the *Ich-Ton* of the zemic, and its identity, for instance, a worry transforms into the helpful love of the neighbour, philanthropy, beauty into aesthetic experience, goodness into solidarity, inner obligation.

However, how should we characterize the representations of the zemic? Sig-zemic? Sign-zemic? Zemic-Sign? What is the difference if 1) zemic S1 appears directly as suprazemic S1, therefore without the mediation of signs or re-presentation? 2) if zemic S1 appears only mediated by the representation i.e. via re-zemic S1 on the suprazemic level? Does it entail mediation offered by culture i.e. that phase in which all, the whole mind (body, person, praxis and value) becomes something cultural? In music this is understandable (see Fig. 7). For instance, Lang Lang, the Chinese pianist shifts directly from the zemic to

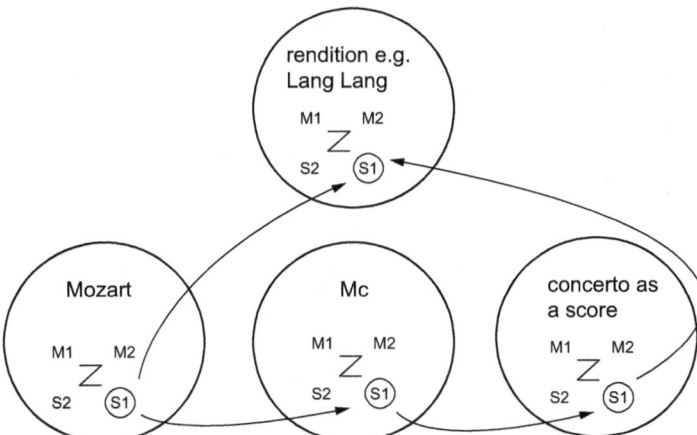

Fig. 7: Interpretation of music via the zemic.

suprazemic without the re-zemic level of European culture and its understanding. Chinese people are able, with their musicality, to infer the suprazemic S1 of music, for instance, the inner experienced aesthetics of Mozart. But does this still take place via a re-zemic?

We might illustrate this by another scheme: there the empirical world consists of two zemic fields; the primary zemic is the same as our *Dasein* (see our first models of existential semiotics, Tarasti 2000: 10); it can be called the in-Zemic, or endo-Zemic world. It signifies, announces, conveys itself as a secondary zemic world which could be called sign-zemic, out-Zemic, exo-Zemic or meta-Zemic. These two form together the empirical world (Fig. 8). For instance the metaphors used in the empirical zemics in the manner of Lakoff's *Metaphors We live By* (Lakoff 1980) are not those metaphors whereby we deal, for instance, with transcendence.

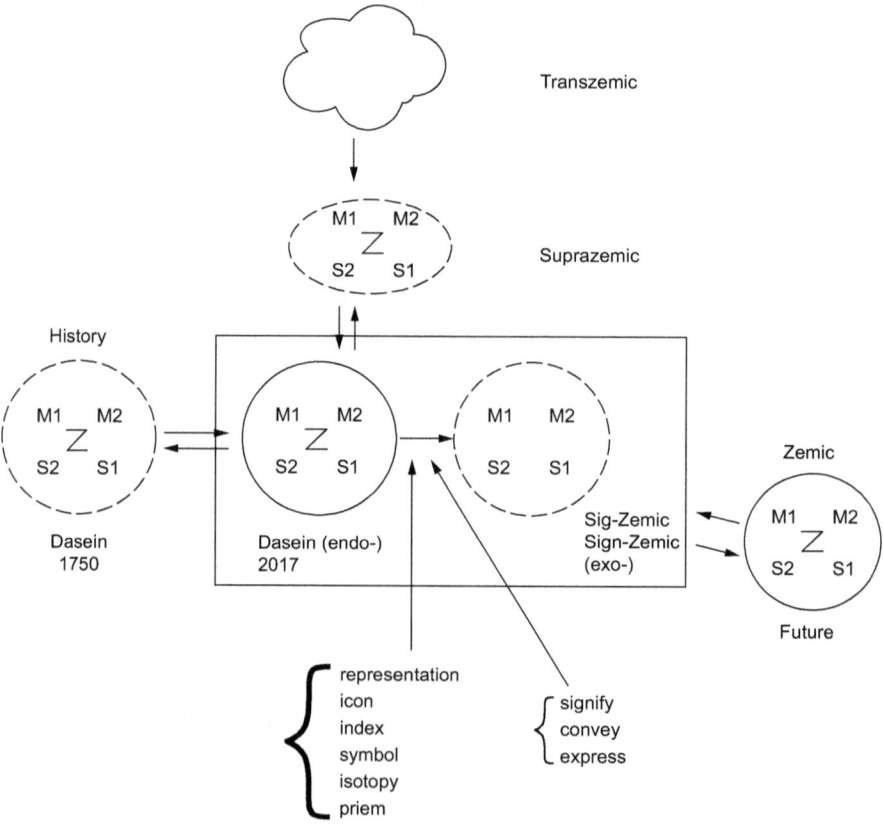

Fig. 8: The whole structure of horizontal and vertical zemic.

This evokes the following questions: 1) can the endo-zemic world be mirrored in the suprazemic (as a Hegelian reflection) without the mediating level of the exo-zemic? If it can, then what kind of transformation takes place therein? 2) or shall we attain the suprazemic only via the exo-zemic? Then, in fact, the model is *mirabile dictu* the same as Peirce's triadic model: object = *Dasein*, representamen = exozemic and interpetant = suprazemic. Yet, here one has to note that the interpetant already contains a seed of existentiality, since behind it looms an interpretant of the higher level or of even the highest or radical transcendence; 3) we can ask: if inside the zemic the modes M1, M2 etc. are perpetually fighting with each other, do we find their reconciliation at the level of exo-zemic already? For instance, writing, composing, painting, performing, acting are exozemic activities whereby we clarify problems of endozemic also psychoanalytically. Young boys lack words to express their emotions, or they are not able to use the verbal channel for their self-expression. Behind the suprazemic is concealed the idea of transcendence, of course, without which this concept cannot be properly understood. In thinking or in semiosis there are, from its point of view, two directions:

> arrow up= transcending starting from the empirical *Dasein*, zemic: our speech gradually becomes metaphorical when we approach this highest level
> arrow down= transcendence which is first encountered as an announcement; for instance, a prophet announces the message of God or Delfi's oracle tells her forecast and, second, it appears in the level of zemic. What is involved is an annunciation which appears in the arts by so many means, not the least in Italian painting, Even the light can get this symbolic epiphanic assignment e.g. in Caravaggio's paintings.

All this looks different depending on which direction our thoughts go. From the latter point of view *Dasein* is mere *Schein*, appearance; but in which sense? Case 1: it is only the end station of transcendence, a metaphor, an unreal, pale, faded reflection. Case 2: the zemic world is so incomplete or so overwhelmingly rich – in which case Greimas's aspectual seme of excessivity is dominant – that we search for another level. We escape from the zemic and construct metalevels of being, as in *Livets stadier* by Kierkeegaard – either organically or by a leap. Yet what is the suprazemic level after all? How could we portray it? Are our aesthetic categories tragical, comical, gracious, dignified, appropriate? Is it the same as metamodalities? Accordingly the zemic world consists of modal situations, but how are they reflected? What is involved is a Hegelian reflection. If, on the zemic level, S1 is justice as a concept, value in the suprazemic appears as noble-mindedness, generosity. If, on the zemic level, we have the category of the tragic, it manifests in the suprazemic as compassion, *Mitleid*, catharsis. So we are again searching for help from Hegel.

5 Hegel's logics

Hegel argues: "Being is immediate. Since knowing wants to clear the truth about what is being as such and for itself, it does not stop, but penetrates through it assuming that behind this being there is still something else than being and that that background constitutes the truth of being" (English translation by the author). As such, this reminds us of Plato and Aristotle's substance; but Hegel continues: "This recognition is mediate knowledge; because it lies not directly in the essence but begins from something else, being, and it has to pass the preceding way leading outside of being or rather the way leaving inside it. Only because the knowledge remembers the immediate being thanks to this mediation it finds the essence." This corresponds to the idea of my earlier existential mode, namely that the subject leaves *Dasein* or transcends and is so shifted outside the zemic as to observe it or to reflect upon it. Later reflection receives from Hegel a more precise meaning. "Language has in the tempus of being preserved the essence as having been in the time, *Wesen = gewesen*, since essence is past but being passed atemporally." Consequently, essence emerges closely from the being itself. On the other hand, to speak about passing away is a reference to the *Phenomenology of spirit*, the prelude to the Science of Logics, in which the absolute is reached only at the end, after all errors. According to Hegel, being remembers its earlier phases and thus becomes essence.

If the absolute was defined first as being, it is now defined as essence. The recognition cannot exclude multiple existences (i.e. the modes of zemic like M1, M2 etc) nor being i.e. pure being; it pushes the reflection, when this pure being presupposes the negation of all limitations, the reminsicence and movement that has purified the immediate being into pure being of the existence. So, here, the negation enters (and affirmation) as existential act whereby our subject is shifted to the level of essence i.e. from the zemic world to the suprazemic. "Being is determined as essence in which all definite and limited being has been negated" – in other words ' definite' means a certain quality of M1, M2 S2 and S1 which rules over everything as their profile, the empirical reality formed by those modes with their emphases. The predicates of the zemic are to the essence a mere external issue. Hegel defines pure essence as a combination of all realities: " . . . Essence is therefore only a product or something done. The external denial which is abstraction lifts away the definition of being from it . . . Essence is therefore not in itself nor for itself, but it is via something else, via external abstracting reflexion, it is for something else." If what is involved is an act of transcending, Hegel states that it is a fully constructed, creation of our subject, no metaphor descending from above. So his view on transcending in the existential sense resorts to our real existence. Hegel does not speak about the question of whose negation and construction we are dealing with i.e. who is the agent here.

However, Hegel says that essence is what it is only thanks to the endless movement of being It is essential being-for-oneself, it is just this negativity. Essence and a complete return to oneself is thus nearest to an essence without a definition. In other words, Hegel claims that it belongs to the movement of the essence that it returns to the being, but now it carries along or remembers the negation it effected. What is involved is an oscillation movement between zemic and suprazemic in our theory. If someone does something correct in the zemic, then by negating this act or rather by affirming it, s/he discovers the essence of justice in the suprazemic. After this realization, s/he returns, changed, to the zemic. It would fit better with negation that our subject be chained in the zemic to certain circumstances, to the dictatorship of conditions as v. Wright once said. But /she now denies them and finds the idea of freedom. Thereafter, when s/he returns to his zemic, s/he acts differently, s/he strives for liberation and sets up, for instance, as a rebel. The everyday life of the human is austere. Yet, the human can find joy, *Freude*, as in Schiller's ode, and when s/he returns, *feuerbetrunken* into his world, s/he encounters there the idea of the fraternity of humankind (Schiller's ode has been sung with the word *Freiheit* which fits here too).

Hegel argues that the predicates of the essence are different from being. We have to speak about them in a different way, to elaborate for them their own metalanguage. Essence, then, is reflected back to being. Essence is between being and concept and constitutes their middle; its movement serves as a shift from being to concept; and, again, the concepts had their place in the framework of the zemic in the category S1, in which values and norms were dwelling. Essence in all its simplicity does not have an existence. But it has to become existence. It is pushing away oneself from itself, a negative attitude to oneself; it therefore sets itself against itself. So this definition is different than in the sphere of being; in other words, in the zemic: the determinants and articulation of the zemic are valid by themselves, self-sufficiently (or via dialogue, when another zemic intervenes with them!), but the predicates of essence live their own lives and want to return to *Dasein* or the zemic world. Hegel had the same idea as early as the *Phenomenology of Spirit*, in which there was the paradoxical thesis that the absolute spirit in order to become absolute had to pass through a long path of mistakes and shortcomings whose end result only was the absolute. Russell said, ironically, about Hegel's absolute:

> Hegel supposed the universe was a concise and coherent unity. . . . his universe was like pudding, if you touched any part of it it started to vibrate. . . . To his mind the idea that the universe consisted of parts was erroneous; the only reality was Absolute and this was

> the name he had given to the God. Hegel's philosophy satisfied me for a while. When its adherents especially McTaggart introduced it to me, he who was my close friend, it seemed to me both charming and tenable (Russell op cit p. 25).

Moreover Hegel focuses then this crucial movement between essence and being:

Essence first appears in itself or as *Schein* or it is a reflection; second, it manifests, *erscheint* and third, it *offenbart sich*. It puts itself into the following predicates:
1. as a simple essence, being in-oneself when it defines itself outside it
2. as stepping into existence according to its existence and appearance
3. as essence which is one with its appearance or as a reality

In the continuation, Hegel states that the essence is refuted being, it is negation of the sphere of being. Therefore, in Hegel, being and essence relate to each other as an other. They both *are* immediately but indifferently to each other. Furthermore, he ponders the appearance which characterizes being before that visit to essence. Being is not-being in the essence, its not-being as such is the negative nature of the essence i.e. essence tells *how the world should be* but, when it is unfortunately *not* that, then being is felt as not-being, emptiness or appearance. This not-being and its inherent negativity are moments of appearance and thus moments of the essence itself.

In the sphere of being there emerges against the mediation the not-being and their truth is becoming. The unessential and apparent live in the sphere of being as residues of being (cf. the facts or 'data' of the empirical world of the zemic). This causes a reflection which is movement of becoming and transferring. Now we get to the core of the problem: how the shift of our subject from the zemic world to the suprazemic level takes place. Nevertheless, Hegel says cryptically that becoming in the essence, its reflective movement, is therefore a movement from nothingness to nothingness and back to itself. The shift or transfer is refuted in its transfer.

Being exists only in the movement of nothingness to nothingness. What does this mean? Hegel answers that it is the same as essence. Essence represents pure negativity which has nothing outside it – just like the primal globe of Plato's *Timaios*: what it could deny but only denies its own negativity. Such a negative change with itself is, for Hegel, the reflection of the absolute. On the other hand, Hegel rejects any psychologising interpretation of his theory. Reflection is understood in general in a subjective sense as a movement of judgement; but what is involved is that its essential predicates are absolutely free and indifferent to each other.

At the end he remarks that reflection is a determined reflection, accordingly essence is definite essence or it is essence which exists as *Wesenheit*. Reflection is the appearance of essence for itself. Yet, this is the nearest Hegel gets in his reflective predicates to the general laws of thought, such as the aforementioned categories of the zemic model i.e logical relation and movement. In turn Hegel suggest that the latter still need a subject for their relationship and this subject is: All or A, which means both everything and every being. Identity is simple immediateness as a refuted immediateness, its negativity is its being. Essence is therefore simple identity with itself. Probably this is enough to show how Hegel's text becomes comprehensible in a new context; it is 'recontextualized' in the framework of existential semiotics. Above, we spoke about errors which the subject experiences or makes on its way to the absolute – in other words, in its relation to its immediate being, the subject recognizes only zemic signs like itself, and correspondingly sees only them in the suprazemic as well. Yet, mistakes are always possible. Something can happen in the circular movement from the immediate zemic being in negation and shift to the level of essences and, from there, back again when one is reflecting the zemic world in the light of notions discovered in the suprazemic. What Jankélévitch called *méconnaissance*, or misunderstanding can. Jankélévith distinguished two species of knowledge: *savoir* and *connaissance*. The Lithuanian-Finnish philosopher Wilhelm Seseman had *wissen* and *kennen*. First, one is close to the suprazemic i.e. knowledge based upon experience. Yet, let us think of the basic situation of our individual – or organism following Uexküll, in its relation to its *Umwelt*. That organism communicates with the surrounding reality, the immediate Other, either by a *Merken* relationship in which it chooses which signs it accepts from the *Umwelt* according to its *Ich-Ton* and, on the other hand, it reacts after this choice, back with its *Wirken* connection. What does it mean to say 'chooses'? Is it deliberate or determined, or reflected or immediate i.e existential or mechanic? The human distinguishes her/himself in that sense from other creatures in that the relationship is noematic. There are many options for errors: one theory of illness is that the subject (organism, *Moi1*) wrongly interprets alien signs and signals as its own and allows them into itself, the organism. Thus the viruses intrude into bodies and cause illnesses. However, at the level of human action subject can interpret signs incorrectly like a protagonist in an ancient tragedy, who understands wrongly the prophecies of the Delfic oracle (Oedipus, Xerxes), since signs can have many interpretations, polysemic, polygenetic (as in the case of Shostakovitch) or the modes of the zemic or elements appear as blended – a struggle goes on inside them concerning what is *marqué* and what is *non-marqué*.

Nevertheless, if we think of what happens inside an organism, reflection on signs on the suprazemic level essential. The worst confusion is caused by the fact that *Wesen* of the suprazemic is mixed with the *Soi* of the zemic (values in *Dasein*). Also *Soi* is abstract – it is only just intelligible, but it is different by its nature. Then there is *méconnaissance*. For instance, some artistic phenomenon is defined as something following the prevailing values of the *Dasein* – 'this is minimalism', 'this is socialist realism' – but the object at the end is not that, but something quite different. Rachmaninov's work is taken as mere entertainment, although it is not that. A musical work can be interpreted as a series of errors programmed by the composer from which we learn the becoming of the work, otherwise the work could not continue. In fact, errors carry music ahead (like the human zemic world as well), since they demand to be corrected. For instance, at the beginning of Mozart's E flat major piano concerto KV 482 – which Panu Heimonen is studying in his doctoral thesis – the D becomes D flat and brings the harmony forth. The same is done by J.S. Bach in his E flat major prelude (The Well-tempered Cl I).

Arnold Schoenberg once said that every tone which is heard after the first one waives the balance of the work, which has to be returned. Paolo Rosato (2013) had a similar idea of the homeostasis of a work. J.S. Bach often modulates via the lowered seventh degree. The turn of the six-four chord of E flat major at the beginning of Beethoven's *Eroica*, E flat – D- C sharp is a radical 'mistake' – but from it started the 'modern' in music as Richard Wagner said. What causes the error? The fact that the Me (*Ich*) of the subject or his zemic profile or *Ur-zemic* favours signs which are like it, similar, identical and not different. Difference is one of the four existential narratives of the zemic: 1) same/different, 2) Z, 3) up/down and 4) dialogicity; Hegel's essence follows these four narratives. Why does the subject make a negation and do something different, as with our composers (above) employing the alien note intruding into the 'normal' or the same in discourse? Because they are unsatisfied; they are driven by a desire to do something of which they do not know even themselves, why. It is the Proppian initial lack, Sartre's *manque*, Greimas' *imperfection*, Plato's longing for a perfect form, a globe. In fact, the zemic 'globe' is already a kind of magical 'globe' or circle which is characteristic also to the play (*Spiel, jeu*) as Mattia Thibault (2017) has shown. In any case, in music we again find illustration for such narrative forces.

In Mozart, the music often falls into sequences which cannot be omitted (e.g. in the C major concerto KV 462, see Fig. 9). In the above mentioned E flat major concerto, the scales continue and continue. Even its beginning is typical regarding our 'error' theory: the first bar is a march – but what is march? It is *Moi1* i.e. corporeal, or it sets us to motion; but at the same time it is a topos of 18th century music or praxis i.e. *Soi2*. And these zemic modes are heard superimposed. Now we would expect the same to be repeated, but no: instead, we hear a sequence again descending or katabasis i.e. a rhetorical figure, but simultaneously there is another topos of *gebundene Stil* in the suspended notes.

What happens? The Zemic model in existential semiotics — 193

Fig. 9: The function of the lowered seventh at a) J.S. Bach and b) Mozart E flat major concerto kV 482, opening bars.

And the playful rhythm in bass puts all in the aesthetic *Soi1* mood of a ludological nature, emphasizing the playfulness. Therefore, what is involved is a linear surprise but also vertical because *Soi2* is connected to play, which is not only aesthetics but a physical activity of *Moi1* and a personal choice of *Moi2*. So the composer creates narrativity by similarity and difference. In any case, in music, the original practices of *Dasein* are resemantized and recontextualised; the horn calls do not function any longer as signals of hunting but as signs of pastorality and sometimes of romantic longing as in *Les Adieux* sonata by Beethoven or in the waltz of the *Rosenkavalier* by Richard Strauss.

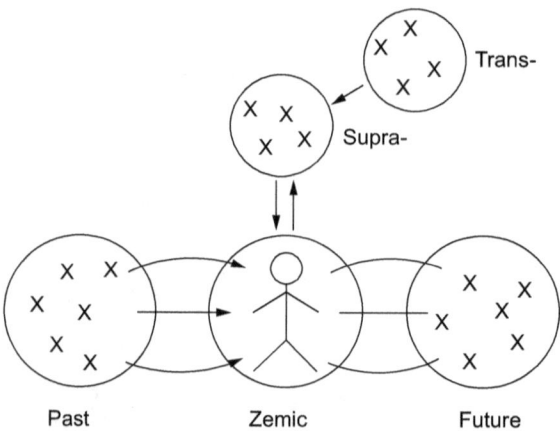

Fig. 10: History and future in their existentiality.

Let us take one step forwards to ponder how our zemic world expands and focus on when we project it in the time line to the past and future (see Fig. 10, above). Does it strengthen its own substance or try, contrarily, to extend in all directions – and, consequently, also towards transcendence? The explorer would thus always discover only his own world, whether we call it American Indians or the Polynesian aboriginals – they are, for her/him, only negations of his/her zemic, not really autonomous substances. Hence our subject is in the centre of being. For them, signs inundate from four directions: form, the now moment, past, future – and transcendence. They are at first mere data for the subject; yet s/he has a preunderstanding, *Vorverständnis*, of what they are. S/hee recognizes in them at least four species: *M1, M2, S2* and *S1*. S/he articulates the *Dasein* or immediate *Umwelt* with them (see Fig. 11). *Dasein*, in turn, consists of act-signs, pre-signs and post-signs. By these categories, our subject can orient her/himself in **what happens** around her/him and inside her/him.

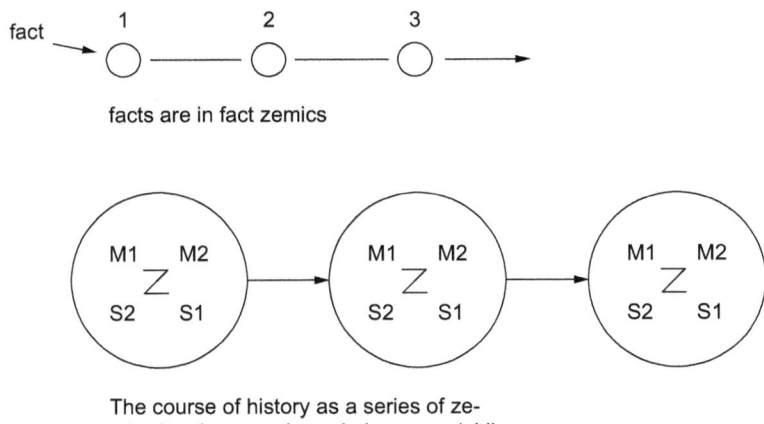

Fig. 11: The zemic, *Umwelt* and history.

Errors emerge due to our passion for likeness or similarity. We suppose that the past world was the same as our zemic world; we presume that the future is the same as present; and we postulate that the zemic stays the same (although we all the time move inside the zemic in two directions). Horisontal narratives are the same, i.e. universals, but they are emphasized, or modalized in diverse manners, in different moments, during the life of a subject (individual or collectivity). Between them can occur conflicts. Can the suprazemic world be *Schein* or illusion or *méconnaissance* or lie? And does the same apply to the transzemic world? What is involved is Peirce's fallibilism or the Hegelian spirit, which is the history of its errors as stated earlier. We speak about the eternal return of history, which is the same as the dominance of the existential narratives and their projection to a disengaged time and place: " . . . such was life in ancient Rome", " . . . Pompeii's last days" (Bulwer-Lytton), etc.

Signs sent by the *Umwelt* make up the world, interpretation and sense. As far as they come from the past, the subject picks up the data and events corresponding to their modes. Insofar as they come from the future, the subject classifies them according to the zemic. What are involved are three taxonomies: now, past and future. But then the subject discovers the inner narratives or movements like/unlike, Z, up/down and dialogicity. They are existential narratives. What is their relationship to the subject and *Umwelt*, to their time, place and subject? This is at the same time a disengagement or shifting away from the centre of the moment now. Narrative starts with a lack or Hegelian negation, the immediacy (Firstness) of being changes into mediated when its *Wesen* is reached. *Wesen* follows those four narratives, or essence appears both vertically and horizontally. Why does a subject make a negation? Because it is unsatisfied; it is driven, but a force to something of which it does not know even itself.

In the centre there are two 'zemics': the *Dasein* or the zemic of the act-signs – and the representation in signs: 'sig-zemic': the empirical focus of our study, something which we obviously cannot doubt, but which we can verify anytime and to anyone. Yet, Gabriel Marcel remarks (1927: 118) that I cannot define myself as a centre afterwards, after my experience . . . I transcend all possible explanation of my own reality. However, everyone can imagine oneself as an object of an ideal historian. If it is so, then it is as possible that this historian can be myself. As Lévi-Strauss once argued, if the human spirit appears in everything it can also appear via myself and via my discourse. Yet, Marcel does not believe in this, albeit he is an existentialist; he says "*Je ne puis pas être mon proper historien*". I cannot be my own historian. But if one would believe in this, no one could for instance write his memories.

Our *Dasein* also consists of its representations as texts, signs, discourses. In this relationship of primary and secondary zemic, also traditional semiotics remains valid: what is involved is the relation between *Zemic1* or object and its representamen *Zemic2* which can be iconic, indexical, symbolic, semic, pre-act- quasi, endo- or exo- signing, or what one might portray by the terms: signify, convey and express. But over this 'box' rises the world of the suprazemic and the Essence, *Wesen* by Hegel or substance by Aristotle. If one wants to be Peircean, one might say that this suprazemic level functions as an interpretant to the two zemics preceding it. Above, it raises still the third trans-zemic world, of which we cannot say anything in this connection. In the linear sense the central zemic box is framed by the supposed zemic world of the History, and likewise the presumed zemic field of the future. To which extent they are zemic is thus an hypothesis,

Let us look at the past. History can be, accordingly, experienced as a series of zemic situations – a kind of chain of them:

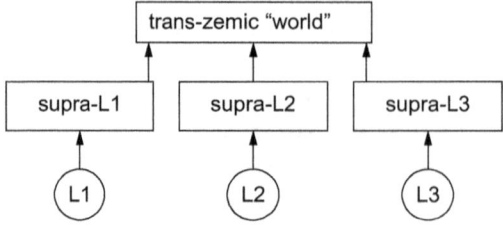

Fig. 12: The chain of history.

When one shifts from one constellation to another, every mode gets old or changes: body, person, praxis or values. From this point of view, there are no 'facts' in the proper sense, but only a quantity of zemics. The Finnish historian Pentti Renvall states poignantly in his treatise *Contemporary Historic Research* (*Nykyajan historiantutkimus,* 1965: 99)

> Every assumption made by a historian, every conclusion to which he arrives, is based upon a gamut of general conceptions of man's common ways of thought, emotional and behavioural manners or of those characteristic answers man gives to impulses, whether they stem from the surrounding nature or from people living around him. He considers plausible only such issues which he judges to be possible for a man, all other things he abandons as an error or misconception. Therefore, both what he considers factual and the interpretation he gives to these facts, is compleletly depending on what he thinks the human nature is and its possibilities. Accordingly, we notice that the view on human nature forms the basic foundation without which no special branch of history can work.

If, therefore, our view of human nature is that it is a kind of zemic world where one necessarily needs those four modes of being, we are certainly entitled to apply it to history. Yet, this will not eliminate the problem that what we in fact are doing here is projecting our own *similarity* onto something different; or then we cannot perhaps get closer to *wie es eigentlich gewesen ist*. Yet, the word *eigentlich* is ambiguous: we can just think that our interpretation of the world is it 'actually' and nothing else. Renvall is conscious of the danger that a historian generalizes his own way of conceiving to concern also other people and times (op. cit. 96). *Je projette*, I project, says Marcel – and this is likewise true for the past as well as the future (Marcel 1927: 151).

Nevertheless, one supposes that a historiographer does not start writing history taking into account only her/his own community. For instance, let us take such a topic as the winter war in 1939 in the history of Finland. Finland has its own narrative about it -the heroic zemic world in which all its modes were mobilized in order to defend the S1 values of Finnish society. On the other side of the borderline it was looked at differently. In one Soviet movie, the break of the war was portrayed as the result of provocation by Finland (a lie now repeated in a Russian new movie just now shown to millions of Russians, arguing moreover that in 1918 the majority of Finns wanted to join the Soviet Union and that now the case with Finland is the same as with the Crimea and Ukraine). So there are facts as such. Yet, in the above mentioned old Soviet movie a touching love story is developed around the event and its protagonists are shown in an altogether moving sympathetic light to the spectator. So there are two different Zemic2 worlds, narratives i.e representations of the primary Zemic1 (war). Let us ponder, too, immigration: immigrants from the East arrive from a completely different zemic world and arrive at a different zemic world of the West, whose structure, i.e. neither substance, nor representations, they recognize. How are these made to blend together?

A historian can have many kinds of prejudices or preconceptions of hermeneutic preunderstandings. They include, according to Renvall, the personal antipathies and sympathies of the scholar, and, on the other hand, group opinions common to the circle in which a scholar lives ('we Finns' or 'we Germans'), the principal views on how historical events should be interpreted and finally the general worldview of the scholar. What would then become a history, if its writer managed to avoid all the three abovementioned errors and proceeded only with a theory on human zemic nature? *Is an existential history possible*? When putting this question, we have to note that not every moment in our zemic process is an existential one. Such moments only occur when our subject rises to the suprazemic level of reflection, in the manner of the Hegelian Essence or *Wesen*. We have the freedom to stop the zemic world any time by way of *a transcendental act of negation or affirmation*. I would like to write the existential history of Europe, à la Stefan Zweig's *Sternstunden der Menschheit*, but this time with a more sophisticated theory of existential ascendence from the zemic to the suprazemic level.

Yet, Renvall also presents the completely relevant (although a little naive sounding) question: to what extent has the human changed during the past? Let us presume that human nature has stayed the same through all ages – it suffices to think only of artworks which talk to us across 2000 years with continuing vivacity and cogency. Then one might think that human nature, which we have dared to call here zemic, is like a principle or axiom on which all focuses. History resumes this human nature or zemic. On the other hand, history unfolds or *ausfaltet* from the zemic (analogously to music, according to the famous theory of Heinrich Schenker who speaks about *Ursatz,* so why not call human nature or zemic the *Ursatz* of all the human's aspirations and acts?). When one reads about the ancient historians Suetonius, Plutarch, Tacitus, Thucydides, etc., one often observes how the history is launched or set forth from the character of some great man. Therefore, much attention is paid to describing him at the levels of *Moi1* and *Moi2*. Yet, if one adopts a somewhat milder view, then it is only said that man's acts are analogous in different times i.e. similar, but not the same in different times. Still, one may go even further and argue that human nature cannot really make an exception from the principle that all is susceptible to change. Renvall states (op. cit. 102): "Human nature is not a definitely fixed and immobile starting point, but it contrarily constitutes an unresolvable problem". On the other hand, our view of the ancient man of antiquity can be limited because his representations in texts do things like that. Therefore they seem to be schematic. Renvall is satisfied to note that human nature is the same – i.e. the zemic – but that the human's goals have changed. What is involved is therefore a noematic, intentional difference. In the existential respect, human nature is that 'perpetual' essence which stays the same, or as Gabriel Marcel has said, "*Ce que le temps ne mord pas*" – that which time does not bite.

What then if the historian declares that s/he writes history from the S1 of the zemic i.e. manifestations of certain ideas and values? An excellent example is found again in the Finnish historic tradition i.e. the *Leading Ideas of the History of the Mankind* by Yrjö-Sakari Yrjö-Koskinen (1960). Particularly interesting in this book is the fact that the author does not seem to know, even himself, what are the 'leading ideas'. He offers as a solution to the Fall of the Roman empire neither the ordinary view on moral decline, or collapse of the army, nor the attack of the barbarians. He especially rejects the last thesis, stating that the Barbarian nations, once in touch with the overwhelming Roman-Hellenic culture, wanted, in fact, to become Romans themselves, as quickly as possible. The explanation was the rise of the idea of a nation and the collapse in general of the idea of a huge realm: "this new idea, namely the national one, had now entered the scene of history and its triumph was the destruction of the Roman empire (op. cit. p. 207)".

According to Yrjö-Koskinen the Roman empire forged all the national peculiarities which had previously strived against this englobing world power in vain. "So the idea of mankind, sense and knowlege of common humanity had got stronger. . . . The common mankind emerged only because all nations had become Romans" (pp. 30–31). The speech about humankind is of course one of the epistemes of Romanticism and the Enlightenment – although as Goethe said: there is no mankind, there are only human beings. Yrjö-Koskinen therefore seems to end at the idea of nationalism as one of the leading ideas of humankind; but, basically he argues differently. As early as the opening chapter, he portrays the victory of Eastern civilization and Rameses of Egypt: "Through these events the general history of mankind has started. The Eastern civilizations and cultures have stepped out of their closed nature . . . . The movement is the primary conditions of progress and now the world had really been put into a motion" (pp. 30–31). It seems, therefore, that the principle of movement is even more important than nationality – and closer to our zemic model and interaction among different zemics i.e. cultures. Accordingly we may think that the primary movement in the historic process can be elucidated by our zemic model.

6 The future in light of the zemic

Can we really forecast the future with our zemic model? The situation concerning the future and the past is in fact the same: signs inundate us – signals, either presigns of the future or postsigns of the past. Marcel asks in which conditions forecasting is possible. To prophesize is the same as to see; what will happen is already present – but in what sense? That which will be is already the other. That other – does it see in advance? I improvise the history, but I know what I want to do with it; I do not only precede the situation, towards which my story is aspiring. I know that it goes so, because I want it (p. 151). What is involved is the teleological principle (op cit p. 119). The 'weak signals' of future investigators which are strange unlike signs of something which does not exist yet.

Could we interpet various future theories in the light of existential semiotics? An excellent source book is the work by Matti Kamppinen, Osmo Kuusi and Sari Söderlund: *Future research. Principles and applications* (Helsinki. SKS 2003). The scholars Elina Hiltunen and Osmo Kuusi have applied a notion borrowed from our theory i.e. that of endo- and exosigns. The international magazine of the field has published an issue about metaphors. Future theories start from the concept of possible worlds, borrowed from philosophers. They are possible and so reachable states of affairs. Are possible worlds a kind of future zemic world which can be forecasted in the sense that their structure – i.e. substance retains the same base of the aforementioned 'universal' principles, likeness/unlikenees, similarity /difference, transcendence, Z and dialogicity? Future scholars would call them invariants, borrowing the idea from Eino Kaila, a Finnish logical empiricist. On the other hand, one can say that inside the zemic the subject is still in the states of M1 and other modes are just forthcoming. Our subjects have a kind of utopian *S1* and they expect it to be concretized until *M1*. For instance if *S1* is communism, then it is expected to be realized on earth all along the pioneers. Yet, the essential is by whose route or paths one reaches the goal. Avenues can be several, when they constitute a network; we need to pay special attention to this. They are semiotically modalized worlds, either particularly desired or necessary (*vouloir, devoir*, will or must).

Furthermore, in the theory, megatrends – which are paths certified by time – are invoked. Agents or actors are an unpredictable element. They are basically alien-psychic, whose mind we can only suppose is something like our own inner zemic world. Values are crucial. Only creatures to whom it is not indifferent to which kind of worlds we are going, can have knowledge about future (p. 38). One might specify that there are two kinds of values: descriptive and prescriptive. Descriptive values are only representations of choices of the zemic world in the sign-Zemics. Again, when those sign values influence act-signs of the zemic world, they are prescriptive. In other words, in future research there is always a certain functional, active aspect. On the other hand values do not exist only inside S1, but they also manifest in how different modes are emphasized or proliferate inside the zemic. Another difficulty is that values in different cultures are often incommensurable. How can zemic1 understand zemic2 which has made certain different choices? From here, one may end up with cultural relativism i.e. different living worlds or zemics which do not have any common point, and none of which represents a privileged standpoint. One might, as a solution, say that each zemic world can, via reflection and negation, move to the suprazemic level and the principle uniting different suprazemics can be found on the transzemic level, one step higher.

In future theory, the concept of emergent reality, borrowed from cybernetics, is used. It is in the zemic model the same as *S1* and also the suprazemic level. But supervenience theory holds true for it i.e. it is dependent on the lower level: *S1* does not exist without *M1 M2* and *S2* and the suprazemic would not exist without the entire zemic. There is no thinking without the brain. Yet this analogy can be risky since, at the same time, we have to reject reductionism, i.e. the idea that we start to talk about emergent worlds in the language of lower levels. Phii phenomena cannot be reduced into fii phenomena. This was discovered as early as the logical empiricists. Ultimately, the future scholars seem to recommend such a world of value, which they call critical realism. It is critical since the focus is on falsification (p. 312). Knowledge is basically believing – just as Greimas said the knowing are islands in the sea of beliefs. Yet, the beliefs have to be well-founded. Humans can reasonably believe in something as long as this the knowledge has not been refuted. According to the postmodernists, knowing is a bundle of competing fictions (p. 307). They think that we may stop the search for the truth, since all phenomena are basically human creations. This can be considered a criticism of positivism. Mind has no contact with reality. However, one has to remember that postmodernism was also a reaction to structuralism and not only to positivism. Finally one forgets in all these new trends that what follows from the fact that reality and knowledge are constructed by humans, namely that the human is totally responsible for them. Or we can enter the existential path.

References

Aristotle. 1994. *Kategoriat tulkinnasta. Teokset I*. Suomentanut Lauri Carlson. Helsinki: Gaudeamus.
Aristotle. 2012. *Metafysiikka. Teokset VI*. Suomentaneet Tuija Jatakari, Kati Näätsaari, Petri Pohjanlehto. Helsinki: Gaudeamus.
Bakhtin, Mikhail. 1981. *The Dialogic Imagination*. Four Essays, Edited by Michael Holquist, Translated by Caryl Emerson and Michael Holquist. Austin: University of Texas Press.
Berti, Enrico. 2014. Aristotele. In Umberto Eco and Riccardo Fedriga: *Storia della Filosofia Dall'Antichità al M edioevo*. 136–169. Milano: Laterza.
Bloch, Ernst. 1985. *Das Prinzip Hoffnung*. Frankfurt am Main: Suhrkamp.
Brunila, Tuukka. 2016. Kurssi kohti transsendenssia, eli Platon ja eksistentiaalisemiotiikka. *Synteesi* 3/2016, s.17–29.
Eco, Umberto and Fedrigas, Riccardo (Eds.) 2004 Storia della Filosofia dall'antichità al Medioeva. Roma, Bari.
Eco, Umberto & Riccardo Fedriga (ed.). 2014. *Storia della Filosofia Dall'Antichità al Medioevo*. Roma, Bari: Giuseppe Laterza.
Greimas, Algirdas Julien. 1979. *Sémiotique. Dictionnaire raisonnée de la théorie du langage*. Paris: Hachette.
Stefania Guerra & Gino Stefani. 2005. *Contatto, Comunicazione, Autismo*. Milano: FrancoAngeli.
Guilford, Joy Paul. 1967. *The Nature of Human Intelligence*. New York: McGraw-Hill.
Hegel, Georg Wilhelm Friedrich. 1969. *Science of logic*. Translated by A.V. Miller. London: George Allen & Unwin Ltd.
Hegel 1972 *Logiikan tiede I*. Suomentanut Eero Tarasti, käsikirjoitus (Finnish translation by Eero Tarasti; unpublished manuscript).
Jankélévitch, Vladimir. 1974. *L'irréversible et la nostalgie*. Paris: Flammarion.
Kamppinen, Matti, Osmo Kuusi & Sari Söderlund (eds.). 2003. *Tulevaisuudentutkimus. Perusteet ja sovellukset. (Future research, Principles and applications)* Helsinki: Suomalaisen Kirjallisuuden Seura.
Lakoff, George & Mark Johnson. 1980. *Metaphors we live by*. Chicago and London: The University of Chicago Press.
Marcel, Gabriel. 1927. *Journal métaphysique*. Paris: Gallimard.
Marcuse, Herbert. 1964. *One-dimensional Man: studies in the ideology of advanced industrial society*. Boston: Beacon Press.
Plato. 1953. *The dialogues of Plato*, vols. II and III. Translated into English with analyses and introductions by Benjamin Jowett. Fourth edition. (Timaeus vol III), (Parmenides vol II). Oxford: Clarendon Press.
Plutarch. 1989. *Kuuluisien miesten elämäkertoja. (Biographies of illustrous men)* Suomentanut Kalle Suuronen. Porvoo, Helsinki, Juva: WSOY.
Rosato, Paolo. 2013. The Organic Principle in Music Analysis. A Semiotic Approach. Acta Semiotica Fennica XLII. Approaches to Musical Semiotics 16. Imatra, Helsinki: Semiotic Society of Finland.
Renvall, Pentti. 1965. *Nykyajan historiantutkimus. (Contemporary historic research)* Porvoo, Helsinki: WSOY.

Russell, Bertrand. 1957. *Muotokuvia muistista ja muita esseitä*. Porvoo, Helsinki: Werner Söderström Osakeyhtiö.
Snellman, Johan Vilhelm. 1932. *Kootut teokset. (Collected works)* Ensimmäinen osa. Filosofisia kirjoituksia. Suomentanut J.E. Salomaa. Porvoo: Werner Söderström Osakeyhtiö.
Tarasti, Eero. 2000. *Existential semiotics*. Bloomington: Indiana University Press.
Thibault, Mattia. 2017. *The meaning of Play. A theory of playfulness, toys and games as cultural semiotic device*. Doctoral dissertation. Dep. di Studi Umanistici PhD Programme in Semiotics and Media. Studies XXIX Cycle. Universitá degli studi di Torino.
Yrjö- Koskinen, Yrjö-Sakari. 1960. *Johtavat aatteet ihmiskunnan historiassa.* (*Leading ideas in the history of mankind*). Helsinki: Otava.
Zweig, Stefan. 1927 *Sternstunden der Menschheit*. (Finnish transl. *Ihmiskunnan tähtihetkiä*, Porvoo, Helsinki: WSOY.

Section 3: **Applications and practical discussions**

Yunhee Lee
Intermedial narrative as communication media: Imagination, narrative, and selfhood from Peirce's semiotic perspective

Abstract: Post-classical narratology developed in two directions: contextualism and cognitivism. Contextualist narrative tends to represent the external world by a cultural and historical parameter, while cognitivist narrative represents the internal world of mental phenomena. Contextualist narratologies have a diachronic view, construing narrative as an instrument to contextualize or historicize, whereas cognitivist narratologies regard narrative as embodied in medium specifics. This paper examines the possible dialogical collaboration of the two directions by looking at the intermediality of narrative between poetry and film. From a Peircean perspective, narrative inquiry has two faces, namely, poetic and rhetoric. I elaborate the relation between "narrative imagination" in poetry and "imagistic narrative" in film from a first-person perspective. Examining their dialogical interaction, I show how narrative form as an impregnator for sense-making is transmitted through medium specifics, entering through poetics and coming out through rhetoric. I conclude that intermedial narrative showcases communication media as a condition for identifying selfhood.

Keywords: narrative, contextualism, cognitivism, intermediality, Peirce

1 Introduction: Intermedial narrative as medium for intercommunication

The theme of the I3th World Congress of the International Association for Semiotic Studies was "Cross-Inter-Multi-Trans", implying a focus on relation and process. We commonly speak of a relation between two things interacting as patient and agent in a dyadic relation: A acting on B and B being acted on by A, and in turn the reverse action. This relation brings about processual thinking according to change of action. The process is associated with time and space. A process allows for the observation of an action in two modes: an active mode

---
Yunhee Lee, Hankuk University of Foreign Studies

https://doi.org/10.1515/9783110857801-011

outwards and a passive mode inwards; in other words, moving forward and being in recess.

As Robert Cooper (2014: 585) states, process implies "approach and withdrawal" as an etymological combination of "pro", which refers to the making and appearance of forms, and "cess", which refers to the disappearance and loss of forms. To this, he adds (Cooper 2014: 585):

> Process thus can be understood as a divided state of being in which human agency is forever suspended between the ceaseless act of making forms present and their constant recession. Process and recess are recursive versions of each other in a world without end.

A human agent is a deliberative subject in relation to an object. The term 'deliberative' in this paper corresponds with Colapietro's 1997: 281 definition of deliberation as "a process of cultivation. The best image for the deliberative subject is that of the gardener who cherishes her flowers (CP 6.289)". This means that the subject is able to observe a dyadic action as semiotic animal, prefiguring a transcendental being as a mediator between subject and object. In this sense the semiotic animal as a transcendental being observes not only the other but also itself in a triadic relation.

In John Deely's interpretation of John Poinsot's *Tractatus de Signis* (1632) ontological relations are presented in a semiotic view. Deely writes: "The analysis of sign — semiotic— provides a point of view that is superior to, that literally transcends, the traditional division of being into what is independent of the mind (*ens reale*) and what is dependent upon it (*ens rationis*), because in the sign, as in experience, both orders of being are found" (Deely 2009a: 193). For Deely the concept of object is the experienced and the experiencing, which introduces the subject of experience. In this way, Deely arrives at the association among three: thing-object-sign. Things are understood as mind-independent being (*ens reale*), objects as things for experience (*ens rationis*) and signs as signifying experiences. This triadic relation of thing-object-sign arguably echoes Peirce's conception of experience, as illustrated by the latter's ontological categories of possibility, actuality, and law. Possibility is the first category, consisting in pure experience, which subsumes such as things of beauty, or, in brief, the first object (*primum cognitum*). The second category is experience proper. It consists, for instance, in the sense of action and reaction. The third category consists in the experience of mediation, comprising, for instance, a sense of learning. Subsuming these three, a sign mediates mind-independent being (*ens reale*) and mind-dependent being (*ens rationis*) for the purpose of inquiry of the first object. Ontological relations and processes are pivotal in Peirce's idea of semiosis, that is, process of sign or sign-actions.

Understood in this light, a relational-processual approach to semiotic animals reveals a panoramic perspective, from phylogeny to ontogeny, regarding developmental processes of a human being. Anthroposemiosis is understood, here, as constituting the human *Umwelt* and, in particular, the foci of this paper are on sign-relations of a specifically human kind: narrative signs in communication media. Thus, for intermedial narrative between image and narrative as communication media, I call the quality of mediation 'mediality of narrative form', the realization of mediation in the narrative medium and the interpretation of mediation with the focus on the narrative genre. Here, by 'communication' I refer to the interpersonal communication between two minds. The interpreting agency of semiotic animals in this model is characterized by semiotic consciousness which transcends the agent him/herself, playing the role of a deliberative subject.

I start by sketching the key terms: media, mediality and intermediality. First of all, media (or medium, in the singular) are understood as being equivalent to the Peircean concept of the sign of a Third or "*Representation* as an element of the Phenomenon" (CP 5.66). Mediality means a quality of mediation (i.e. process) by three modes of signs with their capacities or context, namely, the iconic, the indexical, and the symbolic. Intermediality refers to the interrelationship between two modes of representation, such as image and narrative. Intermediality is a domain of new meaning given the subject's semiotic mediation between imagination and reason, icon and index, fancy and fact, mimesis and reality, private and public, and so on. The act of the intermedial presupposes transmediality through re-presenting the object in a triadic relation of subject-sign-object.

Based on the concepts of sign-relation and process, this paper aims to explicate the intermedial narrative for communication between two minds, resulting in identification of selfhood. To do so, it construes mental processes as operated by narrative imagination and imagistic narrative from the first-person perspective in a Peircean semiotic framework. Therefore, I propose that the function of the narrative sign as a medium for intercommunication is self-discovery. Selfhood is identified through imagined narratives. Given that the work of imagination to construct narratives is realized metaphorically, I focus on the way in which narratives operate as form, medium and genre.

2 Communication according to Peirce

Following Charles Sanders Peirce, a sign is a medium for communication. This notion of sign should not be confused with the sign merely as indexical, or as a signal. Peirce emphasized the character of the sign being "excitant of the same" (EP2: 389). Through this observation, Peirce implied that the mediating function of the sign has a general character for intercommunication between two minds. For Peirce, two communicating minds are not entirely distinct. Rather, they should be understood as one, as quasi-minds taking the role of utterer and interpreter in turn. Both utterer and interpreter must be capable of being determined by a sign, thus each having an interpretant established within it. James Liszka (1996: 90) writes that

> in this context, the utterer is capable of engendering what Peirce calls an *intentional interpretant*, (LW 196), that is, the sign which the utterer is, is in some sense intended or designed for the purpose of communication, and the interpreter is capable of engendering what he calls an *effectual interpretant*, that is, the interpreter can be affected by the sign that the utterer is.

In this view, intercommunication is not possible unless human beings participate in the actions of signs and processes, providing the interpretant with agency.

Under this condition, "there must be something transmitted between utterer and interpreter" and "what is transmitted between them must be something which is capable of establishing common interpretants in both utterer and interpreter" (Liszka 1996: 89). According to Peirce, a communicational interpretant is a determination of what Peirce (Hardwick 1977: 196–197) called the "*commens*" of the common mind; that is, the two minds of utterer and interpreter are welded for communication, through which a form is transmitted. For Peirce, a Form is understood as a Quality or Idea which he frames in a quasi-Platonic sense of form (CP 2.228). Peirce states that "The Form that is communicated does not necessarily cease to be in one thing when it comes to be in a different thing, because its being is a being of the predicate"(EP 2:544). He also states that "two minds in communication are [. . .] 'at one', that is, are properly one mind in that part of them". Therefore to the question, "Is this new scientific concept of a Sign not to recognize the connection of every sign with two minds?" the answer is: "go on to recognize that every sign, – or, at any rate, nearly every one– is a determination of something of the general nature of a mind, which we may call the 'quasi-mind'" (EP 2:389). This process reveals mental action in intercommunication through which a Form is communicated between the two minds of the general nature (EP 2: 389; 544).

3 Semiosic mediators: Imagination, metaphor, and narrative

The concept of sign as medium for intercommunication can be thought more simply as a medium that connects subject and object. The medium is a triadic system centralizing its function of symbolic mediation in a result which is understood as an artifact. In this model, subject and object replace utterer and interpreter in the communicative condition where something is to be transmitted. This is semiotic mediation of activity. The essential role of the artifact for communication is therefore as mediator between subject and object.

This view of mediation was also important for Vygotsky. He posited (Vygotsky 1978: 55) that humans are characterized by the internalization of higher psychological functions through the mediating activity of signs and tools. He distinguished tool from sign in this way:

> The tool's function is to serve as the conductor of human influence on the object of activity; it is *externally* oriented; it must lead to changes in objects. It is a means by which human external activity is aimed at mastering, and triumphing over, nature. The sign, on the other hand, changes nothing in the object of a psychological operation. It is a means of internal activity aimed at mastering oneself; the sign is *internally* oriented.

At the same time, Vygotsky stressed the importance of the tie between external and internal activities. Consequently, his concept of mediated activity illustrates that the processes of internalization consist in a series of transformations. Thus, an external activity is transformed into an internal one; an interpersonal process is transformed into an intrapersonal one (Vygotsky 1978: 56–57). For Vygotsky, a sign as a means of an indirect (mediated) activity refers to a language.

Within this communicative condition, I would like to discuss three different modes of mediation as a form of experience: namely, imagination, metaphor, and narrative, particularly as regards their role and function in relation to mind. These forms of experience, of course, are interconnected.

Jacob Bronowski stated that "every act of imagination is the discovery of likenesses between two things which were thought unlike" (1978:109). As such, he argues that

> All acts of imagination . . . take the closed system, they inspect it, they manipulate it and then they find something which had not been put into the system so far. They open the system up, they introduce new likenesses, whether it is Shakespeare saying, "My Mistress eyes are nothing like the Sunne" or it is Newton saying that the moon in essence is exactly like a thrown apple (Bronowski 1978: 110).

Bronowski's remarks shed light on essential features of imagination in three aspects: imagination can connect two things from different realms based on similarity; the act of imagination involves a subject's deliberative action to understand an object; the act of imagination is manifested in the form of metaphor as a hypothesis, which is related to a perceptual act, and thus, using a Peircean term, abduction.

These aspects of imagination are supported by Vygotsky's experimental psychology. Consider Vygotsky's discussion of the development of imagination in a child. He claims that imagination is connected with realistic thinking. This means that thinking and imagination are intimately connected with the acquisition of speech (Vygotsky 1987: 348). Therefore, imagination is integrated within realistic – or mimetic, as opposed to imaginative or fantastical – thinking. Imagination is not restricted to realistic thinking, therefore. It departs from reality. Through imagination we can construct images, but those images are constructed with relation to reality (Vygotsky 1987: 349).

The act of imagination is thus understood as mediating between images from reality and those from memory, constructing new images by unifying these two. Images from reality are immediate and images from memory are 'mediate'; semiotically speaking, the former is an index and the latter is an icon. The former images are associated with vision and the latter images are associated with perception and the verbal. In this way, imagination as mental activity mediates between the subjective world and the objective world as fancy and fact. Therefore, the role of imagination is a source of constructing a creative metaphor of the sign as a hypothetical inference, representing mental action in parallelism.

According to Julian Jaynes, "there are thus always two terms in metaphor, the thing to be described, which I shall call the *metaphrand*, and the thing or relation used to elucidate it, which I shall call the *metaphier*" (Jaynes 1976: 48). The two terms can be understood as belonging to the two realms of consciousness: the immediate and the mediate in mental action. In relation to narrative, Ricoeur (1988) argues that metaphoric thinking – the "as if" mode – underpins narrativity, as based on analogical ontology. The relation of metaphor and narrative is, therefore, expressed as "seeing as" and "being as". Henry Venema (2000: 107) explains the relation in this manner: "Both historical and fictional narratives refigure experience under this rule of analogy, that is, under the rule of emplotment governed by the logic of metaphor that reconnects art to life through the transformation of "seeing as" into "being as"". Metaphor and narrative show mental action in a similar way regarding a topological aspect, connecting the perceptual and the ontological realms. Both operate through the act of imagination in light of topological features, moving from one point to the other based on resemblance. Narrative imagination works through applying logico-scientific thinking to actual realistic thinking. The logico-scientific (paradigmatic) mode of thinking (Bruner 1986) corresponds to Peirce's concept of scientific imagination, which is associated with what Peirce called abstraction or prescission, the separation of Secondness in thought (EP 2:270). Bruner (1986:13) stated that when the logico-scientific mode of thinking is applied to real thinking, it becomes a story-like or narrative mode of thinking, forming a hypothesis. In this regard, narrative imagination refers to scientific imagination (abstraction) which is applied to realistic thinking. In this sense, narrative imagination is understood as hypostatic abstraction.

Henry Venema claims that Ricoeur failed to provide an explicit explanation of the process of transformation of metaphor into narrative. In other words, Ricoeur's theory does not explain how a metaphoric narrative can transform art into life for the purposes of acquiring narrative identity (Venema 2000: 112). Nevertheless, Venema also states that Ricoeur's concept of narrative identity "is crucial not only for explaining the process of the narrativization of experience but also for understanding Ricoeur's formulation of selfhood as developed in *Oneself as Another*" (Venema 2000: 112). In light of Venema's observation, I would like to add some other directions for developing Ricoeur's concepts of selfhood and narrative identity. The origin of knowledge including self-knowledge consists in imagination and precisely in narrative imagination which is conducted by a subject's deliberative and voluntary act of imagination. Thus, subjectivity within a narrative world can be transformed into narrative identity. Therefore, the subject's experience from the first-person perspective is more crucial to analysing narrative than an attempt to understand the general phenomenon of imagination would be.

Selfhood as developed by oneself as another can be possible only where the self is acting as an agent for interpreting oneself by means of observing other and discovering itself within the other as a general idea. Helmut Pape explains Peirce's logical idealism through a subjective unity of logical operation and its special case in the thesis, "I think here and now that", which always demarcates the largest possible scope of propositional functions (Pape 1997: 164). For this reason, he suggests that we can add a sort of transcendental prefix 'I, here, now' to any string of symbols representing our reading of a formula which indicates the fact that there was an unrepresented subjective unity whose operation in the background caused this interpretation, thus understanding the sequence of formal expressions and scientific facts (Pape 1997:164). Therefore, I-here-now, as mind-dependent being (*ens rationis*), is fused with you-there-then, as mind-independent being (*ens reale*).

This idea is supported by Peirce's ontological categories of I, IT, and THOU being the early version of his categories. According to Max Fisch, Peirce abandoned these terms as *names* for his categories as he later found better fitting technical terms (Peirce 1982: xxx). The terms are Firstness, Secondness, and Thirdness, which are understood as positive qualitative possibility, actuality, and law, respectively. In 1861, Peirce wrote in the book entitled, *I, IT, and THOU*: "I here, for the first time, begin a development of these conceptions . . . THOU is an IT in which there is another I. I looks in, It looks out, Thou looks *through*, out and in again" (Peirce 1982: xxix). Max Fisch commented on this: "For the first time, it becomes emphatic and clear that THOU presupposes IT and IT presupposes I. That is the reason for the difference between categorical and grammatical order" (Peirce 1982: xxix). In another place, Peirce remarked: "First, there was the egotistical stage when man arbitrarily imagined perfection, now is the idistical stage when he observes it. Hereafter must be the more glorious tuisical stage when he shall be in communion with her" (Peirce 1958: 13). William James also commented on Peirce's idea of THOU, delineating it in this manner: "The *thou* idea, as Peirce calls it, dominates an entire realm of mental phenomena, embracing poetry, all direct intuition of nature, scientific *instincts*, relations of man to man, morality &c. *All analysis* must be into a triad; *me & it* require the complement of *thou*." (Peirce 1982: xxix)

This relationship of three categories and mental processes will be discussed in the following section on the esthetic experience and the first-person perspective. So far, though, we have examined two modes of mediation: imagination and metaphor. Now, we turn to the more complex mediator, namely, narrative. Narrative is more complex because it connects the subjective and objective world through a voluntary act of the subject. Ricoeur stated that mimesis was a metaphor of reality. According to Aristotle, mimesis is life in action, which is represented by an artifact of narrative. When an act of imagination connecting scientific imagination with narrative imagination is realized in the form of metaphor, "a=b", a way of understanding the objective world is connected with the inner world.

The subject sees or takes something as something else, so as to form a hypothesis. The subject's perception through focalization is already a generalized perception, extending seeing from one closed system to the other system. At this point, the important thing is the subject's experience of narrativization, promoting the tendency to see him/herself as a protagonist in a possible world. Narrative as a sign of possibility or a sign of fact or a sign of reason is revealed by a form of mediality, mediation, and focalization, respectively. Because of narrative bearing as a sign system, narrative in an art form can become a proper mode of intercommunication where the subject can identify selfhood, undergoing three modes of narrative experience: mediality through narrative imagination; mediation through imagistic narrative; and focalization through the subject's narrating activity, constructing the narratives of self. These three features of narrative process are categorized as a form, medium, and genre through which the subject's experience of narrativization allows the subject to attain knowledge of the self. I will discuss these three points in detail later on.

To recapitulate, there are three modes of mediator: namely, imagination, metaphor, and narrative. They are characterized by the role of connecting two different realms based on the three grades of the subject's experience for thinking. Imagination acts as a mode of thinking which connects the mediate conception and the immediate conception. The sentence "The stove is black" in Peirce's example (MS. 403 [1893]) shows that the immediate consciousness of 'the stove' is mediated with the mediate consciousness of 'black' or 'blackness' which has a verbal feature. This act of imagination can be understood as private thinking, disconnected from the public; however, it is 'narrative imagination' that connects the private with reality, as we have seen above; otherwise, it will be called hallucination, according to Peirce (CP 5. 402).

From Peirce's semiotic perspective, metaphor has two features; firstly, the hypoicon which is from a phenomenological viewpoint, and secondly, the metaicon, from an ontological viewpoint. Michael Cabot Haley argues that the metaicon, being a *type*, an abstract third among Firsts, is "a *possible law,* a governing archetypal pattern in embryo as it were, a real and present possibility even before it is actualized in nature, let alone actualized in the metaphorical assertion" (1988: 34). Then he suggests that the metaicon might be a sort of final cause in the evolution of metaphorical thought in poetry and in language. This idea of the metaicon can be understood through Peirce's thesis of "every true poem is a sound argument" (CP 5.119). Considering the metaphor as hypoicon is an exemplification of a *pure* icon as opposed to a metaicon which has the symbolic feature of working by way of interpretation of a dyadic relation of sign-and-object, thus transcending itself by discovering a law between its components.

A narrative sign is an extended metaphor by way of showing and telling, by engaging the subject's experience of narrativization. In this sense, a narrative sign plays an important role of mediator, the medium for intercommunication between two minds. As Ricoeur suggests, a narrative world as mimesis of reality is highly developed as a sign system, so as to affect and change the subject's experience.

In a mediated activity model of subject-artifact-object, the narrative artifact (an art form) is understood as a psychological tool for the higher mental processes in order for us to understand the objective world. To do so, the subject's deliberative act of imagination is a source of mental activity for generalizing ideas for intercommunication (see Colapietro 1997: 262–288). Consequently, first-person access to a narrative world enables one to enact the subject's experience of narrativization characterized by 'being as', thus identifying selfhood where the self has the three roles of protagonist, observer, and agent.

4 Esthetic experience and the first-person perspective

John Kaag (2014: 208–209) mentions that the role of imagination in Peirce is related to esthetic experience, involved with creativity, epistemology, and logical mental processes from the imaginative "Thou" idea. For Peirce, imagination is a vital factor in mathematics, which is the highest level in a hierarchical system in sciences of discovery. The power of imagination is a source of human creativity and novelty. It is a ground for forming a hypothesis based on discovery of similarity in difference. Kaag relates the power of imagination with esthetic experience. For Peirce, esthetics is a study of what makes things admirable and he defines it as a normative science, positioned below phenomenology in a hierarchical system (cp. 1.91). Logic and ethics are subclasses of a normative science. The three are related to each other hierarchically. Thus, logic presupposes ethics, which in turn presupposes esthetics, dealing with what is truth in the realms of thinking, action, and feeling. Esthetic experience, thus, allows us to understand things of beauty both phenomenologically and experientially for discovering truth. For Peirce, quality of beauty includes ideals, which are perceived as reason or concrete reasonableness in the universe. Viewing esthetics as a normative science, the subject's experiences from sense, imagination, perception, and conception are central to understanding beauty and interpreting the meaning of beauty throughout the subject's esthetic experience.

As we have seen, the work of imagination and metaphor is connected with realistic thinking or the physical world of body, producing unity with the fictional world. Esthetic experience necessarily requires the first-person perspective on the objective world. This does not mean solipsism, but is based on the mental activity of imagination through metaphoric formation, "seeing as". With the first-person perspective by way of a narrative world, the experiencing "I", the subject of esthetic experience is a mediator between two different worlds of fact and fancy, connecting them by similarity. Thus, the mental processes of the subject are not only psychological but also logical in the sense that the experiencing "I" with subjectivity of inwardness and autonomy can control self-control, playing the role of a transcendental being (see Colapietro 1989: chap. 5). In other words, the subject from the first-person perspective also functions as an in-between being, connecting the objective with the subjective.

For this reason, the first-person perspective is a semiotic device for logical mental process to understand the objective world by means of the subject's experience, consequently leading to the discovery of the subjective world.

As Lynne Baker argues (2013: chap. 6), there are two stages of the first-person perspective: namely, a rudimentary stage and a robust stage: animals develop the first-person perspective only at a rudimentary stage, where there is no self-consciousness and no symbolic mode of semiotic consciousness; that stage contains a signal or an indexical mode of symptom for communication. Human animals are characterized by a robust stage of the first-person perspective through which self-consciousness arises, allowing one to proceed to the attainment of self-concept.

The first-person perspective is not confined to the effect of empathy. It moves beyond empathy through the act of imagination, "being as" in a narrative world. The first-person perspective aims for joint attention, producing consensus in a form transmitted during the act of intercommunication. Now the subject position becomes fully engaged with a narrative world by which reality is delineated. This means that, as Deely posited (cf. 2009b: chap. 9), the concept of intersubjectivity is insufficient for explaining the in-betweenness of being in the process of self-interpretation. At this point, the crucial matter is the experientiality of the subject, which is featured as expressing, representing, and interpreting.

Accordingly, a sign of imagination, metaphor, and narrative operates in anthropomorphism. The sign can be known by humans even when asserting something without meaning. So, for Peirce, "we cannot have any idea that is not anthropomorphic" (*The New Elements of Mathematics* 4: 313, cited in de Waal 2013:135). Esthetic experience is thus tied to the first-person perspective in understanding 'reality', which is expressed in an artifact such as poetry, cinema, and personal writings. While investigating imagination in Peirce's semiotics, Kaag posited that understanding imagination requires various dimensions of organic processes, for instance, the physical, the biological, the social, the cognitive, the philosophical, the ontological, and the psychological (Kaag 2014: 13–24). Similarly, Dennis Sepper (2013: 447) sees imagination in Peirce's semiotics as a theory of conceptual topology: topologies of Aristotle's inward senses and Kant's concept serve to focus on and unify the manifold of sensibility. Sepper notes (2013: 447; emphasis added), additionally, that "the mind moves in the field of *experience*". Accordingly, Sepper emphasizes experience as a course of life, thinking through the imagination: "One experience leads to another, because experience is saturated with an implicit logic destined for development, and all 'conclusions' will eventually be drawn and implemented" (Sepper 2013: 448). The point he is making is relevant to the present paper's perspective on narrative imagination and imagistic narrative, focusing on the subject's deliberative act of imagination, which is the centre of subjectivity.

Peirce categorizes experience under three headings, according to a mode of being: first, pure experience of quality which cannot be analyzed; rather it is forced upon us, affecting us, producing a sense of feeling; second, experience of existence, which is a form of sensation and volition through a double-sided consciousness; third, experience of law, which appears as a sense of learning and mediation (CP 7.524–538). These modes of experience are thus undertaken by the act of imagination. Esthetic experience of narrative is categorized by form, medium, and genre, according to Peirce's three categories of ontology as interpreted here. The act of imagination, with its syntactical and transcendental character, serves to form a conception from perception, thereby developing the subject's mind. Esthetic experience from a semiotic viewpoint entails that the subject's experience is also understood as a form, not as content or a psychological feature. Consequently, the subject's experience expresses a general character from esthetic experience.

4.1 Narrative imagination in poetry: The autobiographical self

When we talk about poetry as verbal media, poetry as artifact mediates subject and object. Poetry expresses a poet's mind as his/her subjective experience of the objective world. What the poet expresses is their feelings and emotions, thinking toward the objective world. Feelings and emotions are not an event but a state and, for this reason, poetry does not fit the form of narrative. Narrative is normally understood as representation of human action and is composed of character, event, sequence, time, space, motive, and intention. However, unlike narrative as medium, poetry can be understood as a narrative form for mediality, a transmitting quality of the objective world, functioning differently with respect to the mind, conceptualizing or generalizing feelings of the subject's experience.

The subject's entry into the objective world makes it possible to have poetic imagination; and, yet, imagination needs the subject's experience with reality so as to attain the meaning of a poem. At this point for a poet, s/he constructs a narrative world in which the poet resides as the experiencing "I" for a protagonist, telling his/her own story. In this sense, the poem is regarded as an autobiographical narrative. From the first-person perspective at the autobiographical stage of the subject's experience of narrativization, the experiencing "I" is the centre of a universe from which "I" is regarded as a protagonist in a narrative world: that is, a metaphor of reality. Therefore, a protagonist expressed in the poetic world by narrative imagination points to the experiencing "I" in reality by narrating "I". As a result, it leads to understanding who "I" is.

Following Whitehead, for the poet, trees are symbols to understand and the words are the meaning. He concentrates on the trees in order to get at the words (1927: 12). Therefore, the experiencing "I" and the narrating "I" correspond to symbol and meaning, respectively, which become as one, revealing the poet's consciousness, that is, symbolic reference. Whitehead explained symbolic reference as "the active synthetic element contributed by the nature of the percipient" (Whitehead 1927: 8). In this process the poet sees things with his/her own subjective lenses as Emerson said (Emerson and Thoreau 2015: chap. 14). But the poet's subjective world does not imply a private thought because of metaphoric thinking through which the poet draws a similar quality between the poetic world and reality. Accordingly, his poem transmits a form in a poetic object which excites the reader's mind. The poet, I believe, possesses an innate sensibility to perceive things of beauty. A narrative world that the poet creates is capable of mediating between the poet and the reader by means of narrative imagination. Thus, narrative imagination enables both the poet and the reader to reside in a possible world through which a form is transmitted between them. Narrative imagination in mental processes is a key element for the subject's experience of narrativization for joint attention or building sympathy between two minds.

According to Peirce, the conjugation "is", the conception of being, is understood as two modes of being: "actually is" and "would be" (EP 1: 2). Narrative imagination consists of the syntactic structure of space and time which involves past and present. Paradigmatic thinking amounts to reproductive imagination which is associated with memory. According to Vygotsky's experimental psychology, thinking and its development in childhood are tied to memory. So "for the very young child, to think means to remember . . . we see such a close connection between these two psychological functions" (1978: 50). This memory applies to the present in order to foster unity with the purpose of constructing narrative imagination. As a mode of thought, narrative imagination unifies subject-sign and predicate-sign, which are indexical and iconic, respectively. Thus, the unity of two signs being connected, the conjugated "is", produces a different interpretation of the sign. Therefore, there could be a sign of possibility, or a sign of actuality, or a sign of law, dependent on the interpretant's collateral experience. The conception of being as the two modes of "actually is" and "would be" is thus cognizant of the unity of the subject's sense experience and the subject's conception of mental processes in order to produce a new meaning. In fact, poetry as a mediator between a possible world and reality connects the two realms based on agreement with the verb between "actually is" and "would be". This forms a hypothesis which is undertaken in the subject's experience of poetry.

Let us think of narrative imagination in poetry, concerning the relationship between a poet and his own poem. C. S. Lewis is known not as a poet but as a literary critic and author of tales. Two writers in particular wrote about how Lewis's poetic imagination affected his thinking and influenced him throughout his career as literary critic and writer. First, Roland M. Kawano (2004) delineates Lewis as "the public poet". According to him, Lewis's first calling was poet and he wrote some poems including the war poems 'Spirits in Bondage' (1919) and his long narrative poem 'Dymer' (1926). Kawano writes, "By distinguishing the private and public character of Milton, Lewis found a way to separate what Milton might have said to friends around a fireplace from what he would have said to an audience" (2004: 2). The public character and conventions of poetry interested Lewis and this public character appeared in his poetry. For Lewis, the private conception of poetry, using esoteric metaphors, is too private to transmit truth and thus it does not appear to be communicable. In his book *An Experiment in Criticism,* Lewis's critique of modern poems was that they were too difficult for readers to understand because such poems were too willing to deliberately separate themselves from prose and they seemed to emphasize the form itself (Lewis 1961: 95–103).

At first, Lewis's poetic imagination seems to focus only on the public character of poetry, putting an emphasis on story, pattern and convention, neglecting the private character of feelings and emotions from the inner world. However, his inner world becomes unified with his outward creation using analogy, image, symbol, and allegory, which is reflected in his prose. This idea of Lewis's poetic imagination developed through writing activity, both poetry and prose. Peter J. Schakel (1984) explained clearly the relationship of imagination and reason by illustrating how Lewis' poetic imagination becomes unified with reason following each period of writing activity. As a poet in his teens and twenties, Lewis was struggling with imagination; then, at the time when he was a critic and story writer in his thirties, imagination served his writing of prose; as an apologist in his forties, reason functioned as his master; and toward the end of his life, in his fifties and sixties, as autobiographer and personal writer, reason and imagination became reconciled and united.

As Kawano's book argues, Lewis was always a poet, manifesting narrative imagination throughout his writing activity with a deliberative act of unifying imagination with reason. This is an important point: that imagination is not a private element alone; otherwise it would be hallucination when it is not understood or interpreted by verbal thinking in communication. In this sense, a poet who expresses personal feelings transmits general ideas in life, like a prophet. Peirce (1958: 13) writes:

> The poet in our days – and the true poet is the true prophet – personifies everything, not rhetorically but in his own feeling. He tells us that he feels an affinity for nature, and loves the stone or the drop of water. But the time is coming when there shall be no more poetry, for that which was poetically divined shall be scientifically known. It is true that the progress of science may die away, but then its essence will have been extracted. This cessation itself will give us time to see that cosmos, that esthetic view of science which Humboldt prematurely conceived.

Thus, narrative imagination expressed by the poet's feeling creates a poetic world where both the poet and the reader can reside together in the subject's experience as protagonist. Accordingly, poetry as medium for intercommunication transmits quality or a form in an object between them.

4.2 Imagistic narrative in cinema: The biographical self

Unlike poetry, cinema commonly uses a narrative form as medium of communication; however, it functions as servant to objective images on the screen. There is a certain distance between a director and his creation and there is a camera in-between. Narrative imagination is expressed as a metaphor of reality on the screen. Even though the director makes images, the images seem to be elusive and alienated from the director's eyes. Visual signs of cinematic images give rise to different effects on the subject's experience, as compared to the verbal sign which is associated with consciousness. In the case of cinema, images show themselves while the director is telling another story: as if images are acting, whereas the director is observing them. Unlike a poet who acts as a protagonist expressing their inner world by creating a poetic world, the role of a movie director is as observer of a cinematic world, that is, an imagistic narrative world. Signs on the screen reflect life by pointing to reality. Both a movie director and the audience play the role of observer, which leads to the subject's esthetic experience of the cinema. So, both director and audience experience the object of images throughout narrativization for understanding the implicit meaning of imagistic narrative.

In phenomenology, images involve spontaneity and chance, away from the director's intention of telling. For this reason, image and narrative are complementary but they are distinct from each other, generating imaginative power through deflection of seeing. The images show and the director and audience observe them through dialogical interaction with signs on the screen. In this way, the subject's experience of narrativization focuses on perception with focalization: that is, where to see and what to perceive.

Another important feature of the cinema image is that it is necessarily mediated by the third-person perspective. There has been some experimental endeavour to produce the first-person perspective by using special camera work. This is an irrelevant point in the discussion of the narrative sign for intercommunication. Instead, the first-person perspective functions as a semiotic device, involving psychological and logical mental processes through which narrative imagination creates a possible world, applying indexicality based on conscious activity. Therefore, an indexical relationship connects "I" with "you" or "it"; "here" with "there"; "now" with "then". Eventually, "seeing as" becomes "being as" through the subject's conscious activity of semiosis.

As I explained, narrative imagination of mental action involves subjectivity through which the subject becomes the experiencing "I" in relation with an object in a dialogic way. In this respect, the subject of the experiencing "I" as an observer is in a dialogic relation with the object of the image on the screen. Through this mental activity, the subject conceptualizes who "I" is, discovering a self-concept by understanding a general character within the image.

Cinema, which is a verbal narrative medium incorporated with visual narrative, allows us to see and observe both the outward creation and the inner world by way of dialectic images of icon and index, producing a double-sided consciousness. Poetry expresses qualities in an object, whereas cinema reveals relations between the things. In view of this, the relationship of a director and his/her film represents the subject-object relationship. Observing the cinematic image as a narrative from the first-person perspective, the subject traverses between the fictional and the real because the cinematic fictional world points things out to reality. Indeed, Colapietro argues that literature functions as a reagent index, pointing things out to reality and allowing one to interpret the meaning in life (2009: 109–133). Accordingly, esthetic experience of the cinematic image provides a two-sided consciousness of reality and fiction. This double consciousness with cognitive power furnishes one with the observational acts of seeing and delineates the other as objectively as possible from the first-person perspective.

Consider the relationship from one particular director's experience. Hong, Sang-Soo, a Korean movie director, is known for his essayistic or autobiographical film making. From the first-person perspective, he observes his creation as the other's work. In fact, he sees himself as somebody entering into a dialogical relation with the image on the screen. Even though his film is autobiographical and from the first-person perspective, it becomes biographical in writing about himself as another person while observing him and the character in the cinema residing in a narrative world points to himself alone in reality for the purpose of reflecting.

4.3 Self-narratives in personal writing: The personal self

From the first-person narrative, the subject's experience culminates in conceptualizing a self by virtue of narrative imagination through dialogic relation with imagistic narrative on the screen. A transcendental self as agent can control its mental activity. Following Colapietro (1997: 281), who holds that "The complex signs indicative of the deliberative subject no less than of the dynamic object are, in the context of semiotics itself, such forms *par excellence*. They are both integral parts of this general theory (the deliberative subject no less than the dynamical object), if only it is considered in its full scope", the deliberative subject and the dynamical object become one in the process of the narrative sign as if mind-independent and mind-dependent are mixed in a mental activity. While imagistic narrative on the screen focuses on the dialectic and dialogic relation, self-narrative leads to interpretative activity whose focal point is a perspective which is associated with the subject's intention or purpose, focalizing narratives of self for intercommunication.

From the expressing "I" through the observing "I", the subject attains self-identity by interpreting the "I". Sense, imagination, perception, thinking, and conception all work together to transmit a form between minds. For this reason, self-narratives are really manifested in a verbal form. Michel de Montaigne, who created an intersubjective literary style of mediation – the essay – is an exemplary case of self-narrative. He was an autonomous, responsible subject of experience in his own life story and also a loving, caring, and deliberative observer of others, expressing himself. He used a self as an agent for interpretation of himself. His creation thus became an all-time classic, his *Essays*. He strived to form a balance between two different things in every possible situation, such as humans and animals; nature and culture; imagination and reason; and so on. Self-interpretation allows us to distinguish an objective "I" from an experiencing "I" through observing others in that the objective "I" is presupposed in the other. This process and relation are described in Peirce's categories of "I, IT, and THOU", as I have mentioned above.

5 Conclusion: Intermedial narrative for identifying selfhood

As we have seen from narrative sign as medium for communication, narrative functions to discover the self by implementation of the first-person perspective. The central point is subjectivity, which is characterized by inwardness and autonomy. Mediators, namely imagination, metaphor, and narrative, are incorporated in certain media such as poetry, cinema, and self-narratives in a verbal essay. Viewing narrative from Peirce's semiotic perspective, the narrative sign is categorized by narrative form as mediality in Firstness, the narrative medium as mediation in secondness, and the narrative genre as focalization in thirdness. According to these ontological categories of narrative, the actual modes appeared as narrative imagination, imagistic narrative, and self-narratives in a form of narrative sign in general.

Intermedia between poetry and cinema are grounded upon narrative imagination and imagistic narrative. That is, narrative thinking through the imagination and image is transmitted by virtue of remediation of narrative. Therefore, remedial or intermedial narrative means a dialogical interaction between image and narrative by means of imagination. In this regard, intermediality can be understood as transmediality. In fact, "inter" (in-between being) presupposes "trans" (meta being) in light of anthroposemiosis where a self transcends him/herself. As Emerson said, man recognizes his status in the Fall of Man, failing to see things directly (Emerson and Thoreau 2015: chap. 14). We cannot see what our eyes see; there is always mediation by our inner being. We cannot reach knowledge of an object because the object is dynamical in relation to the subject's own lenses. Thus, truth and reality are not directly approachable by a human being. But the hope consists in the human intellect by which we are able to connect things to develop a tendency to be general through imagination and reason. The conception of being is manifested in the word "is", connecting ideas and concepts in a form of hypothesis. We connect the inner world with the outer world, self and other, for the purpose of generalization of ideas to reach the highest good.

All human actions are initiated from imagination, connecting the world of fancy with the world of fact, therefore acting "as" an actor in a play. We act and perform each role in a drama with subjectivity of being acted on by and acting on other. But with actions in drama without a transcendental self through which the actor imagines and desires the effect of his action in the process and relation with other, the concept of subjectivity is empty. In this sense, we understand that we are a processual being, moving forwards, receding, and transforming with subjectivity, being responsible to the other in a teleological way. This is called a triadic action in Peirce's semiotics.

Thus, the human *Umwelt* is characterized by a narrative world, where the storytelling animal makes meaning out of vagueness to attain a generality through varying narrative activity within intercommunication. Intermedial processes and relations in mental action between narrative imagination, imagistic narrative, and self-narratives develop the subject's esthetic experience and activity into narrative identity by re-storying and refiguring the prefigured story, accordingly identifying selfhood.

References

Baker, Lynne Rudder. 2013. *Naturalism and the first-person perspective*. New York: Oxford University Press.
Bronowski, Jacob. 1978. *The origins of knowledge and imagination*. New Haven and London: Yale University Press.
Bruner, Jerome. 1986. *Actual minds, possible worlds*, Cambridge, Massachusetts and London: Harvard University Press.
Colapietro, Vincent M. 1989. *Peirce's approach to the self: a semiotic perspective on human subjectivity*. Buffalo: State University of New York Press.
Colapietro, Vincent M. 1997. The Dynamical Object and the Deliberative Subject. In Jacqueline Brunning & Paul Forster (eds.), *The Rule of Reason: The Philosophy of Charles Sanders Peirce*, 262–288. Toronto: University of Toronto Press.
Colapietro, Vincent M. 2009. Pointing things out: exploring the indexical dimensions of literary texts. In Harri Veivo, Christina Ljungberg & Jorgen Dines Johansen (eds.), *Redefining literary semiotics*. 109–133. Cambridge: Cambridge Scholars Publishing.
Cooper, Robert. 2014. Process and reality. In Jenny Helin, Tor Hernes, Daniel Hjorth & Robin Holt (eds.), *The Oxford Handbook of Process Philosophy and Organization Studies*, 585–604. Oxford: Oxford University Press. Kindle Edition.
de Montaigne, Michel. 1993. *The complete essays*. Harmondsworth: Penguin Books. Kindle Edition.
de Waal, Cornelis. 2013. *Peirce: A guide for the perplexed*. London and New York: Bloomsbury.
Deely, John. 2009a. *Realism for the 21st Century: A John Deely Reader*, Paul Cobley (ed.), Scranton, Pennsylvania; London, England: Scranton University Press.
Deely, John. 2009b. *Purely objective reality*. Berlin and New York: Mouton de Gruyter.
Emerson, Ralph W. & Henry D. Thoreau. 2015. Experience. In *Self-reliance and other essays: With Walden* (Kindle Location 3464). Titan Read. Kindle Edition.
Haley, Michael C. 1988. *The semeiosis of poetic metaphor*. Bloomington, Indianapolis: Indiana University Press.
Hardwick, Charles S. (ed.). 1977. *Semiotics and significs. The correspondence between Charles S. Peirce and Victoria Lady Welby*. Bloomington: Indiana University Press.
Hong, Sang-Soo. 2015. *Right now, wrong then*. Seoul: Jeonwon Film Company.
Hong, Sang-Soo. 2017. *On the beach at night alone*. Seoul: Jeonwon Film Company.

Jaynes, Julian. 1976. *The origin of consciousness in the breakdown of the bicameral mind*. Boston: Houghton Mifflin.
Kaag, John. 2014. *Thinking through the Imagination: Aesthetics in human cognition*. New York: Fordham University Press.
Kawano, Roland M. 2004. *C. S. Lewis: Always a poet*. Lanham; Boulder, New York & Toronto; Oxford: University Press of America.
Lewis, Clive Staples. 1961. *An experiment in criticism*. Cambridge: Cambridge University Press.
Liszka, James Jacob. 1996. *A general introduction to the semeiotic of Charles Sanders Peirce*. Bloomington; Indianapolis: Indiana University Press.
Pape, Helmut. 1997. The logical structure of idealism: C. S. Peirce's search for a logic of mental processes. In Jacqueline Brunning & Paul Forster (eds.), *The rule of reason: The philosophy of Charles Sanders Peirce*, 153–184. Toronto; Buffalo; London: University of Toronto Press.
Peirce, Charles S. 1931–1958. *Collected papers of Charles S. Peirce*, 8 vols., eds. Charles Hartshorne & Paul Weiss (vols.1–6); Arthur W. Burks (vols.7–8). Cambridge, MA: Harvard University Press. [CP refers to Collected Papers, followed by volume and paragraph number].
Peirce, Charles S. 1958. *Charles S. Peirce: Selected writings (Values in a universe of chance)*. Philip P. Wiener (ed.). New York: Dover Publications.
Peirce, Charles S. 1976. *The new elements of mathematics*, 4 Vols. in 5. Carolyn Eisele (ed.) The Hague: Mouton.
Peirce, Charles S. 1982. *Writings of Charles S. Peirce: A chronological edition*. vol. 1 Bloomington: Indiana University Press.
Peirce, Charles S. 1992. *The essential Peirce: Selected philosophical writings*, vol. 1 (1867–1893). Nathan Houser & Christian J. W. Kloesel (eds.), Bloomington and Indianapolis: Indiana University Press. [EP refers to *The Essential Peirce: Selected Philosophical Writings*, followed by volume and page number].
Peirce, Charles S. 1998. *The essential Peirce: Selected philosophical writings*, vol. 2 (1893–1913). The Peirce Edition Project (ed.). Bloomington and Indianapolis: Indiana University Press. [EP refers to *The Essential Peirce: Selected Philosophical Writings*, followed by volume and page number].
Ricoeur, Paul. 1988. *Time and narrative* vol.3, Kathleen Blamey & David Pellauer (trans.), Chicago and London: University of Chicago Press.
Schakel, Peter J. 1984. *Reason and imagination in C. S. Lewis: A study of Till We Have Faces*, Grand Rapids, Michigan: William B. Eerdmans Publishing Company.
Sepper, Dennis L. 2013. *Understanding imagination: The reason of images*, Dordrecht: Springer.
Venema, Henry I. 2000. *Identifying selfhood: imagination, narrative, and hermeneutics in the thought of Paul Ricoeur*. Buffalo: State University of New York Press.
Vygotsky, Lev S. 1978. *Mind in society: The development of higher psychological processes*, Michael Cole, Vera John-Steiner, Sylvia Scribner & Ellen Souberman (eds.), Cambridge, MA: Harvard University Press.
Vygotsky, Lev S. 1987. *The collected works of L.S. Vygotsky: Problems of general psychology*, vol. 1., Robert W. Rieber and Aaron S. Carton (eds.), New York and London: Plenum Press.
Whitehead, Alfred N. 1927. *Symbolism: Its meaning and effect*. New York: Macmillan.

Mariana Neț
Icons of modernity in *belle époque* Bucharest
The semiotics of city guides and yearbooks, foreign travellers' *memoirs*, postcards and cinema

Abstract: The basic assumption of this essay is that a city can be compared with other cities, but first and foremost, it should be compared with itself, with its own past and with its present ideals and realities, its sources and outcomes.

The era roughly extending between 1880 and 1914, usually known in Europe as *la Belle Epoque*, was a turning point in the development of the city of Bucharest. During this time Romania's capital city turned into a modern, Western European type of city in many respects.[1] Histories and monographs account for its rapid progress, its many urban improvements. So do several foreign travelers' accounts. Many of these texts testify to the plurality of lifestyles and world views in turn-of-the-century Bucharest.

Keywords: semiotics, icons, intermediality, Belle Epoque, Bucharest

1 Introduction

Conventionally, *la Belle Epoque*[2] extends during the last decades of the "long" nineteenth century, between 1880 and 1914. It was a time when city life blossomed and, hence urban lifestyles stood out. It was also the time when most urban facilities emerged and were, in part, implemented. Among them range new materials for street paving (macadam, asphalt), sidewalks, electric lighting (outdoors), running water, sewers, public transport within the city (i.e. tramways), as well as new communication media (the telephone, phonograph) and

---

1 Modernization was incomplete and did not cover the whole surface of the city, but this does not concern us here.
2 In Central European countries, *la Belle Epoque* is better known as *fin de siècle*.

Mariana Neț, Romanian Academy, Bucharest, Romania

https://doi.org/10.1515/9783110857801-012

pastimes (the cinema). All these urban facilities addressed especially the middle class,[3] whose well-being was therefore improved.

Such urban facilities were introduced in virtually all European and American cities; owing to their presence, throughout the latter half of the nineteenth century and increasingly so during the *Belle Epoque*, cities were practically reinvented, which is to say, modernized. In this context, Bucharest took advantage of its opportunity at becoming a modern city, too. The (partial) implementation of urban facilities rapidly transformed it from a little more than a medieval borough into a modern European city.

This paper presents the main icons[4] of modernity in the city of Bucharest during the *Belle Epoque*.[5] as shown in various media, i.e. city guides and yearbooks, foreign travellers' *memoirs*, postcards and cinema. These media products simultaneously emerged during the last decades of the "long century." They supplied complementary information, testifying to a mixture of modernity and tradition.

2 The city of Bucharest and "the culture of impersonality"

One of the basic characteristics of the modern city was pointed out and described by Thomas Bender:

> The modern city is marked by its capacity to generate public life, not as a periodic and formalized public ritual, as in the medieval and early modern city, but as an ongoing aspect of ordinary daily life. [. . .] What characterizes the modern metropolis is the creation of a significant culture of impersonality, a social world of strangers in continuous but limited association. (Bender 1988: 262)

---

[3] The members of the "upper" classes did profit by such facilities but they could have easily done without them as well, since they could enlist paid help to discharge the functions of urban facilities. The "lower" classes, on the other hand, did not count much for the administrations of the time.

[4] The term *icon* has here the "classical" meaning conferred on it by Charles S. Peirce. Vincent M. Colapietro explains it in a nutshell: "A term used by Charles S. Peirce to designate a specific type of sign [. . .] in which the sign vehicle represents its object by virtue of a resemblance or similarity. [. . .] If a sign is connected with its object by virtue of a resemblance to that object, it is an icon." (Colapietro 1993: 114–115) The specific icons this text refers to are either visual images of various parts of Bucharest (reproduced by photographs and movies) or verbal descriptions thereof (excerpted from city guides, yearbooks and memoirs).

[5] Several data included and commented upon here are also to be found in a relatively recent book of mine (Neţ 2016), where they are discussed from a different perspective and in a different context.

This "culture of impersonality," and modern city life in general, was enhanced by the fact that more and more people appropriated specific rules of conviviality, viz. politeness.

In effect, the concepts of "city life" and "good manners" are connected even etymologically: *civility* derives from *civis, -is* (Lat. "citizen"), *politeness* comes from *polis* (Gr. "city"), while *urbanity* is based on *urbs, -is* (Lat. "city").

Figure 1 illustrates a facet of daily life in the city. It shows an image of Calea Victoriei, the main avenue in Romania's capital city. The camera focuses on the three men who seem to be engaged in a conversation on the foreground left. By their gait and demeanour, the men are deemed to belong to the middle class. They seem to be engaged in a presumably spontaneous verbal intercourse and at least the one with his back to the wall looks like an "observer" of the street and the possible events thereon, viz. as a kind of *flâneur*. The image illustrates an instance of the "culture of impersonality", viz. of *modern* city life in Bucharest.

Fig. 1: View of Calea Victoriei towards Frascatti Hotel (1906). Collection of Bogdan Iordănescu

The one-minute film *10 mai 1897* (cf. Rîpeanu [1991] 2007) is another example of the same effect. The film was directed by Paul Menu[6] and produced by "L'Indépendance roumaine" studios. The film's subtitle is a synopsis of its contents.

---

6 Paul Menu was a former member of the Frères Lumière's team. He made some three dozen movies in Bucharest; most of them were destroyed in Communist times. In the evenings, the movies made during the day could be watched in the windows of "L'Indépendance roumaine" club, also located on Calea Victoriei, actually quite close to the place where the image in Fig. 1 was taken.

It runs: "Sa Majesté la reine en calèche et Sa Majesté le roi à cheval revenant au Palais".[7] The film shows the carriages of Queen Elisabeta and of her ladies-in-waiting accompanied by King Carol I[8] and the high officers of the Romanian Army, on horseback. The carriages and cavaliers pass on one of the main boulevards in Bucharest, while a fairly large number of people – both men and women – are assembled on the sidewalk and watch the procession. It is these people – presumably, most of them unbeknownst to each other but involved in the same "event" – which provide proof of what Thomas Bender called "the culture of impersonality". The people on the sidewalk obviously belong to the middle class; the members of the aristocracy and of the *haute bourgeoisie* did not need to cluster on sidewalks to watch the Royal Family pass, while members of the poorer classes would have been dressed differently.

3 *Belle Epoque* Bucharest: Between "the gates of the Orient" and "the little Paris"

Throughout the latter half of the nineteenth century, and increasingly so during the *Belle Epoque,* two clichés used to circulate about the city of Bucharest. Some people considered it as a city lying "at the gates of the Orient"; others dubbed it "the little Paris". Both clichés were devised not by locals, but by Western Europeans. Only later did Romanians appropriate them. Conventionally, the cliché about "the gates of the Orient" applied to *traditional* images and lifestyles in Romania's capital city, while the cliché considering Bucharest as "the little Paris" applied to the icons of *modernity* therein. It is worth mentioning that *Călăusa Capitalei şi a Expoziţiei* (1906: 25), which came out in the jubilee year 1906,[9] on the occasion of the national exhibition opened in "Carol I Park," explicitly referred to "the names by which strangers had first dubbed Bucharest, i.e. *the little Paris, the city of joy,* etc".

Thus, the "actors" of the day could watch themselves on screen at nightfall. This assertion is true for all the 200-odd films made in Romania between 1897 and 1914, most of them destroyed.

7 Her Majesty the queen, in a carriage, and his Majesty the king, [mounted] on a horse, return to the Palace.

8 Carol I von Hohenzollern-Sigmaringen (1866–1914) was first reigning Prince (1866–1881) then King of Romania (1881–1914). He was married to Elizabeth (Rom. Elisabeta) de Wied.

9 It celebrated 25 years since Romania had been a kingdom, 40 years since Carol I had been on the throne and 1800 years since Dacia had been conquered by the Romans and included in the Roman Empire.

While the cliché "Bucharest is the little Paris" mostly referred to the architecture of, for example, many administrative buildings,[10] several private residences, restaurants, cafés and boulevards, it also referred to cultural events and to lifestyles. Scrutinizing the media of the time reveals various constituents of corresponding lifestyles. The activity of skating is an example. Starting with the turn of the nineteenth century it has been a popular pastime in Europe and the United States. Figure 2 shows an image of young people skating on the lake in Cișmigiu Park.[11] The one-minute film *Patinage sur le lac de Cișmigiu* (cf. Rîpeanu [1991] 2007, director: Nicolae Barbelian, producer: "Carmen Sylva" studios), which dates from 1913, dwells on the same topic. It shows a group of aristocratic young men and women involved in skating on the frozen lake but also quite often looking at the camera, therefore concerned with their image thus "immortalized" and conveyed to future generations. It seems that these young aristocrats show an understanding of the cinematic medium and its documentary function. In this postcard and in this brief movie Bucharest was definitely (though implicitly) presented as a "little Paris".

Fig. 2: Skating on Cișmigiu Lake (ca 1900).
Courtesy of the Romanian Academy Library

---

10 Most buildings dating from the period under discussion are in eclectic French style.
11 Cișmigiu Park, projected by the Austrian landscaper W. Meyer and located in downtown Bucharest, dates from 1846. It was the first *public* park in Europe.

A lot of images – especially those reproduced on postcards (cf. *infra*) – show the speedy development of transport, as well as the co-existence of old and new means of transportation. Photographs feature both public transport like tramways, taxis and hackney coaches, and private ones like carts, bicycles, coaches and automobiles. It is often difficult to distinguish between public coaches and taxis, on the one hand, and private coaches and automobiles, on the other hand, especially if these transportation means are in motion. However, the guess may be pretty accurate if they are stationed, as it happens in the case of Fig. 3, discussed below.

The postcard in Fig. 3 is a photograph of the National Theatre Square. It occupied a central location in the city, and, as noticeable in the image, it then hosted the main taxi station. All existing means of public transport convened in the Theatre Square, as this image bears testimony. Also, the presence of the theatre in this context, I argue, suggests the stage-like character of street life in Bucharest.

But the most wonderful turn-of-the-century invention was definitely the "flying machine". The presence of the airplane in a community was an undoubted sign of modernity. The brief movie *Blériot*[12] *fait une démonstration à Bucarest* (cf. Rîpeanu [1991] 2007), a fragment of the (now lost) longer film *Scènes de la vie et du règne du roi Carol I-er* (cf. Rîpeanu 2008: 16–17), is an illustration of this. The movie was directed by Hughes d'Eywo and produced by Pathé Vienna. It was realized on October 18, 1909, i.e. on the very day of Blériot's flying demonstration,[13] which was filmed live. Owing to Blériot's demonstration and to the film and press releases thereof, as well as to the demonstrations, movies and press releases of and about Aurel Vlaicu,[14] Romanians, in general, and Bucharesters in particular, were well acquainted with flying and flying machines.

---

12 Louis Blériot (1872–1936), a French engineer, was one of the first aircraft builders and pilots in the world.
13 Louis Blériot's aircraft was assembled in downtown Bucharest and driven to Băneasa Hyppodrome along Calea Victoriei, the main boulevard of the city. For nearly a week before the demonstrative flights, the aircraft was exhibited in a shred near the hyppodrome, where it could be viewed by hundreds of curious people for a not very low admission fee. Moreover, the day after his arrival in Bucharest, Blériot gave a lecture at the Athenaeum, illustrated by documentary movies.
14 Several Romanians were capable flight pilots at the time. The most outstanding and justly best remembered was Aurel Vlaicu (1882–1913). Vlaicu was born at Binținți, in Transylvania, and studied mechanical engineering in Budapest and Munich. He was a pioneer and inventor of Romanian and world aircraft building. In the summer of 1912 he won two prizes at the International Flying Competition held in Aspen (Austria). The next year he met a tragic death while trying to fly over the Carpathians. Vlaicu's funeral, *Înmormîntarea lui Vlaicu*, was filmed not

Fig. 3: National Theatre Square (ca 1906).
Courtesy of Radu Olteanu

Nevertheless, turn-of-the-century Bucharest was also a city lying "at the gates of the Orient". Badly paved streets and "outdated" means of transportation (e.g. the cart) still existed on a pretty wide scale, while patriarchal lifestyles lingered. The label of being a city which lay "at the gates of the Orient" was applied by several foreign travellers coming from Western Europe. One of them was Raymond Poincaré,[15] who is known to have declared: "Que voulez-vous, nous sommes ici aux portes de l'Orient où tout est pris à la légère . . . ?" [What more do you want, we are here at the gates of the Orient, where everything is taken lightly . . . ?].[16] Derision and superficiality seem to have been among the main characteristics of the city to which the above cliché is/was applied. However, before drawing a conclusion in this respect, one should also keep in mind the statement of another

---

only by Romanian film makers (i.e. "Filmul de artă Leon M. Popescu," image: Gheorghe Ionescu, as well as "România-Film," image: Constantin T. Theodorescu), but also by Gaumont (image: Constantin Ivanovici), and by Pathé (image: Svoboda). By the time of his tragic death, Vlaicu was already a kind of national hero; his panegyric was the subject matter of a documentary movie made by the national film studio "Filmul de Artă Leon M. Popescu" (film direction and image: Gheorghe Ionescu). These films cannot be found and are probably lost.

15 Raymond Poincaré (1860–1934) was several times Prime Minister of the French government, as well as President of France (1913–1920). His statement about Bucharest being "at the gates of the Orient" was made after he had lost a trial there.

16 The source of this quotation is unknown. It was used as a motto to the novel *Craii de Curtea-Veche* [Old-Time Libertines] by Mateiu I. Caragiale (published in 1929).

Frenchman, Ulysse de Marsillac,[17] who, in his *Guide du voyageur à Bucarest* (1877) stated that "Bucarest évoque un Orient de rêve". [Bucharest evokes a dream-like Orient.] (Marsillac 1877: 159). Whether Bucharest evoked a dream-like Orient or just an Orient of superficiality and carelessness, it is hard to say. Probably it evoked both. Traces of Oriental lifestyles and mentalities will be pointed out in the next sections of this text.[18]

4 Modernity and tradition as evoked in guidebooks

The Academy Library in Bucharest holds twenty-eight city guidebooks published between 1871 and 1914. Twenty are in Romanian, two are in German, four in French and two are bilingual (Romanian-German, Romanian-French). The first guidebook for Bucharest was a street guide: *Guid de toate stradele așezate pe alfabet* [Alphabetic guidebook of all streets]. It came out in 1871. It was preceded by the inclusion of Bucharest in *Atlas des grandes villes du monde,* a monumental work which was published in Paris in 1870.[19] This detail is significant. It suggests that Romanians always had some reticence about promoting their own image and assets; in order to do this, they have always waited for an encouragement from abroad. Further proof to this effect: the first guidebook proper, *Guide du voyageur à Bucarest* (1877, cf. *supra*), was authored by Ulysse de Marsillac (cf. *supra*), a Frenchman who had made his home in Bucharest.[20]

---

17 Ulysse de Marsillac (1821–1877) was a French intellectual self-exiled in Bucharest, where he wrote several books and articles describing the city and its lifestyles.
18 One can detect here traces of what a century later, Edward Said would refer to as the Western Europeans patronizing representations of a generic "Orient": "Europeans invented 'the exotic East' and the 'inscrutable Orient', which are cultural representations of peoples and things, considered inferior to the peoples and things of the West". (Said 1978: 38).
19 It mentions the main public, administrative and religious buildings (e.g. the Royal Palace, the ministries, the Préfecture de Police, the City Hall, the National Bank, the Arsenal, the National Theatre, the Military Hospital, the Court of Accounts, a few historical churches, the Synagogue, but omits a few others (e.g. the Museum of Natural History, the Pinacothèque).
20 The main reason for Romanians' reticence to self-promotion consisted in the long centuries of Ottoman (or Hungarian) dominance in the Romanian countries (see also Boia 2012, *inter alii*), which had long-lasting (though sometimes unacknowledged) effects on their mentalities. Their late coming on the "market" of self-promotion was yet another reason. Nowadays, the same reticence is an outcome of long-lasting destructions made in Communist and Post-Communist times, and a reaction against nationalistic views held by some Romanians.

The next guidebook of the city, *Guide-manuel de l'étranger à Bucarest,* was published two years later, in 1879. Afterwards, a guidebook was issued almost every year. The Western character of the city was noticed in a guidebook published immediately after the War of Independence (1877–1878), being therefore one of the first of its kind, *Guide-Manuel de l'étranger à Bucarest* (1879: 17). This guide remarked that the whole city was illuminated by the use of gas, and in this way it stood apart from most Oriental cities, where public lighting, if it did exist, was quite rudimentary. On the other hand, the same guidebook pointed out that by its pitiable paving and the complete lack of symmetry in the street arrangement, Bucharest was close to Oriental cities.[21]

As to the modernity of the city, *Noua călăusă a Bucurescilor* shows that "all coaches [have] headlights which are lit at night," and specifies that this rule had been "voted and adopted by the City Council [as early as] 1868" (Lungu 1896: 9, 4). All guidebooks and yearbooks refer to the tariff of hackney coaches and omnibuses. The 1890 yearbook is the first work of its kind to dedicate a whole chapter to Bucharest tramways (*Annuaire general de Roumanie* 1890: 126), i.e. to specify at length itineraries and tariffs, and to point out that it was possible to buy a tram pass at a discount price. This last detail was fairly important for stimulating the middle class. The city's European appearance is also emphasized by *Noua călăusă a Bucurescilor* (Lungu 1896: 3), which refers to "the changes triggered by the opening of boulevards". It should be pointed out that this latter characteristic of European urbanism was closely related to the changing lifestyles of the middle class (cf. Benjamin [1982] 1993).

Thus, nearly all guidebooks notice the *contrast* between modernity and tradition in the city of Bucharest. They all refer to the "lack of balance" between the large surface of the city and the small number of its inhabitants. The first example to this effect was excerpted from *Călăusa Capitalei și a Expoziției,* a guidebook of the city issued on the occasion of the already mentioned Jubilee Exhibition held in 1906:

---

21 While a present-day reader might be tempted to look upon such a characterization of the "Orient" in terms of Said's criticism of Western "superiority" over the "East" (see note 20), at the end of the 19th century Romanians did not think much at Oriental cultural values and could not possibly share the Westerners' (basically British) "imperialist" attitude towards the East. For most turn-of-the-century Romanians the generic "Orient" suggested the long centuries of Ottoman domination, which they had been subject to and had just relinquished or were about to relinquish. If anything, Romanians' feelings towards the "Orient" might have been termed as "anti-imperialist" (i.e. anti-Ottoman) much rather than "imperialist". However, it is also a fact that, in their quest of a different, modern identity, Romanians gladly accepted what might be called French "cultural imperialism". Things and circumstances were, certainly, more intricate than this and deserve an in-depth analysis, which however is far from the point of this essay.

> Această lipsă de echilibru [între suprafața orașului și numărul locuitorilor] este în favoarea orașului, pentru că numai astfel se pot vedea, în plin centru, case înconjurate de curți și grădini mari, care-i conferă capitalei României un aspect pitoresc, care, până la un punct, o caracterizează. Altă trăsătură distinctivă a Bucureștiului este amestecul de elemente apusene și orientale: clădiri impunătoare așezate lângă (din ce în ce mai puține) case care te duc cu gândul la timpuri apuse (*Călăusa Capitalei și a Expoziției* 1906: 1).
>
> [This lack of balance [between the surface of the city and the number of its inhabitants] is in favour of the city, for it is only owing to it that one can see, in the very centre, houses surrounded by big gardens and courtyards, conferring the capital city of Romania a picturesque appearance, which, up to a certain point, is characteristic. Yet another distinctive feature of Bucharest is the mixture of Western elements and Oriental ones, i.e. impressive buildings by the side of (fewer and fewer) houses that make one think of times of yore.] (*Călăusa Capitalei și a Expoziției* 1906: 1)

The above-quoted fragment is conclusive enough. It points out the perceived contrast between "West" and "East", between modernity and tradition and the "charm" held by large courtyards and gardens, as well as the tendency to leave such traces of the past behind and to transform the city into a truly modern one.

This transformation would entail providing lodgings for a quadruple number of inhabitants, as another guidebook had pointed out a quarter of a century before:

> Dacă terenul ar fi fost folosit corespunzător, orașul ar fi putut număra astăzi 1.000.000 de locuitori; în situația de față numără numai 250.000" (*Guide-manuel de l'étranger à Bucarest* 1879: 16).
>
> [Had the ground been adequately made use of, the city could have now counted 1,000,000 inhabitants; as it is, it only counts 250,000.] (*Guide-manuel de l'étranger à Bucarest* 1879: 16)

A contemporary reader infers that, in spite of their charm and ecological advantages, the large courtyards and gardens and the low density of population per square metre were a hindrance to the complete modernization of the city: under the circumstances, it was difficult to instal too many sewers and/or telephones. During the *Belle Epoque*, Bucharest was obviously a border city. However, its "Westernization" was a constant concern of city officials, or so the guidebooks showed it to be.

Historian Adrian Majuru explains that the reason Bucharest used to be called "the little Paris" was because of its speedy and spectacular rate of development (cf. Majuru 2007: 40), among other things. In effect, all the modern works presenting the city of Bucharest by 1900 emphasized the progress registered by the city in a really short time. In the 1882 *Annuaire général de Roumanie*, the author notes:

> La physionomie de Bucarest a complètement changé. Les rues sont toujours tortueuses, mais elles sont mieux pavées pour les piétons. (*Annuaire général de Roumanie* 1882: 171)

> [The physiognomy of Bucharest has completely changed. Its streets are still tortuous, but they are better paved and more convenient to passers-by.] (*Annuaire general de Roumanie* 1882: 171)

Progress was a daily phenomenon in Bucharest then, so obvious that it was possible to make optimistic forecasts for the near future of the city. The following assertion from the same work, *Annuaire général de Roumanie,* is symptomatic in this respect:

> [. . .] dans quelques années, tous les vestiges de l'ancienne ville auront disparu et Bucarest aura pris l'apparence d'une cité d'Occident – tout en conservant son caractère particulier qu'il serait vraiment dommage qu'elle perdit". (*Annuaire général de Roumanie* 1882: 171)

> [[. . .] in a couple of years, all traces of the old city will have disappeared and Bucharest will look like a Western European city, while preserving its specific character, which it would be a real pity to lose.] (*Annuaire général de Roumanie* 1882: 171)

Thus, nearly all guidebooks and yearbooks of Bucharest show progress to have been a constant, daily phenomenon in the city and point out a few of its landmarks. Since Romanians had the implicit "choice" between "East" and "West", they did choose West, as guidebooks and yearbooks show.

5 The population

By the end of the nineteenth century, Bucharest was a cosmopolitan city, according to the standards of the time.[22] This is testified by statistics and surveys, as well by yearbooks and city guides.

For instance, the 1877 guide states:

> Bucarest est une ville cosmopolite. Le nombre des étrangers qui y résident et y trafiquent est relativement très grand. Français, Allemands, Hongrois, Polonais, Suisses etc. se partagent à peu près toutes les branches du commerce, l'épicerie exceptée. [. . .] La colonie grecque détient surtout le commerce des céréales. [. . .] La colonie juive enfin,

---

22 It preserved this character until the end of World War II.

ici comme partout, part de la haute Banque pour descendre jusqu'au bric-à-brac. (*Guide-Manuel du voyageur à Bucarest* 1879: 20)

[Bucharest is a cosmopolitan city. The number of foreigners residing and working here is fairly big. French, Germans, Hungarians, Poles, Swiss, etc. are present in all branches of trade, except grocery. [. . .] The Greek colony is primarily active in the trade of cereals. [. . .] The Jewish colony, here as everywhere else, illustrates several levels, from high finance to the bric-à-brac.] (*Guide-Manuel du voyageur à Bucarest* 1879: 20)

The information conveyed here is factually accurate. The census of 1900 shows the population of Bucharest to have been 282,071 inhabitants, out of which 186,683 were Romanians, 43,318 were Jews, 38,660 came from the Austro-Hungarian Empire[23] and 13,530 belonged to other nationalities and ethnic groups. From this point of view, the guidebook issued in 1911 (cf. Boermer & Vahrig 1911: 9) was even more specific. It referred to the 1910 survey, according to which Bucharest counted 299,420 inhabitants,[24] one third of which were foreign-born (cf. *supra*).

According to historian Adrian Majuru (cf. Majuru 2007: 40), it was owing to the fact that Bucharest was a multi-ethnic city, and foreign-born elements belonged to the middle class, that the city could be urbanized and modernized successfully, while still remaining a cosmopolitan city. In a book published a decade ago, historian Andrei Pippidi deals fleetingly with this phenomenon. The author cites a foreign traveler who said that in 1868 most of the middle class in Bucharest was foreign-born, having been "imported" by the native aristocracy in order to occupy public positions, because foreigners could represent no danger to the privileges of the aristocracy (cf. Pippidi 2008: 132). The information supplied by guidebooks was accurate; the authors of guidebooks were well-informed.

6 A modern and Narcissist city

Towards the end of the long century, Bucharest referred to itself through all possible media. A survey of its treatment in cinema and guidebooks was provided

---

23 This number also included the Romanians from Transylvania (at the time belonging to the Austro-Hungarian Empire).
24 The number of inhabitants varies with the source.

above. Besides, several travel memoirs,[25] three histories[26] and two monographs[27] of Bucharest were also written during the *Belle Epoque*. Fiction[28] located in Bucharest, and in which the city or some of its landmarks discharged an important function, was also published at the time. It is fairly significant that, while in midcentury the city was represented as a corrupt and crime-filled place, in which progress was morally harmful, as the century drew to a close the image of Bucharest became more and more objective and matter-of-fact. Sometimes, an image of the city is treated with mild irony, as happens in musical comedies.[29]

Nevertheless, the first songs[30] dedicated to Bucharest were composed only after World War I. Also, the city was not yet represented in painting. The first paintings and graphics featuring Bucharest, as well, were only realized in the *postbellum* era. Until then, Bucharest was amply represented in photographs reproduced on postcards (cf. *infra*).

7 Bucharest on postcards

This brief survey of a few images of Bucharest on postcards shows what the city was like, the way it was represented, what those images conveyed then and what they convey now, namely *reality* and *appearance* in *Belle Epoque* Bucharest.

---

25 To give only the best-known example, Ulysse de Marsillac wrote *De Peste à Bucarest. Notes de voyage*. It came out in 1869. The image of the city was far from flattering. But eight years later the same author published the already quoted *Guide du voyageur à Bucarest*, which explicitly noticed the tremendous progress registered in the city.
26 Dimitrie Papazoglu published *Histoire des débuts de la ville de Bucarest* (1870) and *Histoire de la fondation de la ville de Bucarest* (1871), while G. I. Ionescu-Gion is the author of *Histoire de Bucarest* (1899).
27 Ion Licherdopol's monograph is titled *Bucarest* (1889). Frédéric Damé's unfinished monograph *Bucarest en 1906* was published in 1907, a year after his death. It is a monumental work, in many respects still valid.
28 Matei Millo's *Prăpăstiile Bucureștilor* [The Abysses of Bucharest] (1858) and *Apele de la Văcărești* [The Waters of Văcărești] (1872), Ion Ghica's *Convorbiri economice* [Talks on Economy] (1879) and especially I.L. Caragiale's comedies *O noapte furtunoasă* [Stormy Night] (1879) and *D'ale carnavalului* [Carnival Scenes] (1885), as well as his *Momente și schițe* [Momentous Sketches] (1900) are among the best known pieces.
29 The most famous example is *Obor – Gara de Nord* [Obor Market – Northern Railway Station] by Dan and Emil Ciachir. Its partition has been lost.
30 The only exception was the waltz *Viața la București* [Life in Bucharest] by the famous Iosif Ivanovich (1845–1928).

The 'system' of postcards was introduced in Romania in 1873.[31] The first Romanian *illustrated* postcard was issued on August 29, 1894.[32] Soon afterwards, on October 5, 1894, "Carol Müller" bookstore, located in downtown Bucharest, announced that they would soon begin selling the first illustrated postcards issued in Romania. From 1894 to 1896 postcards reproduced drawings. After 1896 they used to bear the logo "Salutări din Bucuresci" [Greetings from Bucharest]. In the two decades separating 1894 from 1914 some 400-odd postcards[33] were issued. They showed representative public buildings, statues,[34] hotels,[35] the University, high schools[36] (see Fig. 4), public parks and gardens[37] markets.[38]

8 On boulevards

Fairly often, the images reproduced on postcards featured human elements, too. It is also a fact that during the first decade of the twentieth century many postcards resembled film images. At the beginning of modern visual media, not only did movie images remind people of photographs, but the reverse was just as true. Postcards were both "romantic" and true-to-life; they offer proof of the photographers' skill, as well as of the represented people's *savoir-faire*. The image in Fig. 5 is an example of this. The postcard's caption mentions that it represents Capșa House.[39] The photograph also features some two-dozen people from the upper middle-class walking at leisure on the sidewalk. The segment of Calea Victoriei between Capșa House and the Royal Palace was the most fashionable "promenade" in downtown Bucharest. It was never deserted, especially in the afternoon.

---

31 A postcard was then a stamped piece of cardboard with a small drawing in a corner; brief messages could be handwritten on the back of this piece of cardboard, as well as in a small square on the front.
32 It represented a peasant woman, in traditional dress, in Cișmigiu Park.
33 The exact number is difficult to know. No museum has an exhaustive collection and no entire collection is available to researchers from outside the museum. Nor are most private collectors too willing to collaborate with researchers.
34 22 statues were unveiled in Bucharest between 1866 and 1916.
35 The most famous were Grand Hôtel du Boulevard (opened in 1867), Hôtel Métropole (1870) and Grand Hôtel de France (1882).
36 E.g. "Lazăr" high school (for boys), "Central" high school (for girls), etc.
37 E.g. Cișmigiu Park (1846), "Carol" Park (1906), etc.
38 Bibescu-Vodă market was often represented.
39 Capșa House (café, restaurant and luxury hotel) was the most famous establishment of its kind in *Belle Epoque* Bucharest. It was located on Calea Victoriei, the main avenue in the city.

Fig. 4: "Lazăr" high school (around 1900).
Courtesy of Cezar Petre Buiumaci

Fig. 5: Capșa House (after 1907).
Courtesy of the Museum of the City of Bucharest

The newly opened boulevards,[40] an unmistakable token of modernity, were also a favourite subject of postcards.[41] Views concentrate on street life and everything it involves: people, sidewalks, electric street lamps, transportation means. Such postcards are fairly relevant because, although the boulevards in Bucharest were relatively few, they were one of the city's acknowledged assets and locals felt proud of having such infrastructure. The aforementioned guidebooks provide proof to this effect. The images featuring boulevards are usually based on the interplay of perspectives and yield *theatrical*, scenic effects. Postcards representing 1900 Bucharest tend to represent everyday life accurately.

Figure 6 offers an example in this respect. Ostensibly, it represents the "Ministry of War". Actually, it is a minimalist image of "Carol I" Boulevard at the turn of the century, featuring only one piece of each and every essential element of a modern boulevard, viz. a building in the new style Haussmann had recently established (the "Ministry of War," on the left), a partial view of the Ministry of Public Domains, in an eclectic French style (on the right), electric street lamps, and an electric streetcar. The human touch is given by a few figures in the background, who look as if they had already interacted with the boulevard and duly appropriated it. At the beginning of the twentieth century it was enough for representations to *suggest* a boulevard, there was no need to actually *show* it.

Bulevardul Carol I

Fig. 6: "Carol I" Boulevard.
From the collection of Infarom Publishing

---

40 Calea Victoriei [Victory Avenue] dates from 1701.
41 Academy Boulevard dates from 1870, Elisabeta Boulevard and Carol I Boulevard were opened in 1871.

Many postcards dating from the turn of the nineteenth century have several variants. Often, these variants are meant to illustrate two different "identities" of the same boulevard. Figs. 7 and 8 reproduce two views of the former Colței Boulevard, which, from 1894 on, was called Lascăr Catargiu Boulevard. The postcard shown in Fig. 7 entered circulation in 1910. It reproduces a street-level image of Colței Boulevard. The viewer can see villas and palaces on both sides, the flower beds in the middle of the boulevard, trees on both sidewalks, cubic pavement and the electric bulbs, several pedestrians (both men and women), a bicycle rider, as well as two people on horseback. Several transportation means of the time, from the electric streetcar to a couple of horse-driven carts and the already mentioned bicycle, are also featured by this image, which presents a typical view of a turn-of-the-century European boulevard.

Fig. 7: Colței Boulevard.
Courtesy of Cezar Petre Buiumaci

Figure 8 features only a partial view of the same boulevard.[42] The image focuses on a couple of villas and palaces, as well as a few trees on the left sidewalk, all seen in a mildly diagonal perspective. This view suggests a peaceful residential neighbourhood much more than a boulevard in a busy city. In actual fact, both images were true to life. Turn-of-the-century Lascăr Catargiu Boulevard was both a modern boulevard – situated on the North-South axis – in a busy city, where vehicles, of many types, and people crossed paths, and a relatively peaceful residential area. The name of Colței Boulevard changed several times in the last

---

42 Now called Lascăr Catargiu.

Fig. 8: Lascăr Catargiu Boulevard.
Courtesy of Radu Olteanu

hundred years, but it has preserved some of the same characteristics to-date. This ambivalent status is strengthened by the fact that the boulevard connected boisterous downtown Bucharest to Kisseleff Avenue, where horse races were held and other leisure activities took place. Lascăr Catargiu Boulevard was an extension of both the busy and elegant downtown and the leisurely, elegant Kisseleff Avenue.

9 Popular neighbourhoods

Some of the postcards issued during the *Belle Epoque* feature "popular" neighbourhoods in the city, i.e. streets inhabited by members of the lower middle class (merchants, craftsmen, etc.).[43] The reproduction of these images is also a sign that the lower middle class had started to arouse interest in most officials, artists and dealers. Parts of the city which had been quite overlooked before

---

[43] The choice of such neighborhoods was probably dictated by financial reasons. Lower middle-class people were also beginning to travel through the country, all the more so as many of them originated from the countryside, which they visited on a regular basis. They also corresponded, sometimes by postcards, with their relatives from the countryside and/or from other towns and cities. Consequently, it was important that some postcards should represent parts of the city which were familiar to that particular segment of population.

were now being photographed and it appears that Bucharesters took pride in them. It is also relevant that photographers focused on those segments where buildings had two levels (not a very frequent characteristic of Romanian cities in those times). Almost always, a tram would be seen moving along, a detail which was by no means irrelevant. Just before World War I, tram riding was a lifestyle in Bucharest. In 1913, the city counted more tram riders than Bremen, Amsterdam, Strasbourg or Berlin, though less than Paris, Bordeaux, New York or Detroit (cf. Parusi 2007: 477).

The last two postcards discussed here (Figs. 9 and 10) represent "Sfântu Gheorghe" Square, which is the Kilometre Zero of Bucharest. This neighbourhood had been always inhabited by the lower middle class. However, at the end of the nineteenth century the Kilometre Zero was also the terminus of all tramways, including the electric one. The presence of the small statue in the centre of these images is well accounted for: in 1906, the city of Bucharest had received, as a gift from the city of Rome, a copy of *Lupa Capitolina*, the symbol of Latinity. The monument was placed at the Kilometre Zero and thus endowed this neighbourhood with a new symbolic value.

Figure 9 has a spectacular character. The human element is most important and it occupies half of the space on the cardboard. Men are everywhere, they occupy the foreground. One can say that the human element is more important than the two-story buildings, the church, the electric tram, and the statue of the she-wolf taken together. The characters, all male, have an impeccable gait and are flawlessly dressed. They probably belong to the upper classes. The image testifies to the fact that, thanks to the statue of the she-wolf, and the electric tram, the Kilometre Zero, a traditionally lower middle-class neighborhood, was being taken over by élites. One is entitled to suppose that the precise image reproduced by Fig. 9 could have been staged.

A postcard issued at the same time by a different publisher (see Fig. 10) representing the same square from the opposite side (the she-wolf is now looking right, the tramway is in front of the monument, and there is no church tower in the background), seen from above and slightly from the left angle is by far less keen on details, distances, angles, viz. it is just as realistic, but obviously less "artistic".

However, the reason for considering the postcards shown in Figs. 9 and 10 in parallel is not so much an aesthetic one. In the insight of Figs. 9, 10, testifies to Bucharesters' concern with what their city looked like, viz. their wish to modernize it, to make it resemble Western European cities. While this concern is far less obvious in Fig. 10, it still is present: notice the open perspective created by the street going up in the background, as well as the presence of all the aforementioned elements of modernity.

Fig. 9: "Sfântu Gherghe" Square.
Courtesy of the National Museum of History of Romania

Fig. 10: "Sfântu Gheorghe" Square.
Courtesy of Cezar Petre Buiumaci

10 Conclusions

Belle Epoque Bucharest had many faces; it presented viewers with multifarious aspects. Its representations in the media of the time show that Bucharesters admired their city and were proud of it; at the very least, they were encouraged to do so by the institutions who had commissioned the postcards. Histories and monographs devoted to the city show its rapid progress and its many urban improvements. So do films and postcards. So do several foreign travellers' accounts. Obviously, some parts of the city were more developed than others, while many citizens still clung to semi-rural lifestyles and the rural imaginary was still powerful.

Often, there are several media representations and several views of the same spot; in such cases, the connotations of each and every representation are different. The interpretation is in the eyes of the beholder; it is, as always, a negotiation between the promoter and the viewer of each image. The plurality of city views is also a vivid sign of the plurality of lifestyles and world views in modern Bucharest. It is a token of aesthetic democracy and of democracy *tout court*. Most views, irrespective of the medium presenting them, can be interpreted as examples of the "culture of impersonality" (cf. *supra*), which is one of the main features of modernity.

References

Anonymous. 1882. *Annuaire général de Roumanie*. Bucarest: Bureaux de l'Annuaire.
Anonymous. 1890. *Annuaire général de Roumanie*. Bucarest: Bureaux de l'Annuaire.
Bender, Thomas. 1988. Metropolitan life and the making of public culture. In John Hull Mollenkopf (ed.), *Power, culture, and place. Essays on New York City*. 262–271. New York: Russell Sage Foundation.
Benjamin, Walter. [1982] 1993. *Paris, capitale du XIXe siècle. Le livre des passages*. (2nd édn). Paris: Editions du Cerf.
Boermer, Edwin & F. Vahrig. 1911. *Quo vadis? Noul plan al orașului București*. București: Albert Baer.
Boia, Lucian. 2012. *De ce este România altfel?* București: Humanitas.
∗∗∗ 1906. *București. Călăusa capitalei și a expoziției*. București: Stabilimentul de arte grafice"Adevărul".
Caragiale, Mateiu. [1929] 2017. *Craii de Curtea-Veche*. București: Humanitas.
Colapietro, Vincent M. 1993. *Glossary of semiotics*. New York: Paragon House.
∗∗∗1879. *Guide-manuel de l'étranger à Bucarest*. Bucuresci: Imprimerie de la Cour.
Lungu, George I. 1896. *Noua călăusă a Bucurescilor*. Bucuresci: Tipografia "Gutenberg". Joeph Göbl.
Majuru, Adrian. 2007. *București. Povestea unei geografii umane*. București: Institutul cultural român.
Marsillac, Ulysse de. 1877. *Guide du voyageur à Bucarest*. Bucarest: Imprimerie de la cour (Ouvriers associés).

Neț, Mariana. 2016. *Once upon two cities. A parallel between New York City and Bucharest by 1900*. Champaign, IL: Common Ground.
Parusi, Gheorghe. 2007. *Cronologia Bucureștilor*. București: Compania.
Pippidi, Andrei. 2008. *Case și oameni din București*. București: Humanitas.
Rîpeanu, Bujor. 2008. *Filmat în România. Filmul documentar 1897–1947*. București: Meronia.
Rîpeanu, Bujor. [1991] 2007. *1897–1938. Images pour l'histoire de la Roumanie*. Episode I. 1897–1918. 2. "18 octobre 1909 Blériot fait une démonstration à Bucarest". București: Editura Video, DVD.
Said, Edward. 1978. *Orientalism*. New York: Vintage Books.

Donna E. West
Glimpses into Peircean event imaging: Episode-simulation as a scaffold for right-guessing

Abstract: Peirce's concept of virtual habit, (1909: MS 620), constitutes a scaffold for abductive reasoning. Notable is how virtual habit compel the conduct employed to avert anticipated consequences. Virtual habits surface as vivid action-images, so specific that they qualify as determinations, soon to be enacted. Although they do not rise to the level of habit, in that repetition has not yet materialized, they serve a higher calling, inciting novel hypotheses, particularly in children (habit-change). Vivid, episodic memories emerge at 3;0 when index differentiates the where of event scenes. These memories are constructed when index hastens the application of logic to cause-effect scenarios, such that spatial relations suggest a logic for event frames/scenes, in line with Schacter and Addis' 2007 Constructive Episodic Simulation Hypothesis. This inquiry shows how Peirce's concept of virtual habit (compelling, episodic images) constitutes the most effective preparation for implementing novel inferences.

Keywords: Peirce, virtual habit, episodic memory, inferencing

1 Introduction

This lecture explores the semiosis of event representations, particularly how mental pictures take on a sequential character in ontogeny. Peirce's Ten-Fold Division of Signs sheds particular light on how index and icon are instrumental in conceiving moving action aggregates. Attention is widely accorded to utilization of indexical signs and their interpretants which aptly represent both action relations, and resultative states of affairs. Emphasis is placed on alterations made in the interpretant within the first five years (meanings, effects) consequent to event-image innovations. Peirce's ten-fold division of signs advocates that deictic (often dialogic) meanings/effects of action schemas constitutes the ultimate event interpretant, and that index is the sign most implicated in this episode-building process. Support for this claim is grounded securely in Peirce's Dicisign and Pheme (1903; 1906; 1908: 8.337–339), because the development of

Donna E. West, State University of New York at Cortland

https://doi.org/10.1515/9783110857801-013

images as propositions/assertions/arguments depends largely upon whether they function as Phemes and Dicisigns. In fact, it is the interpretant of the Pheme and Dicisign which, in making explicit a proposition, can likewise imply assertions and arguments. They do so because they consist in indexes together with icons which have the power to influence others' complexions of mind by implying recommendations for courses of belief and action.

This account provides evidence in support of Peirce's latest semiotic division. It illustrates how children's early event representations become associated with increasingly more objective, logical interpretants – from events whose effects impinge upon the self, to those which are other-centric. Empirical findings will demonstrate that children's event representations emerge as single goal driven events, then expand into deictic, two ordered reciprocal events featuring space and time coordinates. Only after signs depict episodic components, incorporating allocentric location points, can event interpretants suggest imperative/subjunctive meanings. In this way, new assignments of interpretants give rise to qualitatively different conceptions of event templates, which inform children's inferencing skills. In short, the semiosis of Peirce's interpretant as set forth in his ten-fold division of signs accounts for major advances in children's event representations, given realization of the episodic character of events arrived at when interpretants of scenes imply dynamic motion coordinates. The process often begins with flashes of insight, such that definite icons surface in the mind without planning or measurable deliberation. These flashes consist in what Peirce refers to as virtual habits – sudden salient event images which contain the seeds for suggesting plausible action habits. These pre-lived virtual habits reach status as abductions when interpretants supply objective behavioral directives to diverse event participants. Such directives depict recommendations for novel action-paths (1909: MS 637: 12). Because these virtual habits represent viable suggestions for how to act within definite contexts, their form transcends mere resolutions, qualifying as determinations (MS 611). As such, when virtual habits surface, they constitute propositions, then assertions; and when their episodic directive for the objective other is realized, they reach implied argument status.[1] Nonetheless, matching the same meaning to the event sign between sign users is not a simple process, since it relies not merely upon implied relations between events, but upon unrevealed inferences imposed by

---

1 "A representamen is either a rhema, a proposition, or an argument. An argument is a representamen which separately shows what interpretant it is intended to determine. A proposition is a representamen which is not an argument, but which separately indicates what object it is intended to represent. A rhema is a simple representation without such separate parts" (1903: EP2:204).

two distinct signers which feature such relations. In fact, guessing right for both sign producers and receivers (a major thrust of Peirce's division of signs) requires acting upon implicit knowledge drawn from latent effects between events which signers may or may not notice. As such, discerning relations depends heavily upon phenomenological factors – beyond the scope of direct experience. This is paramount in ascertaining perspective diversity for episodic sign use, given the incompleteness of event relations in the face of employing ego's perspective alone. Absent episodic meanings, the range of event interpretants is limited by the self's own bodily activity – constrained to opportunities or observations of other's opportunities. For this reason, factors which contribute to a consequent event can easily be underdetermined by virtue of a disregard for exogenous experiences – those beyond personal enactment/observation.

The factor most responsible for event semiosis is the emergence of episodic features, incorporating within the interpretant movement of happenings across space and time. This episodic attribute of event signs is derived particularly from the growth of the interpretant as set forth in Peirce's 1908 letter to Lady Welby and in MS 620 generated in 1909. Here Peirce elucidates the dialogic influence of index, as gate-keeper to measure others' perspectives – their shifting physical and psychological relations to objects and other participants. The semiosis of event meanings as episodic ultimately emanates from their objective character, but begins with appreciation for ins and outs (inside or outside) events. This dialogic complexion of event signs which index affords, introduces into the interpretant a subjunctive character, making accessible projections of self into other orientations. In furtherance of episode as diverse path-finder, Index legitimizes reference to possible happenings. In sum, Index's role as gate-keeper in episode-building raises it to a new height in semiosis – affording prominence to the sway of participant event slots in ontogeny. The indexical function informs event motility by drawing attention to times and places of participant roles. It highlights the spatial, participatory, and temporal features relevant within and across event frames. This progression requires at least rudimentary consciousness of aspectual features (telicity, dynamicity), as well as an appreciation for the events' purposes/goals. Anticipating how, where, and when events begin and conclude, is paramount to the realization of the event's purpose/goal, since, according to Bauer (2006: 384), it constitutes the basis upon which episodes are constructed.

2 The development of episodic thought

Infants must first perceive the event's situatedness, spatial and temporal boundaries, prior to constructing episodes wherein objects and participants' orientation and motility are integrated. Quinn and Intraub (2007: 331) found that as young as 0;3 spatial boundary extension skills are operational, in that their infants habituated (looked less) at pictures depicting a wider panorama, beyond a narrow visual field. Quinn and Intraub assume that looking longer at a narrow slice of occupied space (than a wider scene) indicates onset of memory of implicit boundaries, e.g. corners or windows in a room. The stimuli consisted of a teddy in a corner (both wide and narrow views), without any obvious border around the teddy. In looking longer at the narrower scene, infants imposed their own spatial boundaries.

At 0;6, infants recognized not merely where scenes end, but paths – looking longer at actions depicting motion toward destinations. Moreover, looking was discontinued when paths were blocked, as well as when they concluded. These findings demonstrate that infants at this age encode some notion of objective path trajectories. This is relevant to event relations in that recognition of end of paths demonstrates the emergence of near and beyond space. Apprehension of motion along paths evidences knowledge of feature distinctiveness and continuity, foundational to apprehension of where events begin, who participates in them, and where they end. Recognition of the beginning and end of paths demonstrates expectations regarding event structure – how single events are connected with others to form aggregate structures/episodes. According to Baillargeon (1986), at 0;6, infants realize that objects proceeding along a path can be stopped if blocked by another object. Although at 0;6 children recognize where motion events end, e.g., when objects stop at the end of a path or when they are prevented from proceeding further, they fail to demonstrate episodic thought, given the lack of continuity across events – relating a happening along one path to a resultative state of another. The non-episodic character of memory at this age is likewise demonstrated by children's actual enactments, not merely by looking-time. At 0;6 infants reproduce path-like gestures with physical movement of their own body, demarcating a beginning and an end point. Nonetheless, their gestures (head movement) at this age are merely imitative (Meltzoff and Moore 1977; Barr, Dowden, and Hayne 1996). Infants' gestures at this age are arguably non-episodic, in that they do not show clear evidence that they encode behavioral trajectories intrinsic to particular objects. Moreover, infants' gestures only constitute immediate reproductions, since little, if any time, intervened between observation of the model and reproductions. In short, despite recognition of graphical arrays at 0;3 (Quinn and Intraub 2007: 331) and spatial boundaries at 0;6 (Baillargeon 1986), infants lack the skill (which index ultimately affords) to unite event features into an integrated behavioral course. Rather, actions resemble automatic bundles performed unconsciously – lacking logical connections across constituent actions. Furthermore, classification of actions/states into event types (giving, putting) is likewise absent at this juncture.

These event classifications are defined by predictable directional templates, e.g., the source, path and goal in a provide-like scenario, where giving represents the source, carrying an object through directed space the path, and arriving at the auspices of the intended receiver the goal. But, Until memory can situate the components of these procedures, individuating and consolidating events are not operational. Despite the means to differentiate when individual events begin and conclude evidenced by discerning blocked path scenarios, episodic thought is still undeveloped, because it lacks logical connections across referent points. Connecting these referent points is facilitated when children bundle events into classes, because recognition that events can cohere semantically with other happenings – forming single event structures which contain several similar procedures obviates the episodic aspects of events (proceeding from origin, path, to goal). Children eventually classify these action/stative relations when event aggregates are understood as kinds, consonant with encoding into syntactic and pragmatic templates. In this way, children discern that it is not merely the endpoint which determines whether events fit into the same template, but other factors internal to the event, e.g., participant roles.

Factors external to the event under consideration likewise contribute to how events are classified, e.g., other events which can preempt the emergence of the original event. Internal factors typically entail semantic roles (agents, receivers, instruments) whose intentions bring the relations of the event into existence, or into sharper focus. Accordingly, whether events express conditions affecting other parties is a consequence of discerning the interpretant of the event sign –constructing potential pragmatic effects from relations holding among participants. In other words, building the episodic character of events entails well-founded conjectures: as to how event types are likely to play out, who constitute their initiators/benefactors, and the like. Such shadows of meaning exist in the interpretant from its outset, ordinarily characterizing the events progression. This meaning potential, referred to as "provenation" (Deely 2009: 29; Deely 2012: 156) is responsible for more advanced meanings which exist invisibly from the interpretant's origin. Essentially, the caliber of events' interpretants (how objects are utilized, or how actions suggest other actions/states of affairs) create profiles. The inception of the meaning begins at the very moment that meaning/effects are first assigned to the event sign.

The upshot is that even primitive interpretants of event signs, e.g., uni-directional motion, invite more elaborated interpretants, e.g., bi-directional templates consisting in episodes. These event interpretants pre-exist the onset of language, in that the realization of where object/participant trajectories begin and conclude (telicity) alone (without symbolic sign use) gives rise to expectations of event slots and their relations. As such, notice of how event initiation/termination identifies individual events and their participant roles (orchestrated by index) informs the construction of episodes. The function of indexical representations does not stop there: it supersedes practical determinations, hastening logical reasoning by inferring which internal event components must be discarded in subsequent uses, and which can be implied/explicit.

Noticing spatial boundaries constitutes the touchstone only in the process of thinking episodically. Episodic thought entails apprehending telicity – the point where an array/action ends, and where beyond near space/present time begins (cf. Vendler 1967 for an elaboration of telicity). It is critical to recognize that for infants apprehension of boundaries defines space containment; nonetheless, spatial containment is but one component toward notice of temporal progressivity/sequentiality. Unless contiguous qualia are apprehended as first filling, then superseding individual fields, events (actions, states of affairs) fail to reach muster as episodes. Accordingly, perceiving events as episodes first requires recognition of space as occupied (incorporating objects/participants and their qualia); afterward determining how to unite bounded events characterizes more refined episodic thought –reflecting a more expanded relational character. In short, the principle of purposive, contiguous motion through space is one of the most primary advancements in determining event relations, because its operation actually fills space while extending time, suggesting plausible explanations of how event components are related.

At 0;6, after objects have been associated with place and identity attributes, in object files, (Leslie, Xu, Tremoulet, and Scholl 1998: 11; Leslie and Káldy 2007: 117) their iconic representations still fail to reach muster to qualify as episodic. Unlike episodic sequences, location/color/shape, define event representations in a static way only at this age. Until event representations supersede individual relations to predict which objects/participants are present to effectuate the event, the representation does not incorporate the dynamicity which episodes naturally afford. This dynamicity intimates logical relations which further obviate practical event sequencing, i.e., suggesting likely resultative events. Consciously tracing internal practical factors, such as participant roles, can have far-reaching logical benefits – hastening plausible predictions of concurrent or resultative events. To think episodically, children must eventually recognize that individual events suggest what is about to transpire, i.e., contribution to a consequence, though this is a lengthy process. As mentioned earlier, infants' reproductions of single gestures (head movement) are non-episodic; they do not suggest consequent states of affairs, since spatial boundaries only, not temporal ones, have been internalized. Even apprehension of relations between objects and locations ("object index" at 0;6, Leslie et al 1998) does not give rise to the recognition of events as moving toward a logical end, because the relations which these skills express are static. Hence, apprehension of single locations or actions on the part of infants cannot directly bridge one occupied space with another to hint at the progressivity necessary to reason whether particular events affect one another.

3 Transitions to episode-building

The association of qualia to objects, operational at 0;9 (Leslie, et al. 1998: 13) facilitates episodic representations, in that it individuates objects in the stream of undifferentiated space, and leads to the apprehension of distinct objects in different spaces. Objects become distinct when they embody certain attributes within a particular space; and qualia embodied in those objects help identify functional relations between objects in different locations. For example, color/shape highlights objects by establishing boundaries (however invisible) between qualia of other objects (other colors, shapes), thereby obviating objects' locations. Despite the suggestive advantage of qualia to imply spatial relations, event construction falls short of an episodic character, because noticing qualia alone fails to invite their inclusion within action templates. This is so given the insufficiency of Firstnesses (in the form of object attributes) to suggest resultative states of affairs. The invasion of phenomenological forces by way of Firstness considerations (culminating in hypostatic abstraction) vitiates the logic required to connect objects and places to moving effects. For this reason, children's construction of object files (the most elementary entity-based memories) fail to highlight object use, leaving predictions of potential paths /goals unconsidered. As simple snapshots of qualia, event representations are not moving, but are spatially and temporally static. Even at 0;9, when infants are "sensitive to individual identities of objects within spatial arrays, they have yet to demonstrate sensitivity to movement trajectories necessary to encode event paths and goals" (Richmond, Zhao, and Burns 2015: 88). Further evidence of infants' limited understanding of event motility is their inability to order visual displays. At 0;11 ordered recall of visual displays (not action events) does not endure beyond one month (Meltzoff 1988: 475; Mandler and McDonough 1995: 471; Bauer, et al. 2006: 382; Bauer, Wenner, Dropik, and Wewerka 2000: 135).[2] This demonstrates that memories still consist largely of single, uni-directional actions, falling short of an episodic character.

Similarly, search and find activities, despite object displacement from the visual field, do not yet sufficiently evidence that infants represent events episodically. Although search for hidden objects emerges at 0;10 (Piaget and Inhelder 1966/1969: 14–15), path-goal representations are still not fully episodic; they are not reliably guided by bi-directional reference-point templates. Only single, uni-directional (the child's own) goal behaviors are illustrated when uncovering objects from hidingplaces. Even more advanced search behaviors (those incorporating additional hiding places in the same search) only reach muster as uni-directional templates, not revealing more than verbatim knowledge of self-to-object locations. With apprehension of sequential space, time and participatory coordinates, children eventually realize that diverse participants/objects can take part in different event frames. Short of this more dialogic skill, attributing even rudimentary episodic status to events is not possible.

Not even when three sequential actions endure in memory (at 2;0) for 24 plus hours (Bauer and Shore 1987; Bauer, et al. 2000: 135) is there sufficient evidence demonstrating that children think episodically. This is so given the unfounded presumption on the part of two and three-year-olds that contemporaneous events possess some logical relationship. The fact that events are spatially and temporally near often misleads younger children to infer a logical relation.

In fact, it is not until event relations are perceived to have a logical order, and are actually reproduced as sequential action schemes after the two-year mark (Wenner and Bauer 1999: 589), that episodic thought is truly operational. Nonetheless, evidence that children bind location with objects in visual arrays between 1;5 and 2;0, and that they remember two sequential events (Richmond, Zhao and Burns (2015) is still insufficient to qualify as episodic. The fact that their subjects looked longer at objects which changed location than at objects substituted in the same place as the original object, still fails to demonstrate that any logical relationship (cause-effect or otherwise) has been applied to the objects. It only suggests that substituting objects in the same array (rather than moving them to other arrays) is an operation which children notice at this age,

---

2 Mandler and McDonough (1995: 471) also observe that their subjects recalled causal events more reliably than arbitrary events. Cf. Mandler (2004: 230–233) for a general discussion of ordered recall in development.

perhaps consequent to increased familiarity. In point of fact, Richmond, et al.'s findings do not go beyond suggesting children's greater comfort with object substitutions, without addressing the issue of object movement or displacement into contiguous events.

To trace the development of episodic thought at 2;0 and beyond, Richmond et al need to explore the emergence of more complex psycho-social skills, such as autonoesis and theory of mind skills. The latter entails how children appreciate diverse perspectives in similar kinds of events. Typically, children transition to this appreciation through self-experiences. These embodied experiences initially allow them to imagine beyond single formulaic points of view when they assume varied participant roles. Diverse first-hand experiences move children into other kinds of event participation (receiverships, and the like) which otherwise might be unattainable. In this way, self-participatory involvement in different kinds of events (causative, ergative) model how actions/states of being depend upon particular orientations, and how these orientations shift from participant to participant, as a moving, episodic structure. In short, assuming diverse paths and orientations via one's own body supplies the directional experience necessary to construct theory of mind consciousness – enhancing knowledge of others' potential role assumption.

At 2;0, children are able to assume a rudimentary form of allocentric perspective (Sluzenski, Newcombe, and Satlow, 2004); their findings indicate that children can select the correct plate under which they recover a reward, despite reorientation to the plates. At different times, children entered an arena from different doors, observing the array of plates from different orientations. Subjects unequivocally demonstrated relational competencies when they accurately located objects despite new orientations (Sluzenski, et al 2004; Ribordy, Jabès, Banta Lavenex and Lavenex 2013: 19). According to Ribordy, et al. (2013), these allocentric skills are critical to a cohesive spatial perspective. Two year old's success locating the target plates after shifting their orientation (despite the absence of landmarks) demonstrates apprehension of space relations over time (the nucleus of episodic thought), consequent to the different perspectives that the children assumed. This allocentric perspective (approaching the object array from different directions) allows children to sequentially experience different spatial relations with object arrays, requiring some prospective thought, in that distal visual cues and other vantage points (points of origin) are integrated (especially within the visual system) to determine changes in event participant orientation and object location. Measuring event relations at this age (2;0) is more reliable than at earlier ages, since enactment utilizing the whole body is not atypical. Moreover, children's enactment of event sequences (three events) one month after a model enacted them (Bauer, et al. 2000: 135) clearly demonstrates memory of relations between two and perhaps three events. This use of the whole body to illustrate movement from one event to another is a quintessential example of how the body becomes the index, providing a compelling directional thrust toward resultative states of affairs. The entire body physically transitions from one action to another, highlighting changes in event relations.

4 The emergence of episodes and autonoesis

Children can employ either of two orientation systems to determine the source for the memory and to bind elements of the spatio-temporal context: an egocentric or allocentric perspective (Ribordy, et al. 2013: 26). The former always precedes the latter in ontogeny for mammals and for other species (Raj and Bell 2010: 387). An egocentric paradigm, discerning paths from the vantage point of self only, is employed utilizing path integration as early as 0;7 (Acredolo 1978). In contrast, utilizing vantage points from another's perspective to determine locations of objects within the event is quintessential to appreciate the objective skill of thinking episodically. These other points of origin may consist of persons or other objects with inherent fronts/backs. Unlike egocentric perspectives, allocentric vantage points require landmark integration; as such, they emerge as late as 1;6, provided that stimuli/locations are familiar (Richmond, Zhao, and Burns 2015: 89). According to Ribordy, et al. (2013: 26) the means to distinguish and remember "closely related spatial locations" improves between 2;0 and 3;6, consequent to maturation of distinct hippocampal circuits. Ribordy, et al. (2013: 22) employed measures beyond looking time to determine whether egocentric or other points of reference were employed to inform subjects' orientation to objects. Certain environmental features were systematically manipulated (presence of opaque curtains, multiple goal locations, and starting positions). These control conditions induced subjects to utilize points of reference other than the self to reorient, hence, measuring the shifting character of motion events. Subjects reentered an arena via different doors across several trials. Consequent to each of their novel orientation to objects (plates), subjects' view of the array altered, accurately matching the actual array. What is still missing in children's perspectival skills to approximate utilization of advanced episodic thought entails attribution of allocentric perspectives to participant event roles, not within arrays whose physical conditions are limited (consonant with those previously shown). Without allocentric perspective-taking, children would lack the means to perceive events/arrays as others perceive them, especially in the face of orientational conflicts/contrasts – particularly when the parties face one another cf. West 2011: 95).

While egocentric paradigms always employ the self as referent point for objects (even when self's orientation is altered), other-centered vantagepoints define allocentric systems, such that objects/persons outside of self likewise determine the location and distance from objects/participants. Children can either enact the event themselves from diverse vantagepoints, or can mentally project themselves or another into the event. The primary advantage of allocentric perspectives is the lack of need to directly take part in the event; and objective inferences are more likely to ensue, ordinarily containing greater validity. For this reason, utilizing allocentric points of view is critical in developing believable episodes, since referent points suitable for all parties are relied upon, independent of locations/orientations.

5 Advantages of perspectival diversity

Unlike the narrowness of egocentric perspectives, paths and goals become part of the equation when utilizing allocentric viewpoints; and perspectives are updated in the face of location and participant changes. The deictic character which requires updating from episode to episode (frequent location and orientation shifts), hastens the manufacture of inferences as to how such shifts (object/person substitutions) redefine the event in question, and how subsequent events, in turn, might be affected. Were the event trajectory to characterize ball-playing, one episode might entail the agent launching a round object along a path, to reach another player at another location, only to reverse the process. Once reaching the receiver, the perspective, together with the event structure alters with the shift -role, mandating recalculation of object distances and object access according to an allocentric viewpoint. Were an observer to utilize an egocentric viewpoint only, distances and orientations of objects at each turn would be measured from ego's place of continual relocation and/or ego's updates in orientation only. Accordingly, the interpretants of index (effects of perceiver's gaze trajectory) would be centered upon where ego is traveling and facing, without reference to how the scene might be interpreted via any other viewpoint, especially those of an objective other.

It is important to stress that until allocentric paradigms inform the perception and encoding/storage/retrieval of events, episodic thought is not fully operational. Until some perspectival objectivity defines logical relations, rationale for how one event precedes/follows another (from a host of viewpoints) is inaccessible – because using logic to explain event relations is unreliable, and often deceptive; and discerning the contribution of events to consequent states of affairs is obscured. In other words, if simple idiosyncratic embodiment is the only/primary consideration, as is the case when employing an egocentric paradigm, effects upon other participants are likely to be foreclosed; and generating plausible inferences (containing valid logical claims) about events to come, is often compromised.

In view of reliance upon ordered recall and orientational posturing within events, episodic memory has a procedural component, in that it charts event sequences (Hayne 2007: 228). It likewise must draw from semantic knowledge (factual knowledge emanating from declarative knowledge) to connect events logically. In this way, episodic memory relies upon both semantic and procedural memory. The procedural components of episodic memory emerge later than do semantic components (Tulving 2005: 11), presumably because they require a clearly established differentiated object system, while semantic memory can feature an undifferentiated world-knowledge-based system.[3]

6 The contribution of Peirce's ten-fold division of signs

A semiotic explanation serves a far more fitting rationale (than does a purely cognitive one) for the late emergence of episodic memory (given its procedural component). For Peirce, indexical signs are characteristically procedural in view of their means to differentiate objects in the spatial array. Consequent to this attentional function, they are the signs most responsible for proposition-making (1906: MS 295:26) (be the propositions implicit or explicit), in that they provide the seeds upon which events cohere. Because propositions state/imply a claim about a state of affairs, they operate to construct events and to unify them into moving logical episodes. Hence, index as proposition refines logical skills, since it individuates events and suggests their relations, allowing the hearer to infer the relation. Unlike symbolic signs, these kinds of situational signs require far more inferencing to determine potential logical event-connections, because they merely hint at the nature of the relations holding between event components. Unlike indexes/icons, symbols express the nature of event relations, making

---

[3] For a discussion of the emergence of declarative and procedural memory, cf. Bauer, de Boer, and Lukowski (2007: 241–243).

inferencing on the part of signers far less necessary. This issue is especially relevant to the development of episodic thought, wherein apprehending relational representations (namely indexes) is central.

Hayne's (2007) and Hayne and Imuta's (2011) findings support the fact that event relations rise to the level of episodic thought. They demonstrate that episode-building depends largely upon the consciousness of the child's own past experiences. The consciousness to which Hayne and Imuta refer supplies the raw material to infer connections across events which index implies. At 3;0, memory of previous hiding places was operational, but not their temporal order. Hayne and Imuta 2011 conclude that although episodic memory begins emerging between 3;0 and 4;0, it is not reliably in place until 4;0, when consciousness of temporal sequences (enhancing memory) is in place. Three-year-olds were able to remember where objects were hidden in a particular room (after observing the hiding process); but not when they were hidden, or who was responsible for hiding them. Four-year-olds were conscious of and were able to recall all three factors of the hiding process (where, when, and whom), indicating that recall of temporal and participant sequences consisting of more than two events require more advanced representational skills than remembering three "where" events. Processing indexical relations sheds particular light on the reason for these ontogenetic distinctions (as set forth in Peirce's ten-fold division of signs), since far less inferential reasoning is necessary to relate co-present objects than to integrate sequential actions. In the former, index implies propositions only, while in the latter it suggests arguments. Inferring a proposition from co-existent entities is cognitively simpler in that only the relations need be constructed; the objects are still before the mind. Conversely, to infer arguments, observers must hold in memory integrated scenes of previous experience in the process of inferring relations among them.

Given that episodic memory requires awareness and recall of temporal sequences, it does not emerge until children unequivocally demonstrate (ordinarily through narration) conscious reconstruction of the events in the order which matches actual experiences (Tulving 2005: 32): "Children's ability to remember how and when and in what setting they learned a new fact can be assessed even more directly [via narratives]. When this is done, findings again suggest a magical number of 4 as the number of years needed to develop a nearly fully operational episodic memory system." Bauer, Stewart, White, and Larkina's (2016) findings similarly indicate that at 4;0, event recall after one week is more accurate when cues (especially location) are provided, compared to uncued recall. In short, although episodic representations begin emerging at 3;0, they continue to be refined even beyond 6;0 (Nelson 1993; Perner and Ruffman 1995: 543; and Tulving 2002: 7).

Here, differing functions of index explain the late acquisition of more full-fledged episodic memory skills – orchestrating the more complex cognitive task of uniting several non-present events into a logical scheme simply by means of having glimpsed previous single conditions. Essentially, children utilize index to infer the relevance of other places, times, and other participants to a previous event or one before the mind. To ascertain a full-fledged episodic memory system, children supersede memory of past temporally ordered events, and utilize past memories to infer future states of affairs, such that contributing events/conditions can be recognized. To make this inferential leap, children must exploit index's ultimate function as Pheme and Dicisign. They first need to associate icons (object qualia) with the definiteness of place and time in the process of proposition-making. Later, children can draw argument-based inferences when recognizing the logical relevance of locations, times and participants roles displaced from the original condition. They eventually exploit place, time, and person coordinates to arrive at plausible conjectures, but often only after measuring how they themselves would respond in discrete but possible scenarios.

The work of Tulving (2002, 2005), Mandler (2004), Hayne (2007), Klein, Cosmides, Costabile, and Mei (2002), Suddendorf, Nielsen, and von Gehlen (2011: 31) and Klein (2015: 12) demonstrates the necessity of projecting the self (even at 4;0 and beyond) into events (prior to projecting others). This skill requires the means to consciously reflect on how resultative events affect particular participants and how they might affect such in the future, namely autonoesis. Wheeler, Stuss, and Tulving (1997: 332) define autonoesis as a system of memory that "renders possible conscious recollection of personal happenings and events from one's past and mental projection of anticipated events into one's subjective future." Wheeler et al.'s definition brings into focus the importance of remembering beyond simple past event sequences, by virtue of building potential event sequences to satisfy a future goal. Autonoesis is necessary for the development of episodic thought, in that it enhances perspectival diversity, and is responsible for uniting actions (especially enabling ones) with their participants and subsequent (yet unrealized) resultative states of affairs.

Although many investigators note the vital role of autonoetic consciousness in episode-building, Tulving's (1985, 1997, 2002 and 2005) insights have been the most influential. Whereas noetic consciousness entails consolidating events which are remembered accurately in their actual and logical sequence (requiring index to supply some rudimentary argument structure), autonoetic consciousness entails the additional skill of remembering how the self traveled, or is likely to travel, through the event sequence (which requires index to suggest future-oriented spatial and temporal conditions for the self). In short, index allows imaging consolidated event sequences (noetic), as well as inserting the self as player in constructed event sequences (autonoetic). But, what truly sets episodic memory apart from autonoesis is the means to further project the self into events experienced by others (not by the self alone), and situating others in subsequent diverse events. In view of this other-based viewpoint, taking allocentric perspectives is vital to thinking episodically – a fact recognized by Szpunar and Tulving (2011: 6) as well as Klein (2015). When children represent the self in past scenarios, and recall the sequence of those scenarios ordinarily during narratives, they are only remembering the happening itself and their own feelings. To truly think episodically (going beyond Tulving's assertions), children must make inferences based upon others' anticipated reactions – a less direct source. As such, children not merely cultivate autonoetic consciousness (insinuating the self only as event participant), but insert others into their perspectives and they, themselves assume the perspectives of the other. Until children consciously incorporate appreciation for diverse perspectives – projecting the self into possible events which others may have experienced, or others into the children's own experiences – episodic memory falls short of its ultimate utility. It must incorporate consciousness of objective points-of-view – to recommend courses of action in immanent episodes, one of Peirce's primary directives for abductive reasoning (1909: MS 637:15).

To make workable recommendations, procedural memory (knowing the steps to reach a goal) must integrate with semantic memory (knowing what to suggest to ascertain a goal). To recommend successful courses of action for diverse others in episodes, children must reason abductively – anticipating participants' likely reactions, and proposing more workable paths of action given the conditions intrinsic to the episodes. This is so, because episodes consist in event frames which hold together by implicit logical affiliation.

In fact, the rather late ontogenesis of episodic memory (Tulving 2005: 11) is likely to be a consequence of the need to integrate procedural with declarative knowledge (the latter is a component of semantic knowledge). Because procedural knowledge cannot ordinarily be "brought to conscious awareness" (Mandler 2004: 46), accessing it and integrating it into perceptual-motor memories requires executive control, not present early on in ontogeny (Baddeley 2007: 148–149). The procedural knowledge necessary for episodic memory, however, is not disconnected from semantic knowledge, since it resides not merely in the spatial but temporal (sequencing) situatedness of the contributing events. In contrast, the autonoetic property of episodic memory relies chiefly upon declarative, semantic knowledge. Its procedural dependence is not insignificant – given its means to coordinate spatial and temporal components (sequencing the where and when of events). In fact, Newcombe, Lloyd, and Balcomb's (2011) analysis is not inconsonant with the inclusion of procedural knowledge in the mix. In short, episodic memory requires integration of procedural with semantic knowledge to organize representations of past and future events pertaining to self and others. To coordinate both kinds of knowledge effectively, children need to have an awareness of the source for their event memories, i.e., how they know the events – from self-observation, or others narratives, and need to exert executive control, utilizing the episodic buffer, to block irrelevant event memories from influencing related abductions.

7 Index as facilitator of episodic thought

Early on in ontogeny, event images are drawn from semantic memory, and are rather undifferentiated, obscuring particular spatial and temporal features. Such images constitute hypoicons; they are static, non-episodic in nature. More particularly, undifferentiated pictures (iconic ones absent the directional focus of index) make salient the impression of the global event, without suggesting logical relations across or within events. With exploitation of index comes differentiation among event components, and increased potentiality to construct other than coincidental relations. Accordingly, Index obviates relevant spatial, temporal, and participant features, rallying them to supply sequential event logic (West 2014: 150–154, 2016b, 2016c). Index obviates procedural aspects of events which are often inexplicit, unconscious, and irretrievable from memory (Mandler 2004: 46). In other words, because index facilitates awareness of relations (even perceptual motor ones), it can convert actions which are ordinarily automatic to conscious awareness. In that index draws attention to spatio-temporal sequences, it can monitor variations in when and where events materialize. It illustrates where propositions by gestural pointing/pronoun use to the object. Making salient propositional meaning of the when of events is far less graphic and more difficult to show, since index must imply comparisons across experiences held in memory, and/or upon tense and adverb suse. For this reason, index's means to draw and shift attention among event features accounts for its indispensability in discerning relational event features. Its import goes beyond establishing new topics/foci of interest. Index's capacity to move the focus to other concurrent objects or to proximate events allows observers to infer event continuity across co-present objects, persons and actions/states of being. It draws paths uniting physical event features to one another, and enhances notice of how one event progresses toward another (West 2016c).

The force of index in building episodes is evident. It coordinates the shifting character of actions and participants, thereby fashioning the objective character of propositions (however implied). It does so initially via directional gaze, head nodding, and body and finger pointing toward the individual subject of the proposition to be communicated. In fact, these gestures feature the primary indexes utilized to exact notice of event components, prior to the onset of language (cf. West 2013: 16–26). During this early stage in development (from 0;6–1;6), index takes the form of gestures, supplying a necessary attentional and directional template to communicate implicit assertions/arguments for partners to follow.

The attentional and directional aspect of Index is obviated in several of its expressed purposes, namely, physical contiguity between sign and object via brute force attention to objects in Secondness (the material world) (1903: 2.248), and an absence of resemblance (iconic) or lawlike (symbolic) relations between sign and object:

> The index asserts nothing; it only says 'There!' It takes hold of our eyes, as it were, and forcibly directs them to a particular object, and there it stops. (1885: 3.361)

Here Peirce highlights the dialogic nature of index: it brutely regulates interactions between sign users, and forcibly aligns the implicit focus of the sign producer with that of the receiver in joint attentional exchanges – emerging at 1;2 (Saylor 2004: 608) just prior to language onset. The sign producer's use of directed gaze toward one then another object/person can convey what is deemed to be the event focus; and shifting the direction of gaze can indicate a subsequent goal for the event, independent of language use. Index's facilitation qualifies the event as proto episode. As such, index fashions implied propositions before they are explicitly produced via language.

In the same year (1885), Peirce extends indexical use to linguistic genres, again emphasizing index's role in relating material objects in the mind of the signer by forcing attention to the subject of discourse (1885: 8.41). Index continues securing attentional foci in language, supported by the fact that children's initial fifty words ordinarily include primary indexes, namely, pronouns, especially the demonstratives "this," and "that" (Clark 2009: 94). These and other pronouns, e.g., "I," "you," continue to initiate the recognition of participant roles within events, emerging at 2;8 (West 2011: 95). The eventual recognition of the deictic character (shifting referents) of these pronouns, e.g., speaker, object near/far from speaker, again reflects index's means to relate participants to their contexts. The pronouns represent the proposition that location of objects is determined by the location and orientation of particular persons who assume particular roles in the discourse (ordinarily speaker), as well as in the event being reported. Establishing, maintaining, and shifting the topic of discourse is Peirce's clearest vision regarding index's relational function, and its status as implied argument. "One of these kinds [of signs] is the *index*, which like a pointing finger exercises a real physiological *force* over the attention, like the power of a mesmerizer, and directs it to a particular object of sense. One such index at least must enter into every proposition, its function being to designate the subject of discourse" (1885: 8.41).[4] Here Peirce determines that the ultimate nature of index is to state propositions for another and to imply arguments, i.e., suggesting to interlocutors novel ways in which events may affect one another. In this way, it serves as a modal operator –compulsively introducing to another mind innovative event organizations. The effect of these novel object relations is two-fold: 1) the establishment of new habits/event coordinations (cf. West 2016a: chapter 13 for an elaboration of index as habit), and 2) to introduce discrete imagined habits into the stream of consciousness, namely, virtual habits (1909: MS 620:[5] 26; cf. Bergman 2016: 192–196; Stjernfelt 2016; and West 2017 for elaborated discussions of virtual habit).

Consequent to index's means to imply practical and logical habits, event participants can be tracked, hastening apprehension of event sequentiality/movement. Index as gesture/Legisign ultimately suggest the progression of events by charting participant contributions, which in turn, hastens determination of resultative states of affairs. In other words, using gestures and/or pronouns provides a first-hand feel for how episodes develop; and how they extend pivotal nuclear events. In this way, index relates features of the context (objects, times, and participants) to other logically relevant contexts. Peirce refines these issues in his 1908 expansion of index:

> *Designatives* (or *Denotatives*), or Indicatives, *Denominatives*, which like a Demonstrative pronoun, or a pointing finger, brutely direct the mental eyeballs of the interpreter to the object in question, which in this case cannot be given by independent reasoning. (1908: 8.35)

Here Peirce not merely reiterates his assertion that index is the primary tool for showcasing new topics/propositions to a single mind, but highlights a newly determined function of index – to imply arguments for the hearer. The upshot is to perpetuate a habit-change – to present a new viable argument to the "mental eyeballs" of other sign users. This validates the far-reaching influence of

---

4 Atkin (2005: 163–164) illuminates these qualities of index and three additional qualities: reference to individuals, independence from interpretation, and asserting nothing. Cf. West (forthcoming) for a further discussion of Index within the construct of the division of signs.

5 "The effectiveness of the virtual habit relatively to that of a real habit is, I say, unquestionably than in proportion to the vividness of the imaginations that induce the former relatively to the vividness of the perceptions . . . " (MS 620: 26).

index as argument and habit changer, in that the claims are for logical and dialogic purposes, not given by "independent reasoning" alone (to satisfy an idiosyncratic standard).

But, Index's role as assertion experiences a lengthy ontogeny: from Pheme, to Dicisign as proposition, finally to Dicisign as implied argument. Peirce's new taxonomy, especially his substitution of "Delome" for argument, demonstrates Index's potency as submitter of assertions:

> The new words I substitute for these ["term," "proposition," and "argument"] (c.1900: MS 142: 6)] are, *Seme, Pheme, and Delome* . . . . It is a division according to the final interpretant. . . . The second member of the triplet, the "Pheme," embraces all capital propositions; but not only capital propositions, but also capital interrogations and commands, whether they be uttered in words or signaled by flags, or trumpeted, or whether they be facts of nature like an earthquake (saying "Get out of here!") or the black vomit in yellow fever (with other symptoms of disease, which virtually declare, or are supposed to declare, some state of health to exist). Such a sign intends or has the air of intending to force some idea (in an interrogation), or some action (in a command), or some belief (in an assertion), upon the interpreter of it, just as if it were the direct and unmodified effect of that which it represents. (1906: MS 295:26)

In its capacity as Pheme, Index directs others' thought germinations and ultimately their assertions through forcing an idea before their mind. As Delome/implied argument, index requests consideration of the plausibility of a future event, or submits for another's adoption a novel assertion in an implied argument for potential adoption. The former has the force of a command, while the latter permits greater liberality, such that the party receiving the informational index has the freedom to consider the validity of the implied argument, and its congruity with his own logical system.

The influence of index, as an independent device, to structure episodes is vital. It allows a more objective construction of event profiles and relations with the incorporation of the hearer's point of view. In its facilitation of the hearer's viewpoint(s), index is a formidable player in promoting allocentric perspectives – anticipating diverse participant orientations (physical, affective, logical) in imagined locations and at future times (as virtual habits). These more visionary templates create opportunities to submit plausible arguments to a host of hearers, in turn, promoting the transfer of new habits of belief and action. In its role as command and argument submitter, index moderates the development of virtual habits, which hastens the process of abductive reasoning. The implied arguments which Index can submit to the hearer may be considered for contemplation and possible adoption. In short, index reaches across persons, places, and times, (considering diverse hearer's perspectives). In this way, it serves as a modal operator – encouraging others to consider the efficacy of particular arguments. These implied arguments have a logical import – they construct boundaries and connections among episodes, which are often exogenous to the sign user's own actual experiences. In short, the utility of index is far-reaching; it serves as a measure and facilitator to draw potential logical episodic relations. It takes full advantage of allocentric perspective-taking in suggesting different event relations – unexperienced, but within the realm of real possibility.[6] In short, index constitutes a long-term action organizer, in simulating diverse orientations to events (inside, outside), and in energizing participants with the insight and foresight to infer novel event relations.

8 Conclusion

This account asserts that semiotic determinants, particularly Index, drive the relational cognitions necessary for episode-building, reaching beyond autonoetic consciousness. The meanings/effects (interpretants) associated with Index at distinct points in development reveal the state of children's implicit knowledge regarding the spatial and temporal coordinates bound to events. In ontogeny, events are first represented as spatial coordinates, object-location coordinations. These more static snapshots of events constitute a rather iconic means of representing events to the exclusion of the indexical function. The fact that infants recognize boundaries and supersede them at such young ages demonstrates that spatial telicity is a primary competency; but, without the attentional and directional quality afforded by index, noticing movement and orientational shifts would be an arduous affair. Once spatial relations of events are characterized by index, such that attentional and action schemes control, interpretants are informed by attentional and directional attributes – obviating movement and sequential happenings. But, only when Index is supported by Logical interpretants, affording more objective event coordinations, can children truly think episodically, superseding self-conscious experiences by representationalizing sequences as participant paths toward goals. This process (from spatial to temporal to participant binding) traces how indexical signs (consequent to their interpretant potential) obviate the physical and logical relations holding between objects and event participants.

---

6 Peirce's notion of possibility is taken from his concept of virtual habit – an image in the mind so vivid that it represents a course of action one step away from being implemented (MS 620; West 2017).

In short, in Peirce's ten-fold division of signs, Index applies maximum logical congruity to events, when it implies arguments. This capacity exploits index's ultimate function as deictic organizer – by cementing locations, times, and participants to event templates, enabling episode construction. This view of index as a tool determining event contiguity facilitates measurement of event motion and sequentiality, necessary to episodic representations. It marks the origin, path, and end-point. In short, index supplies the raw material to develop coherent episodes which incorporate logical features consonant with diverse and shifting points of view.

References

Acredolo, Linda. 1978. Development of spatial orientation in infancy. *Developmental psychology* 14(3), 224–234.
Atkin, Albert. 2005. Peirce on the index and indexical reference. *Transactions of the Charles S. Peirce Society* 16(1), 161–188.
Baddeley, Alan. 2007. *Working memory, thought, and action*. Oxford: Oxford University Press.
Baillargeon, Renee. 1986. Representing the existence and the location of hidden objects: Object permanence in 6- and 8-month-old infants. *Cognition* 23, 21–41.
Barr, Rachel, Anne Dowden, & Harlene Hayne. 1996. Developmental change in deferred imitation by 6- to 24-month-old infants. *Infant behavior and development* 19(2), 159–170.
Bergman, Mats. 2016. Habit-change as ultimate interpretant. In Donna E. West & Myrdene Anderson (eds.), *Consensus on Peirce's concept of habit: Before and beyond consciousness*. 171–197. New York: Springer.
Bauer, Patricia & Cecelia Shore. 1987. Making a memorable event: Effects of familiarization and organization on young children's recall of action sequences. *Cognitive development* 2 (4): 327–338.
Bauer, Patricia, Rebekah Stewart, Elizabeth White, & Marina Larkina. 2016. A place for every event and every event in its place: Memory for locations and activities by 4-year-old children. *Journal of cognition and development* 17 (2): 244–263.
Bauer, Patricia, Jennifer Wenner, Patricia Dropik, & Sandi Wewerka. 2000. Parameters of remembering and forgetting in the transition from infancy to early childhood. *Monographs of the Society for Research in Child Development* 65(4): 1–204.
Bauer, Patricia. 2006. Constructing a past in infancy: A neuro-developmental account. *Trends in cognitive sciences* 10(4), 175–181.
Bauer, Patricia, Tracy de Boer, & Angela Lukowski. 2007. In the language of multiple memory systems: defining and describing developments in long-term declarative memory. In Lisa M. Oakes & Patricia J. Bauer (eds.), *Short and long-term memory in infancy and early childhood*, 240–270. Oxford: Oxford University Press.
Clark, Eve. 2009. *First language acquisition* (2nd Ed.). New York: Cambridge University Press.
Deely, John. 2009. *Purely objective reality*. Berlin: Walter de Gruyter.
Deely, John. 2012. Toward a postmodern recovery of "person". *Espiritu* 61(143), 147–165.

Hayne, Harlene. 2007. Infant memory development: New questions, new answers. In Lisa M. Oakes & Patricia J. Bauer (eds.), *Short and long-term memory in infancy and early childhood: Taking the first steps toward remembering*, 209–239. Oxford: Oxford University Press.

Hayne, Harlene & Kana Imuta. 2011. Episodic Memory in 3 and 4 year old children. *Developmental psychology*, 53(3) 317–322.

Klein, Stan, Leda Cosmides, Kristi Costabile, & Lisa Mei. 2002. Is there something special about the self? A neuropsychological case study. *Journal of research in personality 36*(5), 490–506.

Klein, Stan. 2015) What memory is. *Crosswires* 1, 1–38.

Leslie, Alan & Zsuzsa Káldy. 2007. Things to remember: Limits, codes, and the development of object working memory in the first year. In Lisa M. Oakes & Patricia J. Bauer (eds.), *Short and long term memory in infancy and early childhood*, 103–125. Oxford: Oxford University Press.

Leslie, Alan, Fei Xu, Patrice Tremoulet, & Brian Scholl. 1998. Indexing and the object concept: Developing "what" and "where" systems. *Trends in cognitive sciences 2*, 10–18.

Mandler, Jean. 2004. *The foundations of mind: origins of conceptual thought*. Oxford: Oxford University Press.

Mandler, Jean, & Laraine McDonough. 1995. Long-term recall of event sequences in infancy. *Journal of experimental child psychology*, 59(3), 457–474.

Meltzoff, Andrew N. 1988. Infant imitation and memory: Nine-month-olds in immediate and deferred tests. *Child development 59*(1), 217–225.

Meltzoff, Andrew, & M. Keith Moore. 1977. Imitation of facial and manual gestures by human neonates. *Science 198*(4312), 75–78.

Nelson, Katherine. 1993. The psychological and social origins of autobiographical memory. *Psychological science 4*, 7–14.

Newcombe, Nora, Marianne Lloyd, & Frances Balcomb. 2011. Contextualizing the development of recollection. In Simona Ghetti & Patricia J. Bauer (eds.), *Origins and development of recollection: perspectives from psychology and neuroscience*, 73–100. Oxford: Oxford University Press.

Peirce, Charles S. 1867–1913. *Collected papers of Charles Sanders Peirce*. Vols. 1–6 edited by Charles Hartshorne & Paul Weiss. Cambridge, Massachusetts: Harvard University Press, 1931–1966. Vols. 7–8 edited by Arthur Burks. Cambridge, Massachusetts: Harvard University Press, 1958.

Peirce, Charles S. 1867–1913. *The essential Peirce: Selected philosophical writings*. Vol. 1, Nathan Houser & Christian Kloesel (eds.) Vol. 2, Peirce Edition Project, (eds.). Bloomington: University of Indiana Press, 1992–1998.

Peirce, Charles S. 1867–1913. Unpublished manuscripts are dated according to the *Annotated catalogue of the papers of Charles S. Peirce*, ed. Richard Robin (Amherst: University of Massachusetts Press, 1967), and confirmed by the Peirce Edition Project (Indiana University-Purdue University at Indianapolis).

Perner, Josef & Thomas Ruffman. 1995. Episodic memory and autonoetic consciousness: Developmental evidence and a theory of childhood amnesia. *Journal of experimental child psychology 59*, 516–548.

Piaget, Jean & Bärbel Inhelder. 1966/1969. *The psychology of the child*. H. Weaver, trans. New York: Basic Books.

Quinn, Paul & Helen Intraub. 2007. Perceiving "outside the box" occurs early in development: Evidence for boundary extension in three- to seven-month-old infants. *Child development* 78(1), 324–334.
Raj, Vinaya & Martha Bell. 2010. Cognitive processes supporting episodic memory formation in childhood: The role of source memory, binding, and executive functioning. *Developmental review 30*, 384–402.
Ribordy, Farfalla, Adeline Jabès, Pamela Banta Lavenex, & Pierre Lavenex. 2013. Development of allocentric spatial memory abilities in children from 18 months to 5 years of age. *Cognitive psychology 66*, 1–29.
Richmond, Jenny, Jenna Zhao, & Mary Burns. 2015. What goes where? Eye tracking reveals spatial relational memory during infancy. *Journal of experimental child psychology 130*, 79–91.
Saylor, Megan. 2004. Twelve- and 16-month-old infants recognize properties of mentioned absent things. *Developmental science 7*(5), 599–611.
Sluzenski, Julia, Nora Newcombe, & Eric Satlow. 2004. Knowing where things are in the second year of life: Implications for hippocampal development. *Journal of cognitive neuroscience, 16*(8), 1443–1451.
Stjernfelt, Frederik. 2016. Dicisigns and habits: implicit propositions and habit-taking in Peirce's pragmatism. In Donna E. West & Myrdene Anderson (eds.), *Consensus on Peirce's concept of habit: Before and beyond consciousness*, (Studies in Applied Philosophy, Epistemology and Rational Ethics [SAPERE]), 241–262. New York: Springer.
Suddendorf, Thomas, Mark Nielsen, & Rebecca von Gehlen. 2011. Children's capacity to remember a novel problem and to secure a future solution. *Developmental science 14*(1), 26–33.
Szpunar, Karl & Endel Tulving. 2011. Varieties of future experience. In M. Bar (Ed.), *Predictions in the brain: Using our past to generate a Future*. 3–12. Oxford: Oxford University Press.
Tulving, Endel (1985). How many memory systems are there? *American Psychologist* 40(4), 385–398.
Tulving, Endel. 2002. Episodic memory: From mind to brain. *Annual review of psychology 53*, 1–25.
Tulving, Endel. 2005. Episodic memory and autonoesis: Uniquely human? In Herbert S. Terrace & Janet Metcalfe (eds.), *The missing link in cognition: origins of self-reflective consciousness*, 3–56. Oxford: Oxford University Press.
Vendler, Zeno. 1967. *Linguistics in philosophy*. Ithaca: Cornell University Press.
Wenner, Jennifer, & Patricia Bauer. 1999. Bringing order to the arbitrary: One-to two-year-olds' recall of event sequences. *Infant behavior and development, 22*(4), 585–590.
West, Donna. 2011. Deixis as a symbolic phenomenon. *Linguistik online 50*(6), 89–100.
West, Donna. 2013. *Deictic imaginings: Semiosis at work and at play*. Heidelberg: Springer-Verlag.
West, Donna. 2014. Perspective switching as event affordance: The ontogeny of abductive reasoning. *Cognitive semiotics 7*(2), 149–175.
West, Donna. 2016a. Indexical scaffolds to habit-formation. In Donna West & Myrdene Anderson (eds.), *Consensus on Peirce's concept of habit: Before and beyond consciousness*, 215–240. Heidelberg: Springer-Verlag.
West, Donna. 2016b. Toward the final interpretant in children's pretense scenarios. In J. Pelkey & S. Walsh-Matthews (eds.), *Semiotics 2015*, 205–214. Charlottesville, VA: Philosophy Documentation Center Press.

West, Donna. 2016c. Peirce's creative hallucinations in the ontogeny of abductive reasoning. *Public journal of semiotics 7*(2), 51–72.

West, Donna. 2017. Virtual habit as episode-builder in the inferencing process. *Cognitive semiotics 10*(1), 55–75.

West, Donna. Forthcoming. Index as scaffold to logical and final interpretants. *Semiotica* special issue on Peirce's Division of Signs.

Wheeler, Mark, Donald Stuss & Endel Tulving. 1997. Toward a theory of episodic memory: The frontal lobes and autonoetic consciousness. *Psychological bulletin 121*(3), 331–354.

Juha Ojala
Development of agency as semiotic empowerment: A Peircean analysis

Abstract: The chapter provides a naturalist-pragmatist analysis of agency and its development across the continuum of biological and social processes of signification using Peircean tools such as phaneroscopic categories, semiotic triangle, the tenfold Sign, as well as inquiry, habits, representation, and hard and soft facts.

The sensorimotor agent is a simple semiotic system: an organism with "direct coupling" with the environment. The embodied basis of its learning enables the development of agency. Meaning is located in habits of action, as habits allow for the prediction of future. Through hard and soft facts, we negotiate our position in the world. For that, inquiry involves constant evaluation of the relation of the Signs of ourselves and other Objects, including other subjects. The communicative revelation empowers the instrumental agent to claim the semiotic space of opportunities to operate with signs for self and for others to interpret, reaching the full extent of semiotic agency.

Keywords: agency, inquiry, Peirce, semiosis, mind

1 Introduction

The theme *"Cross–Inter–Multi–Trans"* aptly points to the complex of relations and interactions in signifying processes, both within and across them.[1] Signs are ubiquitous, and semiotics, as a scientific discipline with long and diverse traditions, examines the signs, their essence, operation, meanings, and values from sociocultural practices to biophysical processes and back. Somewhere in between that bipolar distinction – as far as the distinction within the continuum ought to be made at all – is the individual, each with their own ways of participating in signifying processes, of perceiving the qualities of the world

---

[1] The article is based on a master lecture given at the 13th IASS-AIS World congress of semiotics *"Cross–Inter–Multi–Trans"*, June 26–30, 2017, at the International semiotics institute and Kaunas technological university, Kaunas, Lithuania.

Juha Ojala, Sibelius Academy of Uniarts Helsinki

https://doi.org/10.1515/9783110857801-014

and of engaging in action upon the objects of the world, thereby functioning, growing and living in the world of relations, interactions, and meanings. From the humanist perspective, that is where the bottom line is, finally: how the human being is, acts, and exists in the world of signs, meanings, and signifying processes.

The signifying processes are practices, *praxis,* in that they are actual, habitual, and contextual. Praxis takes place only through *action,* activity of an *agent:* a change, a difference – a vicissitude (CP 1.336) – is a necessary condition for signification. That activity takes more or less established and dynamically changing, habitual forms – *habits* – of acting, perceiving and interpreting, of encoding, mediating, and decoding the signs. How, or what kind of habits are involved in the processes, clearly depends on what kind of *situations,* acts, or events constitute the complex of relations between the individual, and the world, including the others – and on what kind of habits are at the agent's disposal, that is, on the agent's semiotic capacity to act.

In many ways, then, action and *agency* are at the core of these important issues of signifying processes. Consequently, vast bodies of research have been pursued on a variety of related issues. Instead of, e.g., reviewing and synthesizing that literature, what now follows is a synopsis, a naturalist-pragmatist synoptic analysis of the notion of *agency* and its development across the biological and social continuum of signifying processes, with Peircean tools such as inquiry, habits, and the semiotic triangle, as well as the tenfold division of the Sign. Thereby, the problem of agency is here considered a semiotic problem. Action being central in many ways to Peirce's pragmatism and in his semeiotic theory, the Peircean approach seems appropriate for the analysis of agency. The monism across the biological and social comes with the underlying naturalist pragmatism. However, in terms of development, I am now not making distinctions between phylogenetic *versus* ontogenetic development. I shall rather focus on the systemic view of semiosis.

My personal interests in engaging with semiotics primarily have to do with signification *of and in* music, as well as signification *of and in* learning, in very practical matters of music education. In terms of both practices and special sciences of music and learning, one of the central viewpoints if not the main one, is that of *agency.* Also, both music and learning are sociocultural practices and biophysical processes. Neither learning (or growth) nor musicking (or the arts at large) are ultimately inseparable from one another, nor from semiosis in general. Therefore, towards the end of the article, I shall briefly discuss agency in music and learning as an example.

2 The phaneroscopic categories and inquiry

Before getting to agency, let us briefly summarize the Peircean arsenal. The *phaneroscopic categories* serve as an axiomatic basis that permeates the Peircean tools (Ojala 2009: 17, 248), phaneroscopy being Peirce's "phenomenology", and category "an element of phenomena of the first rank of generality" (CP 5.43), irreducible classes by which phenomena can be divided. Of the three categories, *Firstness* is characterized by immediacy, possibility, potentiality, lack of reaction or analysis, spontaneity, feeling, and unreachability. In contrast, *Secondness* is accredited with duality, particularity and individuality, action and reaction, struggle and effort, brute force, fact, and existence. Finally, *Thirdness* is attributed with mediation, law, generality, habit, connection, continuity, thinking, representation, and prediction. (See, e.g., CP 1.300–353, CP 8.327–332; Bergman 2004: 133–170; Short 2007: 60–90; Ojala 2009: 248–257).

While the viewpoint of phaneroscopy may seem to be the experiential "within", it is also tightly connected with the actual world, and ultimately describes the subject in the world of relations, interactions, and meanings. In order to address the dynamic and complex interplay between the subject and the world – and the signifying process, or *semiosis* – Peirce's notion of *inquiry* is handy. The gist is that a living organism (as an actual object among other actual objects of the world) is engaged in interaction with its environment by means of perception and action. Each action is an instantiation of an organism's habits of action and more or less affects the objects of the world, contributing to its situations. The encountered situations, their objects, and their features can more or less be perceived, and interpreted. It is noteworthy that the situations include the organism itself, as well. The perception and interpretation of the situations accumulates into experience: according to Pentti Määttänen (2015: 23) "[e]xperience is, generally speaking, orientating to possible future experiences on the ground of past practical experience". (In this sense, the accumulative experience should be distinguished from particular sense experience, or feeling.) Interpretation may yield further habits of action, enforce existing habits, or lead to adjustment of the habits. Namely, any incongruence or mismatch between the existing habits and the interpretation of situations raises what Peirce calls "irritation of doubt that causes a struggle to attain a state of belief" (CP 5.374). Inquiry ceases when a satisfactory state of belief is attained, until further mismatch causes further irritation of doubt, and the cycle of inquiry begins again. According to Määttänen (2015: ix), "[h]abits are beliefs, but they are not internal units, properties of the brain or the body. Habits are modes of interaction, structured schemes of action, which are formed when action accommodates to objective conditions of action. Habits become beliefs about those conditions of action."

This process where the organism asymptotically adapts to the environment is what inquiry in a broad sense is about (see e.g. CP 5.374–384; Ojala 2009: 25–34). Indeed, semiosis is an adaptive process of inquiry. Noting that as far as the environment and the organism are in continuous change, consequently the habits, the beliefs are in continuous change, as well.[2] This dynamic, cyclic system of practical inquiry (as opposed to scientific inquiry) can be illustrated by the *semiotic triangle* (Fig. 1; Määttänen 1993: 40–54; Ojala 2009: 267–270, 2018; cf. e.g. Ogden and Richards 1936: 11; Merrell 1997: 10–22; CP 2.264, 4.310, 8.376).

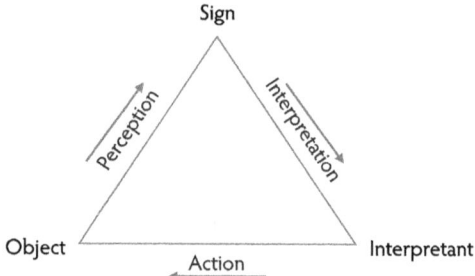

Fig. 1: The semiotic triangle.

The semiotic triangle portrays the Peircean notion of the Sign. According to Peirce (CP 2.274),

> A *Sign*, or *Representamen*, is a First which stands in such a genuine triadic relation to a Second, called its *Object*, as to be capable of determining a Third, called its *Interpretant*, to assume the same triadic relation to its Object in which it stands itself to the same Object.

The Sign is "determined by an Object", and the Sign determines "an idea in a person's mind" termed "the *Interpretant* of the sign" which "is thereby mediately determined by that Object" (CP 8.343). Since the habits of action – meanings – are a result of the process of perception and interpretation, i.e., of the triadic relation of the Sign, to grasp the notion of agency from the semiotic perspective, a further examination of the Sign is necessary.

---

2 Here, beliefs, habits, and meanings – even truth – become conflated. Beliefs are habits of action, meanings are located in habits of action. Likewise, inquiry, semiosis and logic become fused to one another (CP 2.227: "Logic, in its general sense, is, as I believe I have shown, only another name for semiotic (σημειωτικέ), the quasi-necessary, or formal, doctrine of signs.").

3 The tenfold sign

Peirce's ten classes of Signs are based on three trichotomies, each following his phaneroscopic categories of Firstness, Secondness, and Thirdness, displaying the trifurcation into categories of possibility, existence, and law in each of the three Correlates of the Sign. The three Correlates, corresponding to the triadic relation of the Sign, are the Sign itself, its relation with its Object, and its relation with its Interpretant. (CP 2.243–264) Tab. 1 gives a summary of the divisions of the Sign, based on the three tripartitions. It also gives the six transitions between the classes (Ojala 2009: 308, 2006, 2010).

Tab. 1: Summary of the division of the Sign to ten classes.

Category → ↓ Correlate		First	Transition	Second	Transition	Third
1st	Sign in itself	Qualisign	Manifestation	Sinsign	Definition	Legisign
2nd	Sign– Object	Icon	Selection	Index	Correlation	Symbol
3rd	Sign–Interpretant	Rheme	Binding	Dicent	Understanding	Argument

The ten classes are traditionally depicted as triangles, but due to the three interlinked trichotomies, it is better to think of them as a three-dimensional model of the full-fledged Sign (Fig. 2).

I start by observing the First correlate, the Sign in itself. A Qualisign differs from a Sinsign in that a Qualisign is "a quality which is a Sign" (CP 2.244), but since it is a First in all respects, it can "only form a sign through being actually embodied" (CP 2.245). As the potential of the Qualisign is *manifested,* it becomes a Sinsign, that actually contributes to a Sign. It is "an actual existent thing or event which is a sign" (CP 2.245). Sinsigns exist as particular instances. However, although actually existent, alone it stands in relation to nothing, except for the qualities it embodies. It needs to be in relation with other Sinsigns, i.e., with a relevant accumulation of Sinsigns. This takes us to Thirdness of the First correlate: the law-like character of the Legisign. A Sinsign is consequential and functional only in relation to a corresponding Legisign, which reciprocally needs its Sinsign (its replica, as Peirce called it) in order to signify (CP 2.246). Hence, each Sinsign is *defined* by Legisign, and reciprocally, each Legisign may be affected by the particular Sinsign.

As regards the Second correlate, the relation of the Sign with its Object, first, an Icon denotes its Object "merely by virtue of characters of its own", regardless

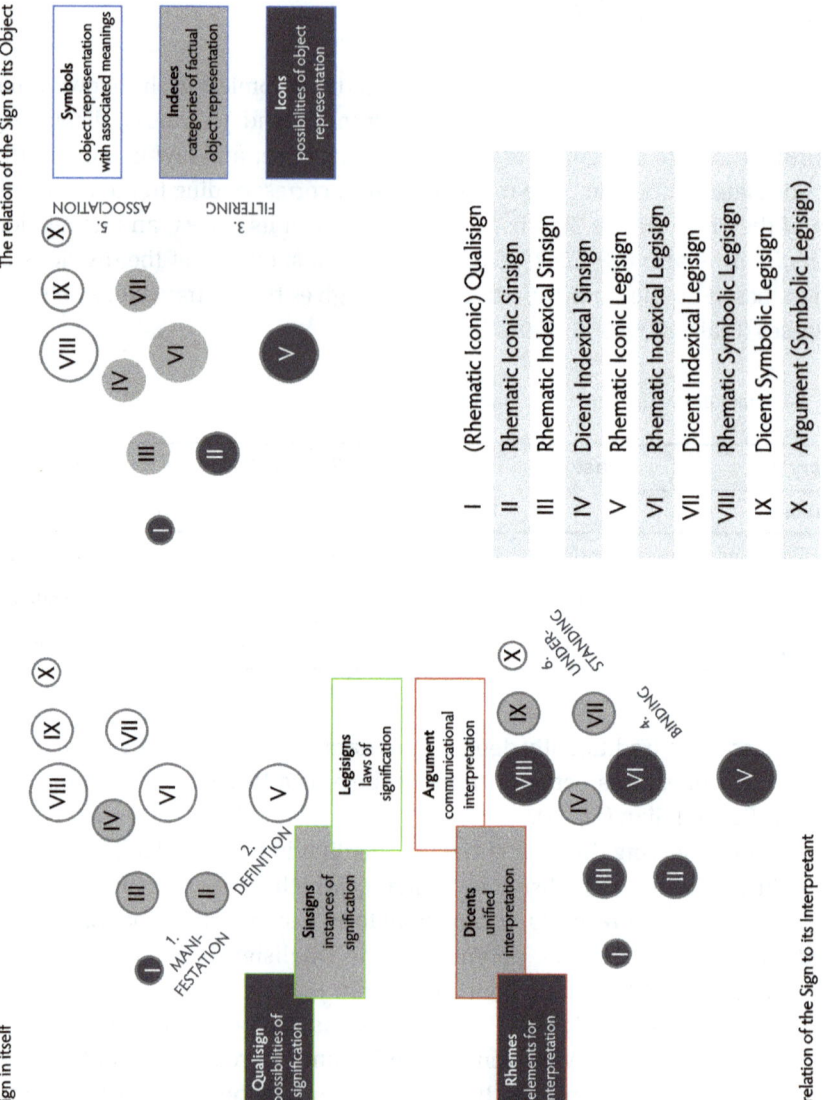

Fig. 2: A three-dimensional model of the tenfold Sign, with the three viewpoints of the three correlates.

of "whether any such Object actually exists or not" (CP 2.247), while, second, an Index "denotes by virtue of being really affected" by its Object (CP 2.248). In other words, while Icons are only a possibility for representing the Object, Indices have a real connection between "the sign and the thing signified", i.e. the Object of the Sign (see e.g. CP 1.372, CP 2.299). Although Peirce gave examples of a weathercock being an Index, as it is affected by wind (CP 2.286, CP 2.428), he also pointed out, that (MS 797: 10; quoted in Bergman 2004: 426) "I have defined index or indication as a sign by virtue of physical connection. Experiential connection would be more explicit; for I mean by physical connection that the sign occurs in our experience in relation to the when and where of the object it represents."

This points towards understanding the Index (when a thought-sign) as a Sign that distinguishes between the qualities manifested in Sinsign at large and those pertaining to the particular Object of the Sign. That is, in moving from Icon to Index, the qualities meaningful for representing the Object have been *selected, filtered* from those that are not. This emerging ability to represent selected qualities and objects of the world is clearly pivotal for semiosis – and for developing agency.

Symbols, in turn, consist in Indices thrown together – *symballein,* as Peirce (CP 2.297) pointed out, that is, Indices *associated, correlated* with other Indices. This opens an avenue for going beyond a factual representation of the world, extending to the genuinely subjective experience.

Concerning the Third correlate, the relation of the Sign with its Interpretant, Rhemes are Firsts, in that they are potential, in terms of interpretation of the Object, but not more. The qualities of the Object may be manifested, but they are not yet *unified, bound* together in order to enable the interpretation of the Sign as the Object. According to Peirce, a Rheme may "afford some information; but it is not interpreted as doing so" (CP 2.250), while a Dicent sign is "a Sign of actual existence" (CP 2.251). Finally, the Argument extends the associative character of the Symbols to a metalevel in the sense, that the interpretation extends to the very processes themselves, revealing the semiotic (communicative, interactive) character of Sign in the process. Peirce described the Argument as "a Sign which is understood to represent its Object in its character as Sign" (CP 2.252). We will get back to the ten classes after discussing the notion of agency below.

4 Agency and the sensorimotor agent

The Oxford English Dictionary defines *'agency'* (in the current sense) as "ability or capacity to act or exert power" and as "action or intervention producing a particular effect; means, instrumentality, mediation" or "such action embodied or personified; a being or thing that acts to produce a particular effect or result" – which is by and large common sense.

In Anthony Giddens's social structuration theory and stratification model (1984: 2–40), agency, together with action, meaning and subjectivity, is in interplay with social structures, and the interplay of individual actors and societal structures dynamically constitutes the social practices ordered across space and time. For Giddens (1979: 55), agency "does not refer to a series of discrete acts combined together, but to *a continuous flow of conduct*". The concept of agency involves "'intervention' in a potentially malleable object-world" and "relates directly to the more generalized notion of *Praxis*" (Giddens 1979: 56, emphases original).

In Albert Bandura's social cognitive theory, beliefs of personal efficacy are the foundation for motivation, well-being, and accomplishments, while at the same time agency and social structures are also interdependent. Bandura (2006: 3–5, 2001: 6–11) lists four core features of agency: intentionality, forethought, self-regulation by self-reactive influence, and self-reflectiveness about one's capabilities. Within this interdependency, Bandura (2006: 5) distinguishes between individual, proxy and collective modes of agency.

Carrie Noland (2009: 9) defines, first, *embodiment* as "the process whereby collective behaviors and beliefs, acquired through acculturation, are rendered individual and 'lived' at the level of the body", and subsequently, *agency* as "the power to alter those acquired behaviors and beliefs for purposes that may be reactive (resistant) or collaborative (innovative) in kind", embodiment appearing subordinate to acculturation.

The current pragmatist and semiotic perspective quite happily agrees with social and embodied views of agency, namely with the idea of dynamic equality between agent and structure or reflexivity and structuration present in the Giddensian theory. This gives weight to self-reflection, contextuality and temporality surpassing the beliefs of personal efficacy presented by Bandura, and with the perspective of embodied (and situated, and distributed) cognitive science of "the close interrelatedness of the so-called 'biological' and 'cultural' aspects" (Lindblom 2015: 2), in which cognition is "forever leaking out into its local surroundings" (Clark 1997: 82). Reciprocally "the objects of environment belong to the functional organization of mind" (Määttänen 1993: 17), making the borderline between 'us' and the 'world' *fuzzy*, and finally, non-existent.

This interplay, that produces the social subjects and their agency, and its role in the origin and development of the process of signification, and the emerging *semiotic empowerment* deserve a closer look. At the simplest stage, it is better not to talk about agent or subject. Instead, the interplay first consists of an organism reacting to stimulus, a "direct coupling" as Peter Gärdenfors

(2000: 122) put it, functioning as what Philip Johnson-Laird (1983: 403–405) called a Craikian automaton or Pentti Määttänen (1993: 64–69) the s-model (for *spatial* model), from rudimentary perception or preperception to predetermined re-action, unsophisticated action. Input is simply mapped to output, more or less in a fixed way. This has been traditionally exemplified by the gill and syphon withdrawal reflex of the *aplysia californica*, the Californian sea hare (e.g., Castellucci and Kandel 1976; Churchland 1992: 70–77). Yet each of us has traces of this kind of direct coupling, for instance, as the vestibulo-ocular reflex that controls the eye-movement of the moving head (cf. Angelaki and Cullen 2008).

Here, a distinction should be made between causation and determination: At this point, the mapping of the input to the output is both causal, in that the one causes the other due to the solid ontological (and epistemological) connection of the organism and the actual world (hence naturalism without the Cartesian divide). The mapping is also relatively deterministic, in that (the quality and quantity of) the output is a relatively simple *function* of the input. However, as the system of signification develops and grows from the simple interplay of organism and other objects into a semiotic process of perception, interpretation and action, depicted by the expansion of the direct coupling into the semiotic triangle (Fig. 3), the dependency of the output on the input – or at that stage: the dependency of the interpretation on the perception – becomes immensely more complex and less predictable. However, even then, the causality prevails, due to the strong ontological and thereby solid epistemological connection.

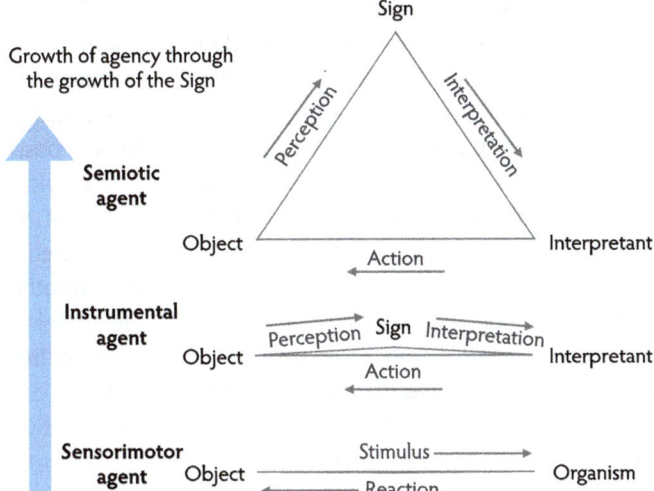

Fig. 3: The growth of agency from the "direct coupling" of sensorimotor agent to the semiotic triangle of semiotic agent.

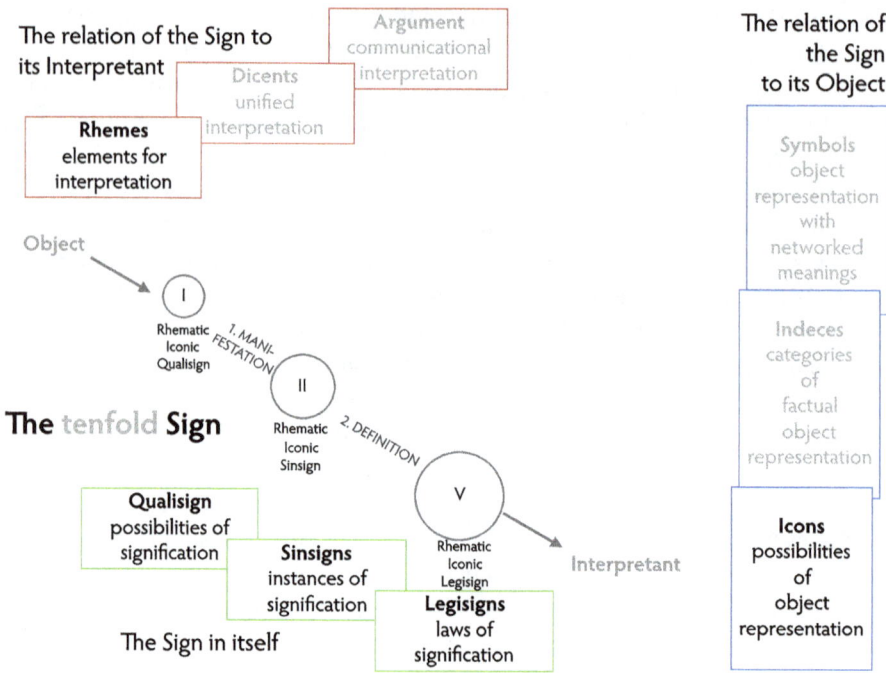

Fig. 4: The simple semiotic system of sensorimotor agent.

A system of a sensorimotor agent, i.e., an organism with a "direct coupling" with the environment, is a simple semiotic system (Fig. 4). There is no fully functional Sign to speak of, and instead of deliberate action based on the interpretation of the sign produced in the perception of the object, the organism (vs. subject, at this point) simply reacts to stimulus. In terms of Peirce's tenfold Sign, the sensorimotor agent operates on *rhematic icons*, but not more: The Sign in itself has the possibilities, instances, and laws of signification, albeit rudimentary, but is not capable of making *subjective, contextual* selections of features critical to the objects of the world, nor is therefore capable of representing the (f)actual objects, nor interpreting the situations of the world in unified let alone communicational ways. In other words, there are *no indices or symbols, nor dicents or argument*. This deterministic signifying mechanism *may* rupture into a fully developed system, to the "indirect modes" of cognition (Gärdenfors 2000: 122) as the habits of reacting evolve into habits of perception, thinking, and action. It is evident that there need be both biophysical mechanisms allowing this and sufficient "environmental pressure" (from the interaction with objects of the world) to drive such expansion.

5 Sensorimotor inquiry, habit, and learning

Given the sensorimotor agent, habits can be construed as the loci of meaning, although there seems to be no distinction between habits of perception, thinking, and action. Let us now return to the tenfold Sign, to consider agency from the semiotic viewpoint in closer detail. As noted, the possibilities of semiosis in Qualisign are causally *manifested* – embodied – as the particular, actual, but temporally volatile Sinsigns. Sinsigns alone are not *meaningful* unless correlated to others and thereby *defined* in relation to the dynamic patterns or the law-like Legisigns which are reciprocally determined by them.

This kind of sensorimotor inquiry is the embodied basis of learning, which makes it possible to develop agency. The sensorimotor agent is capable of developing meanings as habits of action through the interplay of action upon objects and the perception of objects, and the interplay of Sinsign and Legisigns. It is thereby capable of learning – as far as learning is understood functionally as emerging and developing habits of action (see CP 7.536; and for *edusemiotics* e.g. Houser 1987; De Tienne 2003; Olteanu 2015; Semetsky 2017a; Ojala 2018), as changes of behavior that serve the adaptation and functioning of the learner in the world.[3] Reversely, the sensorimotor agent is also capable of forgetting (albeit the processes may be simple, such as the habituation and sensitization in the case of the sea hare gill and syphon withdraw reflex).

This resonates with the pragmatist view of meaning being located in the habits of action. In Peirce's words, "[t]he whole function of thought is to produce habits of action" (CP 5.400). Habits are beliefs, habits are meanings, and vice versa (cf. Määttänen 2015: 29–35). The law-like character of the Legisign is crucial, because in addition to defining the Sinsign, it expands semiosis beyond the here and now of the Sinsign into comprehensive temporality, enabling the accumulation of past experience and anticipation of future situations. According to Peirce (CP 2.148), "every habit has, or is, a general law. Whatever is truly general refers to the indefinite future; for the past contains only a certain collection of such cases that have occurred," and the "mode of being" of the law, is *"esse in futuro"*. This opportunity to rely on habits (a.k.a. meanings of object of the world, or beliefs concerning the *logic* of the world) allows us to make (more or less successful) predictions of the future, based on our accumulated experience. As Pentti Määttänen (2015: 12) put it: "The world is experienced as possibilities of action (affordances), and the object of experience and knowledge is the

---

[3] At this point, the personal pronouns such as 'she' or 'he' are not applicable, as there is no subject.

relationship between two experienced situations: the present situation here and now and the future situation that is an outcome of some way of acting."

According to Gärdenfors (2000: 122), the only way the more refined decision procedures, beyond those triggered by perceptions alone, can be created, is "with the aid of the experience of the agent". Gärdenfors (2000: 122) also emphasized the very pragmatist principles in stating, that "[t]o be useful, the procedures should not only be applicable to known cases, but should *generalize* to new situations as well," which points to the law-like characteristics of the Legisigns and habits of action. As far as the environmental pressure and inquiry as the driving force necessary for the survival or well-being of the organism are concerned, Gärdenfors (2000: 123) furthermore asserted that "[i]f the agent realizes that it has made a mistake, it will adjust the application rules for the concepts that led to the error". This, again, is in harmony with the notion of inquiry, driven by fallibility of beliefs (and habits), and the "irritation of doubt that causes a struggle to attain a state of belief" (CP 5.374). The ever-lasting inquiry entails continuing processes of action and perception, resulting in accumulation of experience, and thereby – when successful – further development, learning and growth of the signifying system, involving the remaining seven classes of Sign.[4] If there is biological potential for growth, the growth of semiosis may result in *semiotic rupture,* in breaking up of the deterministic signifying mechanism into a fully developed system of signification, and agency.

6 From sensorimotor system to factual representation

The key distinction between the rudimentary sensorimotor and the more developed semiotic process is *representation*. The semiotic rupture from the sensorimotor semiosis results from growth into factually re-presenting the world, its objects and their qualities. This is clearly beneficial for the organism, if biologically possible, and hence its growth to subject and a true agent, when possible. Namely, with the more "indirect modes" of cognition, i.e., with more accurate and complex representation, by virtue of the more complex Sign, the organism may better not only represent the world, but also predict its events and situations, its actions. Clearly, developed agency in the form of intentional, goal-oriented and reflective action on objects of the world (versus random, fortuitous

---

4 Hence also John Dewey's notion of learning by doing (e.g. MW 4.178–188; Semetsky 2017b).

action) is only possible if there is an ability to represent the objects. As noted, the whole function of thought is to produce habits, and those habits go beyond the immediate temporality (a Second), extending to anticipation, prediction (a Third). The preparedness for future situations, improves the chances of successful action – agency, which in turn again increases opportunities to interact, perceive and, in turn, represent and interpret. In other words, there is a kind of positive learning cycle to be formed.

This development requires that features essential for (sufficiently accurate or rewarding) representation are adequately *selected, filtered* out from the chaotic, continuous stream of perception, and that the perceived – or selected features of different qualities are *bound* together into representations of objects of the world (Fig. 5).[5] This becomes a transition from the Peircean possibility of Firstness to the actuality of Secondness both in the relation of the Sign to its

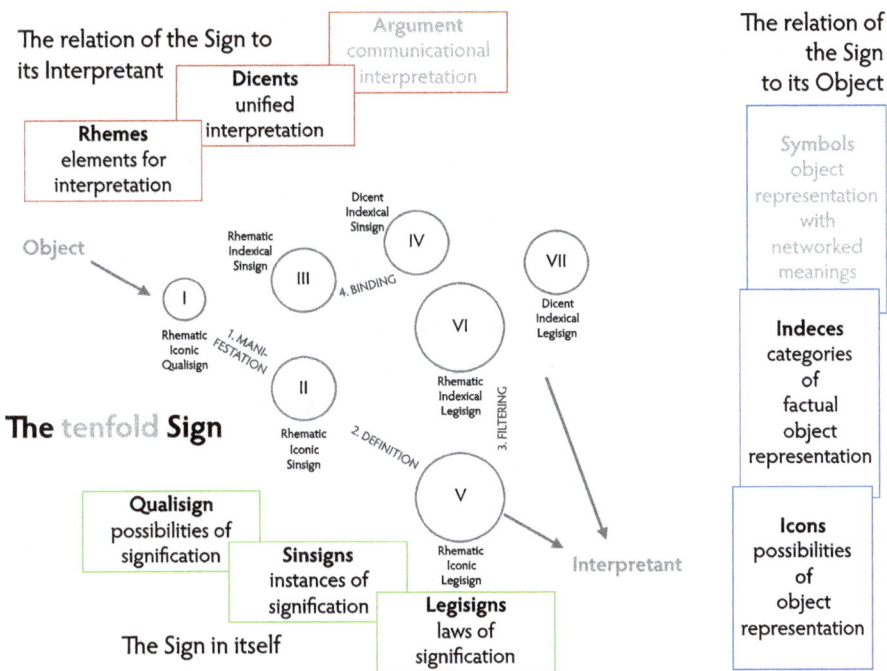

Fig. 5: The intermediate semiotic system of agent capable of representation.

---

5 The choice of the word connects and corresponds with the 'binding problem' in psychology, cognitive science, and philosophy of mind. See, e.g., Cleeremans 2003.

Object and, subsequently, in the relation of the Sign to its Interpretant. In brief, the Sign expands from Icons to Indices and from Rhemes to Dicents.

By this point, the changes in Legisigns, the patterns and laws for defining Sinsigns, have been affected by the perceivable qualities of the Objects. Already the Iconic Legisign (of simple semiotic system) serves as a rudimentary accumulation of experience. However, once the rules for filtering and binding are formed, the perceptual–interpretative process becomes more complex and more dependent on the particular history of the semiosis – *experience* – i.e., on the existing and emerging beliefs and meanings. Habits become habits of perception, action, and thinking when the interplay of mutual determination between the Sinsigns and Legisigns continues and the semiotic triangle grows to include the remaining classes of Sign. There is interplay or feedback between what could be called higher and lower levels of semiosis. This is parallel to the system implementing semiosis in animals, i.e. natural neural networks, which constitute complex systems with ascending and descending (or sensory and motor, afferent and efferent) pathways, so that the "higher" levels affect the processing of the "lower" ones, while the "lower" ones feed the "higher" ones (see, e.g., Valenta and Fiala 2012).

With the rupture that expands the semiotic triangle from the "direct coupling" to subjective representation of the world, we approach the everlasting topic of nature and nurture, the roles of the biological or physical possibilities and constraints versus the influence of the environment, including those of other subjects and their agency. We eventually approach the topic of self-reflectivity and metacognition, as well, that is, the self-regulation of developing the habits of feeling, thought, and action.

The ways in which factual objects become represented depend on what the qualities of objects in the world are available for perception and interpretation (and clearly on the organism's perceptual abilities as well). It is fundamentally important to note that for semiosis, this also includes the organism itself as an object in the world – which is the basis for the representation and understanding of organism itself, the self and subjectivity.

7 Apparent but false duality of processing

Note that in the three-dimensional model of Peirce's tenfold Sign, there are no Sinsigns at the level of Symbols. The Sinsigns are indeed signs of *particular* qualities of Object (Rhematic Icons), selected qualities (Rhematic Indices) and selected qualities bound together for the unified representation of Object (Dicent

Indexical Sinsigns), which are Seconds "on all accounts" (CP 2.243–264), that is, in terms of all three Correlates of the Sign. The Sinsigns are all defined by their mutual relations with the corresponding Legisigns. In this sense, the Legisigns, as laws, are the locus and constitution of the representations, the accumulating experience, meanings, and habits – beyond the interpretation of the volatile Sign of a particular situation of the world.

As noted earlier, once we have the factual representation of the Object with the particular (Sin)signs, both in terms of selected features (Rhematic Indices) and a unified interpretation of the features representing the Object (Dicent Indices), these representations, that is, the Legisigns corresponding to the Sinsigns, may be associated, thrown together with Legisigns representing *other* Objects, thus forming Symbols in the Peircean sense. (This is why no Sinsigns are necessary on the Symbolic level of the model.) Symbols are about the relations, connections, a.k.a. *associations* of represented objects and their features (Fig. 6).

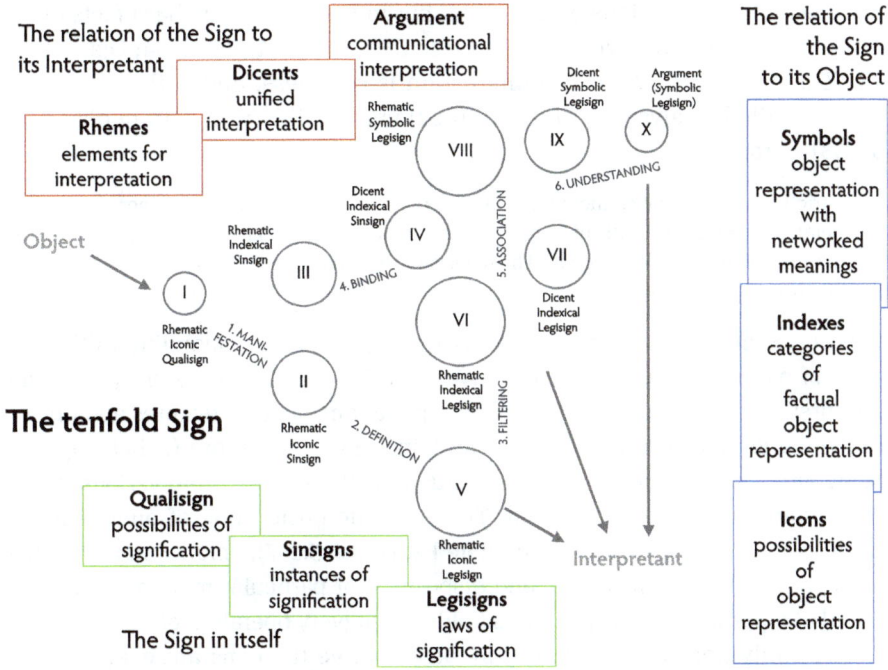

Fig. 6: The complex semiotic system of semiotic agent.

Among all the Objects of the world being represented, there is one kind that is exceptional: the organism itself as Object of the Sign. It appears there would be some kind of dual processing going on. However, in closer analysis that distinction ends up being not only nebulous but lacking any true separation. Yet, this duality appears along the lines of endogenic and exogenic semiosis discussed in various ways by e.g. Thomas Sebeok (2001) and Jesper Hoffmeyer (1992), or even Eero Tarasti (2015: 66–69). In terms of the existential notions of Soi and Moi: on the one hand, we perceive and interpret Signs the Objects of which are whatever there is in the environment present to us, but, on the other, we perceive and interpret Signs whose (dynamical) Object is our own body, ourselves as organisms.

The latter appears somewhat different from the former in that the living body of the organism, embodying semiosis, is always present, constantly perceived, active in continuous processes of perception and action. The objects of the world are always present, by persistently exerting their brute force and hard facts upon us (due to causality). In regard to action, we are, on the one hand, capable of locomotion within the limits of our physique (and suitable tools). On the other hand, we are capable of causing changes in objects, their features, and in situations of the world, but in both cases, the hard facts of the causal world resist our will and effort (see CP 1.324, CP 1.375–1.384; Ojala 2009: 73, 252; Määttänen 1993). The interaction is ceaseless, and without going to more detailed analysis, it suffices to summarize this in Määttänen's (2015: 57–58) words:

> Strictly speaking one cannot talk about interaction in terms of only the other party of this relation. The correct unit of analysis is the interactive system as a whole. In this sense mind extends outside the body. The objects of the environment belong to "the functional organization of mind".

Through Symbols, through associating the Legisigns corresponding to the Sinsigns of particular situations of ourselves and the world, we constantly relate the interpretations of ourselves with our interpretations of other features and objects of the world, and thereby evaluate our being-in-the-world, our (beliefs of) wellbeing and survival, and interpret the situations through and into various, sometimes competing habits of action. This semiotic positioning of oneself in the world is the locus of *emotions*. To quote Peirce (CP 5.247), emotions are "relative to the particular circumstances and disposition of particular man [or woman, or other] at a particular time", and this holds for "[e]very operation of the mind".

Not only does the process of inquiry involve the constant evaluation of the relation of the Signs of *our bodies, ourselves* with those of other *Objects*: the evaluation encompasses the relation with other *subjects* of the world through their perceivable features, as well. In brief, emotions are our means for inquiring into and negotiating our position in the world of our own and of the others, the socially shared world.

8 Tool usage, soft facts, and agency

Just as there is no actual distinction between the self and the world, there is no final, distinctive borderline between others and self. The development of social relations is rooted in the bodily, causal relations of Objects, and our perception and interpretation of them. As we grasp physical objects and study their features, properties, we learn them and we learn to use them (since the meaning of the object is the habit of action it ensues). Manifested habits of action have their consequences on the objects of action, and those ramifications of actions are there for us to perceive and interpret. Due to the causality of the actual objects, the ramifications of action upon objects are logical and consistent. At this point, the emerging subject functions as an *instrumental agent*. Using objects also has ramifications we may not at first know of – consequences that are either beneficial or not, and those consequences, again, we attach to the representation of the object. However, as we grow into representing the objects and situations more efficiently, we surpass mere trial-and-error cycles and develop habits of action that are about (more or less intentional) testing, examining, inquiring into the objects and the world. Children's play is a prime example of this. Even at rudimentary levels, objects – such as sound – can be used as tools, as means for achieving goals.

Think of a baby crying, for instance. A baby may use crying in order to achieve a state of affairs where a caregiver is present. John Dewey (LW 10:68) illustrated the pragmatic maxim through a baby's cry as an intrinsically expressive act (see also, e.g., Nakayama 2015; Winnicott [1960] 1982; Ojala 2009: 338):

> At first a baby weeps, just as it turns its head to follow light; there is an inner urge but nothing to express. As the infant matures, he learns that particular acts effect different consequences, that, for example, he gets attention if he cries, and that smiling induces another definite response from those about him. He thus begins to be aware of the meaning of what he does. As he grasps the meaning of an act at first performed from sheer internal pressure, he becomes capable of acts of true expression.

In this case, the baby is an instrumental agent, producing sound in order to use it – intentionally or not, at first – as a Sign, as a tool to affect the caregiver's action, and their habits of action. The perception of the revealed outcomes of action upon objects is the basis of *tool usage*, of learning how to use tools, and of learning the habits of learning tool usage. In Piaget's terms, these are concrete operations becoming abstract operations.

What we can do with inanimate objects is of course constrained by their physical properties and our abilities to manipulate them. Once we learn to manipulate or interact with an inanimate object in certain ways (i.e., develop the pertinent habits of action), we can more or less rely on those habits until we encounter an object of the same category with different properties that redefine the category, i.e., update or reform the relevant Legisigns, beliefs, and habits.

Animate objects, that is, other organisms and subjects (with the so-called "free will") are less predictable. Whereas we must comply with the *hard facts* of inanimate objects, other subjects may more or less comply with our actions: our and their *social facts are soft*. To quote Määttänen (2007: 458),

> Social facts are also objective, but in a different way than hard facts. – –. From the Peircean point of view these soft facts exist as habits of social action, and from an individual's viewpoint the social practices and habits are perfectly objective. But there is still a difference. The objectivity of hard facts is the objectivity of physical bodies, but soft facts (social habits) are not physical bodies.

To this he adds (2007: 458) that: "As habits of action the soft facts are not only facts but also beliefs." In brief, the soft social facts are the beliefs, the habits of others, the outcome of their processes of signification. Hard facts of the actual objects in the world afford (enable and delimit) our actions, our agency in ways based on the features and causal relations of the objects. The social facts do the same, through the objects of the actual world (since there is no direct, immaterial connection from one mind to another), but in a soft way. That is, in social interaction we can negotiate the affordances and constraints, depending on our counterparts. For instance, the early stages of infancy are (hopefully always) protected by good-enough caretakers, so that, from the baby's viewpoint, they can sufficiently sustain their beliefs of *omnipotency*: the world as interpreted by them simply complies to their wishes.

As children develop representations of themselves as organisms, outcomes of their actions as contrasted to actions of others, and the various inconsistencies versus consistencies in interaction with not only objects but with other subjects (that is, mutually non-complying versus complying soft facts of interaction), a phase of a relative separation of self from others occurs. The last transition on the path of semiotic empowerment to agency is the *understanding* of the social interaction as communicative – a theory of mind. In that transition from the Dicent Legisign to the Argument, the difference between noncompliance of the hard facts of inanimate objects without semiotic agency and the relative negotiable compliance of the soft facts of other semiotic agents is revealed. That, in turn, reveals the process of interaction, and semiosis itself becomes the Object of the Sign. In this respect, the Argument is indeed "a Sign which is understood to represent its Object in its character as Sign" (CP 2.252).

The continuing negotiation of the subject's position in the socially shared world is similar to the notion of negotiating identity in various contexts throughout life, in the sense of Stuart Hall's (1996) notion of postmodern subject. In education, the soft facts connect closely to Vygotsky's (1978) notion of *zone of proximal development* and to *scaffolding*: optimally, the needs of learner are complied with, but only to the point that the learning situation affords successful action and the development of habit of action as an achievement from the learning situation. This applies both to formal and informal learning. Once the habit of action regarding the learning situation is formed, supporting the action is no longer needed, and the learner is capable of acting independently. Enabled by the communicative revelation of the Argument, this goes beyond claiming an actual space for action, to claiming a *semiotic space* by the subject: acquiring sets of possibilities of signifying encounters with others in the world, the afforded and constrained opportunities for acting and producing signs for self and for others to perceive and interpret, the full extent of *semiotic agency*.

The communicative revelation is also a step to joint action, including action coordinated towards joint goals, with matching meanings. For successful co-action, it is necessary to negotiate the tasks and roles between the agents. In learning that, that is, in the process of social growth, the soft facts mediate the bilateral and multilateral positions in each particular situation, and are, again, interpreted through the interplay of Sinsigns and Legisigns. Through the negotiations, the subject develops *an agency repertoire* for the joint action and social situations: a selection of habits of action, where the subject assumes subordinate, equal, or superordinate positions, with contextually varying degree of autonomy for action – regardless of whether the resulting power issues in social positions become explicit or remain implicit. Through inquiry, the semiotic system is self-regulatory, even in this respect.

9 Existence, mind, and inference

The semiotic model of agency is now quite complete. To recapitulate: in the process of inquiry, depicted by the semiotic triangle, the Sign of the Object is interpreted, producing the habits of action. The tenfold model of the Sign covers the stages and transitions of semiosis from the potential of the Qualisign to the communicative understanding of the Argument. The law-like character of

Legisigns overcomes the temporal volatility of particular Sinsigns, and enables the continuity of semiosis and inquiry. Through semiosis, we are able to more or less anticipate and predict future situations. From this perspective, it is appropriate to understand 'mind' as the competence or ability of predicting and guiding organisms' action in the world, as based on the developed representations thereof, i.e., habits (cf. Colapietro 1989: 110; Ojala 2009: 13).

We negotiate habits for social action, identities and our positions in semiotic space through soft facts. We form beliefs of ourselves and others as more or less similar subjects, as members of social groups, as representatives of cultures. In the process, we also negotiate our positions within social networks and thereby shape our identities, which still, from the Peircean viewpoint, are the conglomeration of Legisigns, the accumulated experience, our habits of action. As inquiry continues, our representation of the world becomes (presumably) more precise (I dare say more truthful), and we become better prepared to *be, act* and *exist* in the world. In other words, as we grow, we become empowered from sensorimotor agency to instrumental agency, and further to semiotic agency. (This is the optimistic view.)

The world we inhabit constantly changes. Our habits are based on experiencing the world as it has been present to us, which is bounded within the qualitatively and quantitatively limited situations we encounter. They are constrained by our imperfect abilities to perceive and interpret situations. (This puts the optimistic view into a more realistic perspective.) In developing our agency, do we just have to wait until we are exposed to particular situations of the world, to be able to gain experience and develop habits regarding the objects, others, and situations of the world *as they may be* in the future? If action is *deduced* from developed habits of action, and habits, in turn, are produced by interpretation in semiosis – in *induction* from percepts, where does new knowledge lie, beyond merely adapting to the *status quo*? The answer to this question resides in the notion of *abduction*, hypothetical inference. According to Peirce, whereas "induction does nothing but determine a value, and deduction merely evolves the necessary consequences of a pure hypothesis", "[a]bduction is the process of forming an explanatory hypothesis", "the only logical operation which introduces any new idea" (CP 5.171; see also CP 2.270, CP 5.145, CP 5.603, CP 5.172; Paavola 2006).

Hypotheses, of course, are well-known to researchers in certain research methodologies (and perhaps from Peirce's theory of perceptual judgment). However, there are also more common – perhaps more important forms of abduction. Children's play was already mentioned: the make-believe, the imaginative aspects of it are abductive inquiry into *possible* situations of the world.

Other forms of *transcending the actual world* and creating virtual worlds can be found in music and other arts.

10 A glimpse of agency and music

Given the scope of this article, it is both impossible and unnecessary to truly delve into agency from the viewpoint of music and the arts. However, there are be two matters worth considering. The first one is about musical agency. At least in the Western World, and evidently increasingly elsewhere as well, the agentive access to the virtual worlds of music is limited. Music is ubiquitous, and the majority of people listen to music (in singular), but what musics (in plural) are accessible may severely depend on, or even be dictated by the commercially-oriented mechanisms of music and media industry. Music industry, per se, is not necessarily evil, but there is a problem with its limited agency: we live an age of *consumer culture* in music, rather than *participatory culture*, where each member of society would, in principle, have equal agency in *producing, performing, and creating* the kind of virtual worlds they themselves find meaningful to explore and enjoy. While this by no means excludes or diminishes the value of expertise in music, musical agency is not *democratic*, although it might need to be: should not each individual have equal access to the semiotic space for semiotic agency, as a matter of equal opportunities? That is something the field of music education is actively working on, globally, education being the path to empowering individuals and societies into agency. (On practical terms, this means, among other things, increased role of composing in Western music education.)

The second point is about agency in music: How does music mean? How does the praxis of the virtual worlds of music come into being, so that they produce experiences in others to the point that music is ubiquitous? There is no unresolvable mystery, although more research is needed. Much has already been done, by researchers such as Márta Grabócz, Joan Grimalt, Robert Hatten, Jean-Marie Jacono, the late Raymond Monelle, Eero Tarasti, and many more in the International Musical Signification Project.

In that context, I suggested an approach that incorporates cognitive metaphor theory into musical semiosis (e.g. Ojala 2009). In music, the perceptual features of sound (as dynamical Object) are detached from their origin (we do not listen to sound as per identifying their source). Once so liberated for interpretation, we use a variety of quality dimensions (such as timbre, dynamics, rhythm, pitch, melody, harmony etc.) combined together to form temporally evolving complex sound objects and situations, acts, and events (see Tarasti 1998). Perhaps due to anthropocentric empathy, these acoustic situations get listened to as virtual situations, as articulations of narratives, that is, as metaphors of unfolding situations, acts and events corresponding to those in the accumulated experience of ourselves or other subjects. We hear Signs of ourselves and others in the virtual situations of music. The virtual situations are perceived similarly enough to the perceived situations of the actual world to constitute meaningful experience. However, the landscape, the *virtual space* created by the metaphorical action in music does not consist of hard facts in the sense that the virtual world or its virtual subjects could actually become broken or hurt (albeit sound is an actual, physical, causal phenomenon). In this sense, music serves as a laboratory, it is a playground, it is a world of make-believe, a world of hypotheses and abduction that goes beyond the semiosis in the regular actual world. By living through the musical narratives (broadly taken), we may gain virtual experiences of acts, events, situations that do not necessarily have direct counterparts in the actual world – or deal with the aspects of the actual world safely, since music is unbreakable and can be created anew, adjusted to produce the wanted experience, again and again. This makes agency in music an efficient tool for further inquiry and semiotic empowerment. Similar can by all means be said about other arts.

11 To conclude

This has been a rough outline of the development of agency from the point of view of Peirce's semiotics and pragmatism. I did not go into details or even examples, apart from the brief consideration of music. I did not deal with the spatiality and temporality of semiosis in detail, nor with cognitive metaphors, conceptual spaces, or conceptual blending, nor with the embodiment in its five tiers. These all are topics and theories underlying this text, but beyond the scope here. There is much to be done, e.g., in drawing together research on embodied cognition and thought-signs, which is where Peirce's semiotics focusses on, but is not limited to. I placed emphasis on Peirce's notion of the tenfold Sign and the six transitions between the ten classes in order to convey systematically how agency develops from mere reaction to object representation and further to self-aware and self-regulated activity, ramifications of which are understood. I hope the approach also illustrates how semiotics may serve as a solidifying theory in this kind of topic cluster – agency, growth and meaning – which encompasses a variety of research disciplines. From this Peircean perspective, the development of agency can well be understood as a problem of semiotic empowerment.

References

Angelaki, Dora & Kathleen Cullen. 2008. Vestibular system: The many facets of a multimodal sense. *Annual Review of Neuroscience* 31. 125–150.
Bandura, Albert. 2001. Social cognitive theory: An agentic perspective. *Annual Review of Psychology* 52. 1–26.
Bandura, Albert. 2006. Adolescent development from an agentic perspective. In Frank Pajares & Timothy Urdan (eds.), *Self-efficacy beliefs of adolescents*, 1–43. Greenwich, CN: IAP – Information Age.
Bergman, Mats. 2004. *Fields of signification: Explorations in Charles S. Peirce's theory of signs.* (Philosophical studies from the University of Helsinki 6.) Helsinki: University of Helsinki.
Castellucci, Vincent & Eric Kandel. 1976. Presynaptic facilitation as a mechanism for behavioral sensitization in Aplysia. *Nature* 194. 1176–1178.
Churchland, Patricia Smith. 1992. *Neurophilosophy: Toward a unified science of the mind/brain*. Cambridge, MA: The MIT Press.
Clark, Andy. 1997. *Being there: Putting brain, body, and world together again*. Cambridge, MA: Bradford.
Cleeremans, Axel (ed.). 2003. *The unity of consciousness: Binding, integration, and dissociation*. Oxford: Oxford University Press.
Colapietro, Vincent. 1989. *Peirce's approach to the self: A semiotic perspective on human subjectivity*. Albany: State University of New York Press.
CP = Peirce, Charles S., Charles Hartshorne, Paul Weiss, and Arthur W. Burks. (eds.). 1931–1958. *The Collected Papers of Charles Sanders Peirce*. (Electronic edition.) Charlottsville, VA: InteLex.
De Tienne, André. 2003. Learning *qua* semiosis. *S.E.E.D. Journal* 3(3). 37–53.
Dewey MW 4 = The Middle Works of John Dewey, volume 4, Essays on pragmatism and truth, 1907–1909, edited by Jo Ann Boydston. Carbondale: Southern Illinois University Press.
Gärdenfors, Peter. 2000. *Conceptual spaces: The geometry of thought*. Cambridge, MA: MIT Press.
Giddens, Anthony. 1979. *Central problems in social theory: action, structure and contradiction in social analysis*. London: Macmillan.
Giddens, Anthony. 1984. *The constitution of society: Outline of the theory of structuration*. Berkeley: University of California Press.
Hall, Stuart. 1996. The question of cultural identity. In Stuart Hall, David Held, Don Hubert & Kenneth Thompson (eds.), *Modernity: An introduction to modern societies*, 595–634. Malden, MA: Blackwell.
Hoffmeyer, Jesper. 1992. Some semiotic aspects of the psycho-physical relation: The endo-exosemiotic boundary. In Thomas A. Sebeok and Jean Umiker-Sebeok (eds.), *Biosemiotics: The Semiotic Web 1991*, 101–124. Berlin: Mouton de Gruyter.

Houser, Nathan. 1987. Toward a Peircean semiotic theory of learning. *The American Journal of Semiotics* 5(2). 251–274.
Johnson-Laird, Philip. 1983. *Mental models: Towards a cognitive science of language, inference, and consciousness.* Cambridge, MA: Harvard University Press.
Lakoff, George, and Mark Johnson. 1999. *Philosophy in the flesh.* New York: Basic Books.
Lindblom, Jessica. 2015. *Embodied social cognition.* Cham: Springer.
Määttänen, Pentti. 1993. *Action and experience: A naturalistic approach to cognition.* Helsinki: Suomalainen tiedeakatemia.
Määttänen, Pentti (2007) Semiotics of Space: Peirce and Lefebvre. *Semiotica* 166. 453–461.
Määttänen, Pentti. 2015. *Mind in action: Experience and embodied cognition in pragmatism.* Cham: Springer.
Merrell, Floyd. 1997. *Peirce, signs, and meaning.* Toronto: University of Toronto Press.
Nakayama, Hiroko. 2015. Emergence of *amae* crying in early infancy as a possible social communication tool between infants and mothers. *Infant Behavior & Development* 40. 122–130.
Noland, Carrie. 2009. *Agency and embodiment: Performing gestures/producing culture.* Cambridge, MA: Harvard University Press.
Ogden, Charles K., and Ivor A. Richards. 1936. *The meaning of meaning.* (8th edition.) New York: Harcourt, Brace & World.
Ojala, Juha. 2006. Peirce's ten classes of Signs and spatiality in semiosis. In Eero Tarasti (ed.), *Music and the Arts*, volume 1, 199–209. Imatra: International Semiotics Institute.
Ojala, Juha. 2009. *Space in musical semiosis: An abductive theory of the musical composition process.* Imatra: International Semiotics Institute. http://urn.fi/URN:ISBN:978-952-5431-28-5 (26 Jan, 2018.)
Ojala, Juha. 2010. Before and after the emergence of musical thought-signs. In Lina Navickaitė-Martinelli (ed.), *Before and after music*, 173–182. Vilnius: Lithuanian Academy of Music and Theatre.
Ojala, Juha. 2020. Musical semiosis as a process of learning and growth. In Esti Sheinberg & William Dougherty (eds.), *The Routledge handbook of music signification*, 299–309. London: Routledge.
Olteanu, Alin. 2015. *Philosophy of education in the semiotics of Charles Peirce: A cosmology of learning and loving.* Bern: Peter Lang.
Paavola, Sami. 2006. *On the origin of ideas: An abductivist approach to discovery.* (Philosophical studies from the University of Helsinki 15.) Helsinki: University of Helsinki.
Sebeok, Thomas A. 2001. *Global semiotics.* Bloomington: Indiana University Press.
Semetsky, Inna (ed.). 2017a. *Edusemiotics: A handbook.* Singapore: Springer.
Semetsky, Inna. 2017b. The embodied mind: Education as the transformation of habits. In Inna Semetsky (ed.), *Edusemiotics: A handbook*, 137–150. Singapore: Springer.
Short, Thomas L. 2007. *Peirce's theory of Signs.* Cambridge: Cambridge University Press.
Tarasti, Eero 1998. Signs as acts and events: An essay on musical situations. In Gino Stefani, Eero Tarasti and Luca Marconi (eds.), *Musical signification: Between rhetoric and pragmatics*, 39–62. (Proceedings of the 5th international congress on musical signification.) Imatra & Bologna: International Semiotics Institute & CLUEB.

Tarasti, Eero. 2015. *Sein und Schein: Explorations in existential semiotics*. Berlin: De Gruyter Mouton.
Valenta, Jiří & Pavel Fiala. 2012. *Central nervous system: Overview of anatomy*. Prague: Karolinum Press.
Vygotsky, L.S. 1978. *Mind in society*. Cambridge, MA: Harvard University Press.
Winnicott, Donald Woods. [1960] 1982. The theory of parent-infant relationship. In J. D. Sutherland (ed.), *Maturational processes and the facilitating environment*, 37–55. London: Hogarth Press.

José Enrique Finol
On the corposphere: Body, eroticism and pornography

Abstract: In this paper we discuss the concepts of eroticism and pornography in a broader vision than is usually the case in much scholarship. We propose a vision of these two concepts from a semiotic perspective and within a frame that proceeds from a phenomenological concept of the body. We will also correlate these concepts with those of coquetry and flirtation, in a way that will allow us to better understand a series of cultural ways of looking at the body and speaking of it. The concepts of body motion and body rest will also help to frame the senses of eroticism and pornography.

Keywords: body, eroticism, pornography, coquetry, flirtation

1 Introduction: Erotic body / Pornographic body

There is a now old and long discussion on the concepts of eroticism and pornography. It is about expressions and meanings of the body that are not opposed or contradictory, but that often overlap. Eco, for example, signaled that to distinguish an erotic movie from a pornographic one only needs to see if they abound in "dead time" (Eco, 1994); and Nubiola differentiates the two concepts using the criterion of finality: "Works of pornography are those that are made, commercialized, and consumed as sexual stimulants (. . .); it is about commercial products designed to produce or elicit sexual stimulation from the audience, embodying their sexual fantasies" (2014: online). Pornography has also been related to the promotion and increase of sexual violence. One of the most famous examples concerns the serial rape cases in New Delhi, Gandhi Nagar and Badarpur, India, where it was revealed that the accused "had watched pornographic film [sic] before they sexually assaulted the girl. It evoked intellectuals to argue that pornography incites rape and violence against women in India . . . A section of feminists urge that pornography is the result and cause of sex inequality, the objectification of women, and violence against women" (Roul, 2013). This typical form of evidence is in distinct contrast to the argument of some intellectuals who have claimed that pornography should be tolerated as a way of promoting freedom of speech.

José Enrique Finol, Universidad de Lima, Perú

https://doi.org/10.1515/9783110857801-015

One of the classic studies of eroticism is that of Bataille, who proposed to find unity, concert, and cohesion between "the voluptuous and the saint", whose philosophical perspective, however, tells us very little, at least intelligibly, about how eroticism is conceived today. On the one hand, Bataille (2010 [1957]: 277) affirmed: "I do not say that eroticism is the most important". On the other hand, on the same page, he claimed that "it is the personal problem for excellence. It is, at the same time, the universal problem for excellence", "it is situated at the top of the human spirit", "the supreme philosophical (. . .) coinciding with the peak of the erotic". Bataille confused eroticism with carnal sexual enjoyment, effectively, and, as such, he related it with death. In our view, eroticism is an anterior enjoyment, imagined, closer to the territory of the possibility than realization. We believe, however, that we can salvage the relation between eroticism and religious ecstasy from his work: "There are flagrant similarities, or even equivalencies and exchanges, between the systems of erotic and mystical effusion" (122).

Ziomek relates pornography – a word of Greek origin composed of two morphemes: πόρνη or "*pórnē*", prostitute; and γράφειν or *gráphein*, to record, to write, to illustrate – to eroticism. This an erroneous point of view, to our understanding, as pornography should be related with sex, but not with reproduction, as we explain below. Perceiving that pornography is difficult to define, Ziomek characterizes it as three complementary forms:
1) pornography is not at all formed by eroticism in nature, which is to say, pornography is a sphere of culture; the pornographic can only be an image of the erotic, to be exact: a presentation of the same, that is, a text;
2) pornography is the polar negative in the series of erotic texts;
3) pornography uses means of characteristic expression as an art, but it does not have artistic value (1990: 8).

We believe, however, that if indeed pornography, at least initially, "does not have artistic value" – since it is not, in its origin, its own primary interest – today pornographic photography, for example, is frequently considered to contain works of art. As Jones suggests, "The distinction between erotic art and pornography is often debated, but rarely agreed upon. As western society becomes increasingly liberal, art becomes more experimental and the distribution of porn, commonplace. As a result art and pornography continue to merge" (1976, n/p). Maes goes further:

> Sexual experiences involve the deepest corners of ourselves and are among the most intense, powerful, emotional, and profound experiences we have. If pornography, which offers the most direct representation of, and access to, such experiences, can in principle

be lifted into the realm of art . . . then I think we have every reason to encourage artists to attempt just that, to make intense, powerful, and profound works of pornographic art and rescue this much-maligned genre from the clutches of the seedy porn-barons (Maes in Jones, 1976).

If there are no clear boundaries between pornography and art, it follows, then, that it is not through artistic criteria that pornography and eroticism can be differentiated, nor, as Zodiak does, can we ascribe the pornographic, nor the erotic, in the process of reception or in what he calls "facsimilation".

For Moia, in the pornographic scene "Woman's pleasure (?) – and its culmination: the orgasm – appears only as the demonstration of male power, whose quantity and quality matters to the other" (1980: 85). She later continues:

> It behooves us, to clarify the contrast, to give some definitions that are used in the masculine discourse: 'The erotic: libidinal beauty; the pornographic: functional loyalty'. J.M. Lo Duca; 'Pornography does not mean sexuality as much as its representation . . . the look that is directed upon itself', G. Lapouge; 'pornography is a story of an ideology around the transmitted sexuality of media', O. Massotta; 'Eroticism reigns when it can be suggestion, allusion, even inclusive obsession', J.M. Lo Duca; 'Pornography consists of making money with sex . . . eroticism tries to elucidate the mechanisms of pleasure through that "knowledge effect" specifically 'artistic creation', B. Muldworff. The citations come from *Ucriona* (Moia, 1980: 86–87).

According to Giménez Gatto, "the erotic is associated, principally, with the visual drive, the desire to see never quite satisfied, the game of presence and absence, of the visible and invisible. In return, the pornographic performs a disappearance from the absence in the image, everything is visible, and the image is offered, without veils, to the voracity of the look" (2011a: 124).

For feminist theory, the masculine body and the feminine body are neither in symmetric relation nor equal, except that the former controls and dominates the latter, while using it as a pattern for its own measurement: "Now, the woman's function in sexual phallo-cratic economy is the *benchmark* of sexual virility. Without this 'measure' it would be impossible (?) for the man to establish a hierarchical scale, the only rule of their game" (Moia, 1980: 85). As a consequence, pornography appears as its own masculine body control and as the submission of the feminine body: "The masculine system of presentation/representation of desire with its insistence on erection/penetration/discharge, not including woman's pleasure. Pornography clearly shows us that it is not for pleasure, but our mission/submission (his pleasure: our mission) in an imaginary of body and desire that is not ours" (Moia, 1980:86).

Nevertheless, women may at times also construct their own erotic-sexual game to achieve their purposes, a strategy as ancient as the great Greek playwright Aristophanes (450 BCE – 385 BCE). In Aristophanes' famous work,

Lysistrata, Greek women oblige men to quit warring and to make peace with their enemies; they refuse to have sexual relations and tempt the men by using powerful erotic strategies: "We need only sit indoors with painted cheeks, and meet our mates lightly clad in transparent gowns, and perfectly depilated; they will get their tools up and wish to fuck us, but we will refuse them, and they will hasten to make peace, I am convinced of that" (Aristophanes, 411 BCE: 7).

To better understand eroticism, it is useful to relate it to feminine coquetry, a practice studied by the neo-Kantian sociologist Georg Simmel (1858–1918), for whom

> the property and peculiarity of flirtation consists of producing likability and desire via typical antithesis and synthesis, offering and refusing simultaneously or successively, saying yes and no 'as from afar', through symbols and insinuations, giving without getting, or, to express one's self in platonic terms, maintaining the opposites of possession and non-possession, while making them feel both in one act (2008: 54).

Feminine flirtation, Simmel adds, implies a game of "half-covered", the main reason being to generate "the charm of liberty and dominion" (2008: 60); and its primary conclusion would be to add, subjugate, and be desired. Thus, just as corporal practices are based on eroticism, so too is "flirtation conducted with complete 'finality' but rejects the '*fin*' to which this conduct would ultimately lead, and encloses it in *subjective pleasure of the game*" (2008: 64, emphasis added). Flirtation and the erotic, therefore, share the same conditions of the game, of retracted bids, temptation, and stimulus of the imagination, regarding what is possible. Both practices utilize an enormous codified repertoire of signs and phrases that the transmitter and receiver alike know. However, while flirtation uses signs with greater emphasis and, mainly, involving sigs centred around the face (winks, grimaces, glances, smiles, etc.), eroticism mostly uses corporal signs centered on the erogenous zones (hip swaying, spread legs, caressing one's self, the back, etc.).

On the other hand, flirtation is not necessarily a promise of carnal enjoyment, but a promise of love and romance, while eroticism is a practice that points only toward carnal pleasure, towards non-reproductive sex, an invitation in which the offer is more toward the real than the imaginary. If we relate *coquetry*, *eroticism*, and *pornography* we can say that in the frame of imaginary passion, a progression that went from platonic love, in one extreme, to carnal sex, in another, we would have the former nearer to platonic love and the third nearer to carnal sex, while eroticism would be the middle road between the two. The scheme below illustrates the chain of dependence:

Platonic love → flirtation → EROTICISM → pornography → carnal sex

While this model supposes semiotic boundaries between some phenomena and others that point towards the intelligibility of these three practices, we know that in reality, the experience is always richer and more varied than any model; often these borders overlap, are combined and mixed to create a sometimes unexpected individual richness.

Defining and delimiting concepts such as eroticism and pornography which are subject to ideological, religious, and philosophical variables, is a difficult task. It involves a complicated process of signification and communication that can only be made intelligible if concepts are analyzed as a dynamic whole, in which – in principle several components interact. I propose the following distinctions:

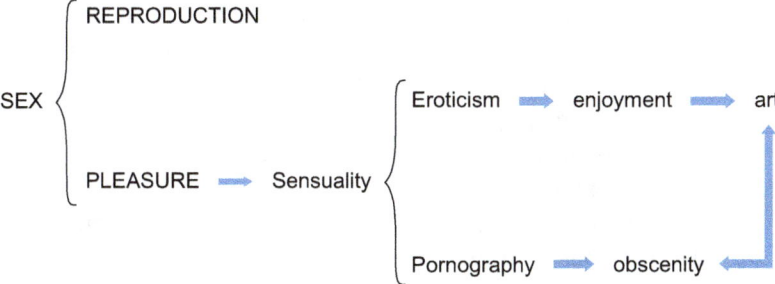

These components, here organized in a reductionist manner, overlap and interdetermined so that their boundaries are fuzzy and difficult to sift through. However, it is important to designate some differences. In receptive processes, for example, while eroticism can affect all perceptual forms – sight, touch, smell, taste, sound – pornography is, predominantly, of a visual character, although it is also found in sound recordings or what we call pornophony.[1] Its history reveals that it was a derivation of erotic dancing but really solidified with the invention of photography and, later, with film and video. Also, while eroticism's

---

[1] Some authors have spoken about *pornophony* not to refer to a "pornographic music" but, above all, to the utilization of recordings of human voices expressing sexual enjoyment. "*Pornophony* is not music, nor bad, nor good, but a genre of sound recording and sound icon (in this case, of the human voice as a symptom of orgasmic release)" (Ziomek, 1990: 2). Zorzoli notes that "We call *pornophony* as pornography broadcasted through radio, television, telephone, and film" (2000: 82). One variation of *pornophony* is what it is called *auralism*, which is defined by the Urban Dictionary as "a sexual fetish defined as sexual arousal or excitement caused by sound, to be compared with voyeurism. This sound might be music, a voice, the actual sounds of sex itself, or other sounds, and may include enjoyment from listening to others having sex. As with most fetishes, in some cases it is simply a small additional turn-on, and in others it is a requirement to sexual gratification".

own imaginaries update semiotic processes concerning fantasy games, to spiritual and intellectual enjoyment, pornography's imaginaries emphasize carnal visual enjoyment, namely the sexual. Obviously, the limits between one and the other are insistent, fuzzy, and involve transitions that are random.

From a semiotic perspective, the difference between pornography and eroticism is not *in* the body itself, but in its expressive practice, that is to say in the set of bodily signs that are favoured in the message, in communication. Thus, to approximate a distinction between eroticism and pornography it will be necessary to take into account: a) the sign systems that bodily performance updates in any determined moment (motion, glances, gestures, clothing, ornaments); b) the specific situation (scenery: lights, music, colors, objects, devices); c) the circumstances (actors, times, places); d) the context (text, subtext, hypertext); e) the mediations (sounds, visuals, audio-visuals); f) the narrative organization (sequentiality: introduction, development, outcome). By correlating the concepts of sex, eroticism, and pornography, we could argue that eroticism favours body signs and veils, obfuscates, hides, and postpones sexual pleasure itself. Pornography, on the other hand, favors sex as a reference, explicitly pointing it out, while at the same time, ignoring or minimizing symbols of eroticism.

Striptease, together with expressions like *pole dance* exploits eroticism, hence its extensive use of bodily signs. It is characterized by a *narrative organization* that goes from the covered to the uncovered or, better, from the hidden to the visible: it is a progressive body unveiling that follows a classic syntax and that is structured around time and physical space. In regard to time, the performance is characterized by a predominance of slowness. The body acts parsimoniously, a characteristic that seeks to exploit the semiosis of visual desire and that makes motion particularly articulated, generally to music equally parsimonious and slow. In regard to the body and physical space, striptease follows three main directionalities. The first relates to the unveiling of body zones, a process that goes from the most visible to the most hidden, or from what is permitted to be seen to what is not permitted, and that has sex as a completion point, be the performer woman, man, or other. In this directionality, clothing is a powerful signification that the dancer is hiding. It is precisely the hidden, not the seen, that the eyes are looking to uncover. Here, clothes meet the function of the veil, an element that, as Fabbri (2004) states, "possesses the strength of a philosophical and aesthetic metaphor; it is a rhetorical device, comparable to those that separate the literal meaning of the tropes that adorn and cover it". As an outmost expression of eroticism striptease works also over distance and the visual: "The erotic scene is founded on the distance" (Giménez Gatto 2011b: 69). I add that the distance at stake is considerably long, a characteristic that differentiates eroticism from pornography, the latter acting over a short distance, over the proximity of the camera that leaves nothing to imagination.

The second directionality is that which allows the dancer to articulate arm and leg movements in a manner that highlights the most erogenous areas of the body: bust, hips, and mouth. It is precisely because they are the areas of most erotic significance that the arms, legs, and their movements articulate in order to highlight themselves. The third directionality is that of the glances of the ballerina (herself) which transition constantly between those glances which she directs at her own body and those which she directs at the gazes of those who watch her, a directionality which seeks to construct a feigned complicity of passion between the one and the other. That passionate collusion built with semiotic looks differs, for example, from those who look, in the framework of a museum or gallery, establishing respect for the artistic nude, where a more intellectual, more rational connection predominates.

If classic striptease was based upon the active unveiling of body garments by the *stripper*, today also another type of passive striptease is practiced. In this case, the spectators assume an active role and take off, often with their teeth, the *stripper's* garments. At its core, striptease is based on a moral and social transgression, on a rupture of cultural encoding and of geographies of the body, a rupture from permitted to prohibited, that avails itself from bodily boundaries, from the intimate made public, from the invisible made visible. For this study, we examined three mainstream striptease performances, available on YouTube. The first is done by Demi Moore, in *Striptease* (1996), directed by Andrew Bergman; the second is Jamie Lee Curtis in *True Lies* (1994), a work of James Cameron; and the third is from Jennifer Aniston found in *We're the Millers* (2013), Rawson Marshall Thurber directing. In the first, Demi Moore, "excessively" dressed, with a male suit, hat, and tie, performs a dynamic transition from the worn to the unworn, from the covered to the uncovered, from masculine appearance to feminine reality. Following a classic progression that goes from the least corporally erotic to the most erotic, a progression that, like every striptease, bolsters expectations and stirs desires. Jamie Lee Curtis, instead, simulates being a stripper, while in the movie's narrative she is a secretary, and, as a consequence, distorts the general model of the dance and executes a sort of anti-striptease: it is comical and clumsy, while still erotic. Jennifer Aniston's performance also breaks the dance's outline. Even though she uses her own bodily rhetoric – aggressive looks, feline pose, intense shaking – she is forced to perform the striptease, it is a pretense to overcome her captors. These three performative variants, in spite of being fictional examples, demonstrate the wealth of body codes – motions, gestures, looks, clothing – and the para-corporal – music, space, choreography, lights – that have an immense expressive and communicative capacity. In these three cases, the dancers use a pole that has a phallic connotation. This symbol was most exploited in the first case, which is explained because, justly, this is a case of real striptease and not merely a simulation, as occurs in the second and third cases.

2 Body: Motion and rest

> Is our body not but an object
> and, as such, does it not need just as well to be
> analyzed under the relationship between
> rest and motion?
> Maurice Merleau-Ponty (1945)

The dialectic between rest and motion is one of the most complicated signification structures of the body. In this dialectic, the body creates complicated phrases comprised from its own daily actions to the most artistic forms. The repertoire of motile possibilities is extensive and its systematization has been of great interest both for the medical and the social sciences. Plato was concerned by the distinction between motion and rest and related these with the concept of uniformity: "Motion is not found in any way to be consistent (. . .) We will assume that rest resides in uniformity and motion in the absence of uniformity" (1979:1153).

One of the classic works of systematization within the study of motion comes from the psychologist Robert S. Woodworth, who studied the processes of bodily motion perception and its production from a functionalist perspective. In regard to the former, Woodworth points out the relevance of "the position in which motion is made, the direction, duration, time and length, the force executed and the resistance opposed" (1907: 163). As for its production, Woodworth classifies motion as reflections, habits, idea-engines, and volitions, but insists that motion is a oneness and that in everything "there are reflective elements, others habitual, and others that can be voluntary" (1907: 237).

Ossona classified types of motion into organic, expressive-instinctive, utilitarian, involuntary and imitative (in Medellín, 2013: 3–4). The first type refers to motions that an infant does with its extremities; the expressive-instinctive are manifested for the first time when the neonate wishes to express pain, discomfort, hunger, etc. This includes head turning, not only including the extremities. Utilitarian motions are developed by the child in order to grab or get nearby objects that they find satisfying, for example, as stemming from the need to feed. Involuntary motions are somatic responses to unexpected situations and are intended to protect against real or imaginary accidents. Finally, imitative motions allow the neonate to acquire and develop bodily communication codes that will facilitate the achievement of their own ends. We could add creative and innovative motion to this classification, feeding off the already mentioned types, since they point towards the construction of new significations and the resolution of new communicative needs. This regards new semiotic strategies that, chiefly, respond to utilitarian needs of daily life and, secondly, seek to resolve aesthetic and expressive needs, a territory through which artistic motions enter. (When the creation or renewal of motions occurs in the predominantly pragmatic framework of everyday life we talk about Microkinesics, while when such forms of creativity occur in art and ceremony we are speaking of Macrokinesics).

Within the set of body motions, Saramago, discussin gestures, introduces the notion of subgesture:

> The whole truth claims that we be attentive to the multiple scintillating subgestures that go behind the gesture (. . .) because subgestures are the fine print in the contract, which are hard to decipher are there. It would not surprise us if the analysis, identification and classification of subgestures turned out, individually and as a whole, to be one of the most fruitful branches of general semiotic science" (Saramago, 2007: 55–56).

A gesture spotting-algorithm, like the one created by Alon, Athitsos, and Sclaroff (2005) allows users to accurately mark the subgestures that the body movement, in a major or minor frequency, uses in specific context. This also contributes to classifying and interpreting gesture communication.[2] Elaboration of a more detailed code of gestures and subgestures in erotic and pornographic expressions of body movement and rest will facilitate accurate descriptions, differentiations and interpretations of bodily communication.

For some authors *corporal posture* is a reflection of personality (Psycho-Semiotics). For others, it influences the way one thinks of one's self and the opinion others have about that person. A semiotic of *corporal posture* that is not limited by the absence of motion, conceives posture not as passive but active, capable of entering in a dialogical game with the individual and with those around him or her, capable of signifying.

The definition of *posture* is associated with the concept of *demeanour*, to which Flores (2009) dedicated an interesting lexicographical (Spanish, French, and English), semiotic and phenomenological study. The lexicographical study reveals a series of common semantic features in the three languages: "1) corporality,

---

[2] "Gesture spotting is a special case of the more general pattern spotting problem, where the goal is to find the boundaries (start points and endpoints) of patterns of interest in a long input signal. Pattern spotting has been applied to different types of input including text, speech, and image sequences" (Alon, Athitsos, and Sclaroff 2005: 2).

2) appearance, 3) posture, 4) how he moves, 5) how he normally behaves, 6) origin or education of the person, 7) assessment (of value)" (Flores, 2009:85). In all three languages, the notion of demeanour is extremely rich and complex, and so in it are not only expressed communicative strategies, but also cultural values that are socialized through the tongue and that configure certain views of the body.

For Flores, posture and the body have a comparable relation to that of tongue and speech. Therefore, demeanour "is realization while posture is virtuality" (2009: 93). However, in spite of the fact that "Demeanor is a property that is attributed to the phenomenal body" it is also "an appearance directed to others, a part of the communicative axis that links the holder with the observer. Demeanor is considered as a form of bodily expression" (2009: 92), deeply rooted in the individual and seen by recipients as strongly expressive of personality, which, according to the author, reveals that these attributes of a character are more of a symptom and not a sign.

From an anthroposemiotic perspective, the *motion-rest* model should be enriched and expanded beyond *itself*, for when the context of which the body partakes daily is seen, where it actually performs, we see that the spectrum of movement is much more complicated and its possibilities increased. First, that model should correlate, at least, with temporal, spatial, and actorial dimensions. Concerning the temporal or chronometric dimension, motion and rest are strongly charged, among others, by variables like speed and duration, alternation and continuity, rhythm, cadence and pause, and permanence or eventuality. Regarding the spatial or proxemic dimension, it will be necessary to analyze direction and distance, verticality and horizontality, angles and planes, territorialities assumed by the self or other (that Lyman and Scott, for example, classify in public, domestic, interactional, and body spaces – in Nöth, 1990: 413). In regard to the actorial dimension, the *motion-rest* model should develop from formal categories like emitter-receiver and object-subject, but also in relation to semantic variables that place actors in hierarchies, classes, functions, genres, occupations, etc. Secondly, the *motion-rest* model should expand into socio-cultural variables of ethnographic contexts where the body acts so that the systematization of data, the analysis and interpretations, are the product of a dialogue with 'reality' and not with the expression of "universal" models.

In dealing with eroticism and pornography, on the one hand, and with motion and rest, on the other, we find that different semiotic mechanisms differentiate one from another. When motion is at work in erotic practices it is usually characterized by slowness, implicitness and delicacy; while when motion is at work in pornographic practices it is generally characterized by quickness, explicitness and indelicacy. Of course, overlaps occur at every moment and in every case, but I think that these three criteria will help to differentiate eroticism and pornography when dealing with motion.

At the same time, when rest is at work in erotic practices it is usually characterized by implicitness, imagination, and promise. When rest is at work in pornographic practices it is usually characterized by explicitness, reality, and offering. These two images illustrate the differences:

Fig. 1: Eroticism and pornography. Eroticism. Taken from https://i.ytimg.com/vi/GklrOYttPOU/maxresdefault.jpg. Pornography. Taken from https://www.flickr.com/photos/cheshir/5286915548.

3 Final remarks

Finally, I raise some questions for later consideration about research on the semiotic ways that the body expresses itself. To begin with, what are the relations between posture and eroticism? What are the relations between posture and pornography? What are the particularities that codes of body posture renew in eroticism and pornography?

It is a fact that in the recent history of practices and representations of masculine and feminine bodies their extreme oppositions have been consistently reduced in ways that thirty years ago were unimaginable. For my father, for instance, the use of earrings by men was some kind of "aberration", which was, at that time, almost unanimously condemned by society. The same process of reduction and annihilation of semiotic distances between masculine and feminine occurred at the level of eroticism and pornography, a fact that is striking, for example, in the relationship between art and pornography. Future research should delve deeply into the social and cultural contexts that facilitate and promote such changes, since their analysis will allow for a better understanding of the uses, representations and practices of the body in contemporary societies.

References

Alon, Jonathan, Vassilis Athitsos, & Stan Sclaroff. 2005. Accurate and Efficient Gesture Spotting via Pruning and Subgesture Reasoning. *Proc. ICCV HCI Workshop*. http://www.cs.bu.edu/techreports/pdf/2005-020-gesture-spotting.pdf accessed 13 January 2018.
Aristófanes. 411 b. C. *Lisístrata*. https://www.librodot.com. Visited on 07/04/2014.
Bataille, Georges. 2010. *El Erotismo*. Buenos Aires: Tusquets.
Eco, Umberto. 1994 *Segundo diario mínimo*. Barcelona: Lumen.
Fabbri, Paolo. 2004. Pensieri del corpo nudo. In P. Weiermaier (ed.), *Il nudo tra ideale e realtà*, Milano: Artificio Skira. Available at http://www.paolofabbri.it/saggi/nudo.html
Flores, Roberto. 2009. Postura y porte. Ensayo de semiótica lexicográfica. *Antropología. Boletín Oficial del Instituto Nacional de Antropología e Historia*, 87: 78–94.
Galimberti, Umberto. 2009 [1983]. *Il corpo*. Milano: Feltrinelli.
Giménez Gatto, Fabián. 2011a. *Erótica de la banalidad. Simulaciones, Abyecciones, Eyaculaciones*. México: Fontamara – Universidad Autónoma de Querétaro.
Giménez Gatto, Fabián. 2011b. Parapornografía o la puesta en escena del deseo. In Ramón del Baño Ibáñez & Lucia Molatore (eds.), *Los nuevos círculos del nuevo infierno*. México: Universidad Autónoma de Querétaro/Miguel Ángel Porrúa Editores, 69–83.
Jones, Allen. 1976. *Art and Pornography*. http://www.tate.org.uk/art/art-and-pornography. Visited on 12/06/2017.
Medellín, Ana. 2013. Del cuerpo formado de signos, al lenguaje del cuerpo que se transforma en signo: el mundo de sentido que emerge de la percepción corporal en un fenómeno escénico. Communication at the VIII Congreso Internacional Chileno de Semiótica, Chillán, Chile, 9–11 octubre.
Merleau-Ponty, Marcel 1945, Phénoménologie de la perception, Paris: Gallimard; Phenomenology of Perception, Donald Landes (trans.), London: Routledge, 2012.
Moia, Martha I. 1980. Mujer y Pornografía. www.raco.cat/index. Visited on 04/05/2013.
Nöth, Winfried. 1990. *Handbook of Semiotics*. Bloomington: Indiana University Press.
Nubiola, Jaime. 2014. Erotismo y pornografía. In M. Lluch (ed.), *Bases antropológicas y culturales de la formación universitaria*. Pamplona: Eunsa. www.unav.es/users/Articulo69a.html. Visited on 07/04/2014.
Platón. 1979. *Obras Completas*. Madrid: Aguilar.
Roul, Kamalakanta. 2013. Semiotics of Pornographic Violence. *Mainstream*, Vol. LII, No 1, December 28, 2013. http://www.mainstreamweekly.net/article4674.html
Saramago, José. 2007. *Manual de pintura y caligrafía*. Madrid: Punto de Lectura.
Simmel, Georg. 2008. *De la esencia de la cultura*. Buenos Aires: Prometeo Libros.
Woodworth, Robert S. 1907. *El Movimiento*. Madrid: Daniel Jorro Editor.
Ziomek, Jerzy. 1990. La pornografía y lo obsceno. *Criterios* 25–28: 244–264.
Zorzoli, Alicia. 2000. *¿Y ahora qué hago?* Madrid: Mundo Hispano.

Zdzisław Wąsik
Natural and cultural layers in the discursive becoming of language as a semiotic system

Abstract: The subject matter of this paper constitutes a historical-evolutionary approach to language as an individual property of its speakers and learners. Language, here, is viewed from the perspective of its 'becoming' in ecologically determined speech communities. The notion of becoming is referred to as the continuous changeability of language through its discursive realization in texts, understood as collective assemblages of meaningful enunciations, as well as through transgenerational transmissions of inborn linguistic aptitudes and conventionally established means of verbal signification and communication.

The discussion starts with an enumeration of observable and inferrable modes in which language exists as a semiotic system against the background of divergent evolutionism or convergent diffusionism, stating that languages have a mixed character while splitting up into new branches, or influencing each other through the dissemination of changes. The semiotic expressivity of humans is shown to be a conflation, or a set of binary relations, formed by a multiplicity of interconnected points, or linkage positions, in intentional productions and utilizations of verbal signs, referring to virtual, or actual, things and states of affairs, which form the signified and communicated reality of everyday life. Thus, the natural and cultural layers of language are regarded as potential tiers originating from the innate character of the speech faculty. This faculty is embedded in the hereditarily neuronal centres of human brains enabling people to communicate by the use of verbal means of signification through the implementation of certain physiological techniques. It is assumed that these layers might have emerged as a result of evolutionary adaptations of human organisms to their natural and artificial surroundings, through the extension of communicational abilities that already existed in their genetic memory.

Zdzisław Wąsik, Professor Senior at Adam Mickiewicz University, Poznań; Professor at WSB University in Wrocław & President of the Scientific Council of the Discipline Linguistics in the Research Federation of WSB–DSW Universities, Gdańsk

https://doi.org/10.1515/9783110857801-016

1 On the heteronomy of language and its autonomization in use and cognition

1.1 Heteronomous conditionings of language

To begin, language as a system of verbal signs is heteronomous by nature. Nevertheless, it can be made autonomous as a tool of communication through the acceptance of social norms, or as an object of study through the choice of investigative perspectives. When a given language has been established as a unified lexical and grammatical system, it possesses only a relative autonomy. While acquiring the state of autonomy, a given language, or rather its standard variety becomes independent from its individual users as a shared means of communication. What is being recognized and shared by communities as a normal state in a language is imposed upon its members by virtue of social sanctions. The pressure of society, expressed, for instance, in rejection and acceptance, punishment and reward, or stigma and charisma, decides that the individual language user adjusts him- or herself to common rules, without being authorized to introduce any changes in the collective character of the semiotic system formed by conventions of "phatic" communities (cf. Wąsik 2016: 277).

The factor of relativeness explains the occurrence of multilingualism and the differentiation of language users into minorities and majorities while indicating that a particular language is subjected, in its genesis and functioning, to customs and conventions. The use of language depends upon the agreement of individuals and communities, situated hierarchically on various social strata, who contribute to the development of a shared means of communication proportionally to the degree of their standardization and codification.

Thus, language as a tool of information exchange must be made independent of individuals while providing patterns of standard realizations, which has to be followed by descendants of those users who have given rise to its origins and development. The facts that some speech communities get rid, or are deprived, of their own native vernacular, or that a given foreign language can become the property of many communicative communities, speaks also in favour of the idea of separating languages from individuals and social groups.

1.2 Exposing the multiaspectuality of language

1.2.1 Modes of existence and forms of manifestation of language

In determining the autonomous status of the system of language, the most important problem lies in the selection of an appropriate perspective concerning the existence modes of the investigative object of linguistics. On account of the concrete and mental, static and dynamic, substantial and relational manifestation of language as a property of human beings, the object of linguistic study, reconstituted in agreement with the principles of hard-science linguistics by Victor Huse Yngve (1986), may be specified in terms of at least one of six separate existence modes (as discussed in Wąsik 2016: 84–86).

(1) Language manifests itself in socially accepted patterns of vocal sound waves, which are articulated by speakers and segmented by hearers as the verbal means of individual signification and interindividual communication;
(2) Language sustains itself in the consciousness of speakers/hearers as the mental equivalents of vocal sound waves, which are processed and interpreted as verbal means of individual signification and interindividual communication;
(3) Language recurs in the concrete speaking and hearing activities of individuals who possess physiological endowments for the production and reception of vocal sound waves as the significative means of interindividual communication;
(4) Language endures in the mental sign-processing and sign-interpreting activities of individuals who possess communicational abilities which allow them to create and recognize vocal sound waves, and their sensorially perceivable surrogates, as significative means being distinguishable from each other, grammatically correct, semantically meaningful and pragmatically appropriate to respective contexts and situations;
(5) Language is deducible from the socially abstracted networks of relational values of significative means, which are externalized by individual communicators in their concrete speaking and hearing activities;
(6) Language is assumable from the networks of associations between mental equivalents of significative means and their relational values, which are internalized by individual communicators in their sign-processing and sign-interpreting activities.

It should be noted that all the above enumerated six existence modes of language constitute intra-organismic and extra-organismic properties of communicating individuals. In opposition to speech processes, thoughts or networks of associations, which depend upon the physiological and mental capabilities or competencies of individual communicators, only the sets of externalized patterns of verbal products, as well as their relational properties, become independent from the will of particular members of certain collectivities when they function as a means of social communication.

However, in the real world, language as a property of collectivity does not constitute a set of empirical data. It may be only assumed as a theoretical construct consisting of the interindividual means and contents of communication that are typified from observable changes in individuals when they are engaged in communicating activities. What can concretely be singled out are no more than referential behaviours of communicators, and their interpretational practices have to be mentally inferred from the shared knowledge of communication participants.

Accordingly, in the physical dimension, communicating individuals are linked with each other interpersonally through sound waves and energy flow, or their multimodal surrogates, carried out in their sending and receiving activities. What is more, in the logical dimension, intersubjective links come into being through the mutual understanding of people when communicating individuals negotiate and confirm the meaning of verbal means through interpretative practices and referential behaviour on the basis of internally concluded commonalities of experience or knowledge about the same domain of reference.

Considering the role of language in the formation of interpersonal collectivities of those who speak and listen to each other and intersubjective collectivities of those who communicate with and understand each other, one can distinguish after Elżbieta Magdalena Wąsik (2010: 55–56), on the basis of observable and concluded similarities in their referential behaviour and their interpretational activities, two additional existence modes of language where: in the first dimension, communicating individuals are linked externally by sound waves and energy flow and, in the second, they are united internally by commonalities of experience or knowledge about the same domain of reference.

(7) Language unites people in concretely observable dynamic interactions when the communicating individuals produce, emit, perceive and receive meaning carriers in the form of sound waves and their surrogate codes through a respective physical channel;
(8) Language can be deduced from the intersubjective linkages that occur between individual communication participants when they understand or interpret received meaning carriers in the same way, referring them to the common extralingual reality known to each other separately.

Apart from the observable interpersonal links related to the use of language, which come into being through the exchange of energy flow being sent and received, and the assumable intersubjective links, which are connected with the same domain of reference being inferred by communication participants, there are also interorganismic links to be taken into consideration, namely the linguistic faculties inherited genetically. Therefore, alluding to the ascertainments of biological anthropologists one is entitled to assume that language exists also in the generational memory of organisms in the form of cultural memes.

Worth mentioning is a hypothesis attributed to Edward Sapir and Benjamin Lee Whorf that the perception of extralingual reality is determined by the structure of a given language (cf. Whorf 1956). To be exposed is also the claim regarding the innate faculty of language about the genotype-phenotype interplay in the genetic code of organisms put forward by Marc D. Hauser, Noam Avram Chomsky and W. Tecumseh Fitch (2002), and the presence of primitive semantic patterns in the *lingua mentalis*, advocated by Anna Wierzbicka (1972, 1980). This begs also for a discussion of the concept of exaptation on the basis of the work of Stephen Jay Gould and Elisabeth S. Vrba (1982). These conceptions allow us to formulate a statement about the additional two existence modes of language.

(9) Language is possible due to the innate speech faculty localized in genetically specialized neuronal centres of human brains to communicate by using vocal systems of verbal means with threefold duality patterns structure and sequential segmentation while implementing complex physiological techniques of articulation and audition.

(10) Language has emerged as a result of evolutionary changes of animal organisms adapting to their natural and artificial surroundings through the extension of their communicative abilities preexisting in their genetic memory as a set of primitive and more developed verbal means.

1.2.2 Inherent and relational of properties of language in the domain of scientific investigation

The subject matter of linguistics and the non-linguistic science of language constitutes individual/collective dimensions of language as a property of its speakers/learners viewed from the perspective of its temporal changeability and spatial variability in environmentally determined communicative collectivities through the transgenerational transmission of inborn speech faculties and conventionally established verbal signs. Therefore, for detaching the scope of investigative domains of linguistics and its neighbouring disciplines, it will be essential to summarize (cf. Wąsik, 2016: 84–92) all modalities in which language, as a set of extraorganismic and intraorganismic properties of its speakers and learners, i.e., as observable and inferable meaning-bearers, exists, manifests, sustains, lasts and/or endures, etc. in (1) externalized speech products, (2) internalized thought products, (3) concrete processes of articulation and audition, (4) mental aptitudes of sign-creation and sign-interpretation, (5), relationships between verbal signs, their meaning, and use, (6) mental associations between verbal signs, (7) observable links between interpersonal collectivities, (8) assumable links between intersubjective collectivities, (9) physiological and intellectual endowments of human individuals, and (10) genetic codes transmitted in the evolution of the human species.

Accordingly, to separate the investigative domain of linguistics from the domain studied by non-linguistic disciplines, it is enough to observe the distinction between language "as an object" and language "as a relational property" of other objects of study. In consequence, practitioners of linguistic disciplines should be aware of the fact when they observe the extrasystemic properties of languages conditioned by external environments, and when they detach the systemic-structural properties of a particular language from its environment.

To begin with the neighbouring disciplines of linguistics, as far as the object of anthropology is concerned, the scientist may be curious about what the definitional attributes of the category of human being are. For a psychologist, the performance of language abilities can be treated as a clue to how the mind (psyche), being the principal object of his/her study, operates. Furthermore, in the sociology of language, the social group (society) is a formal object of study and the language spoken by this group serves as a criterion determining its scope. Accordingly, one can consider that language can be studied from the viewpoint of non-linguistic sciences in the ecology of humans, i.e., in the communicative settings of individuals and collectivities (cf. Wąsik 2016: 89).

Linguistics proper studies language as a principal object, but sometimes in relation to its ecological settings and sometimes in abstraction from the ecology in which it functions. In a broader dimension, heteronomies of language – studied by neighbouring disciplines, such as, for instance, anthropology, psychology, and sociology – are assigned as properties of the formal object of linguistic studies, namely, as that of anthropolinguistics, psycholinguistics, and sociolinguistics. In these "ecolinguistic" disciplines, language constitutes the main object of study, and humanity; mind or society are used as criteria embracing the scope of objects studied in the domains of the so-called heteronomous linguistics (cf. Wąsik 2016: 89).

In a narrower dimension, so-called autonomous linguistics claims to study linguistic facts solely on the intra-systemic ground. Linguists make generalizations about the systemic properties of language as a whole or describe and compare systems of particular languages of the world while abstracting them from the ecology of their individual speakers, social groups, or ethnic, national, or international communities. Consequently, the division of autonomous linguistics into the domains of general linguistics and particular linguistics is a consequence of the distinction between a theoretical approach to the systemic properties of language as a definitional model and a material one to languages as ecologically determined specimens.

Regarding the subject matter of autonomous linguistics, one has to take into account that the language-as-a-definitional model is not to be equated with the properties characterizing all languages of the world or a selected language in particular. It is also not "language in itself" which is specified in terms of observational statements which is the subject matter of comparative linguistics. Correspondingly, systemic properties of ecologically determined languages are studied by typological linguistics in search of their primary and secondary, universal and exclusive, isomorphous and allomorphous manifestation forms, and in historical linguistics – their origin and evolution, separation and unification, continuity or disappearance of structures which realize respective communicative functions (cf. Wąsik 2016: 90).

1.2.3 Conceptual levels in the understanding of language as a model, system and relational network

For the reason that theories depend on certain authorized viewpoints, one has to acknowledge that language as a theoretical construct does not exist really. Nor can it be abstracted from any hitherto existing language. Distinguishing the uncountable "language" as a theoretical construct from countable "languages" as empirical data, linguists have to be aware that language understood as a definitional model is not to be equated with the properties common for all languages of the world or with the properties characteristic of one language in particular.

Taking a structural-systemic perspective, we can distinguish three conceptual levels in the hierarchy of investigative objects: (1) language in general – language in particular, (2) language *ex definition* – language *in abstracto* – language *in concreto*, and, furthermore, (3) language as a theoretical construct – language as an inductive generalization – language as an autonomous sociolect – language as a heteronomous idiolect. Language, in general, can be understood either as language *ex definitione*, i.e., a theoretical construct on a hypothetical–deductive basis or as language *in abstracto*, i.e., a generalization of inductively observed language properties in time and space. Furthermore, the language in particular, seen as synonymous with language *in concreto*, may be specified either as a shared means of verbal signification and communication, autonomized collectively by virtue of social functions, or as a linguistic idiosystem without interindividual norm principles.

To summarize the discussion about heteronomous existence modes of language and its autonomization in their use and cognition, one can conclude that not only linguists are able to autonomize their object of study. Any heteronomy of language can be made autonomous from any (inter)disciplinary point of view (cf Wąsik 2016: 94–95).

2 Semiotic universals of language in animal and human communication

The subject matter of this subpart constitutes the author's (cf. Wąsik 2016: 151–164) classificatory elaborations and extensions of Charles Francis Hockett's (1959a /1958/, 1959b, 1960a, 1960b, 1966/1963/), Stuart A. Altmann's (1962), Hockett's and Altmann's (1968) as well as Charles Egerton Osgood's (1980) approaches to defining characteristics of speech derivable from the contrast between verbal and non-verbal means of communication in the universe of animals and humans. Accordingly, semiotic universals of language have been divided into four groups: (I) form and structure of language, (II) substances of codes and channels of communication, (III) cognitive faculties and communicational abilities of human beings across cultures and generations, (IV) relationships between the signifying and signified sides of verbal means as well as between verbal means and their users.

2.1 The structural-systemic set of semiotic universals of language

Group I embraces systemic properties of language making up the domain of linguistic studies, such as: *semantic referentiality* where the semantic function of verbal signs results from their reference to extra-semiotic reality and the relation between signs and their referents always repeats in a similar way although always in new contexts; *conventional arbitrariness* – the relationship between verbal signs and their referents is not natural by origin but depends upon the social usage and customs conditioned by free and non-motivated choices; *discrete distinctiveness* – verbal means are not continuous and global but articulated and segmented as mutually distinguishable and replaceable contextual entities, units or constructions; *double articulateness* – verbal means can be divided into the smallest meaningful text elements (morphemes) and smallest diacritic text elements (phonemes); *morphological duality* – verbal means can be divided into two classes of signs as entities and categories, i.e., grammatical and lexical morphemes; *bipartite significance* – verbal means as textual constituents of predication frames can be divided, on the syntactic level, into sentences and word phrases that realize, on the logical and semantic level, both the function of propositions and the function of concepts; *functional and compositional hierarchicality* – on the subordinating level, text elements of lower order function within entities, units or constructions of higher order, as phonemes, morphemes, semantemes, words, phrases, sentences, utterances, discourses and texts, and, on the superordinating level, text elements of higher order consist at least of one entity, unit or construction of lower order, as text, discourse, utterance, sentence, phrase, word, semanteme, morpheme, and phoneme; *binary isomorphism of text structures* – segmental text structures, as syllable, stem, word, phrase, clause, sentence, are isomorphous as to their binary forms consisting of a constitutive component and an accessory component; for a syllable, the constitutive component is a vowel or semivowel, for a stem – a lexical morpheme, for a word – a stem, for a phrase – a determined word, for a clause – verbal phrase, for a sentence – the main clause; accessory, in turn, for a syllable is a consonant, for a stem – a derivational affix, for a word – an inflectional ending, for a phrase – a determining word, for a clause – a nominal phrase, for a sentence – a subordinated clause; *syntagmatic integrativity and paradigmatic commutability* – verbal signs can create entities, units and constructions appearing as segments and/or suprasegmental features; *combinatorial-productive openness* – the system of language functions as an open system, so that its users have the opportunity to produce an infinite number of signs from a finite number of simple elements and conventionally established phraseological constructions.

The specification of characteristic features of language that belong to the domain of linguistics can lead to the formulation of its semiotic definition when language is confronted with other systems of communication on the basis of the *genus proximum* of the linguistic sign among the other semiotic objects. Examined at the syntagmatic level of utterances and locutions, both simple signs and composed signs are regarded as complex signs of a higher order as to their global meaning, where the sum of their components does not equal the sum of their partial meanings. All meaningful forms as simple signs or composed signs are considered as members of the same paradigm when they replace each other within the same context of locutions and/or utterances.

2.2 Phonic realization of linguistic texts in speech as non-systemic properties of language

Non-systemic properties of language constituting group II should be relegated to the interest of physical acoustics. The object of study is reduced here to non-systemic properties of speech sounds, as follows: *vocal-auditory*, verbal signs have a phonic character; they are emitted through the vocal tract and received by ear; *centrifugal transmission and directional reception* – sound waves expand in all directions, but they are received from that direction in which the listener finds himself; *evanescence in time* – phonic substances of speech sounds due to physical laws are transitory and volatile; *linear integration over time* – receivers apprehend sound waves as a sequence of segments arranged in a line.

2.3 Extrasystemic properties of language as an investigative object of the neighbouring disciplines of linguistics

Groups III and IV, in turn, pertain to extrasystemic properties of the language studied by human-centred semiotics. Group III has been précised in the following order: (15) *interchangeability of sender-receiver roles* stating that the communicating individual who can be both a sender and a receiver of his or her signs and the signs of other individuals can produce, perceive and reproduce their own or foreign signs as many times as they want; *complete (total) feedback* – the sender, while speaking, can not only simultaneously perceive reactions of others, but she can also react to the form and content of what she emits her-self; which also gives them the possibility of controlling and/or correcting their errors; *cultural transmission* – languages are not genetically inherited, but generationally transferred through education and participation in culture; *creativity, learnability and forgetability* – as far as speech faculties can be inherited, every representative of the species *Homo sapiens*, understood also as *Homo animal symbolicum* (cf. Wąsik 2016: 124), cannot only acquire every language but also create her own linguistic system, or forget a given language which they have learned; *translatability* – the feature of learnability implies also the feature of translatability of every language learned by users as a second, third or fourth, and so forth, language; *conventionally determined changeability in time and variability in space* – bearers of a given language, as members of communicative communities can contribute, on the basis of social agreement or contacts between different languages or their different varieties, not only to the formation of new but also to mixed languages or their new functional and stylistic varieties as well as new expressions and utterances never heard before in a given language, etc.

Group IV encompasses: *specialization* stating that language has developed to perform various semantic and non-semantic functions; *contextuality* – the meanings of verbal means specify themselves in dependence of environments; *translocation* (displacement) – users of a given language may speak about things remote in time and space; *metadesignation* – a language may serve to speak about the language as an object of reality; *prevarication* – the extralingual reality of verbal signs can be both true and false, observed and inferred, as well as imagined and real, and the like; *pragmaticity* – linguistic utterances can be interpreted directly according to their locutionary meaning, or indirectly as exerting an impact upon receivers due to their illocutionary force; *intentionality* – senders can deliberately manipulate with a sense of utterances; *transparency* or *opacity* – the meaning of expressions are either overt or covert when their receivers understand them immediately or interpret them only through paraphrases; *gestalticity* – verbal means possess a producer-oriented recognizable shape; *fossilization* (lexicalization) – verbal signs strive to become independent from their derivational meanings, motivation or etymology (see Wąsik 2016: 161–162).

Among the most relevant species-specific properties of animals (including humans in communication) identified in the research on the semiotic universals of language, the following pair of oppositions might be enumerated: immutability vs. interchangeability of sender-receiver roles, innateness vs. experientiality in generational acquisition and transmission; naturalness of signaling means vs. conventionality of origin, constancy or variability and stability or changeability of language; boundedness vs. displacement facility in time and space; instinctiveness vs. intentionality; globality vs. continuity or segmentability and discreteness of patterning, etc. (cf. Wąsik 2016: 230).

3 Merging synchrony with diachrony in functional and evolutionary descriptions of language

In this section, a synchronic view of language as a system of signs will be juxtaposed with diachronic conceptions, pertaining to the kinship relationships among languages. Against the background of divergent evolutionism and convergent diffusionism, stating that languages have a mixed character while splitting up both into new branches, and while influencing each other through the dissemination of changes, this paper, which aims at explaining the changeability and variability of languages, will consider the applicative value of the metaphor of the rhizome, proposed by Gilles Deleuze and Félix Guattari in 1976, along with the metaphor of assemblage in the first place created afterward as a parallel term in 1980.

In keeping with the original definitions, the notion of assemblage will be specified as an aggregation, or arrangement, of any kinds of heterogeneous things and states of affairs, being thematically concatenated with human expressivity manifested in the intentional production and utilization of verbal signs, referring to virtual, or actual, things and states of affairs, which form the signified and communicated reality of everyday life; whereas the notion of rhizome will be referred to a kind of conflation, or a set of binary relations, formed by a multiplicity of interconnected points, or positions. As regards the speaker-centred view of the becoming of language, the question will be posed how it comes into being due to its discursive realization through collective assemblages of enunciations.

Accordingly, discourse will be referred to expressions/utterances that link communicating individuals in group interactions as physical persons and psychical subjects into interpersonal and intersubjective collectivities when they create and interpret the meanings embodied in material meaning-bearers. In such a context, the natural and cultural layers of discourses will be shown as an inherited potential of individuals owing to an innate speech faculty localized in the genetically specialized neuronal centres of human brains to communicate by using the verbal means of signification through the implementation of certain physiological techniques. Such layers might have emerged as a result of evolutionary adaptations of animal organisms to their natural and artificial surroundings through the extension of their communicational abilities preexisting in their genetic memory.

3.1 Linguistic views of changeability and variability of languages

In this subsection, the evolution of languages and changes in languages will be briefly presented from the perspectives of different theories that are known in historical linguistics, under such labels as genealogical tree theory, wave theory, stratal theory, cultural transfers and linguistic interferences, as well as the metaphor of roofing languages in contact situations.

3.1.1 The genealogical tree theory of language evolution and distribution

The so-called genealogical tree of languages, dealing with the kinship of Germanic and Indo-European languages, was elaborated by August Schleicher (1848, 1850). Explaining the grounds of divergence occurring between cognate languages which are genetically related, it made use of a metaphor comparing languages to people in a biological family tree (German *Stammbaumtheorie*), or in a subsequent modification, to species in a phylogenetic tree of evolutionary taxonomy.

3.1.2 The wave theory of language diversification and unification

The so-called 'wave theory' (German *Wellentheorie*) was presented by Johannes Schmidt in his work on the kinship relationships among Indo-European languages, explaining the structural convergence between historically remote languages. The wave theory presented a model of language change in which a new language feature or a new combination of language features spreads from a central region of origin in continuously weakening concentric circles, similar to the waves created when a stone is thrown into a body of water.

3.1.3 The stratal theory of language growth and decay

The term *substrate* (cf. Lat. *stratum* 'a cover', 'a surface') was applied, at first, by Graziadio Isaia Ascoli (1881–1882 /1881/, 1886), for explaining the changes, which took place in the Latin language spoken in various parts of the Roman Empire. It was accepted in linguistics in the sense of an original language, upon which the language of invading peoples was superposed.

The name *superstrate*, used in the sciences of language, has been employed in relation to the language of peoples invading a given territory. It was proposed by Walter von Wartburg (1932) in his lecture on the cause of split of Galloromania into two language territories: French and Provençal, delivered at the session of the Saxon Academy of Sciences on May 18, 1932, in Leipzig.

The term *adstrate*, in turn, was initiated (in the same year) by Marius François Valkhoff (1932) in his work pertaining to the acculturation of elements by a given language from a foreign one.

3.1.4 Cultural transfers and linguistic interferences in contact situations

Scrutiny of the phenomenon of verbal interference is a heritage of Uriel Weinreich's work of 1953, under the title *Languages in Contact*. It was Robert Lado who popularized, from 1957 onwards, in his work *Linguistics Across Cultures*, the notion of interference for the aims of applied linguistics. While cultural transfers are outcomes of collective intercourses and borrowings, interferences have a solipsistic character, as far as they occur in the mental spaces of individuals.

Linguistic interferences occurring in the mind of second-language learners are based on the reduction of image schemata, composed of concepts and sound patterns, to their equivalents from the first language previously acquired in a natural way. In short, interference can be described as an influence of the first-language patterns upon the patterns which are processed mentally and physiologically in the second language.

Linguistic interferences may be considered in terms of positive or negative transfers. The latter is the source of errors in the acquisition of a foreign language. However, verbal interference takes place not in the system of a language but in the text-processing activities of communicating individuals who transfer mental patterns of meaning-carriers and their interpretations as meaning-bearers from the competence of one language to the performance of another, from the discursive patterns of one language to the discursive practices of another one.

3.1.5 The metaphor of roofing languages in contact situations

Another term for interrelationships between languages and their varieties was the metaphor of "roof". It was a German sociologist of language, Heinz Kloss, who utilized in his work the roof-related metaphors, according to which certain languages or dialects can cover other languages or dialects and certain others appear in the role of being covered (cf. 1978 /1952/: 20–22).

Kloss distinguished between: (1) "hedged" (Germ. *gehegt*) or "roofed" dialects (*überdacht*) and (2) "wild" dialects (wild), which should be recognized as "not-roofed" (dachlos). Cultivated languages develop within the borders of a hedge in the garden (*im Gehege*) determined by a given written language. Their bearers use a written variety of cultural languages as a superordinate language in relation to given dialects.

Wild dialects are deprived of this cultivating influence of a cultural language closely related to them by birth. Their users utilize at the same time a written language, being to a lesser degree cognate or totally non-cognate with dialects they speak in everyday communication. Non-roofed means exchange in verbal contacts tend to accept foreign borrowings, or spontaneous innovations of individual character. These exchanges become less and less similar to the written language, being related from a linguistic point of view, including also further varieties.

3.2 Appreciating the assemblage-and-rhizome-oriented conceptions of language performance and change

Against the background of linguistic theories, one might pose at least two questions with regard to the notions of French *agencement*, translated into English as "assemblage", and French *rhizome*, rendered in English with the same orthographic stem as "rhizome". The initial question would refer to the definition of language as a set of both mental and concrete signs or texts, with the characterization of language as a set of enunciative assemblages. The reply to the question about the defining properties of language would be decisive, in consequence, for posing a conclusive question in order to specify whether language is a social product (with a hold on the point of its existence) or a social process (understood in terms of its becoming), namely: "What is new and productive in the rhizomatic conception of change in the performative function language as an assemblage of enunciation?"

3.2.1 Towards understanding language as an assemblage of enunciation

In interdisciplinary studies, scientists collect various linguistic data to support those scientific disciplines, the main object of which belongs to functional environments of languages. As an alternative for strictly linguistic studies, the subject matter of which has been language in itself, practitioners of language sciences have switched their interest to studies conducted from the perspective of neighbouring disciplines (cf. Wąsik 2016: 82). Linguists concerned with the social and abstract character of language have usually defined it either as a set of mental signs composed of concepts and sound patterns that are shared by all members of a particular speech community, as postulated by Ferdinand de Saussure (1916); or a set of concrete types of verbal means of signification that are used for communicating about extra-linguistic reality, following the functionalist principles of Karl Ludwig Bühler (1965 /1934/) and Leon Zawadowski (1966).

In the approaches of isolationists, natural languages are reduced to "stages" and stages identified with "systems". Integrationists, in turn, investigate actual lay speakers, as they cooperate communicatively and interactively with other members of social groupings, such as inter-individual, public and mass aggregations of local or global, national or international communities connected by blood kinship or ethnic descent, common profession or confession, and shared means of signification or cognition – communication rather than language (Harris 1981). In such an integrational and interdisciplinary context, one might also include the pragmatic position of Gilles Deleuze and Félix Guattari (1987 [1980]: 89) to language as a "collective assemblage of enunciation" as fruitful and innovative. The notion of language as an assemblage of enunciation might be placed in the context of social discourses as particular acts of speech communication embedded in sign-processing activities.

3.2.2 The philosophy of becoming in the processual view of life

To explain the origin of Deleuze's notion of "becoming" one has to refer to its sources going back to the famous πάντα ῥεῖ 'everything flows', attributed to Heraclitus c. 500 B.C. from Greek Antiquity (cf., as translated by Philip Wheelwright, 1959: 29, Chapter II. Universal Flux, Fragments 20 and 21, "20. Everything flows and nothing abides; everything gives way and nothing stays fixed."; "21. You cannot step twice into the same river, for other waters are continually flowing on", summarized in the concluding note "all things that we say 'exist' are really in process of becoming"). Nevertheless, Heraclitus was known to Deleuze (1983 [1962]) solely through the mediation of Friedrich Nietzsche's works (1990 [1899] & 2007 /1994/ [1887]). Valuable here also is the reference to the collective anthology edited by Christa Davis Acampora with her husband Ralph R. Acampora (2004). Ultimately, decisive for further discussion in this paper, is Wheelwright's interpretation of Fragment 6 "Much learning does not teach understanding" (1959: 19) which means that "we come to know reality not by merely knowing about it (cf. Fr. 6), but by becoming of its nature."

4 The discursive becoming of language in the enunciative pragmatics of social communication

With the focus on the theory of becoming, it is important to consider the notions of discourse and discursive practices, introduced by Michel Foucault (1972 [1969], 1971 [1971]), having been implemented in sociologically-oriented studies on human relationships and their linguistic manifestations. Foucault's approach benefited, however, both from the language-in-use and utterance-centred turn, called in France *pragmatique énonciative* 'enunciative pragmatics', which took place within poststructuralist linguistics and social sciences.

4.1 Alluding to the concept of discourse and discursive practices

Foucault proceeded from a brief description of *discourse*, defining it "sometimes as the general domain of all statements, sometimes as an individualizable group of statements, and sometimes as a regulated practice that accounts for a number of statements" (1972: 80). In the more individualized sense, according to some linguistic rules governing all the utterances of a determined language in terms of a specific formation that groups the enunciation of statements similar in kind, "discourse is constituted by a group of sequences of signs, in so far as they are statements, that is, in so far as they can be assigned particular modalities of existence" (Foucault 1972: 107). Worth mentioning is Foucault's opinion that the rules governing discursive practices do not "define the dumb existence of reality, nor the canonical use of vocabulary, but the ordering of objects" (1972: 49). As far as the human being as the subject of the discourse is concerned, one cannot assume, following Foucault's reasoning, that s/he plays a synthesizing or unifying function but, contrarily, "the various enunciative modalities manifest his dispersion. To the various statuses, the various sites, the various positions he can occupy or be given when making a discourse" (1972: 54).

Consequently, Foucault argues that "discourses and their systematic ordering are not only the ultimate state, the final result of a long and often sinuous development involving language (*langue*) and thought, empirical experience and categories, the lived and ideal necessities, the contingency of events and the play of formal constraints" (1972: 84). One can accept, after Foucault, that the communicating individual always remains "within the dimension of discourse" (1972: 85).

Analyzing the dependencies between language, social reality, and the human individual as a social subject, thoughts, and ideas, as well as science and knowledge, against the background of historical and cultural settings, Foucault maintained that all are constructed discursive-*ly*: they come into being through discursive practices and within fixed, definite discursive formations. What matters in the investigative approach proposed by Foucault are the ways of thinking and believing rooted in language and grounded in the historical tradition and social and institutional order which can be uncovered through discourse studies. Foucault's conviction that discursive practices construct human reality, that they systematically form the objects of speech, implies that the words of speech themselves are not used to designate things but to create social order.

Adhering to Foucault's philosophy for the purposes and literary studies (cf. Wąsik 2016: 271–272), one can refer the term *discourse* to socially- and culturally-determined properties of the types of texts or text-processing activities characterizing the domains of language use in human communication. Seen from the perspective of cultural and communicational sciences, discourse might be specified in terms of semiotic codes and processes that link communicating selves into individual members of social groupings. Taking part in group interactions, the communicating selves as observable persons and inferable subjects are linked into interpersonal and intersubjective collectivities when they create and interpret the inferable meanings, which are embodied in material bearers forming the nonverbal or verbal means and modes of human understanding.

4.2 Languages as discursive assemblages of enunciation in natural and cultural environments

The subject matter of this subsection is the existential modes of assemblages considered in terms of how they are formed as semiotic objects in the environments of animals (including humans). The term *assemblage*, known from English translations and often misinterpreted, will be explained in relation to the original French term *agencement*, which means an arrangement of concrete elements and relational aspects. As Deleuze and Guattari claim, there are two kinds of arrangements which co-occur in reality: on the one hand, "a machinic assemblage of bodies, of actions and passions, an intermingling of bodies reacting to one another", and, on the other, "a collective assemblage of enunciation, of acts and statements, of incorporeal transformations attributed to bodies" (1987: 88). Furthermore, assemblages are specified as bipolar sets of enunciations and bodies: "The assemblage has two poles or vectors: one vector is oriented toward the strata, upon which it distributes territorialities, relative deterritorializations, and reterritorializations; the other is oriented toward the plane of consistency or destratification, upon which it conjugates processes of deterritorialization, carrying them to the absolute of the earth" (Deleuze & Guattari 1987: 145).

Thus, when Deleuze asks "What is an assemblage?", he answers that it is "a multiplicity which is made up of heterogeneous terms and which establishes liaisons, relations between them", stressing that its "only unity is that of a co-functioning . . . It is never filiations which are important, but alliances, alloys;

these are not successions, lines of descent, but contagions, epidemics, the wind" (Deleuze and Parnet 2002: 69). More explicitly, he notes that: "There are states of things, states of bodies . . . but also statements, regimes of statements: signs are organized in a new way, new formulations appear, a new style for new gestures", etc. (Deleuze and Parnet 2002: 70–71]).

4.3 Rhizomatic layers of human nature and culture in discursively shaped languages

4.3.1 On the notion of rhizome in nature and culture

Summarizing "the principal characteristic of a rhizome", Deleuze and Guattari (1987: 21) state that: "unlike trees or their roots, the rhizome connects any point to any other point, and its traits are not necessarily linked to traits of the same nature; it brings into play very different regimes of signs, and even nonsign states." The authors add: "It constitutes linear multiplicities with n dimensions having neither subject nor object, which can be laid out on a plane of consistency, and from which the one is always subtracted". As regards its changeability: "Unlike a structure, which is defined by a set of points and positions, the rhizome is made only of lines; lines of segmentarity and stratification as its dimensions, and the line of flight or deterritorialization as the maximum dimension after which the multiplicity undergoes metamorphosis, changes in nature". Defining the rhizome, Deleuze and Guattari say that these "lines, or lineaments" of a rhizome should be treated as "localizable linkages between points and positions". In their view: "The rhizome operates by variation, expansion, conquest, capture, offshoots. Unlike the graphic arts, drawing, or photography, unlike tracings, the rhizome pertains to a map that must be produced, constructed, a map that is always detachable, connectable, reversible, modifiable, and has multiple entryways and exits and its own lines of flight." Specified in terms of "antigenealogy", which "is a short-term memory, or antimemory" in the depiction of authors, "the rhizome is an acentered, nonhierarchical, nonsignifying system without a General and without an organizing memory or central automaton, defined solely by a circulation of states." (Deleuze & Guattari 1987: 21).

4.3.2 Assemblages of enunciation as a discursively becoming phenomenon

Subsequently, the issue of *assemblage* might be associated with an interdisciplinary framework of discourse studies. Special attention should be paid to the formation of discursive assemblages in the lifeworld of human subjects as participants of social communication.

In view of the enunciative formation of discursive assemblages in the lifeworld of human subjects as participants of social communication, primary attention should be devoted to semiotic codes and processes that link communicating individuals taking part in group interactions as observable persons and inferable subjects, into interpersonal and intersubjective collectivities when they create and interpret the inferable meanings which are embodied in material bearers forming the nonverbal or verbal means and modes of human understanding.

Since languages manifest themselves in individual and collective forms as the sets of extraorganismic and intraorganismic properties of their speakers and learners, they should be viewed from an evolutionist perspective according to their becoming in discursively determined domains of human life-worlds. These linguistic properties of humans are transgenerationally transmitted through epigenetic inheritance of inborn speech faculties of individuals and through the cultural tradition of conventionally established verbal signs of social groupings.

Correspondingly, semiotic objects, regarded as the realization of language and culture in various discursive domains of human communication, should be detached from interest spheres, or thematic preferences of people. Hence, on account of various forms of interactions, the communicational collectivities could be examined within the scope of discursive communities in relation to their constitutive elements as parts of communicational systems, individuals playing certain roles of participants in group communication, nonverbal and verbal means, channels and communicational settings.

Semiotic properties of communicating individuals participating in discursive communities are changeable, depending on biological, psychical, social, cultural, and other ecological conditionings, which co-determine the modes of their functioning and the direction of their development. Because the discursive communities of a lower order are situated within the communities of higher order, the autonomy principle refers here to the self-government of a small-group, applying its own laws and functioning within the larger structures of a particular discursive community.

In the real world, language and culture, as properties of collectivity, do not constitute only sets of observable data; they may be only imagined as consisting of the means and contents of interpersonal communication and intersubjective signification that are typified from observable changes in individuals when they are engaged in communicating activities. What can concretely be singled out are no more than referential behaviours of communicators, and their interpretational practices have to be mentally inferred from the shared knowledge of communication participants.

Thus, in the physical dimension, communicating selves are linked with each other as persons through sensible meaning-bearers carried out in their sending and receiving activities. In the logical dimension, intersubjective links come into being through the mutual understanding of people when the communication participants negotiate and confirm the extrinsic meaning of nonverbal and verbal means through interpretative practices and referential behaviour on the basis of internally concluded commonalities of experience or knowledge about the same domain of reference.

In keeping with the assumption that there are also interorganismic links due to not only linguistic faculties but also cultural faculties inherited genetically, according to the ascertainments of biologically and anthropologically inclined semioticians one may be entitled to assume that discourses exist also in the generational memory of human organisms in the form of mental memes or biosemiotic texts (cf. Dawkins 1976, 1982; Dennett 1991, 1995, 1996; Blackmore 1998, 1999; with special reference to Kull 2000a, 2000b).

It could be assumed that a participant of social communication as such must be able to simultaneously and interchangeably function in various discursive environments. While paraphrasing the metaphor of polyglotism applied to culture, one could finally state that the communicating individual, as a "cultural polyglot", must be able to cope with texts from different cultures, i.e., he/she must know how to communicate in and understand a "multiplicity of cultural languages". Hence, he/she must be described as possessing so-called intercultural competence.

To conclude, the rhizomatic layers of discourses may be found in the enunciative aptitudes of human organisms, inherited generationally through genetic codes of nature and transmitted through semiotic codes of culture. Such layers of biological and anthropological rhizomes might have developed genetic memory due to the cultural evolution of languages.

The rhizomatic reflection of human nature and culture in the development of language may be searched as semiotic traces against the background of comparative linguistic studies, as discussed hitherto in the author's work on the word as a trace of man (Wąsik 2010, with the definitions offered in Webster 1997 /1995/ [1992]) against the background of philosophical explorations in the philosophy of symbolic forms posited by Ernst Cassirer (1955 [1923]). To appreciate rhizome-centred reasoning, it will be enough to consider at least two examples of words or naming systems in pursuing how their rhizomatic links to various spheres of the human lifeworld in time and space across generations and traditions might be analyzed, specifically *money* and *Saturday*.

Starting with *money*, this word stands etymologically to the Latin *pecuniary* (adj.) c. 1500, from the Latin *pecuniarius* 'pertaining to money', from *pecunia* 'money, property, wealth', from *pecu* '*cattle, flock'*, from Proto Indo-European root **peku-* "wealth, movable property, livestock" (source of Sanskrit *pasu-* 'cattle', Gothic *faihu* 'money, fortune', Old English *feoh* 'cattle, money'). In the sense of the Latin word *pecunia* derived from "cattle" or "flock" (herd) as the translational equivalent for "money" may found in the linkage with the famous saying *pecunia non olet* ('money does not stink') and its assumed author whose name may be found in a respective online dictionary. Since this saying belongs to phraseology, it has also an English equivalent in the proverb *where there's muck there's brass* (Yorkshire, Britain) 'There is money to be made in unpleasant dirty jobs'. But *money* has also other links to *mint* 'place where money is coined', early 15c., from Old English *mynet* 'coin, coinage, money' (8c.), from West Germanic **munita* (source also of Old Saxon *munita*, Old Frisian *menote*, Middle Dutch *munte*, Old High German *munizza*, German *münze*), from Latin *moneta* 'mint'. Earlier word for 'place where money is coined' was *minter* (early 12c.). The general sense of 'a vast sum of money' is from the 1650s. In other contexts, *money* is related to monetary and banking systems and their translations as well as valuations in various countries and languages of the world. Not to be overlooked are also various forms of payments, by cheques, treasury bills, promissory notes, credit card or wire transfers, etc.

As regards *Saturday*, derived in Latin as the day of *Saturn* from the Hellenic Astrology (the day of *Kronos*), which stands in relation the counting and naming systems of the days of the week, as in Portuguese Sexta-feira ("sexto dia" 'sixth day'), in Latvian *sestdiena* ('6th day') or seventh Star in the Chinese Astrology, it used to be connected with the Biblical *Sabbath*, Polish *sobota*. What is remarkable that Scandinavians used to name *Saturday* as a bathing day in very early times (cf. Old Norse laugardagr, *laug* 'bad'; Old Danish *løverdag*). It has been borrowed also by Finns as *lauantai*. Worth noting is also the link of *Saturday* to other counting and naming systems of the year's seasons and months. Furthermore, the naming systems of the division of time and space are related to various forms of counting in the languages and cultures of the world.

The evolution of languages and changes in languages have been discussed in historical linguistics from the perspectives of different theories, such as, for example, genealogical tree theory, wave theory, stratal theory, cultural transfers, and linguistic interferences, the metaphor of roofing languages in contact situations. Against the background of various theories of language evolutions, one can undoubtedly recognize an added value in the conception of the rhizomatic development of language as an assemblage of enunciation. From such a viewpoint, the changeability and variability of languages may be appreciated as depending upon the differentiation of humankind in phylogenesis and ontogenesis and the evolution of the human lifeworld in natural and cultural dimensions. In fact, the rhizomatic view of language change unites all hitherto discussed approaches that link the becomings of language as an organism in the metaphorical sense to all observable and assumed properties of human selves as persons and subjects.

References

Acampora, Christa Davis & Ralph R Acampora (eds.). 2004. *A Nietzschean bestiary: Becoming animal beyond docile and brutal*. New York: Rowman and Littlefield.

Altmann, Stuart A. 1962. A field study of the sociobiology of rhesus monkeys, Macaca mulatta. *Annals of the New York Academy of Sciences* (= *The Relatives of Man: Modern Studies of the Relation of the Evolution of Nonhuman Primates to Human Evolution*) 102: 338–435.

Altmann, Stuart A. 1967. The structure of primate social communication. In Stuart A. Altman (ed.), *social communication among primates*. 325–362. Chicago, IL: University of Chicago Press.

Ascoli, Graziadio Isaia. 1881–1882 /1881/. Lettere glottologiche. *Revista di Filologia e d'Istruzione Classica* X (): 1–71 /*Una lettera glottologica*. Torino: E. Loescher/.

Ascoli, Graziadio Isaia. 1886. *Due recenti lettere glottologiche e una poscritta nuova*. Roma: E. Loescher.

Blackmore, Susan J. 1998. Imitation and the definition of a meme. *Journal of Memetics – Evolutionary Models of Information Transmission* 2.2: 159–170.

Blackmore, Susan J. 1999. *The meme machine*. Oxford [Oxfordshire], UK: Oxford University Press.

Bühler, Karl (Ludwig).1965 /1934/. *Sprachtheorie. Die Darstellungsfunktion der Sprache*. Zweite Auflage (Second edition). Stuttgart: Gustav Fischer Verlag, 1965 / Jena: Gustav Fischer Verlag, 1934/.

Cassirer, Ernst. 1955 [1923]. *Philosophie der symbolischen Formen*. Erster Teil. *Die Sprache* (*Zur Phänomenologie der sprachlichen Form*). Berlin: Bruno Cassirer [*The philosophy of symbolic forms*. Vol. I: *Language*. Trans. Ralph Manheim. New Haven, CT: Yale University Press].

Dawkins, (Clinton) Richard. 1976. *The selfish gene*. Oxford, UK: Oxford University Press,

Dawkins, (Clinton) Richard. 1982. *The extended phenotype*. Oxford, UK: Oxford University Press.

Deleuze, Gilles & Claire Parnet. 2002 /1987/ [1977]. *Dialogues* II. Trans. Hugh Tomlinson, Barbara Habberjam, London: The Athlone Press /New York: Columbia University Press [*Dialogues*. Paris: Flammarion].

Deleuze, Gilles & Félix Guattari. 1976. *Rhizome*. Paris: Les Éditions de Minuit.

Deleuze, Gilles & Félix Guattari. 1987 [1980]. *A thousand plateaus*. Trans. Brian Massumi. Minneapolis, MN: University of Minnesota Press [*Mille plateaux*. Paris: Éditions de Minuit, 1980].

Deleuze, Gilles. 1983 [1962]. *Nietzsche and philosophy*. Trans. Hugh Tomlinson. New York: Columbia University Press [*Nietzsche et la philosophie*. Paris: Presses universitaires de France].
Dennett, Daniel. 1991. *Consciousness explained*. Boston, MA: Little, Brown & Co.
Dennett, Daniel. 1995. *Darwin's dangerous idea: Evolution and the meanings of life*. New York, NY: Simon & Schuster.
Dennett, Daniel. 1996. *Kinds of minds: Toward an understanding of consciousness*. New York, NY: Basic Books.
Foucault, Michel. 1971 [1971]. "Discourse on language", trans. Rupert Swyer. Social Science Information 10/2 (April 1971). 7–30 [L'ordre du discours. Paris : Éditions Gallimard].
Foucault, Michel 1972 [1969], The archaeology of knowledge, trans. Alan M. Sheridan Smith. London, UK: Tavistock Publications [Archéologie du savoir. Paris : Éditions Gallimard].
Gould, Stephen Jay & Elisabeth S. Vrba. 1982. Exaptation – a missing term in the sience of form. *Paleobiology* 8.1: 4–15.
Harris, Roy. 1981. *The language myth*. London: Duckworth.
Hauser, Marc D., Noam (Avram) Chomsky & W. Tecumseh Fitch. 2002. The faculty of language: What is it, Who has it, and how did it evolve. *Science* 298.5598: 1569–1579.
Hockett, Charles F(rancis). 1959a /1958/. *A course in modern linguistics*. Second printing. New York, NY: Macmillan.
Hockett, Charles F(rancis). 1959b. Animal 'languages' and human language. In James N. Spuhler (ed.), *The evolution of man's capacity for culture*. 32–39. Detroit, MI: Wayne State University Press.
Hockett, Charles F(rancis). 1960a. Logical considerations in the study of animal communication. In Westley E. Lanyon and William N. Tavolga (eds.), *Animal sounds and communication*. 392–430. Washington, DC: American Institute of Biological Sciences.
Hockett, Charles F(rancis) 1960b. The origin of speech. *Scientific American* 203 (9): 89–96.
Hockett, Charles F(rancis). 1966 /1963/. The problem of universals in language. In Joseph H. Greenberg (ed.), *Universals in language*. Second edition. 1–29. Cambridge, MA: The Massachusetts Institute of Technology Press.
Hockett, Charles F(rancis) & Stuart A. Altmann. 1968. A note on design features. In Thomas A (lbert) Sebeok (ed.), *Animal communication techniques of study and results of research*. 61–72. Bloomington, IN: Indiana University Press.
Kloss, Heinz. 1978 /1952/. *Die Entwicklung neuer germanischen Kultursprachen seit 1800*. Zweite Auflage. Düsseldorf: Schwann /Die Entwicklung neuer germanischen Sprachen von 1800 bis 1950. München: Schwann/.
Kull, Kalevi. 2000a. Copy versus translate, meme versus sign: Development of biological textuality. *European Journal for Semiotic Studies* 12.1: 101–120.
Kull, Kalevi. 2000b. Organisms can be proud to have been their own designers. *Cybernetics and Human Knowing* 7.1: 44–55.
Lado, Robert. 1957. *Linguistics across cultures*. Ann Arbor, MI: University of Michigan Press.
Nietzsche, Friedrich. 1990 [1899]. *Twilight of the idols, or, how to philosophize with a hammer*. Trans. Reginald John Hollingdale. London: Penguin Classics [*Götzen-Dämmerung oder Wie man mit dem Hammer philosophiert*. Lepizig: Verlag von C. G. Nauman].
Nietzsche, Friedrich. 2007 /1994/ [1887]. *On the genealogy of morality*. Ed. Keith Ansell-Pearson. Trans. Carol Diethe. Revised edition. New York: Cambridge University Press [*Zur Genealogie der Moral*. Leipzig: Verlag von C. G. Nauman].

Osgood, Charles E(gerton). 1980. What is a language. In Irmengard Rauch & Gerard F. Carr (eds.), *The signifying animal*. 9–50. Bloomington: Indiana University Press.
Saussure, Ferdinand de. 1922 /1916/. *Cours de linguistique générale*. Publié par Charles Bally et Albert Sechehaye. Avec la collaboration de Albert Riedlinger. Deuxième édition. Paris: Payot, /Lausanne, Paris: Payot/.
Schleicher, August. 1848. *Sprachvergleichende Untersuchungen. Zur vergleichenden Sprachgeschichte*. (2 Bände). Bonn: H. B. Koenig.
Schleicher, August. 1850. *Linguistische Untersuchungen*. 2. Teil: *Die Sprachen Europas in systematischer Übersicht*. Bonn, H. B. König.
Schmidt, Johannes. 1872. *Die Verwandtschaftsverhältnisse der indogermanischen Sprachen*. Weimar: H. Böhlau.
Valkhoff, Marius F(rançois). 1932. *Latijn, Romaans, Roemeens*. Amersfoort: Valkhoff & Co.,
Wartburg, Walther von. 1932. Die Ursache des Auseinanderfallens der Galloromania in zwei Sprachgebiete: Französisch und Provenzalisch. Vortrag gehalten in der Sitzung der Philologisch-Historischen Klasse der Sächsischen Akademie der Wissenschaften zu Leipzig vom 18. Mai 1932. Forschungen und Fortschritte 8.21.: 268–269.
Wąsik, Zdzisław. 2010. The word as a trace of man. In Daina Teters (ed.), Riga: *Metamorphoses of the world: Traces, shadows, reflections, echoes, and metaphors*, 108–121. Riga: Technical University of Riga.
Wąsik, Zdzisław. 2016. *From grammar to discourse: Towards a solipsistic paradigm of semiotics* (Filologia Angielska 50). Poznań: Adam Mickiewicz University Press.
Webster. 1997 /1995/ [1992]. *Webster's College Dictionary*. Second edition of the revised edition, New York, NY: Random House /Revised edition, 1995/ [First edition, 1992].
Weinreich, Uriel. 1974 /1953/. *Languages in contact. Findings and problems*. With a preface by André Martinet. Eighth printing. The Hague, Paris: Mouton /New York, NY: Linguistic Circle of New York/.
Wheelwright, Philip. 1959. *Heraclitus*. Princeton, NJ: Princeton University Press.
Whorf, Benjamin Lee. 1956. *Language, thought, and reality*. Selected Writings of Benjamin Lee Whorf, ed. & introd. John B. Caroll. Foreword Stuart Chase. Cambridge, MA: The Massachusetts Institute of Technology Press.
Wierzbicka, Anna. 1972 [1969]. *Semantic Primitives*. Trans. Anna Wierzbicka. John Besemeres. Frankfurt am Main: Athenäum [Based on the Polish edition: *Dociekania semantyczne* (Semantic inquiries). Warszawa: Zakład Narodowy imienia Ossolińskich].
Wierzbicka, Anna. 1980. *Lingua mentalis: The semantics of natural language*. Sydney, New York, NY: Academic Press.
Yngve, Victor H(use). 1986. *From grammar to science. New foundations for general linguistics*. Amsterdam: John Benjamins.
Zawadowski, Leon. 1966. *Lingwistyczna teoria języka* (A linguistic theory of language). Warszawa: Państwowe Wydawnictwo Naukowe.

Index

abduction X, 69–71, 177, 212, 249–50, 263–4, 267, 292–4
actant 46–8, 54–5, 131, 151, 156, 161, 166
Actor Network Theory 130–1
aesthetic(s) 45, 78, 91, 103, 170–5, 185–7, 194, 245, 247, 304, 307
affordances VIII, 129, 132, 136–7, 144, 283–4, 290
agency X–XI, 17, 32–3, 43, 45–6, 131–2, 143, 208–10, 273–98
agriculture 130, 142
algorithm 41, 46, 63, 117, 307
Altmann S.A. 318
Allen, C. 19–20, 22
Anthropocene VI, VII, 54, 57, 75, 77–8, 80, 84–5
anthropology IX, 41, 132, 133, 151–67, 171, 315, 316, 331
Aquinas, T. 23
assemblage 322, 325–326, 328
archetype 51, 215
argument (Peircean sign function) 66–70, 250, 261–2, 265–9, 277, 279, 282, 290, 291
Aristotle 19, 25, 26 n. 1, 30, 31, 49, 91–3, 180–4, 188, 196, 214, 217
Aspect, A. 49
Atlan, H. 53

Baker, L. 217
Bakhtin, M. M. 152, 176, 182
Bankov, K. VIII
barbarism VII, 75–85, 175, 199
Barbieri, M. 22
Barthes, R. 5
Bataille, G. 300
Bateson, G. 17, 18, 32, 132
Baudelaire, C. 119
Bauer P. 251, 256, 260 n. 3, 261
Belle Epoque X, 227–228, 230, 236, 239, 240 n. 39, 246
Bender, T. 228, 230
Berthelot, M. 43
Betancourt, M. 124–5

Big Bang 39, 50, 51
biodiversity 104, 129
biology VI, 13–44, 53, 89
biosemiotics 13–34, 129–46
biosphere VII, 28, 52
biotranslation *see* translation
Bitcoin 117–8
Born, M. 44
Brier, S. 22
Brøndal, V. 48 n. 1
Bronowski, J. 211
Bruner J. 213
Bruni, L. 22
Buddhism 98
butterfly effect 52
Bühler K. L. 325

Calabrese, O. 7
Cartesian VII, 26, 59, 60–65, 72, 90, 281
cogito VII, 59, 61
chemistry 14, 15, 16, 18, 22, 52, 53, 78, 175
Christianity 153, 155
Clark E. 265
Clark A. 280
Clayton, P. 53
Climate change 4, 77, 78, 129, 131
Cobley, P. 33, 132
code 5, 9, 10, 15, 20, 23, 129, 132, 136, 138, 140, 143–5, 166, 169, 305, 307, 309, 314–5, 316, 318, 328, 330–1
Colapietro, V. 215–216, 222–223, 228 n. 4, 292
cognition IX–X, 19, 42, 46–8, 60–1, 64, 70–1, 104, 113, 132, 140, 172, 207, 217, 22, 260–2, 268, 280, 282, 284, 286, 293–4, 312, 318, 326
cognitive science 71, 280, 285 n. 5
communication VI, X, XI, 15, 75, 82, 89, 97, 105, 112, 115, 118, 123–4, 132, 134–46, 162, 167, 172, 174–7, 191, 209–225, 227, 265, 273, 279, 282, 290, 291–2, 303–5, 307–8, 311–32
complexity VII, 29 n. 5, 39, 52–7, 76, 83, 84, 102, 133

constraints 29, 31–3, 140, 286, 290, 327
Conway-Morris, S. 52
consciousness 16, 50, 83, 97, 100, 141, 179, 209, 212, 215, 217–219, 221–222, 251, 257, 261–263, 266, 268
Cooper, R. 208
Courtés, J. 45, 47
Costa de Beauregard, O. 49–50
Creatura 17, 18, 22 n. 2, 32
critical realism 202
Crutzen, P. 78
culture 75–85, 90, 95, 118–9, 121, 129, 131–3, 135, 136, 142, 144–5, 171, 174–5, 177, 185, 186, 199, 201, 223, 228, 229–30, 247, 292, 293, 300, 318, 320, 324, 329–32
cybernetics 89, 133, 201; *see also* systems theory

d'Espagnat, B. 45
Damasio, A. 39
Darwin, C. 19, 20, 22, 43, 51, 54, 56
Dasein 120, 186–96
de Duve, C. 51
Deacon, T. 22, 28–30, 32–3
Deconstruction 114, 119–20
Deely, J. VI, 23–9, 33, 90, 208, 217
Deleuze G. 322, 326, 328–329
Democritus 408
Denton, M. 51
Derrida, J. 95, 99, 113, 119–21, 126
Descartes, R. VII, 26, 52, 59–73
determinism VII, 42, 43, 44, 52, 53, 56, 131, 281, 282, 284
Detienne, M. 47
Dewey, J. 171, 284 n. 4, 289
dialogue 30, 75–85, 91, 130, 172, 174, 176–7, 189, 308
Diamond, J. 130
dicent (dicisign) 66–7, 249–50, 262, 267, 277, 279, 282, 286–7, 290
dualism, duality VII, VIII, 23, 25–6, 33, 49, 54, 59–73, 89, 90–4, 96–7, 275, 288–9, 315, 318–9
Dyer, A. W. 118–9
Dyson, F. 50

Eco, U. 5, 8, 10, 11, 113, 115, 180, 299
ecolinguistics 141
economics VIII, 84, 111–26
ecosemiotics VIII–IX, 129–46
edusemiotics 91–107, 283, 296
eroticism 299–304, 308, 309
Einstein, A. 43–4, 49, 51, 94
emergence VII, IX, 14–15, 30–33, 39, 52–6, 63, 64, 169, 171, 201, 135, 182, 251–3, 257–60
empiricism VII, 89, 91–5, 102–4, 200–1
Enlightenment 71, 199
entropy 53
enunciation IX, 151–2, 162–7, 311, 322, 325–33
environment VII–IX, XI, 10, 17, 22, 28, 40, 43, 46, 52, 78, 90, 103, 112, 129–46, 160, 173, 180, 258, 273, 275–6, 282, 284, 286, 288, 315, 316, 321, 325, 331
Epicurus 40
epistemology V, X, 23, 26, 27, 39, 41, 45, 61, 81, 84, 91, 135, 216, 281
ethics 84, 91, 103, 123, 216

Facebook 123
Fairclough, N. 92
Farina, A. 137
Favareau, D. VI
film X, 4, 9–10, 89, 123, 207–22, 228 n. 4, 229–33, 240, 247, 299, 303, 305
finiousity 29–33
Finol, J.E. XI
Firstness 95, 100, 195, 214, 224, 255, 275, 277, 285
Fisch, M. 213–214
Flores R. 307–308
Fontanille, J. IX, 7
Foucault 72, 326–328
– Marcel, G. 170, 196, 199

Gauchet, M. 77
Giddens A. 280
Gibson, J. J. 132–3
gift 11–23, 155–9, 164, 166–7, 174, 245
Gleicher, D. 123–4
Gödel, K. 44, 49

Goetzmann, W. 113, 121
Google 122
Gould, S. J. 40
Graziadio I. A. 323
Greimas, A. J. VIII, IX, 4, 5, 6, 7–10, 11, 45, 48 n. 1, 55, 131, 151–67, 170–1, 182, 187, 192, 201
Guattari F. 322, 326, 328–329

habit X, XI, 97, 98–9, 100, 104, 140, 169, 156–69, 273–6, 282–92, 296, 306
Haldane, J.B.S. 19
Haley, M.C. 215
Hall, S. 219
Hamilton, C. 77
Hayne H. 252, 260–262, 311, 315, 322, 329, 331
Hegel, G. W. F. 41, 170–6, 182, 185, 187–98
Heidegger (Heideggerian), M. VIII, 111, 113, 119–21, 171
Heisenberg, W. 49
Hertz, H. 24, 28
Hilbert, D. 43, 49
Hjelmslev, L. 48 n. 1
Hockett C. F. 318
Hoffmeyer, J. 17–18, 22, 32, 134, 288
homology VII, 48, 111, 120–1
Hornborg, A. 133
Hulswit, M. 30–3
humanism 96–8
humanities 6, 7, 89, 106, 118, 131–3, 145

IASS V, 4–5, 8, 15, 35, 273 n. 1
icon, iconicity IX, 66–70, 99, 115, 131, 186, 196, 209, 212, 215, 219, 222, 227–47, 249–50, 254, 260, 262, 264, 265, 268, 277–9, 282, 286–7, 303
idealism 24, 34, 91, 102, 104, 213
ideology 79, 122, 132, 135, 301, 303
imagination X, 56, 119, 207, 209, 211–225, 302, 305, 309
index (Peircean sign function) X, 66–71, 99, 131, 137–8, 140, 186, 196, 209, 212, 217, 219, 222, 249–55, 258–69, 279, 287
Ingold, T. 47
intentionality VI, 22, 46–52, 280, 321

interdisciplinarity 90, 113, 325–6, 330; *see also* transdisciplinarity
intermediality 207–25, 227–45
internet 79, 112, 113, 116, 122, 125, 175
internet of things 77, 126
interpretant 5, 28, 96, 187, 196, 210, 219, 249–251, 253–254, 259, 267, 268
Intraub 252
Islam 153, 155

Jacob, F. 24
Jakobson, R. 48 n. 1
Jaynes, J. 212
Johnson, M. 70
Johnson-Laird, P. 281
Jullien, F. 47
Judaism 153, 155, 238
Jung, C. G. 17
Jüssi, F. 135

Kaag, J. 216–217
Kandel, E. 16
Kant, I. 60–1, 93, 94, 217, 302, 24 n. 2
Kask, E. 145
Kauffman, S. 22, 29, 30, 53–4
Kawano, R.M. 220
Klein 262–263
Kloss H. 324
Komárek, S. 141
Koopman, C. 95
Kristeva, J. 152
Kuhn, T. S. 34
Kull, K. 19, 22, 133, 143
Kurzweil, R. 79

Lado R. 324
Lakoff, G. 70, 186
Landowski, Eric VII, 7, 161
Lang, A. 133
language VI, X, 3–11, 16, 44, 54, 57, 75–6, 83, 92–3, 96–8, 113, 118, 121, 124 132, 135, 141, 143, 162, 183, 188, 201, 211, 215, 254, 265, 307–8, 312–33
Laplace, P.-S. 43, 52, 56
Latour, B. 48, 130–1
Law, J. 131

law (legal requirement) 185, 330
laws (principles, codes) 6, 13, 17, 21, 22 n. 1,
    28 n. 4, 30, 31–2, 39–43, 50, 53–4,
    68–9, 79, 81–2, 183, 191, 208, 214, 215,
    218, 219, 265, 275, 277, 282–4, 286,
    287, 291–2, 320
Lederman, L. 72–3
Lee, Y. IX
legisign 66–7, 226, 277, 283–4, 2868,
    290–2
Lee, Y. IX
Leone, M. VI
Lepassar, J. 145
Lessing, G. E. 153–4
Leucippus 40
Lévi-Strauss, C. 48 n. 1, 151, 170, 196
Lewis, C.S. 220
linguistics 48 n. 1, 151, 313, 315–17, 319,
    320–32
Lotman, J. 5, 114, 171, 175
Low, D. 142
Lyotard, J.-F. 103
– de Maintenon, M. (Françoise
    d'Aubigné) 119

Majuru, A. 236, 238
Maran, T. VIII–IX
Markoš, A. 22
Martinelli, D. 6
Marsillac, U. de 234, 239 n. 25
Marx, K. 116, 118
Mauss, M. 113, 164
Mayr, E. 18–20, 22 n. 1, 23
Määttänen P. 275–276, 280–281, 283, 288,
    290
media studies VI, IX, 89, 151–168
mediation VII, IX, XI, 23, 63, 656, 72, 96, 114,
    118, 119, 129, 133, 136–8, 142, 151–2,
    159–64, 172, 183, 185, 187, 188, 190, 195,
    208–25, 274–6, 280, 291, 304 326
memory 10, 134–136, 140, 165–166, 171,
    179, 212, 219, 249, 252–253, 256, 258,
    260–264
Merleau-Ponty M. 306
metaphor 10, 16, 20, 51, 52, 70, 72, 79, 144,
    154, 157, 174, 186–8, 200, 209–24,
    293–4, 304, 322–4, 331–3

metaphysics VIII, 33, 61, 81, 92–3, 114, 119,
    180–1
Mettrie, J. O. de la 63
Michelangelo 61
Miles, L. 98
model VII, IX, 22, 32, 41, 43, 47, 50, 52 n. 1,
    53, 55, 56, 59, 60–5, 70, 76, 84, 93,
    95–100, 103–5, 112, 129–46, 151, 162–4,
    169–201, 209, 211, 215, 252, 257–8,
    277, 280, 281, 286, 287, 291, 303, 305,
    308, 317, 323
Moia M.I. 301
modelling 40. 48, 50, 93, 95, 97, 135, 136,
    139, 141, 143, 144, 145
Modernism 71–3
– cosmodernism 84
money VIII, 107, 111–26, 301, 332
Monod, J. 19, 42, 44, 56
Montaigne, M. de 61, 223
Morin, E. 53, 56
music 20, 158, 169, 175, 179, 185–186, 192,
    194, 198, 239, 274, 293–294, 303 n. 1,
    304–305

narrative IX, X, 45–6, 121, 131, 143–4,
    151–168, 170, 192, 195–7, 207–25,
    261, 263–4, 294, 304–5
narratology IX, 151–168, 207–25
Neț, M. X
Newton, I. 17, 18, 43, 94, 131
Nicolescu, B. VII, 80, 83
Nietzsche F. 326
Noble, D. 22
Noland, C. 280
nominalism VI, 13, 25
Nöth, W. 133

Oakeshott, M. 105
Ockham, William of VI, 13, 25, 50
Ojala, J. X–XI, 275–277, 283, 288–289,
    292–293
Olteanu, A. 91, 99, 101–102, 283
ontology 23, 27, 33, 99, 121, 130, 132,
    134,145, 212, 218
Osgood, C. E. 318

panterrorism VII, 75–7, 80, 84–5
Peirce, C. S. VII, X, IX, 4, 5, 11, 24, 28–34, 59–60, 62–9, 90–1, 95–6, 99, 133, 137, 142, 177, 187, 195–6, 207–25, 228 n. 4, 249–69, 273–295
Percy, W. 119
Petitimbert, Jean-Paul VII
pheme 249–250, 262, 267
philosophy VII, 8, 9, 5, 23–4, 25–34, 40, 46, 48, 53, 56, 60–73, 75, 77, 80, 84, 98, 90–95, 104, 113, 118–9, 120–1, 162, 169–201, 217, 300, 303, 304, 326–31
philosophy of mind 285 n. 5
philosophy of science VII, 52
physics 14, 16, 17, 18, 19, 22, 33, 50, 55, 72, 89, 93, 94
–quantum physics 44, 49, 81, 83
–astrophysics 53
Piaget, J. 102, 105, 178, 290
Pittendrigh, C. 18, 19
Planck, M. 50
Plato 30–1, 91–3, 171–7, 182, 188, 190, 192, 210, 302–3, 306, 310
Pleroma 17, 18, 22 n. 2, 32
poetry X, 84, 106, 207, 214–5, 217, 218–24
Poinsot, J. 24, 208
Polanyi, M. 132
pornography XI, 4, 299–310
Posner, R. 138
postmodernism 201
poststructuralism 95, 327
pragmatics 112, 133, 326–33
pragmatism 113, 274, 294
Prigogine, I. 30, 53, 56
Puura, I. 139

Quinn 252
qualisign 66, 277, 283, 291
quantum physics *see* physics

realism VI, 13–35
reductionism VII, 14, 15, 22, 52–3, 55, 59, 201, 303
religion 6, 8, 76, 77, 80, 84, 93, 99–100, 126, 153–5, 234 n. 19, 300, 303
remediation IX, 151–2, 224

representamen 138, 140, 187, 196, 260 n. 1, 276
rheme 66, 250 n. 1, 277, 279, 282, 286–288
Ribordy F. 258
Ricoeur, P. 113, 121, 163–4, 212–15
Rifkin, J. 113, 114, 123

Saussure 5, 48 n. 1, 95, 115, 162–3, 177, 325
Saramago, J. 307
Schleicher, A. 323
Schrödinger, E. 49
Sebeok, T. A. 90, 138, 288
Secondness 95, 100, 213, 214, 224, 265, 275, 277, 285
self-organisation 53–5, 144
semiocide X, 129, 136, 139, 140, 145
semiology 5, 95
semiosis V, 5, 13, 17, 22, 90–91, 95, 97–98, 100–101, 104, 131, 133, 137, 141, 143, 161–166, 187, 208, 222, 249–251, 274–276, 279, 283–284, 286, 288, 291–294, 304
Semiotica 91
semiotic pollution IX, 129, 138–40
Sepper, D. 217
Sexton, R. L. 117
Shakespeare, W. 61, 106, 211
Shank, G. VII
Shapiro, J. 22
Short, T. L. 30–3
Siewers, A. K. 135
Sign Systems Studies 133
sinsign 66, 277, 279, 283, 286–8, 291, 292
Simmel G. 302
sixth mass extinction VII, 57, 130
social sciences 53, 61, 89, 90, 306, 327
socialist realism 192
Sperber, D. 162–7
Spretnak, C. 133
Stables, A. VII, 90–91, 102–103, 105
Sterne, L. 47
Stjernfelt, F. 15–6, 20, 22, 33, 97
structuralism IX, 48 n. 1, 85, 99, 113, 151, 174, 178, 180, 201
symbol (Peircean sign function) 66–71, 99, 186, 199, 209, 254, 260–1, 265, 277, 279, 282, 286, 287–8

syntagmatic 159, 161–6, 319
syntax 46, 47, 48, 54, 55, 97, 155, 304
systems theory VII

Tarasti, E. IX, 5, 288, 294
Tattersall, I. 54
teleology 22–3, 30, 49–50
Teller, E. 78
Thirdness 27, 28, 30, 95, 100, 214, 224, 275, 277
Thuan, T. X. 50
Tønnessen, M. 140, 142
Toulmin, S. 61
transdisciplinarity VI, 34, 53, 75–85; *see also* interdisciplinarity
transhumanism VII, 75–76, 78–9, 84–5
transhumanism VII, 75, 76, 78, 79–80, 84, 85
translation 62, 76, 320, 332
– biotranslation 136, 139–40, 145
transmission IX, X, 43, 151–67, 207, 210–11, 217–24, 301, 302, 311, 315–16, 320–1, 330–1
– retransmission IX, 151–67
Treviranus, G. R. 13
triadicity VII, 33, 59–73, 95, 96, 187, 208–9, 211, 214, 225, 276–7
Tulving E. 260–263
Turner, V. 47

Umwelt V, 135–40, 191, 194–5, 209, 225

Vernant, J.-P. 47
Venema, H. 212–213
Villeneuve, D. 9
Vinge, V. 78–9
Vygotsky, L. 211–212
von Uexküll, J. 18, 26 n. 3, 137, 140, 191

Wartburg W. 323
Wąsik, Z. XI, 312–313, 315–318, 320–321, 325, 328, 331
Wąsik E. M. 314
Weinberg, S. 39, 40
Welby, V. 96, 251
West, D. X, 259, 264, 265, 266, 268 n. 6
Whitehead, A. N. 219
Wilde, O. 121
Wikipedia 4, 21
Wilson, A. 32
Wittgenstein, L. 97
Woese, C. 14, 15, 18, 33
Wood, L. 78
Woodworth, R. 306

Yngve V.H. 313

Zemic model 169–206
Zawadowski L. 325